Classical CD Library

A Music Lover's Guide to Great Recorded Performances

Foreword by
Lucinda Carver
Music Director and Conductor
Los Angeles Mozart Orchestra

Dhun H Sethna

William C Stivelman

Published by
The Fitzwilliam Press
100 Monterey Lane, Sierra Madre, CA 91024
(626) 355-1296

Library of Congress Cataloging in Publication Data

Sethna, Dhun H. 1948 -
Stivelman, William C. 1955 -

Classical CD Library: A Music Lover's Guide to Great Recorded
Performances / Dhun H Sethna & William C Stivelman
p.   cm.
Includes bibliographical references and indexes
ISBN 0-96-44103-4-6 $16.95

98-093154
CIP

To
My wife Virginia,
Jonathan and Judith
and Diana

- D.H.S.

To
Steven J. Davidson
A rising musical talent
And his parents John and Karen
For tolerating my madness

- W.C.S.

Table of Contents

Acknowledgments - v

Foreword - vii

Prelude - ix

A Note on the Recordings - - - - - - - - - - - - - - - - - - - xii

Index of the Recordings - xiii

Part 1. Great Orchestral & Instrumental Music of the Western World

1. Early Music - 7

2. The Renaissance - 15

3. The Baroque World - 21

4. The Age of Elegance - - - - - - - - - - - - - - - - - - - 45

5. A Time for Revolution - - - - - - - - - - - - - - - - - - - 69

6. Romanticisim - 121

7. A Time to be Free - 163

8. The Age of Opulence - - - - - - - - - - - - - - - - - - - 189

9. Impressionism - 267

10. Modern Music - 289

Part 2. The Lifetime Listening Program

The Life Time Listening Program - - - - - - - - - - - - - - - 319

Appendix

Selected Bibliography - 333

Index - 337

Acknowledgments

I owe my greatest pleasure, the joy of music, to my mother and father who gave me the freedom from age 4 or 5 to discover what I liked on my own, without much direction. It nearly came to homicide; my first dozen recordings were of the same work: Wagner's *Prelude to Die Meistersinger von Nurnberg*, Act I. Apparently, I was carrying out an independent study of comparative performance without knowing it. This led, probably after more than a decade, to the discovery of a second, third and fourth musical work, which ultimately opened my horizons. All these works were orchestral in nature.

I owe a great deal of gratitude to my brother who has routinely chided me for maintaining a vertical rather than a horizontally oriented collection of recordings. Funny thing, however, because whenever I tell him of a new recording I have heard of a work that we had each heard 2,000 times or have 35 recordings of between us (he might have 5 to my 30), he would frown and say, "I don't need another recording of the Beethoven Symphonies!" I have habitually placed a gentleman's bet with my father that my brother would appropriate the recording within the year. He always does, and the experience that he goes through is as if the work is being heard for the first time. He then approaches me and says, "Have you heard such and such a recording? It's unbelievable!" I furrow my brow and say, "Didn't you dismiss that out of hand last year?" He blissfully demonstrates selective amnesia for my earlier recommendation. Oh well!

I am indebted to my colleague Dhun Sethna who apparently feels my fund of knowledge sufficient to expound in the form of a guide book that he has co-authored with me. I still wonder whether or not he is wise. Thanks also to Suzi Robertson for being my "left hand" in the preparation of this manuscript.

W.C.S.

The essays and introductions to the selections are the outcome of syntopical reading whereby many sources have been read as they relate to one another and to the musical piece around which they all revolve. These secondary sources are listed together to form the Bibliography. My sincere gratitude to Avi Shroff, my "bestest" friend, for her insight, wisdom, support and kindness throughout the preparation of this book.

D.H.S.

Foreword

Countless words have been spent by writers both famous and obscure in attempts to verbalize and hence better understand the power and mystery of music in the human experience. Music has the power to effortlessly evoke thoughts, emotions and experiences which are far beyond our ability to articulate. Not only can a great piece of music convey a message which is unique to each and every listener, it also can speak to us differently each time we revisit it. It is a language more powerful than any other; music can speak to every corner of our soul.

As the century draws to a close, we are living at an ever quickening pace, racing along merely to keep up in a very complex and uncertain world. In such an environment, the opportunity to be drawn in by a piece of music that is capable of melting away the angst of the day surrounding it is ever more precious. But for many people, the intimidation of walking into a classical music record store is, if anything, the source of yet more angst! With this book, Dhun Sethna and William Stivelman have provided an invaluable tool for beginning with confidence a basic personal library of classical music recordings.

It is unfortunate that classical music has somehow taken on an elitist stigma whereby, for some ridiculous reason, there is a common misconception that one must have had a certain level of formal study in music to appreciate it. Time and time again I hear the following remark, often in an apologetic tone: "I don't really know much about classical music but I certainly think it is beautiful." The only thing music really requires of us is the willingness to listen, to allow it to work its powers.

W.H. Auden once wrote: "The trouble with music appreciation in general is that people are taught to have too much respect for music; they should be taught to love it instead." It is very clear from this book that both Dhun Sethna and William Stivelman are great lovers of music; it is also very clear that their love is infectious. I certainly hope that no one who reads this book will be immune!

Lucinda Carver
Los Angeles, 1998

Prelude

It has, for long, been held as self evident that the road to education lies through the great books. Yet long before picture-writing was superseded by the alphabet, humankind has expressed itself in the sound of music. The common voice of the human mind has been articulated and has endured through all the great arts, and great music, the most ethereal of all arts, deserves a place in its own right in the home of every cultured family of our time. This book is a guide for lay music lovers who wish to explore classical music on compact discs (CDs), and begin for themselves and their families a home library of the best recorded classical music. It is not meant for the music scholar or the professional musician who would find little that is new in this book. Rather, it is directed to the great and growing army of intelligent men and women, from eighteen to eighty eight, who are penetrated by a vague, uncomfortable sense that the mere solutions to the daily problems of living are not enough, that somewhere worlds of thought and feeling call out for exploration to complete the fullness of that experience called the human condition. Music has a special power to move and even to disturb, and this has something to do with bringing what has been unconscious to consciousness.

The subtitle of this book claims that it encompasses performances of "Great" recorded music. Who is knowing enough and eternal enough to judge things of this kind? Works in music have been labeled "Great" in their own way, in their own time, and for their own reasons, after which the world has often changed its mind. The function and purpose of a piece of music, the expectations that have been placed upon it, and the role of the composer have not been constant. They have varied in different ages and societies.

Yet a few works have stood out because they have had the ability to speak beyond their age, and have offered meaning and inspiration across time.

Some music is great in a private way, and speaks to listeners as thinking, feeling, unique human beings with experiences and emotions and values that are unlike those of any other persons. To them the music speaks of things which it says to no one else, and which can neither be repeated nor explained. Other works have become great in a public way, selected by no one in particular for no one in particular, but determined by reputation and the prominence given to them. No one is responsible for them, and they reflect no one's taste. Such music is a means of understanding our world and ourselves. It contains the feelings and ideas that dominate us without our knowing it. And the music has endured because humankind in every era has been lifted beyond itself by the inspiration of its example. In its company we are still in the ordinary world, but it is the ordinary world transfigured and seen through eyes of wisdom and genius. And some of its vision becomes our own.

There is only one way of reporting on great music, and that is by listening to it. Listening is not the same as hearing. Hearing involves only the effort it takes to open one's ears; listening means opening one's mind and taxing one's intellect. Listening to music is like going on a journey - a journey with many possibilities, including the excitement of sharing the visions and feelings of another age. As with any journey, the better the preparation, the more fulfilling the expedition is likely to be. Traveling is best done with a guide who can help as one acclimatizes to a new environment, and who can point out things that might otherwise go unnoticed. The purpose of this book is to provide such a guide into the world of recorded classical music.

The authors have drawn upon their combined listening and reading experiences as a guide in putting together this collection of outstanding recorded performances. Great care has been exercised in the selection of the works that they felt should be included in a music lover's personal home library. Much thought also went in the choice of the recordings, and the recommendations made are truly outstanding recordings whose magical quality make them a special treasure that is uniquely valuable. The authors do not claim that all the great orchestral music of the West is discussed here, and many readers will be disappointed to find one, at least, of their favorite works missing. Some will be surprised to find music that they had a low opinion of given a place of honor.

The authors felt that the chronological order was the most appropriate organizing principle for a work of this type. It seemed natural to present the styles and expressions of the great composers in the temporal sequence in which they took part in the great musical conversation. The music is almost self selected in the sense that one work leads naturally to another, amplifying, modifying or contradicting it. And though the collection ends in the middle part of our century, the story continues to the present day and will continue in the centuries to follow.

It is unfortunate that guide books to musical recordings blithely ignore the simple fact that to understand any piece of great music involves understanding the logic indigenous to the milieu which made it, and to the limited but well-defined period in history to which it once belonged. Just as the function of the stained glass windows in a church is not to offer to the eyes merely another set of scenes to decipher but also to bring to life the interior space of the church with its hourly metamorphoses in light and expressiveness, so also a musical work should not be viewed in detachment from the ensemble in which it was conceived. The essays and introductions that accompany the collection of recordings presented here cannot pretend to put into the grasp of readers the ensembles as they truly were, but they may furnish a preliminary key to let them into a few corners which are most accessible, and serve as a platform for further inquiry.

This book is the result of a happy collaboration between two music lovers, both physicians. The essays and the introductory notes to the individual orchestral selections were put together by one (D.H.S.) based upon his syntopical reading of many secondary sources which are collectively referenced in the Bibliography, and to them a debt is acknowledged at the outset. The reviews and recommendations of the recorded performances recall a lifetime odyssey of the other (W.C.S.) into the magical and wondrous world of live and recorded classical music. The selections are focused on instrumental and orchestral music; vocal music and opera have for the most part been left out for they have earned books in their own right.

In a way, this book is a natural sequel to a previous work, *Classical Music for Everybody: A Companion to Good Listening* by Dhun H. Sethna (Foreword by Zubin Mehta; The Fitzwilliam Press, 1997) in which, through a collection of over ninety *Listening Notes*, lay music lovers are introduced to the instruments of the orchestra, and a variety of musical styles, forms and genres through an evolutionary journey into the history of music over time. Readers who wish to increase their present understanding and enjoyment of classical music are referred to this companion volume.

A Note on the Recordings

Of all the arts, music is one that requires an intermediary for its projection from creator to observer. All recorded versions of the same musical work are not the same. Love at first sight, or at first hearing, is a dangerous proposition. For, the first experience often engrains in our subconscious the *DIN*, the *echt*, of what the music *should* be, and how it should sound from that point forward. The conditions under which one is exposed to it, such as one's emotions at a particular time of life, the venue of exposure (where it was first heard), the nature of the performance and, in the event of a recorded performance, the engineering and acoustics of that recording are factors that can impact the first experience. All of us as listeners have had our "first exposures," and upon the rehearing of a given work in the hands of another performer, the response may vary from "That isn't right" to utter gratification.

It follows, therefore, that if one is exposed to an inferior recording of a given musical piece, it is possible that the imprinting of that performance in the mind will be jaded for a long time, unless one remains of open mind. In my thirty five years of collecting and listening to recordings, I have had my share of poor recorded performances. And I have failed to enjoy some excellent performances of the same pieces because of my own preconceived expectations.

This compendium of recommended recordings is only an opinion; the opinion of a music lover who has one goal: to be gratified by listening through recordings that accurately and authoritatively depict the composer's intentions, but with the stamp of the personality of the musicians who perform it. I have rarely been interested in perfunctory, musicologically sound, didactic run-throughs of the major repertory. Performances of this nature abound on the major and minor labels that grace Tower Records and the Virgin Megastores. If not in the current catalogs, most entries can be ordered by fax from Tower or Virgin or Music Discount Centers in London, England, among other sources.

The intention of this list is to direct the novice music lover to recordings that have gratified *me* upon repeated hearing, and which are indispensable to *me* as *Desert Island* recordings. References to unavailable, older LPs and cassettes are made as deemed appropriate and practical. The price of a recording was considered secondary in creating this music lover's companion. However, many entries do have a mid-priced if not a budget recommendation which is of high caliber.

W.C.S.

Great Orchestral & Instrumental Music
of the Western World
A Music Lover's Basic Home Library

Index of the Recordings

Early Music
Hildegard von Bingen

1. Gregorian Chant - 12

The Renaissance

Giovanni Pierluigi de Palestrina

2. Mass for Pope Marcellus - - - - - - - - - - - - - - - - - - - 18

The Baroque World
Antonio Vivaldi

3. The Four Seasons - 27

Johann Sebastian Bach

4. Brandenburg Concertos - - - - - - - - - - - - - - - - - - - 28

5. Orchestral Suites - 31

6. Goldberg Variations - 33

7. Mass in B minor - 35

George Frederic Handel

8. Water Music (complete) - - - - - - - - - - - - - - - - - - - 37

9. Royal Fireworks Music - - - - - - - - - - - - - - - - - - - 39

Henry Purcell

10. Dido's Lament (Dido and Aeneas) - - - - - - - - - - - - - 41

The Age of Elegance

Franz Josef Haydn

11. Symphonies 93-104 (London) - - - - - - - - - - - - - - 51

12. String Quartet No. 77 (Emperor) - - - - - - - - - - - - 53

Wolfgang Amadeus Mozart

13. Overtures - 55

14. Symphony No 40 - 57

15. Symphony No. 41 (Jupiter) - - - - - - - - - - - - - - - 59

16. Piano Concerto No. 19, 21, 23 - - - - - - - - - - - - - 60

17. Die Zauberflote - 64

A Time for Revolution

Ludwig van Beethoven

18. Symphony No. 1 - 73

19. Symphony No. 2 - 75

20. Symphony No. 3 (Eroica) - - - - - - - - - - - - - - - - 78

21. Symphony No. 4 - 83

22. Symphony No. 5 - 86

23. Symphony No. 6 (Pastoral) - - - - - - - - - - - - - - - 89

24. Symphony No. 7 - 91

25. Symphony No. 8 - 94

26. Symphony No. 9 (Choral) - - - - - - - - - - - - - - - - 96

27. Overtures - 99

28. Piano Sonatas - 102

29. Piano concerto No. 5 (Emperor) - - - - - - - - - - - - 107

30. Violin concerto - 109

Franz Schubert

31. Symphony No. 5 - 111

32. Symphony No. 8 (Unfinished) - - - - - - - - - - - - - - - 113

33. Symphony No. 9 (Great) - - - - - - - - - - - - - - - - - 115

34. Piano quintet in A (Trout) - - - - - - - - - - - - - - - - 117

The Romantic Period

Hector Berlioz

35. Symphonie fantastique - - - - - - - - - - - - - - - - - - - 126

36. Overtures - 129

Felix Mendelssohn-Bartholdy

37. Symphony No. 3 (Scotch) - - - - - - - - - - - - - - - - - 132

38. Symphony No. 4 (Italian) - - - - - - - - - - - - - - - - - 134

39. Violin concerto in E minor - - - - - - - - - - - - - - - - 136

40. Overtures - 138

Robert Schumann

41. Symphony No. 1 (Spring) - - - - - - - - - - - - - - - - - 140

42. Symphony No. 2 - 142

43. Symphony No. 3 (Rhenische) - - - - - - - - - - - - - - 145

44. Symphony No. 4 - 147

Frederic Chopin

45. Piano Works - 148

Franz Liszt

46. Symphonic Poems - 151

Gioacchino Rossini

47. Overtures - 155

Giacomo Puccini

48. La Boheme - 158

Jean Sibelius

49. Symphony No. 2 - 159

A Time to be Free

Peter Ilyich Tchaikovsky

50. Orchestral Works - 167

Antonin Dvorak

51. Slavonic Dances - 170

Modeste Mussorgsky

52. Pictures at an Exhibition - - - - - - - - - - - - - - - - - 172

Nicolai Rimski-Korsakov

53. Scheherazade - 176

Bedrich Smetana

54. Ma Vlast (complete) - - - - - - - - - - - - - - - - - - - 177

Edvard Grieg

55. Peer Gynt (incidental music) - - - - - - - - - - - - - - - 180

Jean Sibelius

56. Symphonic poems - 182

Guiseppe Verdi

57. Aida - 185

The Age of Opulence
Johann Strauss

58. Waltzes - 191

Anton Bruckner

59. Symphony No 4 (Romantic) - - - - - - - - - - - - - - - - 194

60. Symphony No 7 - 196

Johannes Brahms

61. Symphony No. 1 - 198

62. Symphony No. 2 - 202

63. Symphony No. 3 - 204

64. Symphony No. 4 - 206

65. Piano concertos - 209

66. Violin concerto - 213

67. Orchestral Works - 216

Gustav Mahler

68. Symphony No. 1 (Titan) - - - - - - - - - - - - - - - - 220

69. Symphony No. 2 (Resurrection) - - - - - - - - - - - - 223

Peter Ilyich Tchaikovsky

70. Symphony No. 4 - 225

71. Symphony No. 5 - 228

72. Symphony No. 6 (Pathetique) - - - - - - - - - - - - - 230

73. Piano concerto No. 1 - - - - - - - - - - - - - - - - - 233

74. Violin concerto - 236

75. Ballet music - 238

Antonin Dvorak

76. Symphonies (Nos. 7,8,9) - - - - - - - - - - - - - - - 240

Camille Saint-Saens

77. Symphony No. 3 (Organ) - - - - - - - - - - - - - - - - 246

Georges Bizet

78. Orchestral Works - 249

Richard Wagner

    79. Die Meistersinger von Nurnberg - - - - - - - - - - - - - - - 252

    80. Overtures - 256

Impressionism

Claude Debussy

    81. Orchestral Works - 270

Gustav Holst

    82. The Planets - 273

Ralph Vaughan Williams

    83. Symphony No. 2 (London) - - - - - - - - - - - - - - - - - 274

Maurice Ravel

    84. Orchestral Works - 278

Ottorino Respighi

    85. Orchestral Works - 282

Igor Stravinsky

    86. The Rite of Spring - 284

Modern Music

Richard Strauss

    87. Tone poems - 292

Edward Elgar

    88. Orchestral Works - 297

Igor Stravinsky

    89. Petrushcha - 301

Sergei Rachmaninoff

    90. Symphony No. 2 - 304

    91. Piano concertos - 306

Serge Prokofiev

92. Symphony No 1 (Classical) - - - - - - - - - - - - - - - - 308

Bela Bartok

93. Concerto for Orchestra - - - - - - - - - - - - - - - - - 310

Samuel Barber

94. Adagio for Strings - 312

Aaron Copland

95. Appalachian Spring - - - - - - - - - - - - - - - - - - - 314

Leonard Bernstein

96. West Side Story - 315

Part I

Great Orchestral
&
Instrumental Music
of the Western World

Music, as we know it now, with its broad melodies, its harmonic wealth, dazzling instrumental color and intense expressiveness is the youngest of the arts. The beginning of its present position dates only from the eighteenth century—from Bach. But Bach had predecessors who had for a millennium prepared the ground for its seed. In the Western world, as everywhere else, vocal music preceded the instrumental.

The earliest Western music of which we know many things definitely is the plainsong of the Church. The early congregation loved to linger and dwell on their sacred and precious words such as *Alleluia, Amen,* and *Hosanna.* They longed to express their meanings earnestly and with emotion, and to this end they allowed the words to become extended, sustaining them as long as their voices could allow as if loathe to let go, and then repeating them to reinforce their devotion. The chanters were not concerned with pitch. For what were tones and scales to sober men, who also were in the main ignorant men, knowing little more than how to praise God, and whose psalms were but an overflowing of an earnest heart? The main aim of the early Christian chant was not the exposition of a musical tune but the fervent utterance of holy thought, to profit the soul through the holy words that were declaimed. The tones, the wavering and trembling of their sustained untrained voices, were unimportant.

The arrival of the wandering minstrels supplied the musical moods not germane to the Church, and liberalized the songs of the Church to entertain the common people on themes that reflected the life they led, and on themes of heroism and the love of woman. About 1000 - 1050 AD, the monk Guido d'Arezzo made a landmark contribution by distributing the twenty music notes that were then being used into named groups of six called the hexachords. It was at this time that the art of musical notation became exact enough to indicate rhythm. By 1225, the English had evolved a simple musical form called the *round* that involved musical imitation by repetition. This soon led to a musical form called the *canon*, and musicians put out a voluminous mass of *motets* and *chansons* that employed this type of musical imitation. The folk-songs of the Middle Ages, which happy accident has preserved for us, have all the freshness, melody and rhythmic force that was so conspicuously absent from Church music of the period. And from time to time, some holy brother, less dehumanized than his fellows, had glimpses of the musical possibilities of folk song.

By the year 1400, musical polyphony had matured, and composers were already writing polyphony for wedding celebrations. In the middle of the fifteenth century, Josquin des Pres, perhaps the first great composer, consciously blended the freshness of melody and sense of rhythm from popular music to the principles of counterpoint that had been developed in ecclesiastical music. The result was not only a brilliant display of technique but an ever-growing feeling for musical beauty. Allied to this was a rudimentary taste for realistic effects taking form in an effort to echo the sounds of nature and of human life, at first purely imitative, and afterwards more artistic.

Columbus, Michelangelo and Leonardo da Vinci were well in their prime when Petrucci published, in 1502, some nine hundred of the Flemish and Italian *frotolle* which were the immediate precursor of the *madrigal*. In 1507 came the first publishing of music for the lute. By the time Palestrina (1514-1594) was born, the Amati family were getting ready to make their first violin and Martin Luther was soon to issue the first hymn book. Shakespeare began his career during Palestrina's lifetime and, by the year of his death, Gabrieli had already written music for voices and orchestral instruments, and the Florentines were writing the first music drama. By 1600, the first year of the oratorio, there were already two thousand madrigals in print.

The opening of the seventeenth century, the birth of the opera, saw a revolution in music that has never since been paralleled. With Palestrina and his school, music, as it was then known, had reached a climax of perfection beyond which progress was scarcely perceivable. But the rise of opera and of secular music as a separate entity gave a new complexion to the world of music. The new generation of musical dramatists set forth upon an unknown course, leaving behind them the edifice that Church and secular polyphony had required generations to build. That they in time arrived at a desired port was largely due to the genius of the Italian race for adapting itself to the various difficulties as they arose.

The timetables of history in the arts are seldom fixed and well defined time segments. One of the great errors of the science of history is to seek chronological dividing posts between humankind's great ages. No human tradition is ever wholly lost in the sands of time: evolution is continuous. At no time does a society live entirely in the past or in the future, and the present is seldom anything but a fragile equilibrium between the two. Were it ever possible to reconstruct the continuum of daily life and events from the past, it might be tempting to argue that the sharply defined periods of human history never really existed. The Renaissance, for example, would simply be a continuation of the Middle Ages and, without any distinct break with the past, would just prepare the way into the Baroque era. However, it is in their expression of the esthetic tendencies of a style and culture, be it in Hogarth's earthy engravings, Monteverdi's stunning demonstration of the dramatic possibilities of the *basso continuo*, or Milton's lofty poetry that the great ages of mankind allow definition, and carry in themselves the seeds of further development that permit the past to be divided into comprehensible segments. The *Great Orchestral & Instrumental Music of the Western World* unfolds the story of music over the centuries, from the early Christian times to the modern era.

Early Music

At the dawn of music, poetry and song were one art. Music (Greek: *musice*, "art of the Muses") began its career, like man, by leaning on its surroundings. Music in ancient Greece slavishly followed the meter of poetry. Among the Greek-speaking people of the pagan world, music was regarded not only as an agreeable amusement but also as a higher intellectual and artistic education, and one of the most effective means of cultivating the feelings and character. The great importance they attached to music was apparent from their belief that it was of divine origin. Hermes or Apollo was said to have invented the lyre, Athena the simple flute, and Pan the shepherd's pipes, and many myths, such as those of Amphion and Orpheus, sang of its haunting power and influence. The actual foundation of the music of the Greeks has been ascribed to Terpander (c. 675 BC), of the Aeolian island of Lesbos, who was the first to give true artistry to song by accompanying it with a cithara.

In the beginning, music was subordinate to the words. It was only in this way that an ancient audience could follow the musical representation of the intricate language of a text when sung by a whole choir. There was no music and no poem that was not sung—the impulses which controlled the creation of these two forms of expression were equally potent in each art. The first songs of the pagan era were verses chanted over the tombs of warriors whose brave deeds were recounted and whose memories were invoked. The narrator, heated by draughts of fiery brew, commonly soared in fictional flights and turned fact into legend. Thus arose the golden period of epic chant. It progressed from a purely vocal genre with words, to vocal with instrumental accompaniment, to the purely instrumental or abstract.

Greek music was monodic wherein all voices and instruments sang the same tune. But the subtleties of the tune were readily apparent to imaginative and sensitive listeners who found them to be as vivid and poignant as the most richly scored of modern operas. Critics regarded it as a decline in the art form when, towards the end of the Peloponnesian War, music began to be a more important element than the poetry it accompanied. This change was first introduced in the solos of the Greek tragedies and in their choruses where music raised itself more and more to a free and independent position beside poetry.

In its earliest phase, medieval music and Christian music were one and the same thing. Certainly the Christians did not all at once work out an original new system of musical representation. As always happens, they employed the old means society already had at hand to express new values. The first Christians were converted pagans; their music likewise was pagan music diverted from its contemporary significance. Beginning as an expression of hope for the miraculous by a minority of believers, Christian music became the official music of the age and benefited from the wealth that power brought. Eventually, its content changed. Instead of recording the intimate hopes of the faithful, it proclaimed aloud the doctrine of power.

In the early Christian world, music was fostered jealously by the Church exclusively for worship, and the birth of musical form and structure was wrought within its cloisters. The first explorations in musical form began with the addition of a second human voice in the liturgy as a servile accompaniment to the single-voiced chant, with the second voice always keeping its unaltered and respectful distance. The possibilities of combining several voices (polyphony), independent in melody yet interdependent in harmony, reached their highest levels of precision, dignity and elaboration over the next few centuries. But no matter how exalted or articulate its power, music could be used to express only those feelings that were sanctioned within the Faith, in the austere and somber musical forms of the Church school.

Apart from dance music, most of the music that was written between the years 600 to 1100 (The Middle Ages) was for the voice, and was meant to be sung without any instrumental accompaniment. And by far, the most important genre of this time was the Catholic Mass. Of all the ceremonies in human society, those concerned with religious worship have remained the most profound. The Christian Church has always distinguished between private worship and the liturgy, with the latter being a formal worship enacted by a community coming together to offer thanks to God. The centerpiece of the Christian communal world was the Mass (Latin: *Ite missa est,* Go, you are dismissed). This ritual enactment of the Last Supper was designed to impress upon the ordinary person the assurance and splendor of the spiritual world in contrast to the miseries and uncertainties of everyday existence. A Mass could celebrate a feast day, a saint's birthday, a funeral (*requiem mass*) or a universal event such as Easter or Christmas. The text of the Mass was in Latin which, having open and clear vowels, was particularly well suited for chanting. In a Low Mass, all the words were spoken, but a High Mass (*missa solemnis*) required many sections to be sung. The human voice, with its deep expressiveness and versatility, became the obvious instrument to praise the glory of God in the song of His Church.

The earliest song of the church was the chant (plainchant or plainsong), commonly known as *Gregorian Chant* after Pope Gregory I (540-604). Here, the music of the entire Mass consisted of a single, repetitively chanted line, trance-like and deeply mystical, devoid of any instrumental accompaniment. Instruments were considered to be too distracting and empty, and popular melodies too heretical in their content, to be allowed in communal worship. The earliest chants were, most likely, an accented mode of speech. Each syllable of a Latin text was sung in a steady, balanced, single voice with perhaps a change of pitch, either up or down, at the end of a line. At any moment, only a single note was heard, strong and expressive, and it never lost its devout, somewhat austere, feeling. In any span of time, only a *single* melody, with its unique rhythm and tone color was present, without accompaniments of any kind. Its beauty lay, and still does, in the balanced rise and fall of the lines.

The plainchant was not intended to represent actual men praying in an act of worship. Rather, the sorrow of the Christ, the soul tormented and longing for union with God and salvation were the spiritual issues evoked, and the chant was devoted solely to the mystery of God. The music had about it a strange quality of otherworldliness and timelessness. It appealed to what was highest in the soul, and its beauty and nobility came from the fact that it borrowed little from the world of the senses.

The definite musical structure of the Mass was established in the late Middle Ages by the French composer Machaut. He grouped the sections of a *missa solemnis* into the Ordinary, or unchanged portion, in which the text for the Mass was the same for all occasions, and the Proper, or changing part, where additional text was chosen to suit the event that was being celebrated. The five parts that made up the Ordinary of a Mass were the

Kyrie (Lord have Mercy) sung three times by the congregation, *Gloria* (Glory to God in the highest) based on the song of the angels at the birth of Christ, *Credo* or a statement of faith (beginning with "I believe in one God"), *Sanctus Benedictus* (Holy, holy, holy), and the *Agnus Dei* which was a prayer petitioning for mercy and peace ("Lamb of God, who takest away the sins of the world"). In a *requiem* Mass, the *Gloria* and the *Credo* were omitted, and other hymns and prayers including the *Dies irae* (Day of Wrath) were added. The Ordinary divisions of a Mass, that occurred in every Mass, were the ones that were initially set to music. Such music could then be played at any time whenever that particular text was used. It is this group of five texts of the Ordinary that has been set to music, over the centuries, by the great composers.

The five sections that were added to the Ordinary to form the Proper alternated with the five parts of the Ordinary. The first of these five additions was a musical introduction or *Introit* that opened the Mass and preceded the *Kyrie*, and announced the particular occasion that was being celebrated on that day in the Mass. The next addition was the *Gradual* which followed the *Gloria*, and was originally sung from the step (*gradus*) of a pulpit as the epistle was being moved from one side of the alter to the other. The *Alleluia* (a hymn of praise or verses from the Bible) was added to follow the *Gradual*; the *Offertory* (offering of bread and wine at the altar to God) followed the *Credo*; and the *Communion* (partaking of the consecrated bread and wine) was added to follow the *Agnes Dei* and end the Mass.

A significant advance was made in music between 900 and 1200 when a new concept in singing, called the *organum*, was developed in France. The choir of the Abbey of St Martial at Limoges took to singing certain items of the Mass by splitting the choir into parts, one group singing the original chant and others singing four or five or eight notes below. The idea was simply to introduce a certain amount of decoration into the plain chant that typically involved combining two or more equally important voices or melodies with contrasting pitches. Sometimes, soloist and congregation would alternate; sometimes, the congregation was divided to sing alternate verses and then come together. Over time, the chant developed into a very sophisticated form of free rhythm. About 1300, medieval composers felt that they had so mastered the technical development of polyphony that they believed that they were creating a new art that they called the *ars nova*. And with this term, they relegated the *organum* into the realm of the *ars antiqua* (ancient art).

The typical Mass of the late Middle Ages was based upon a fragment of traditional chant around which two or more voices were made to weave an inventive web. The same chant was commonly used as the basis (called *cantus firmus*) for all the sections of a Mass setting. And, over time, the original chant was so heavily concealed by the musical surrounding of the vocal melodies that it very well went unrecognized by the congregation.

Since the best composers of the time were equally adept at writing music for the glittering and indolent life at court, it was perhaps a small step to use a secular tune, instead of a chant, as the basis for a Mass setting. One of the prolific composers of the time, Guillaume Dufay, actually took the melody of one of his love songs and one of his battle-songs to use as a *cantus firmus!* Such Masses were called "parody" Masses. The greatest composer of the age, Josquin des Pres, created a deeper integration still by requiring the voices to copy each other melodically in counterpoint.

Side by side with plainchant, perhaps even older, perhaps mightily influenced by it, lived folk-song, the song of the people. These ancient songs, though bent beneath several yokes, preserved an image of the life of the people from its birth. They were songs of occasion and songs of ceremony, songs of war, both epic and historical, and songs of village festivals, songs of the farm, of toil, of melancholy evenings in the winter, of women enamored and professional brigands, songs of coarse guffawing laughter and songs of childhood.

The music that follows presents the Gregorian Chant which formed the foundation of church music of the Middle Ages. The secular music of this period is listed in *The Lifetime Listening Program.*

Hildegard von Bingen: Gregorian Chant

Hildegard, born in 1098, was a mystic who entered the Benedictine cloister at Disibodenberg as a child and later became the Abbess. In 1151, she founded her own convent on the Rubertsberg near Bingen. Poetess, biologist, physician, diplomat, mystic seer, monastic reformer—the "Sybil of the Rhine," as Hildegard was then known, was all this! And, in addition, she was an outstanding composer of monophonic chant music.

Hildegard advocated a total healing system that integrated natural medicine with spiritual knowledge and music. She compiled a handbook on nature, the *Physica*, and a handbook on medicine called *Causae et Curae* in which she recommended the use of music, gems and minerals for healing—for example, the cooling effects of jasper placed firmly over the chest, and the healing properties of emeralds were considered to be especially beneficial for diseases of the heart.

The music of Hildegard is purely melodic one-line (monophonic) music consisting of a single, repetitively chanted line, trance-like and deeply mystical, devoid of any instrumental accompaniment. Most of it has survived in the Cistercian monastery at Villers as a collection of lyric poetry set to music. Called the *Symphonia harmonie celestium revelationum* (Symphony of the Harmony of Celestial Revelation), the collection contains her most beautiful and affecting pieces that seek to convey her belief that music, with its suffusion of lyric imagery and tone painting, is the highest form of human activity. To her, music gave concrete form to the positive truths on which rested the solidarity of the members of a well-disciplined social body. It became an instrument of intellectual understanding rather than a soul-stirring witness to the timorous but often heroic faith of individuals—a new intellectual system that modified both the individual representation of destiny as well as the causality of the acts that men performed. It offered to the faithful a painstakingly worked out repertory of attitudes and events which could have meaning for the initiated. The melodic lines flowed freely in her music, blending erotic imagery and an ineffable mystical spirit to mirror the sounds of the heavenly spheres and choirs of angels.

Hildegard's musical corpus includes seventy one works, mostly monophonic liturgical chants devoted to religious feasts or classes of feasts.

This mystic Nun, a captivating figure for believers and non-believers alike, became famous from the CD format only a few years ago. Nearly a millenium after her birth, one of the principal female composers is coming into her own. The diversity of her music is surprising for the time in which she wrote. We have to wait well over half a millenium before we come to women who contributed as much to the musical literature - to the music of Fanny Mendelssohn, Clara Schumann and Mrs. H. H. A. Beach, and they too have had to take a back seat to their male counterparts. Indeed, Felix Mendelssohn and Robert Schumann may well have published the works of the women in their lives as their own just to give their music its well deserved public exposure. Times are not so sordid today, but matters still haven't been completely righted.

Deutsche Harmonia Mundi has been a leader in presenting the musical output of this mysterious woman under its Sequentia pro-duced series. Since 1989 the output has been impressive and worthy; *Symphoniae* (BMG 77020-2RG), *Canticles of Ecstasy* (BMG 05472-77320-2), *Voice of the Blood* (BMG 05472 77346 2), *O Jerusalem* (BMG 05472-77353-2) and finally *Ordo virtutum* (BMG 05472 77394-2) document the output of this amazing composer in a way that no other compendia of releases do, though I would encourage the listener interested in discovering Hildegard through a variety of artists to also search out *Tapestry's Celestial Light* from a recent Telarc recording (CD-80456) which amalgamates her writings and her music. The Telarc disc is the most sonically impressive and may well be a good starting point for those wishing an introduction to Hildegard von Bingen's *oeuvre*.

Don't confuse these musical *meisterwerken* for the Gregorian Chant CDs you see being pushed at your local store. This is highly differentiated, cultivated music worthy of intense study; it is not atmospheric or background music; don't sell it short!

- Canticles of Ecstasy
  HM/BMG Dig 05472 77320-2. Sequentia, Barbara Thornton

The Renaissance

The Renaissance was a time of reawakening in Europe to the culture of Greece and Rome that had been forgotten or neglected from the time that Rome had fallen to the barbarians. It began as a period of attempted reconciliation between classical and Christian teachings that resulted in a vivid revival of the traditions of ancient Greece and Rome, insofar as they did not affect the foundations of Christian faith. And in the process it advocated a new and vital perception of the dignity of man as a rational being apart from theological determinations.

The proper study of mankind now became man, in all the strength and beauty of his own body, the passion and eloquence of his feelings, and the frail majesty of his reason. A just and virtuous life no longer depended upon the Emperor, the Pope, or a monastic renunciation. Man placed the crown and miter on his own head and proclaimed himself the new emperor. Heaven and earth were made for man, but man was made for himself. The whole universe was regarded as a small, finite place, and it was man's place. He alone occupied the center, and his good was the controlling end of all creation.

Though much that was medieval survived in their minds, men felt they were living on the brink of a new and modern age. A brand new type of man emerged, intellectually and politically self-reliant, who called everything in the world into question with an extraordinary and peculiar combination of Utopian fantasy and cool realism. Bold and sweeping ideas became very much a part of the prevailing atmosphere, and wide ranging discussions took place among the nobility and bourgeoisie in the *palazzi* and country houses. The recognition that poetry apart from its supposed prophetic meaning was delightful for its own sake, and that the history of ancient nations, in spite of their paganism, could be used profitably was the first step taken by these pioneers of the new culture.

An important genre in the music of the Renaissance was the music of the Church, and the most characteristic feature of the Mass during the Renaissance was polyphony. No less devotional, the church music of the Renaissance was a coherent musical experience that looked towards both God *and* man. Here was a sweetly melodic *musicke's feaste*, both mystic and colorful, reminiscent of sacred processions and pilgrimages, saints and miracles, the adoration of relics, and all the exuberance that the Latin temperament brought to the Catholic religion. But the atmosphere was typically Italian, as clear as the waters of the Mediterranean and as grand as the Sistine Chapel.

Another significant innovation of the Renaissance in music was the art of orchestration. Very few instruments had been expressly designated in medieval compositions—it was usually up to the performer to work things out with his own resources of instruments. But with the Renaissance, more and more instruments were specifically named on the title pages of musical works, indicating a new and deep concern for instrumental music. The audience was, after all, the consumer of music, and an active effort was made to please the audience by playing the interludes between the verses of a hymn with different instruments—wood winds, brass or strings— because always hearing the same instrument could annoy the listener!

As with the liturgical forms, so with the secular ones. By the fourteenth century, the popular art of song was flourishing everywhere in Europe outside the restrictive walls of the Church. In taverns and village greens, in country fairs and town squares, lively and colorful wandering minstrels expressed their music through words and, if there were not enough singers at hand, through instruments such as the harp, lute or fiddle. Their lyrics sang of their intense joy in living and their devotion to the difficult art of courtly love, illustrating a side of medieval life that was in direct antithesis to the austere spirituality of the chanting monks who were their contemporaries.

The most far-reaching development in the secular music of the time was the evolution of polyphony to give depth to the song. In its more mature form, the basic melody was given in long, held notes, akin to the plainsong in medieval chant, to a lower principal voice called a *tenor* (Latin *tenere*: to hold), while a second voice sang a free-flowing "melismatic" line in shorter notes to adorn the main melody. The tenor was usually too long drawn out to be easily audible as a melody but acted as a fixed reference point for the other freshly composed free melodies, each with its own words, to weave around in a contrapuntal fashion. In such a form, the vocal composition was called a *motet* (French: *mot,* meaning *word)*.

Evidence of the great power of music was soon everywhere. The most cultivated form of secular vocal music during the Renaissance was the *madrigal*, a four- or five-voiced composition usually sung by soloists, rather than by large choruses, that made use of polyphony as well as simple chords. The early meaning of the word *madrigal* is "rustic song" such as might be sung by a shepherd; and the word was first noted in 1332 in a writing of Antonio da Tempo. The Italian madrigal was a descendent of the songs of the wandering minstrels. They were short vocal pieces bound intimately to a poem—at best, and most characteristically, to a Petrarchian sonnet, an isolated stanza from Ariosto, or a lyric by Tasso. Images, moods and affects were translated into musical terms. The finest madrigals were cleverly composed so that a key word or phrase—often amorous or naughty—would suddenly stand out in the musical web of polyphony, and then the busy, often jolly, counterpoint would close in again. Often the madrigalists would imitate the sounds of nature as bird song. The madrigal subject might vary with different writers, but the general style was always the same, being a generally short composition of many parts, a melody for each voice, with the words usually suggesting a quaint imagery, or gaiety, and a fine sense of humor.

The music that follows presents the mainstream of Renaissance church music: the Renaissance Mass. The secular music of the age is listed in *The Lifetime Listening Program.*

Palestrina: Mass for Pope Marcellus

The greatest achievement of Giovanni Pierluigi de Palestrina (1525 - 1594) was to establish a form of music that was to become the standard for the Renaissance Mass. When he accepted the position of *maestro di capella* at Santa Maria Maggiore in Rome, the music of the Church had lost all relation to the services which it was supposed to illustrate. Not only did music completely dominate over the words of the Mass, but it was founded, for the most part, on popular secular melodies to which the words were actually sung. It was not unusual for the most solemn phrases of the *Kyrie*, *Gloria*, *Credo* and *Agnus* to blend along the aisles with the unedifying refrains of a lewd *chanson* of Flanders or Provence, and dance music was played daily on the church organ! A Papal Bull was eventually issued by Pope Marcellus II to reform Church music which required that the words of a mass should be more clearly sung in a suitable manner, with voices so modulated that everything could be both heard and understood properly, and nothing impure or "lascivious" entered into the music of the Church.

The 30 year old Palestrina was ordered to write a Mass as a prototype of the kind of music that should be the sacred office. He composed three Masses and sent them without titles to the Cardinal; it was in the third, afterward known as the *Missa Papae Marcelli*, that the commission felt that Palestrina had at last produced the archetype of ecclesiastical song. The music was inextricably bound to the words and to the acts of adoration which it illustrated; the inner meaning of the Christian religion was everything. The post of composer to the Pontifical choir was created for him in the Vatican by a grateful Pope in honor of this noble achievement, and seven successive pontiffs were to confirm the great composer in this office during their reigns.

Palestrina himself explained that his intention was "to adorn the holy sacrifice of the Mass in a new manner." The technique of counterpoint was suppressed whenever there was any danger that the text might become obscured, and interplay of the parts and frequent repetition of the words were used to convey the text with unfailing clarity. Musical variety was preserved by the ingenious use of every possible combination of the six available voice parts. And the prevailing note of his music was its intense spirituality. Not a touch of the earthy degraded its celestial rapture! It voiced the highest and purest mysticism of the Catholic faith as it had never been voiced before.

Palestrina infused a spiritual quality in his music by taking into account the proper accentuation of the Latin words, and often even their meaning, and by inventing melodies that were smooth and clear in texture, leaving plenty of air and space for the polyphony to flow at a continuous and unbroken pace. All was controlled and calculated in the skillful combination of the elegance of counterpoint and harmony with audibility of text, yet all seemed so wonderfully spontaneous that the ear was beguiled by the "linked sweetness long drawn out" that became the hallmark of the Palestrina style.

The *Missa Papae Marcelli* (*Mass for Pope Marcellus*) falls into the usual five sections: *Kyrie, Gloria, Credo, Sanctus* (including *Benedictus*), and *Agnus Dei.*

The *Kyrie* consists of three distinct sections, each with its own musical development: *Kyrie, eleison* (Lord, have mercy on us); *Christie, eleison* (Christ, have mercy on us), and then once again *Kyrie, eleison.* Long melismas are avoided so as not to obscure the text.

The *Gloria* opens with a solo voice singing in a monophonic Gregorian Chant, and then the choral polyphony takes over beginning with the phrase *Et in terra* (*And on earth*). The movement contains subsections, set off by pauses and by contrasting musical treatment as demonstrated in the section that begins with the words *Qui tollis* (*Thou who takest away*). An especially awesome moment in the music occurs with the words *Jesu Christie*, uttered twice in the *Gloria,* where the singers are allowed to linger over the syllables with an unique majesty and reverence.

Like the *Gloria*, the *Credo* also opens with a solo voice singing in Gregorian Chant following which the choir enters in glorious polyphony. This movement, too, is punctuated by sections, beginning with the words *Et incarnatus est* (*And it was incarnate*) and *Cruci-*

fixus, where the music is made to develop in contrast to the main form.

The *Sanctus* is a marvelous example of graceful polyphony. Of especial interest is the melismatic singing (the singing of many notes to one syllable) in the elongated syllables of the "di" of the word *Benedictus*, and the "ve" of the word *venit*.

The concluding *Agnus Dei* is sung twice to the same music.

To the thousands of serious men and women who have found solace in the songs of the early Church, I have a confession to make. Pivotal as its role has been in the story of great music, I am guilty of procrastination, and have perennially deferred really coming to grips with the music of the medieval times and the Renaissance. And so I find myself unversed even as I am faced with this section to make a suitable recommendation. However, my co-author has come to my rescue and to him I owe the choice presented below.

- Missa Papae Marcelli; Tu es Petrus— ALLEGRI: Miserere
  DG 415 517-2. Westminister Abbey Ch., Preston

The Baroque World

When the French historian Charles de Brossos visited Rome in 1739, his taste was offended by some opulent decoration on the Palazzo Doria Pamphili which he thought was more suitable for tableware than for an official building. He called this type of decoration *baroque*, and thus coined a term that came to be used to describe the artistic spirit of an age. The word Baroque (Portuguese *barroco*: "a pearl distorted"), was originally applied with a sense of disapproval for the arts of the seventeenth century. In contrast to the clarity, unity and proportion of the Renaissance, the Baroque style promoted over-elaborate extravagance with a lesser regularity of form. In music, the Baroque state of mind and the Baroque sound may be regarded as being born at the first performance of the first opera—Jacopo Peri's *Dafne*, in 1597. It reached its zenith of grandeur, pageantry and majestic self-confidence during the 1650s, and probably came to an end with the death of George Frederic Handel in 1759.

The Baroque world was an age of the landed aristocracy that was driven by the pleasures of the chase, the table and the boudoir. It was a giant theater that touched all levels of life, and all that impressed mankind was theatrical. Rubens lavishly painted the rambunctious peasants of the Flemish countryside and the fleshy mythological scenes of flirtation which the Baroque era loved so much, the formidable Bernini intersected sweeping arches with flamboyant columns to form colonnades and alters of breathtaking majesty set ablaze in marble and glass, and a permanent air of scandal and amorous intrigues hovered over the plush drawing rooms of Versailles where the Sun King, Louis XIV, starred in his own ballets at the royal court theater. Baroque music expressed the cheerful fecundity of this age—lucid, spontaneous, melodious, exuberant and embellished, and infused with a tension and movement that added gusto. It reflected the changing moods of individual composers who threw themselves wholly into their work, and enshrined the listeners in a new theatrical splendor.

Blended with the courtly grandeur of Baroque art was a homespun simplicity, and a passionate humanism and an intense devotion that was promoted by the purifying experience of Martin Luther's Reformation. Rembrandt probed deeply for psychological motifs in the persons he painted, Vermeer sought patterns and symbols in his recordings of bourgeois Holland, and Milton wrote with tremendous feeling to justify the ways of God to man. Superstition rode side-by-side with science, destitute misery mingled with extravagant wealth, and religious asceticism arose out of a world given to colorful ceremonials. And much of the music of the Baroque world was outside the dominant theatrical mood. Bach's magnificent works for the organ, his Masses, Passions and Cantatas projected deeply the intensity of the inner vision, and reconciled the significant spiritual problems of the Baroque world.

An increase in the size of musical ensembles distinguished Baroque music from all earlier periods, and music for harpsichord, organ, lute and other chord-playing instruments filled in the harmonies that had been previously supplied by voices. The variety of musical instruments that were pressed into service made it necessary to invent a glue that could bind the new composite music together by a continuous and powerful thong. A solution was at hand in the pert and metallic jangle of the newly refined harpsichord (the keyboard precursor of the piano), and the variety of its tone colors and ample harmonics made it the instrument *par excellence* for such a purpose. The harpsichord was marvelously suited for the spontaneous expression of free fantasy and could, snakelike, turn out patterns of infinite choice and wide emotional range. In addition, it provided the harmonic foundation for the baroque musical glue, called the *basso continuo,* that became the hallmark of the music of this age.

With the emergence of the Baroque, the weight in a musical ensemble clearly shifted to the strings. Whereas the inventory of the chapel of Henry VIII, a century earlier in England, had boasted two hundred and seventy two wind instruments, the Berlin court orchestra in 1667 consisted of twenty two strings and only one wind instrument! Exploitation of the individuality of instruments marked the Baroque style. Baroque composers sometimes made music at four or five levels at once, and intended their listeners to hear what the flutes were doing while also pursuing the violins, and be aware, at the same time, of what was going on in the bass. There was an inherent fascination in the interweaving of two or three or more strands of melody.

The main orchestral genres that were cultivated in the Baroque world were the Baroque *concerto* and the orchestral *suite*. A classical concerto is a composition, usually in three movements, for a solo instrument and orchestra in which the two are made to act as opposing and unequal forces. In its Baroque form called *concerto grosso*, the musical dialogue occurred between a full orchestra (called the *tutti*) on the one hand, and smaller *groups* of instruments (called the *concertino*) instead of a single solo instrument. Unlike the solo-instrument concertos of later times, the Baroque *concerto grosso* was not concerned with a display of virtuosity by the soloists. The *tutti* and the *concertino* were equal partners, and the aim of a *concerto grosso* was to exploit the contrast in sound of the different groups of musical instruments.

The Baroque orchestral *suite* was a collection of dance tunes that were arranged to provide contrast between successive dances. The keyboard suite contributed immensely, and it was a keyboard composer, Froberger, who standardized the order and types of the dances. Eventually, the suite came to be played by an orchestra for its music value alone. It was like being at a dance today where the music is so magnificent that hosts of young people stop dancing entirely to crowd in around the musicians and listen to the band! Another name for a suite was *partita*; in later years, some of the pieces in a suite were given such names as *sinfonia, caprice, burlesque, romance* or *pastoral*.

Opera, like so much in music, owed its foundation largely through accident. When, late in the sixteenth century, a small band of Florentine enthusiasts took upon themselves the task of reviving the lost glories of Greek drama, nothing was farther from their thoughts than the creation of a new art-form. They worked along what they believed to be antiquarian lines; they wrote plays, and because they fancied that Greek drama had been sung, or rather chanted, in a kind of accompanied recitative, they decided to perform their plays in the same way. None of the musical forms then in use were satisfactory for such an experiment, so the composers struck out boldly and produced a new form, a sort of musical speech, that allowed the voice to follow the accents of language but employing musical tone. This declamatory song became known as *recitative*. The men called themselves the *Camerati* (Comrades), and the little "opera" that they assembled (*Dafne*) was eventually performed at the palatial home of Jacopo Corsi in 1594.

If music in pagan times had imitated and stirred the emotions with matchless power, it could be done again. And Baroque composers devoted their attention to the means of emotional expression, experimenting sometimes with great psychological understanding and, over the years, with greater ingenuity and effectiveness. The composer became the dramatist, and the libretto his inspiration and his limitation. The initial efforts were almost entirely set to a bare monotonous recitative, varied at rare intervals by simple passages of choral writing and short instrumental interludes. But over the decade, though the recitative became the fundamental constant element of operatic dramaturgy, the musical interest rose, the solo parts and the choruses became more expressive, and the instrumental sections were made considerably more elaborate. The music became tuneful and charming, the main part of the drama was carried out in expressive dialogue, and the variety of instrumentation created an overwhelming effect. For the first time, the *da capo* was regularly used to give cohesion to the musical fabric of the opera—the first part of an air was repeated after the end of the second part. And to whip the recitative into a passion, the music was harrowed through every available means for tension, from sudden halts and spurting cascades in rhythm to precipitous and intense rises and falls in melodic line.

At first the audience protested against the "unnaturalness" of the performers who sang their conversations instead of speaking them. But musical declamation could appeal to the emotions and imagination in ways spoken lines could not, and before long the Italians adopted to the new genre with an unquenchable enthusiasm. It would serve no good purpose to enumerate the composers who furnished Italy with operas! Hardly a town was without its opera house, for the musical activity throughout the country was amazing. The output of libretti and scores was enormous; everything was instantly staged, cheered, and plundered. Music at that time meant the opera, the opera guided the evolution of the art of music, and the librettist became the universal laureate.

What may be called the first period of Italian opera began with Monterverdi and culminated in Alessandro Scarlatti. Lulli brought Italian traditions to Paris where he grafted them to the *masques* that were already popular at the French courts. Dancing, for which the Italians cared comparatively little, was much appreciated in France, and elaborate ballets became a distinctive feature of Lulli's operas. And the development of the new music-drama reached new heights in England in the operas of Henry Purcell (? 1659 - 1695).

The composers of the Baroque era were a remarkable group. Italy was the principal land of music in the Baroque world. Scarcely had a traveler entered the country when he would become possessed of the musical passion that was devouring the whole nation. There were violinists, instrumental performers and singers in the streets. And one could hear in the public places a shoemaker, a blacksmith or a cabinet maker singing an aria with a correctness and taste which they owed to nature and to the habit of listening. The *concerto grosso* was, if not invented, at least carried to its perfection by the Italian Archangelo Corelli who ranked Handel among his many pupils. After Corelli came Antonio Vivaldi who singularly transformed the *concerto grosso* by giving it the free character of program music. His concerti were grand "impression pictures" in sound where the least change of emotion could make itself easily felt.

Even in Germany, it was clear that both princes and plebeians favored the Italians. Saxony had produced two great giants in Johann Sebastian Bach and George Frederick Handel (they never met, though they were born within eighty miles of each other), but it seemed that the Germans had derived their knowledge of music not from nature, but through study. The love of music was not nearly so ardent or so universal as in Italy, not even along the Rhine that had always claimed to inspire a passion for music. Bach, himself, had enjoyed a respectable reputation among the musicians of his time, but this celebrity never extended beyond a restricted circle. Twenty years after his death, he was remembered in Leipzig as an able organist and teacher who had brought the art of playing the organ to the highest degree of perfection. For Bach's music, the eclipse after his death was virtually total—it was almost as though it had never existed! It had to wait for the youthful Felix Mendelssohn to resurrect his choral works a century later, which gradually accelerated its further revival.

Handel, on the other hand, was more fortunate. His music was genuinely conceived for the people, and he produced in a language that was immediately understood by all, and which expressed those feelings in which all could share. He had always within him a popular vein: Like the orators of old, he had the cult of style and instinct for immediate and vital effect. Handel was never a church musician, and he hardly ever wrote for the church other than what he composed for private chapels or for exceptional events. Whereas critics and historians found in Bach and "his melodious sons" nothing to glorify but their skill as performers of the organ and clavier, the same genres in Handel's works were dramatic and theatrical, and had an astonishing popularity in his own time. Certain arias from his operas were circulated and vulgarized not only in England, but abroad. His thought and instrumental style led him to conceive music for the great masses, wide spaces, and huge audiences.

Open-air music took a prominent place in Baroque English life. The environs of London were full of gardens where, Pepys tells us, "vocal and instrumental concerts vied with the voices of the birds." Handel wrote pieces especially intended for these garden concerts. In his famous *Water Music*, written for the procession of royal barges on the Thames, and his *Royal Fireworks Music* that he composed to accompany a grand fireworks display in London's Green Park, he asserted very definitively the character of open-air music.

With the death of Handel, the Baroque era came to a close. But in the recordings that follow, its music continues to speak to listeners in a voice as clear, and as moving, as it did across the chasm of centuries to the audiences of that age.

Vivaldi: The Four Seasons

Antonio Vivaldi (1675 - 1741), nicknamed *il prete rosso* (the red-haired priest), was a music teacher at a foundling school for girls in Venice, and a master of the Baroque *concerto grosso* form. Even Bach was one of his great admirers—Bach arranged more than twenty of Vivaldi's violin concertos for other instruments such as the harpsichord and organ. Among Vivaldi's voluminous legacy are a set of concerti that were called by the composer *Il Cimento dell' Armonia e dell' Inventioni* (*The Trial of Harmony and Invention*). The first quartet of works in this collection are *The Four Seasons*.

This sparkling music, perhaps the best known work from the Baroque era, is one of the most felicitous examples of program music. Vivaldi wrote the music with great gusto to bring to life the words of four sonnets that he had written, each for one of the four seasons. In his manuscript, each line of the sonnet is printed over the precise music passage that explains it. Vivaldi was also an ingenious exploiter of sound effects, and took an almost childish pleasure in imitating the songs of birds such as the cuckoo, turtle dove and finch. And in this work he gives a free transcription of the sounds that he may have heard over the seasons in the sheltered gardens of his school behind the Grand Canal of Venice. The music itself is vividly explicit, from the bird calls and the arf-arf of a shepherd's dog in *Spring,* the slumbering of a shepherd disturbed by flies in *Summer,* a peasant carousal and a hunt in *Fall*, to shivery winter winds and the chattering of teeth in *Winter*! Some may choose to regard this work as absolute music: a quartet of violin concertos. Each concerto observes the standard format of the Italian concerto of the time, with a fast first movement, a slow second one, and a fast finale.

The Four Seasons is one of the over-represented and over-recorded works in the catalog. It is a disturbing thought that the number of available   recordings is approaching one hundred when other Vivaldi compositions, particularly his sacred music, let alone other far more inventive works than *The Four Seasons*, are shrouded in obscurity. This is something I will never understand! Nonetheless, this work affords excellent exposure to the novitiate and a pleasant refreshment of memory to the advanced listener who has been away from the Baroque for years—so long as one has not been exposed to an overplaying of the work, as it appears far too often in television programs, movies and commercials. Producers beware!

Forget the "big band" full orchestral versions by major orchestras and their *chefs diragenten*. These plodding, syrupy performances should be followed by a death sentence to the conductor for corruption of the music. This is a chamber orchestra-sized work, and should be heard as such. Otherwise, it becomes an unwieldy, marshmallow mass of plush sound, something Vivaldi would probably have rejected out of hand. My personal favorite is an older analog recording played by Neville Marriner and the Academy of St. Martin's-in-the-Fields with Alan Loveday as the solo violinist. This tasteful, idiomatic and elegant performance has stood the test of time since its first release several decades ago, and nothing in my mind has bettered it. Another excellent modern version is by Gidon Kremer with the London Symphony Orchestra and Claudio Abbado, a recording made at the dawn of the digital era by DG but released only in analog form for unknown reasons.

An alternate performance, issued this decade by Trevor Pinnock and the English Concert—a group dedicated to performances in more than idiomatic circumstances with original instruments—bristles with the excitement and verve of how the work more than likely sounded in Vivaldi's own time.

- The Four Seasons
    Argo 414 486-2 Alan Loveday, ASMF, Marriner
- The Four Seasons
    DG 431 172-2. Kremer, LSO, Abbado

Bach: Brandenburg Concertos

The true value of Johann Sebastian Bach (1685 - 1750), regarded by some as the greatest composer of all time, is still enigmatic. When the rest of his world was reveling in the delights of a new toy, the opera, which seemed to all but drive out the ideal of high art and leave sensuous melody as the sole usurper, this German master, like some Egyptian high priest, single-handedly upheld the traditions and spirit of the "learned style" in music in the time of its greatest peril. He filled the old bottles with the new wine of his genius. Like *Janus,* he looked both backwards and into the future. He quietly continued to write his oratorios and organ works and, elaborating on the musical forms and styles that had been used by his predecessors, he raised instrumental music to a strict discipline. And he did all this within the limits of a harassed and ill-paid organist with a family of twenty children in a little German province. Perhaps the greatest value of Bach may be indirect, in the influence that he has had in the world of music through the works of other great masters. For, among composers, there has been but one source that has inexhaustibly provided new ideas over the centuries—Johann Sebastian Bach.

The *Brandenburg Concertos* are the purest product of Bach's instrumental music. Some have called them treasures in the same sense as the Beethoven symphonies. Before his time, instrumental solos in orchestral music had been predominantly limited to the strings. Bach experimented with other instruments, and in the six concertos that he dispatched to the Margrave of Brandenburg, he perfected and summarized the whole art of the Baroque instrumental music form called the *concerto grosso* in which groups of instruments or solo instruments alternate with the whole orchestra. Here is truly lovely music, simple yet so full and rich—at times buoyant, vigorous and vibrant, sparkling and tripping with an elastic step; at times serene and tender and extraordinarily beautiful to the point of poignancy. Some have called this music profoundly nourishing and life-giving, much like the basic simple rhythms of the universe, and the pulse and growth of nature.

Each concerto was written for a different group of instruments that sang the "solo" parts; each was totally different from the others in mood and style. Weird instruments that have fallen out of use since Bach's day give them the peculiar shrill delicacy of the true Baroque. Strings, oboes, bassoons and horns are brought together with the audacity of genius as a kind of solo quartet in the First concerto, a trumpet is featured prominently with splendid fragments of melody in the Second, and the Fifth has an unusually long part for the harpsichord making it, perhaps, the first precursor of the piano concerto. The Third concerto is also unusual in that it uses only strings. It is unlikely that the Margrave ever had any of the works performed—musical gossip says that he failed to appreciate the imagination, enchantment and wealth of originality that marked these pieces. In reality, it appears more than likely that they were just too difficult for the Margrave's orchestra to play!

The *Brandenburg Concerti* have been well served in recorded format for many decades, principally due to orchestral size and the relative ease of "miking" the instrumental forces at play. Original instrument and modern performances abound in the catalog, many at least decent, and many truly excellent.

I remember as a toddler running in circles around the dining room table to the jaunty rhythm of the Third Movement of the Second Concerto, being made nauseous by the repeated encircling of the table (not the music). I learned the recordings first in a performance by Carl Ristenpart conducting the Chamber Orchestra of the Saar on a Nonesuch LP, currently unavailable. And, having heard these works several hundred times apiece, I still revere my Karl Richter recordings on Archiv, and I was truly pleased when they were reissued on CD a number of years ago. They are virile, aggressive readings, far from being Teutonic, and the Munich Bach Orchestra plays brilliantly. The recording, dating from 1967, captures all aspects of each part with ease, and the tempi are typically on the fast side. Richter himself is particularly impressive on the harpsichord in the Fifth Concerto.

Of other modern instruments versions, I would consider Marriner's early and late recordings on Philips with the Academy of St. Martin's-in-the-Fields, the former with Thurston Dart on *continuo*, the latter with many a famous first chair in the orchestra such as Henryk Szeryng and Jean-Pierre Rampal. These are just a hair pallid compared to Richter, but are nonetheless excellent. Of the versions played on original instruments, I can heartily recommend Pinnock's excellent traversal with the English Concert on Archiv—they are brilliantly virtuosic, and are expertly captured by the recording engineers in modern digital sound. Also on Archiv are the rather humorous recordings by Reinhard Goebel and his group of original instrumentalists, the Musica Antiqua Koln. One well known radio announcer in Los Angeles wondered what the rush in these perform-ances was all about: perhaps, the players had to use the toilet facilities imminently! Nonetheless, the performances are lean, swift and sure-footed, and expertly played. They make an exotic recommendation, though not a first choice.

Unfortunately, I'm leaving out excellent recorded versions, and as unfair as this is, no one would go wrong with any of the referenced recordings.

- Brandenburg Concertos Nos 1-6, BWV 1046-51
  Archiv 427 143.2AX2. Munich Bach O, Karl Richter
- Brandenburg Concertos Nos 1-6, BWV 1046-51
  Archiv 423 922AX3. The English Concert, Trevor Pinnock

Bach: Orchestral suites

In the beginning, there were just two kinds of music—the music of the church, and the music of the folk. Folk songs are the wild flowers of music that grow into beauty without cultivation. They are the melodies created by the people themselves in an unconscious effort to entertain or to express their inner feelings, whether of joy, sadness, longing or patriotism. When musical instruments, such as the lute, became sufficiently developed to make it possible for folk tunes to be actually played, the old songs were put together into sets of dance music which were called *suites*. A suite, then, was a collection of fairly short dance forms of various origins. In the hands of Johann Sebastian Bach, the suite reached its final stage, and assumed the rank of "absolute" music whose sole *raison d'être* was being for its own sake, setting the stage for the *sonata* and *symphony* forms of the future.

The four *Orchestral Suites*, that Bach himself called "overtures," rank with his most charming and popular compositions. They are French in style and format, with a pompous slow introduction, a lively main section, and a short pompous conclusion. And the dances, too, are French dances. Here is a merry Bach, blessed with robust health and a happy inward life, preserving for posterity the earthy and lusty dances of the land, full of playfulness and mischief, with frisky rhythms and light-footed melodies that give the music a hearty glow. Some of the songs are of true peasant stock, celebrating the land and its bounty, others are ceremonial, more like a march than a dance, and still some of the music is slow and majestic, courtly and dainty with sophisticated little steps—remembrances of a vanished world of grace and elegance.

There are many great recorded performances of the *Orchestral Suites* from the earliest periods of stereo recording, and some pretty hideous ones. Those to avoid are by the large symphony orchestras (Karajan, Marvansky), and those issued in a variegated form for lute or trio. One should hear this work as the composer intended! The *Suites* stand up well to treatment with either original instrumentation or with modern instruments. I prefer the latter for my own purposes, but the former permit a certain degree of transparency not produced by modern instruments.

Again, I grew up on the late Karl Richter's recordings of Bach. Even his solo organ recitals albums moved me. Alas, the Richter interpretation of the *Orchestral Suites* are not currently available on CD, either as a set of Bach's music or individually. They last appeared on a DG Walkman cassette and Archiv LP, and the reader would be advised to search these out, if at all possible. They are really "rock-em sock-em" versions, much like his interpretations of the *Brandenburg Concerti*.

I would say there's very little to choose between the excellence of Christopher Hogwood's Academy of Ancient Music interpretations on L'Oiseau Lyre, Sigiswald Kuijken's La Petite Bande recordings on Editio Classica, Trevor Pinnock's English Concert performances on Archiv, John Eliot Gardiner's English Baroque Soloists' recordings on Erato, and Philip Pickett's New London Concert recordings on EMI Classics; they all offer modern sound, outstanding academically appropriate instrumental contributions, and the highest quality of academic musical leadership. I have no real choice between them; all are satisfying and impressive.

As mentioned earlier, the modern instrument versions stir my soul a bit more than those played on original instruments. Other than the 1964 recordings by Richter, I would say that Marriner's recordings on Philips are preferable to his later EMI re-recording in digital sound, and certainly far preferable to his earlier performances on Argo Records from 1971. All are with the same orchestra, the Academy of St. Martin's-in-the-Fields. One will always be impressed by Marriner, especially the Philips' rendition. It is solid and exciting, and at mid price, it is a veritable steal.

- Orchestral Suites Nos. 1-4, BWV 1066-9
  Philips 446 533-2, ASMF, Marriner
- Orchestral Suites Nos. 1-4, BWV 1066-9
  Archiv 423 922-2AX3. The English Concert, Pinnock

Bach: Goldberg Variations

Bach was a workman rather than a poet. He was *obliged* to work, and he worked perseveringly. He used to say that whoever worked as hard as he did should succeed quite as well as he did. He wrote a library of music which, a century after his death, took more than ten editors over fifty years to collate. In a sense his work was final and definitive, and whatever genre he chose to illustrate, he summed up so completely in his characteristically Teutonic way that nothing more remained to be said on the subject. In the *Goldberg Variations,* he extended the horizons of keyboard music to imaginative inventions of incomparable scope.

Unlike his other instrumental works in which the interest resides in the charm of its melodic parts, it takes time to savor the gentle and consoling cheerfulness that gives such warmth to these seemingly artificial variations. The theme itself was well known to Bach since he had created it a decade earlier for the *Klavierbuchlein* of his wife, Anna Magdalena. The story goes that a Russian Count fell very ill in Dresden and could not sleep at night, and so he would require his musician, Goldberg, a pupil of Bach, to play the clavichord in an adjoining room until slumber was induced. The pupil appealed to the master, and the Count commissioned Bach to write some clavichord music of a quiet and cheerful character that Goldberg could play for him on sleepless nights. Bach thought that the best thing for the purpose would be a set of variations by reason of the persistence of the same basic harmony throughout. The result was a success! The Count was forever requesting "Dear Goldberg, play me one of *my* variations." Bach, for his part, was amply rewarded with a golden goblet containing 100 Louis d'or.

The *Goldberg Variations* have seen many iterations for harpsichord, piano, organ and chamber orchestra. My preference is for the modern piano, and there are few generally excellent recommendations for this great academic and analytical work of absolute genius. I learned this work only after the death of Glenn Gould, the Canadian pianist, who was a rather unconventional man who abandoned stardom in the concert halls and a classical recording career to live independently and perform for recordings made by the Canadian Broadcasting Company (CBC) as well as studio recordings for CBS (now Sony). Much has been written, and a film made, about his performances of this work, and no wonder! All his several available interpretations, including a live concert at the Salzburg Festival in 1957, are a revelation. The pioneering 1955 monophonic recording for Columbia Masterworks is a monument to Gould in his youth, and it should be heard. The final 1981 recording, however, is for me his most comprehensive statement on the subject, and it is the only performance I truly need for repeated hearings.

Let me say briefly that there are excellent non-Gouldian performances for those who cannot stand his rather metallic piano sound, let alone his miscellaneous musings, all out of key, which CBS desperately tried to block from hitting the microphones. No such luck: these sounds are now a part of history! For those looking for a harpsichord version, I would suggest Trevor Pinnock on Archiv, and the historic RCA recording by Wanda Landowski who put this work on the map in long-playing microgroove. For those interested in modern piano versions, there are excellent recordings by Tatiana Nikolaiev on Hyperion, Andrei Gavilov on DG, and the outstanding academician, Charles Rosen on Sony Classical—the last at budget price.

I still think one needs only the 1981 Gould performance; it's as nearly everything there is to say about the work, and it says it well.

- Goldberg Variations, BWV 988
  Sony MK37779, Glenn Gould (piano)

Bach: Mass in B minor

The Church music of the Reformation stemmed from the more rugged and sturdy temperament of Northern Europe. The titanic conflicts that had attended the Protestant quest for spiritual values created a music of great inward strength with an intense concentration of purpose. Instead of the naiveté and childlike tenderness that had clothed the Renaissance Mass, the earthy Lutheran service was forged from the fresh memory of seasoned and storm-tossed men who had shed their blood on battle fields to uphold their religious convictions. The Baroque Lutheran service did not abandon the Catholic Mass, but shortened it to include only the first two parts, the *Kyrie* and the *Gloria*. These short Masses were appropriate for regular church services. An exception was the great *Mass in B minor* by Johann Sebastian Bach which is a Catholic and not a Lutheran Mass, and incorporates all the divisions of a complete Catholic Mass. Its three hours duration, and its elaborate orchestral accompaniment, make it unsuitable for routine liturgical purposes, and it has been performed, therefore, only as a concert Mass.

It has been proposed that no one can be said to be educated who has not experienced this work. This huge Mass represents the peak of the polyphonic tradition in church music. It is a vivid series of emotional tableaux presented by an organ and orchestra, with choruses ranging from four to eight parts to solos and duets, with each expressing in music the emotional quality of the successive passages of the Mass' text. Some of the choruses are adaptations of music that had been written by Bach for other works, especially his cantatas.

The music of this Mass ranges in mood from ecstatic jubilation to touching simplicity. It is strong and rugged, a song of strength attained through suffering and grief. And the reaction to this music is of wonder, awe and humility. Thus we may react to Bach, but as he himself would have had it, thus we react through Bach to God! The grandeur of the first *Kyrie* that summons the spirit to awareness, and the engulfing *Sanctus* where one stands within the Celestial City, have probably never been surpassed in choral music; in the *Sanctus* and *Osanna,* one part of the chorus is dramatically pitted against another. The contrast between the friction of the *Kyrie* and the serene *Gratias* is polar: the whole world lies between them. On the other hand, there are moments when the music is filled with the most intimate human expression. The solos and duets are typically introduced by an orchestral melody that weaves in and out of the musical texture in polyphonic combination with the solo voices. "My soul," said St. Augustine, "yearns to know this most entangled enigma." The *Mass in B Minor* is Bach's response - Bach uses the fullness of his resources to celebrate the saint's vision of God in heaven and the felicity of the City of God.

Anywhere between fifty and ninety years ago it was customary to perform this work with large orchestra and huge choral forces, resulting in a ponderous, leaden and syrupy memorial to the dead. Unfortunately, the interest level of this music waned substantively because of this approach to perform and record this work. Karajan, Solti, and Klemperer are equally guilty as charged in doing this, despite the fact that each of them have rendered, at moments, both glorious solo performances and plush choral sounds. These, however, are not performances to learn the work by.

I grew up on a modern orchestral version of the work conducted by Karl Richter with the Munich Bach Orchestra, from the mid sixties. This sensible, highly intelligible performance, is not only exciting, but has some heft to it, with solid fundamental bass, brilliant choral accompaniment, and superb choral contributions. I know some will find it to be rather Teutonic, but I maintain that this performance is as close as we can obtain to Bach's intentions based on Richter's close study of the score using modern instrumentation.

For those who must have an original instrument performance, that by John Elliot Gardiner on Archiv and Andrew Parrott on EMI are good alternatives.

There are also two other modern instrument performances, both by the same conductor, on EMI and Philips—the venerable late Eugen Jochum uses a variety of different forces in each performance. Much like Richter, Jochum understands the work, having been bathed in it since childhood. Either of these performances will please, but neither is as aptly captured on tape as the Richter.

- Mass in B Minor, BWV 232
    Archiv 427 155-2AGA2. Munich Bach O, Karl Richter
- Mass in B Minor, BWV 232
    Archiv 415 514-2AH2. English Baroque Soloists, Gardiner

Handel: Water music

What an awkward situation George Frederic Handel (1685 - 1759) found himself in when he heard the news in 1714! A few years earlier, he had deserted his German patron, the Elector of Hanover, and had moved over to the English court where Queen Anne had smiled favorably upon his music, and had assured him a generous annual stipend and prestige in London's fashionable society. Now Queen Anne was dead, and his former patron, the Elector, had arrived in London to become George I, the new King of England! But his influential friends devised a ruse to reconcile the estranged composer with the King.

His Majesty was wont, according to the custom of his day, to entertain the court on the luxurious Royal barge as it sailed up the river Thames to Whitehall and back, accompanied by swarms of ornately bedecked sailboats from which a band of musicians played "water concerts" for their diversion. For one such river party, Handel was instructed to secretly prepare some special music for the occasion. The music, played by fifty musicians on trumpets, horns, bassoons, flutes and strings, created a sensation. The King commanded it to be repeated, twice before and once after supper, and then insisted upon meeting its composer. The truant, Handel, was presented to his former patron, appropriately too conscious of his fault to attempt any excuses. All was forgiven, and Handel was restored to royal favor.

The passage of time has created many ambiguities regarding this popular piece. When was it written? How many pieces were there when the *Water Music* was first played? Exactly what was Handel's orchestration? The original manuscript is lost, and a number of different instrumentations and a number of different editions now exist. Depending on the authority, there are some twenty odd pieces in the French style—a full overture in two parts (first grand, then brisk) followed by a chain of limp and lively dances.

The complete *Water music* consists of three such pieces that Handel had composed for three such excursions along the river. In modern times, they have been edited into two suites that collectively form the *Water Music*. It is light, tuneful and varied, sometimes naive, but always lovely, and consists of a series of more than twenty enchanting dances. It opens with a pompous opera overture; then come dialogues, with echoes of horns and drums to which the brass and the rest of the orchestra respond. Then follow happy and soothing songs whose melodies have continued to entertain audiences, with dances, a hornpipe, and minuets that alternate and contrast with the joyful and powerful fanfares.

The *Water Music* has been brilliantly served in modern sound. It is one of the great high-fidelity spectaculars of the Baroque era, and there are two recordings of the dozens that are listed that come to mind immediately, both of which should be heard if not appropriated. The Los Angeles Chamber Orchestra's first musical director, Sir Neville Marriner, developed this group of musicians into an outstanding ensemble. Its second conductor, Gerard Schwarz, who is now working miracles in Seattle, is responsible for some of the Los Angeles Chamber Orchestra's highest quality output. His recording of the *Water Music*, in first class digital sound as captured at Bridges Auditorium, Claremont College, is a recording I can never be without. The engineering is well nigh perfect. The performance is an absolute joy. As precise as Neville Marriner's Academy of St. Martin's-in-the-Fields' performances are, they pale overall in excitement and enthusiasm to the Schwartz performance. This is a true *Desert Island* contribution to the recorded literature.

For original instrumentation, I recommend Pinnock's outstanding version with the English Concert, Hogwood's version with the Academy of Ancient Music, and Koopman's version with the Amsterdam Baroque Soloists. Another off-the-beaten-track performance is that of Nicholas McGegan, using the Philharmonia Baroque Orchestra recorded by Harmonia Mundi in Tiburon, California. Do avoid versions for brass and large symphony orchestra and conductorless orchestras, as interesting as some of them are. A chamber orchestra will suffice. The noise is loud enough!

- Water Music, Suites 1-3 (complete)
  Delos DCD3010. Los Angeles Chamber O, Gerard Schwarz

Handel: The Royal Fireworks Music

When the war with France was concluded at the treaty of Aix-la-Chapelle, London was ready for a celebration. Handel was commissioned by the King to write the music for the victory party, scheduled to take place in the open in Green Park, London, with glorious fireworks and a thundering royal salute from a hundred and one cannons. And the composer lived up to the occasion! He divided the composition into two parts: an overture, which was a sort of stately, joyous and equestrian march that was to be played before the grand fireworks display, and then five short dance tunes that would be played during the actual display, and which would be immediately appealing to the jubilant crowd of twelve thousand celebrants. Each of the smaller pieces was to be appropriately accompanied by a special fireworks display.

The music itself is superb - self possessed, imperial and impervious to the manic quality of the evening for which it was drafted. It begins explosively, accompanied by the roar of cannons, to set off the rejoicing with invigorating energy. Then there is a serene song, a shepherd's dance, to celebrate the peace, and then the music steps up gaily into a lively old French woodcutter's dance, the *bouree*, followed by the all-time favorite of the people—two minuets. Here, the celebrants in the park could dance to the tune with dainty steps and graceful bows, with the cellos and basses sounding the beat like a drum! The melody of the second minuet is repeated loudly to make a pompous ending for the royal fire work's music.

I must confess not to being an admirer of this work. I enjoy Peter Schickele's parody on the work, *Royal Firewater Music*, by his "discovered composer, PDQ Bach." Nevertheless, this remains a very popular, compelling work for baroque orchestra and is not unlike the *Water Music*, something of a showpiece of its time. The conductorless Orpheus Chamber Orchestra has a direct, unfussy performance which bristles with excitement much as Schwarz' recording of the *Water Music* does. For original instruments, one may wish to consider Pinnock and The English Concert on Archiv.

- Music for the Royal Fireworks
  DG 435 390.2, Orpheus CO

Purcell: Dido's Lament, from Dido and Aeneas

The lasting myths contain in them the lasting problems of man. And Virgilian characters first made their operatic appearance in England in 1689 in Henry Purcell's *Dido and Aeneas*. The characters are as yet innocent; the miniaturized epic begets a comedy of foolish misunderstanding and easy infidelity. The Gods are not moral tutors but mischievous witches who play tricks on the two lovers to procure their consummation. Even an incriminating historical fate is amended in Purcell's opera: Dido, deserted by her conquering hero, melodically entreats her confidante to "Remember me! but ah! forget my fate!" History has shown otherwise: her fate as one of history's casualties *was* remembered by Hannibal as he traveled from Carthage to menace Rome.

Act III begins prophetically with a rude chorus of departing sailors singing their traditional sanguine sea-song of abandoning their women. After a violent scene with Aeneas, Dido's only solace is self indulgence: When Aeneas offers to stay with her after all, she sends him packing and offers herself to another ravisher - "Death invades me." Then Dido, every inch a great queen but very much a vulnerable human being, prepares to mount her funeral pyre.

Two choruses, placed with a brilliant sense of drama, exquisitely frame Dido's agonizing lament, embodying a lifetime of decision. They provide a release of tension, and a new vantage point of balance from which to gauge her cavernous grief. As Aeneas departs, she sings two lines in recitative: "But death, alas, I cannot shun; Death must come when he is gone." Then the chorus, properly silent during their quarrel, comments: "Great minds against themselves conspire, And shun the cure they most desire."

It is musical form that fixes the emotions. No operatic climax has ever been approached with more direct strength, in a more genuinely classic dramatic rhythm than Dido's lament. Though she expresses the wish not to be completely forgotten, she does not desire the wrong she has suffered to embitter the hearts of those who live on. The recitative, "Thy hand, Belinda," moves directly into the great farewell, "When I am laid in earth." As Dido ends her chant and mounts the pyre, the music runs down slowly with an unyielding uncomprehending bass, closing the song with a sense of excruciating force, magnifying the piercing grief of Dido's situation. The lament does not end, but flows into a lovely final chorus as a solemn choral dance that is a supreme expression of grief and resignation, to soften her tragedy and spread her mourning.

Dido and Aeneas is two hundred years old, and not a bit the worse for wear with its spirit, its freshness, its dramatic expression, and its unapproached art of setting English speech to music. It has fared well on long-playing microgroove and CD, and now has the added benefit of being performed with original instruments to enhance the authenticity. Most of my favorite recordings of *Dido* have long since been deleted, and I'm left principally with recommendations from the original instruments.

Christopher Hogwood and his Academy of Ancient Music have made an outstanding recording featuring Katherine Bott and Emma Kirkby which is well worth owning. It is a dramatic performance, at rather apt tempi, and it is utterly delightful. Lynn Dawson as Dido, along with Anne Sophie Von Otter have recorded *Dido* for Archive with the conductor Trevor Pinnock in his English Concert, which is another excellent original instrument choice. Finally, William Christie and Les Arts Florssants have recorded the work for Harmonia Mundi France using J. Feldman as Dido along with G. Laurens filling the mezzo role. This is an excellent performance, and it should be distinguished from an equally excellent performance by the same conductor and orchestra on Erato with Veronique Gens as the soprano Dido. I would recommend that any individual wishing to make a direct comparison of the same conductor in two separate performances of the same work should study these two recordings, as there is much to learn about how different things can be on different days.

John Elliot Gardiner with the English Baroque Soloists and the Monteverdi Choir have also produced an outstanding version with Carolyn Watkinson as Dido. This excellent Philips recording also features additional music by Purcell other than *Dido*. The recording dates from July, 1990, and is also worth owning.

Again, on the subject of Purcell's *Dido and Aeneas*, again with Kirkby as the soprano Dido, Andrew Parrott and the Taverner Players and Taverner Choir have made an excellent recording of the work for Chandos which is relatively recent, and of excellent recorded sound.

In this particular work, I would avoid performances by large symphony orchestras and conductors who are not normally associated with the performance of baroque music. Indeed, although he is intimately associated with the baroque period, I would avoid all of the multiple performances by Nikolaus Harnoncourt for the sledgehammer approach to inflection and dynamism in orchestral performance.

- Dido and Aeneas (complete)
    London 436 992.2. Academy of Ancient Music, Hogwood

The Age of Elegance

As early as 1737, Frederick II of Prussia, then crown prince, wrote to the Prince of Orange: "Handel's best days are over; his mind is exhausted and his taste out of fashion." This may well have been an epitaph for the music of the Baroque world. What was now "in fashion" was a change in style brought about by the transformation of the Baroque opera itself by a new element which was to develop with unexpected rapidity: the symphonic element. Once the orchestra was introduced into drama, the world of music could never remain the same. For, when all the passions of the mind and heart could be represented in pure music merely with instruments without words, the effect was to prove intoxicating.

A severe handicap of Baroque music had been the rigor with which a work had to be unfolded in accordance with the strictest laws of form and structure that seemed to deliberately blight the expression of deep emotions. Not even the personality of Bach or Handel was able to surmount, evade or contradict such an obstacle because of their conscientious obligations to their art. Whereas the expression of emotions requires composers to continue upon a free and undetermined path and not retrace their steps, the laws of Baroque music precluded fluctuations of feelings, consenting to them only on condition that they presented themselves under symmetrical aspects, at moments and in places determined upon beforehand by the dialogue between the *tutti* and the *concertino*. In Baroque music, it was deemed inartistic to express one's individual feeling in an immediate and spontaneous fashion; one had perforce to interpose between oneself and one's feelings a veil of beautiful and impersonal forms.

The new symphonists broke the old framework of what they contemptuously called "the learned style," and liberated thought from the slavery of form. Through them, instrumental music became the supple garment of the living soul, always in movement, perpetually changing with unexpected fluctuations and contrasts. Whereas Baroque music could best be followed by the mind, the newer music, called approvingly the "gallant style," could best be followed by the senses. Whereas Baroque seemed public in private, the new style seemed private even in public. The older ideal had been magnificence and grandeur, the new ideal was grace and a delight in more human things such as flirtation and love, and the beauty of sculptured landscape. Art and music aimed at dispensing pleasure by making pleasure itself their subject. And composers of the new era rose brilliantly to the challenge to blend the "learned" with the "gallant," and fuse grandeur with grace, and extravagance with intimacy, to create the pleasing masterpieces of an age of elegance.

The age of elegance was the world of Maria Theresa and Marie Antoinette, and it reflected the best of times and the worst of times. It was an artificial and unrealistic world, a world of make-believe and game-playing where courtiers played at being shepherds and countesses dressed up as milkmaids. Wit, charm and sentimentality were considered the desired attributes of the day, and though social life had moved away from the large palaces to the intimacy of the *salon* in less imposing country estates, it still retained the conventions of etiquette. It was an age of witty men and seductive women, of irreverent laughter and lovely serenades, of drawing rooms and fox hunts, silk coats and lace ruffles, powdered wigs and elaborate coiffure, rustling silks and graceful folds in hues of apricot, sea green and mignonette that were vividly captured in the paintings of Watteau, Fragonard and Thomas Gainsborough. It was an age of reason and an age of enlightenment—of Voltaire and Montesquieu, of John Locke and Alexander Pope, of Boyle and Lavoisier, and Madame de Pompadour. It was an age of a rising middle class of merchants and mistresses, of *Tom Jones* and *Moll Flanders*. In the final analysis, it was an age of exquisite sensibility that ended in the blood of revolution, an age of reason that ended in an orgy of unreason.

For the most part, the music of the period expressed the playfulness and wit of the times, including its sentimental and artificial view of nature. It was an age that believed that life could be sweet, and its music sang of, and with, that sweetness. The composers of that time aimed to please; they wrote to please their patrons and not themselves or their inspiration, and they wrote commissioned pieces for special occasions and for special persons. In a word, they wrote for the moment, not for posterity. And while the music was sincere and at times intensely personal, it related to the occasion or the person for whom it was commissioned. It was largely separate from the personal feeling and the autobiographical expression of the composer. For, the composer of that time was still a servant who wore his master's livery—a man frequently admired and honored, sometimes well rewarded, but always without question obliged to please his patron or his public. Boccherini, Gluck and Haydn accepted their fate, their surroundings, and their institutions murmuringly. They were glad to be allowed their wages and please their princes. Mozart was the first great musical genius born into a feudal society who dared to be freelance. He was also the first to be inelegant, if not boorish, in an age of elegance.

This was also a period of incomparable enlightenment in the annals of music. It was the time when the sonata form was established and perfected into a level of artistic fulfillment that has remained unsurpassed. It was the time that saw the maturity of the symphony and the string quartet. Haydn was not the inventor of the symphony. Just as an alchemist needs base material before he can transmute it to something more precious, so Haydn needed the primitive but sturdy form of his predecessors to quicken the response of his latent genius. It was the speed and assurance with which he developed this art form that justified his appellation as "the father of the symphony." It is also generally regarded that the six quartets of Haydn's controversial Op. 3 established the form and instrumental treatment that made them the first *true* string quartets—however, the authenticity of this work as being truly that of Haydn has been questioned. "It was from Haydn," claimed Mozart, "that I first learned the true way to compose quartets." Haydn might have made a similar acknowledgment to Mozart regarding the symphony. Writing from the age of nine, Mozart summed up his achievements in this genre in his final three symphonies.

The end of the baroque era saw the demise of the *concerto grosso* form. It was abandoned in favor of a concerto in the classical style for the professional soloist and orchestra. The solo parts were intentionally made difficult to display the uninhibited showmanship and superior technique of the virtuoso player. Vivaldi and Bach, along with other baroque composers, had also written solo concertos for their favorite instruments. The *concertino*, naturally, had been confined to a single type of instrument, and it admittedly had been refined to allow a greater degree of virtuosity. However, these baroque *solo concertos* had retained the principle of competing sonorities that was the hallmark of the *concerto grosso*: the solo instrument and orchestra remained *equal* partners in the music.

With the coming of the age of elegance, the solo concerto developed alongside the symphony as a genre of some length and importance. It made use of the same musical forms as the symphony, predominantly the sonata form, and it was divided into three movements instead of the traditional four—the minuet and trio movement was generally dropped. The majority of the solo concertos written by Haydn and Mozart were for the piano or violin, but Mozart also composed works for the solo clarinet, bassoon, flute and the French horn which are considered to be among the best for these instruments, even though the instruments were in a technically primitive state in his time.

A hallmark of thought in the age of elegance was the idea of extending culture to the ordinary man or woman: human life in the middle social class should be enriched by the arts. And nowhere did this become more ably manifest than in the opera of the age. In Italy, a gayer spirit opened the career of the comic opera (*opera buffa*), and in France, a*n opera comique*, in which songs were interspersed with spoken dialogue in simple stories about common folk, got decisively under way in the Paris "fair theaters." While Italian opera continued to entertain the princes and the plebeians in Germany and England, a middle class public extended their enjoyment to *The Beggars Opera* in London and all over the English country.

The primary themes expressed so trenchantly and creatively in opera were the domestic and social issues of middle level life. The drama and music embodied the fundamental and moral beliefs and values of the scholars of the time, difficult as they may have been for musical or even theatrical realization. The most important of these values was the conviction that human beings could overcome the antagonisms that separated them from one another, and that they had the intellectual and emotional resources to transcend their hostilities and reconcile. Reconciliation became the main argument of operas, a perennial and prominent theme that was explored in detail exhibited in many guises, and was allowed to permeate the musical and the dramatic action thoroughly.

If "reconciliation" was the argument of the opera, one might say that "reason" was its means. Reason was the faculty of mind that disputed the unargued claims of tradition and authority and became the great battle cry of the times, permitting thinkers to construct an adequate view of reality and the world largely by deductive means. The age of elegance (the Enlightenment) celebrated Reason as man's last and best hope in an unfriendly world; the opera celebrated Reason dramatically in the machinations of its principal character and musically in the cleverness of the composer. Viewed psychologically, the opera was an essay on social and domestic conflict and reconciliation. Viewed intellectually, it became a tract on Reason. And the greatest genius who stressed both its psychological and intellectual aspects in dramatic and musical terms was Mozart.

The musical characteristics of the operas of Mozart were its regular, symmetrical and clearly articulated phrases, the steadiness of its pulse, and the transparency and stability of its harmonic organization. The operas were constructed of "numbers": arias, duets, trios, ensembles and choruses. The numbers were separated by a dramatic recitative to become a series of discrete musical events, each with its distinct beginning and end. They were generally composed in a single key and to a fixed rhythm, tempo, and orchestral accompaniment—and, if not that, then in two clearly contrasted sections, one slow, and the other fast. And they characteristically contained melodic material that was repeated several times over. Thus, passages in rest alternated with passages of impulse, and grew in and out of one another in a way that gave a vital impression of leading and arrival. These qualities were carefully refined to calculate climaxes, tensions and balances so that conflict, excitement and flux could be handled within a single musical continuity. Moreover, Mozart experimented with the idea of bringing emotional content into the aria by developing a composite aria form that was comparable to that of the larger ensembles.

The age of elegance has the music of Haydn and Mozart at its core. Much of their music, including their symphonies, was primarily *Hausmusik*—music in and for the house—requiring relatively few instruments. Many of Haydn's symphonies had their first performances in the *salon* of the palace at Esterhazy, and some of Mozart's symphonies were performed in the homes of Viennese music lovers. Music making in the family circle was a cherished activity, and the family string quartet remained an essential part of European aristocratic and middle-class culture. The growing popularity of the piano paralleled Mozart's enthusiasm for the keyboard; throughout his life, the piano received his constant attention, and he wrote for it some of his most beautiful and profound compositions.

The music that follows in these pages is the music of Haydn and Mozart, and it captures the spirit of their times as forcefully and directly today as it did in the age of elegance. It was written to please, to provide immediate and spontaneous enjoyment, and evoke pleasant sensations through its well-balanced, well-ordered nature. Though some have found demonic forces or paroxysms of exaltation in some of Mozart's symphonies, most will derive complete satisfaction on a less intense emotional scale. The music is profound without being self-conscious or introspective, without intending to represent or symbolize violent struggle, exaltations or apotheoses of any kinds. In a word, this music incorporates esthetic and emotional qualities that stand in welcome contrast to the stress and conflicts of our modern world. When Mozart died in 1791, the age of elegance in music died with him.

Haydn: Symphony Nos. 93-104 (London)

No composer's creative lifetime has spanned greater changes in music than that of Franz Joseph Haydn (1732 - 1809). When he was twenty years old, Bach had been dead for only two years, and Handel still had a few more to live. By the time of his death, Beethoven had already written his first six symphonies. In his younger days, the symphony and quartet had been barely distinguishable. When he passed away at the age of seventy seven, he was hailed as the "father" of both these musical genres. And it was during his long lifetime that instrumental music attained its equal rights with the human voice.

Gaiety, lightness, cheerfulness—these have long been accepted as the traits of Haydn's symphonic music. An unequivocal love of life expressed with energy, tenderness and humor, a sense of the open air and a truth to Nature that was part of his peasant birthright—these were Haydn's essential qualities. He could be deeply moving in his tragedy, and he could write with rare intensity, but it was his frequent use of the rhythmic and tuneful Croatian folk-melodies—bright, sensitive and piquant—that enriched this field of his art. They belong to a temper which was marked rather by beauty and imagination than by any sustained breadth of thought, and though they rarely strike fire in the soul, they still sparkle with a perennial magic. The Haydn symphonies are stylized, formal and well bred, perfectly restrained and correctly polite to fit into the simple, leisurely and refined spirit of the age of elegance.

When Haydn left the service of the *Esterhazy* family on the death of his patron Prince Nicholas, he was induced by an entrepreneur, Johann Peter Salomon, to visit London and conduct his new symphonies there. The success of the first six concerts prompted a second trip for which he composed six more works. Together, they form the graceful and exquisitely finished *London Symphonies* which have remained the best expression of the happy spirit and vivacity of his finest music.

Representative of these trips to England are No 92 (*Oxford*), composed for the ceremony at the renowned English university that honored him with a doctorate (not included in the *London* collection);

No 94 (*Surprise*), a charming and playful piece that has an endearing set of variations on a theme of which the first four bars are reminiscent of the popular nursery rhyme *Twinkle, Twinkle Little Star;* No. *98,* which has a beautiful slow movement in which the principal theme is suggestive of *God Save the King;* No. 101 *(Clock)*, where Haydn reproduces in music the ticking of a clock as the background for his flowing melodies in the second movement; and No. 103 (*Drum Roll*), characterized by the startling roll of drums that opens the music. Last of the line is No. 104 *(London)*, Haydn's final essay in the genre and form that he more than anyone had help establish.

The last twelve symphonies of "Papa Haydn" are monuments to be reckoned with when compared to any other composer, and the pleasures derived from their moments of wist, and their buoyant, joyous rhythms and humor are timeless. They have been well served in recorded format since Beecham, whose recordings, though elegant, are neither well played (due to Beecham's distinct non-rehearsal, storytelling technique) nor recorded. Fortunately, those who have respected and studied that conductor's works have delivered for us outstanding cycles of the *Salomon Symphonies*. My all-time favorite recordings are no longer available (those with Leslie Jones and The Little Orchestra of London; Unicorn Records, UK; Nonesuch LP and Advent Chromium Dioxide Musicassettes). They should be sought by avid collectors. Hopefully, they will reappear some day, as they are brilliant in sound and in performance.

Currently available recordings include Abbado's evolving cycle with The Chamber Orchestra of Europe which demonstrates the finest in recorded sound and ensemble. They are simply unbelievable *Desert Island* versions that are available on individual discs. The small-orchestra approach delineates the inner voices of the works much as Haydn would have heard at Esterhaza. I need not say more about them other than they shine from the first moment.

Boxed sets of the *Salomon Symphonies* at mid-price are fortu-nately not in short supply. Eugen Jochum and the LPO recorded the *London Symphonies* in 1971 for DG's *Anniversary of the Symphony.*

This big-band approach resembles Beecham most closely, but the ensemble work equals the accuracy of Abbado and the sound, though recorded in the ambient acoustics of Barking Town Hall, London, is mellifluously clear and precise, not showing its age. Humor abounds. Tempi are on the fast side—Jochum holds back no punches.

Sir Collin Davis achieves a superb meld of Abbado and Jochum with the Amsterdam Concertgebouw Orchestra, using a sizable body of players in the resonant acoustics of the Concertgebouw, and obtains playing of great care and concern with a close-in multiple miking technique in evidence. The performances are at tempo, no more, but bubble with excitement as if the players are discovering a work for the first time.

For those interested in original instrumental versions of the symphonies, Christopher Hogwood and the Academy of Ancient Music (Decca Florilegeum) can be heartily recommended on similar grounds as Davis.

- Symphony Nos 93, 101 (DG 429 776-2); Symphony No. 96; Sinfonia concertante (DG 423 105-2); Symphony Nos. 98, 100 (DG 439 932-2); Symphony Nos 102, 103 (DG 449 204-2)
  Chamber O of Europe, Abbado
  Completion of this cycle is anticipated from DG

Haydn: String Quartet No 77 (Emperor)

It has been said that the string quartet is the most sincere form of musical expression. A symphony is more massive and less subtle, where the great must be presented as the gigantic, and the elusive as the definite. It gives us the monarch on a great state occasion rather than the man. It is for this reason that the true composer, the man, of any period is probably more accurately reflected in his string quartets or his solo concertos than in his symphonies.

Haydn did not invent the string quartet (first and second violins, viola, cello); he made it into an infinitely higher achievement. It was at the encouragement of a devoted amateur musician that he composed his first string quartet. The form so captivated him that over the next few months he brought out one such piece after another. The earliest of his eighty three quartets were but small suites for four string instruments that could be suitable for street serenade parties in Vienna. It was not until he had composed almost forty that he achieved a perfection of form, both graceful and charming, that brought to life each of the four stringed voices, individualized yet unified under a common will. Transparency, neatness and clarity dominated this music which became his happiest and most popular medium. Each instrument had its role, according to the capacity of the instrument and the balance of the part, so that each individual part was neither a solo nor a mere accompaniment to the others. "It was from Haydn," claimed Mozart, "that I first learned the true way to compose quartets." And rightly so, for, the string quartets that Haydn wrote were, both humanly and on the plane of musical thought, his great songs of experience.

The string quartet *Kaiser* (*The Emperor*) is so nicknamed because its slow movement is a set of variations on an *Emperor's Hymn* that Haydn had composed earlier on the occasion of the Emperor's birthday. It was the German equivalent to *God Save the King* that he had heard the English people sing so enthusiastically when he had been in London, and he set his devotion to the kind and upright ruler of his own Fatherland to a simple and touching Croatian melody which the country was to later adopt as its national anthem. There is a majesty about the whole work, a symphonic richness of sound, that springs from the strength, poise and definition of the haunting melodies that seem to move with all the power of some ancestral memory. A story has it that when Napoleon's cannons were bombarding the peaceful suburb in Vienna where Haydn lived, the frail old composer asked to be carried once more to his piano. There, surrounded by his small household, he fired back fiercely in his own way by playing his *Emperor's Hymn* three times—a farewell salute from one of Austria's greatest sons. Four days later, he passed away gently in his sleep.

I regret to admit that I have never seriously looked into the string quartets of the "father" of the genre and I am unable to comment on these performances. Once again, I've sought refuge in my co-author who recommends the much admired budget selection listed here.

- String Quartets Nos 76 (Fifths); 77 (Emperor); 78 (Sunrise), Op. 76/2-4
  Naxos Dig. 8.550129, Kodaly Qt.

Mozart: Overtures

If music be the food of love, then love is also its food. And floating down the stream of Mozart's music, we find out that his songs are truly the food of love. For, beneath all his music we seem to hear a simple demand : "I love you; please love me." Even as a child—and he always remained one—he had an almost morbid need for affection. He loved tenderly those he knew and spoke of them with ardent affection, but there was nothing extravagant or romantic about his love. He merely expressed the sweetness or sadness of affection. Wolfgang Amadeus Mozart (1756 - 1791) is the chosen friend of those who have loved and whose souls are quiet.

His letters show him to be a pleasant and cheerful soul, with the quick sympathies and the gentleness of a child, for he was given to tears and laughter, to teasing, and all the tricks of a warmhearted boy. He was always fidgety and jumping about, nearly killing himself with laughter over anything funny, or even over things that were not so funny. The blood flowed freely in his veins, and often he found merriment in nothing at all. He seemed unaffected by the illness, cares, and terrible distress that made up his lot in life. In his own words, he said that he was always hovering between anxiety and hope, but the music came from an irresistible desire to laugh which he could not conquer, and which he had to satisfy even in the midst of the worst of his troubles. His laughter was very near to tears—those happy tears that well up from a loving nature.

Nowhere is his gaiety and buffoonery, his characteristic gentleness and understanding, more expressed that in the overtures to his operas. The happy mixture of his own qualities—sensibility, shrewd perception, gentleness and self-control—was naturally fitted to understand the differences of character in others and to observe keenly the world that he lived in; and it cost him no effort to reproduce what he saw. His characters are delightful creatures who sing their troubles in rhythmic phrases in their own charming way, striving amid laughter and thoughtless jests to hide the amorous emotion of their hearts, and end up by falling asleep in the midst of their tears with a smile on their faces. The music is filled with love and life and activity, without malice and leaving no aftertaste of bitterness, and it surrounds and envelopes us, clear and full of light. It was in the soft radiance of this light, when he had scarcely begun to unfold the secret of his being, that death took him away at the age of thirty five.

Recordings of the *Overtures* of Mozart are nowhere near as plentiful as they should be. Early listeners of the stereo era were graced with excellent performances by Sir Colin Davis on EMI and Bruno Walter's famous recording on Columbia (now Sony Classical). Later, DG issued a recording of Mozart's Opera Overtures compiled from various performances made by Karl Bohm and the Vienna Philharmonic. It was an excellent, though sonically uneven, traversal of the Overtures which spanned several decades.

Today, nearly three decades later, looking at the list of available recordings, things haven't changed as much as other major orchestral works. The performances by Davis, Walter, and Bohm are still in the catalog, and are all recommendable. Two newcomers, however, are present: Hans Vonk and the Dresden Staatskapelle on budget Laser-Light Classics, and Barry Wordsworth on a Naxos super-budget recording. Both are good, but not particularly distinguished. Leopold Hager, a Professor of Music at the Salzburg Mozartem, has also compiled an excellent amalgam of the Overtures with the English Chamber Orchestra on Novalis at full price. Sir Neville Marriner has compiled a substantial offering of the Overtures as a modern, well recorded version. They are insightful, effervescent performances, and are well recorded. Virtually all the other recordings mentioned are of secondary interest due to their age and somewhat less than elegant engineering and presentation.

- Overtures
  EMI CDC7 47014, ASMF, Marriner

Mozart: Symphony No 40

Much of Mozart's writings were no more than *pieces d'occasion*; many were pretty, more were ingenious, all were charming. He came from Salzburg which is on the road from Venice to Vienna, and there seemed to be something Italian, something sensual and voluptuous, in his nature. But the spirit of the musical life in Vienna, where the public was intoxicated by the elegant pleasures of the court, was not one likely to encourage the writing of music calculated to express the deeper pulses of the human life and soul. Mozart's patrons asked for dances. For the present symphony, his penultimate one, he put aside the exigencies of time and circumstance, and wrote a piece after his own heart, with all his grace and sincerity of feeling. And Mozart was capable of intense feeling. "If any one offends me," he had once remarked, "I must revenge myself, and unless I revenge myself with interest I consider I have only repaid my enemy and not corrected him."

Though he was happy, no life could have been harder than his. He knew sadness in every form; he knew the pangs of mental suffering, the dread of the unknown, and the sadness of a lonely soul. It was a perpetual fight against sickness and misery, and though Death put an end to it, he was able to sustain it because of a strong, kind faith—a calm and peaceful faith, without passion or mysticism. Mozart's soul was youthful and gentle, suffering at times from an excess affectation, yet full of peace that allowed him to remain calm even during events like his mother's death, and when death was approaching him.

The music of this symphony is Mozart's most personal expression, and it has a direct emotional impact. Some have even ventured to call it a confession, but however poignant these expressions may become, they are presented with an incomparable poise and restraint. The dominant mood of this music is pathos, not only where it is agitated, but also where it assumes a kind of uneasy calm, or a smiling pastoral placidity. Some of its melodies are unbearably beautiful, and there is in the last movement an unforgettable shattering moment of threatening disintegration, where the melody is torn to meaningful shreds only to be hastily reassembled. Mozart wrote two versions of this symphony—with and without clarinets.

Symphony No. 40 of Mozart, curiously the only of the last six to be written without tympany, is a glorious, quasi-romantic work. It has been extremely well held in the gramophone since the beginning of the era of recording, and there are many distinguished readings of this work. Fritz Reiner recorded a superlative monophonic version with the Chicago Symphony in the 1950s, which has seen recent reissue on a monophonic RCA CD. In more recent times, Carlo Maria Giulini recorded this symphony for London Records with the New Philharmonia Orchestra in what is perhaps the most elegant statement of this work that I have encountered. It is resplendent sonically, and is tasteful, elegant, and not rushed.

Other modern versions, including Abbado's with the London Symphony Orchestra, Sir Benjamin Britten's reading with the English Chamber Orchestra, and Gerard Schwarz's recording with the Los Angeles Chamber Orchestra are splendid examples of modern stereophonic and early digital versions which merit serious consideration. The Orpheus Chamber Orchestra has recorded an outstanding version for DG but would need to be imported at this time—it is absolutely worth hearing due to its shear beauty and elegance, and the modern sound has not been bettered anywhere. Of original instrument versions, I can heartily recommend those of Christopher Hogwood and the Academy of Ancient Music on London's Florilegium label. Also, Sir Roger Norrington's performance with the London Classical Players on EMI merits attention for its insightfulness, as does Pinnock's with the English Concert for Archiv. If I were to live with one performance of this work, it would have to be that conducted by Giulini, which was not bettered in any way by his more recent recording with the Berlin Philharmonic.

- Symphony Nos. 40, 41
  London 452 889-2 LCS. NPO, Giulini

Mozart: Symphony No 41 (Jupiter)

It is ever an old question, like that of the lost tribes of Israel, on which the world's judgment must forever stay poised. There will always be people who believe that Mozart reached an absolute pinnacle in the art of music, and that all those who followed him marked a descent. The problem is incapable of solution. One thing is certain: every person has a right to think Mozart the greatest. And his greatest work is probably his final symphony.

Hitherto, Mozart had lived in a perpetual Nirvana where he could sing the theme of constant blessedness. But notes of eternal praise fail to sustain interest and become a pointless task. For, a world without the stress of moral strife is very like no world at all—a state of non existence. The chief business of the world is its moral strife and its onward, upward course, and of such a world Mozart became a prophet in the music of his last symphony. Here the master got wind of his own power of special utterance, and reaped all gain of earlier experience, to trace a bold experiment in the realms of more defined emotion. In it the inner Mozart spoke, and he wrote not for the age, but for the ages.

The very opening of this music utters a sense of gravity of the coming epic, an invocation for the right spirit. The atmosphere of suspense continues, gathering more and more heavily as the music takes its course, as if it were all still a prelude to the end. The spirit of the work is one of a vague and perhaps unreasoning cheeriness with a moderation and restraint, and an invariable graciousness in its suggestions of the deeper feelings. And when the music ends in the *Finale*, there is an expression of a real Olympian force, even if there be no Promethean fire. So godlike was the perfection of this work that posterity has dubbed it the *Jupiter* symphony. And with this work, the symphony form itself changed, gaining a degree of breadth, dignity and respect that merged into awe.

The last of the Mozart symphonies, No. 41, has been brilliantly served on records. Many of the same contenders for an excellent Symphony No. 40 repeat themselves for No. 41. Fritz Reiner's recording with the Chicago Symphony simply has to be heard to be believed! The tempi are all on the fast side, and the playing is of such utter genius that this recording, available in stereo on LP, must be heard. Beg, borrow or steal it! It might not be the most sonically elegant of all available, but it sure is a "mind blower" when it comes to playing.

Guilini and the New Philharmonia Orchestra are extremely well served by the London engineers, even though the recording is now over thirty years old. This is one of two great interpretations in my book, and has been recently reissued on CD. Another great recording has come out of the Schwarz-LACO relationship, and this performance, even more than the 40th, rings true to ear. It is fleet of foot, bracing, and yet elegant. The recorded sound is absolutely resplendent, and the entire performance is beyond criticism. It is in some ways reminiscent of the Reiner recording, but in superior sound.

Historically, other great recordings include those by Karl Bohm and the Berlin Philharmonic (not his Vienna Philharmonic remake undertaken later in his life), and those of Sir Neville Marriner and the Academy of St. Martin's-in-the-Fields on Philips (not his EMI remake).

- Symphony Nos 40, 41
    Delos DCD3012, Los Angeles Chamber O, Schwartz
- Symphony No. 40, 41
    London 452 889-2 LCS. NPO, Giulini

Mozart: Piano Concertos (Nos.19, 21, 23)

Mozart lavished his most exquisite care and unstinted inventiveness on his twenty five concertos for piano and orchestra. In his poetic hands, both piano and orchestra knew their place, based upon a mutual respect arising from a well-defined comprehension of one another's functions. The piano could listen patiently through long orchestral passages with unfailing good temper, its good breeding enabling it to withstand even the temptation of clearing its throat. The orchestra, for its part, allowed the preeminence of the piano as a general proposition, and kept its own more unruly members in restraint. Etiquette did not always prevent a bassoon from sly humor, nor a horn from becoming, on occasion, slightly sentimental. But all subscribed to a certain standard of decorous behavior that breathed the very essence of the Viennese spirit and the age of elegance.

Mozart was the prince of concertos. In 1765, during his ninth year, he had arranged three sonata movements: this was his first work in concerto form. The last was a clarinet concerto. In the twenty six intervening years, he composed more than twenty-five works for the keyboard. These pieces are voiceless dramas, full of tension, nobility and pathos, with melodies that are just as alive as his operatic characters. It was this sense of dramatic value recreated in pure instrumental form that revolutionized this genre as an expression of profound personal emotion. And herein lay part of the reason why he could not rely on them to secure a well-paid income—the fashionable public wanted to be entertained, not moved!

Of all his piano concertos, *Concerto No. 19* is the most uniformly cheerful. In its original form, the soloist was supported by a chamber orchestra consisting of flutes, oboes, bassoons, horns and strings. Trumpets and drums were added in a revised version. The first movement is extraordinary in its prodigal allowance of eight themes of which it has been said that the "heard melodies are sweet, but those unheard are sweeter." The second slow movement shows his genius through the deft blending of overlapping themes and the subtle varying of repeats. A brilliant finale brings the music to a close.

Whether goaded by debts and efforts to meet the high rent and expenses of his *Schulerstrasse* residence in Vienna or merely by a feverish creative urge, the *Piano Concerto No. 21* was written with a flurry of no less ten other piano compositions in 1784. This was the busiest period of Mozart's life—he had freed himself from the tyranny of his former employer, the Archbishop of Saltzburg, and was establishing himself in the rough-and-tumble musical world of

Vienna with his new bride. By this time, the concerto form in Mozart's hands had become a medium in which he had succeeded in combining perfect aptness to its special requirements with inexhaustible poetry and originality. He had learned to adorn his concertos with all manner of embroideries and elaboration, and he reserved a place in each piece, usually in the cadenzas, for his unaccompanied free improvisations. Despite its showy sequences and gay flourishes of trumpets and drums, this Concerto is a grave and thoughtful piece, a complete repudiation of glittering concert halls and their shallow patrons. The weepingly romantic theme in the second movement is one of Mozart's most stirring and unforgettable musical utterances.

Piano Concerto No. 23 is the most lyrical. Clarinets set a gracious and conversational mood with linked sweetness, long drawn out. The serene spirit pervading the first movement is overtaken in the second by the sorrows of Niobe! Clarinet and first violin intensify the elegiac mood, the strings play smooth quavers and the wood winds sustain the harmony. A pageant of almost a dozen melodies weave in and out in the succeeding rondo, and the music ends merrily in a series of shimmering dialogues between piano and orchestra.

Many consider Mozart's Piano Concerti to be the standard bearer for the medium, and I am inclined to feel this is true whenever I listen to them. I feel the same way when I listen to Beethoven's Piano Concerti, Haydn's Piano Concerti, and Brahms' Piano Concerti. So the suggestion probably isn't a fair one except at the moment when one is immersed in the medium.

Outstanding interpretations of the Mozart Piano Concerti abound, and in all fairness to the litany of recordings listed in various catalogs (Schwann-Opus, Bielefelder, Gramophone's Gramofile on CD-ROM), I will assert that the listener would go wrong with NONE of the following in virtually any of the Mozart Concerti, whether they be complete or incomplete cycles:

Casadesus/Szell, Sony Classical; Serkin/Szell/Schneider, Sony Classical; Perahia (pianist and conductor) English Chamber Orchestra, Sony Classical; Ashkenazy (pianist and conductor) Philharmonia

Orchestra, London; Uchida/Tate/English Chamber Orchestra, Philips; Curzon/Britten/Kertesz/ECO-LSO, London; Gulda/Abbado/VPO, DG; Pires/Abbado/COE DG; Previn (pianist and conductor) VPO, Philips; Brendel/Marriner/Academy of St Martin's in the Fields, Philips; Pollini/Bohm/VPO, DG; Goode/Orpheus Chamber Orchestra, Nonesuch; de Laroccha/Davis/English Chamber Orchestra, BMG/RCA.

Avoid like the plague: Geza Anda, once referred to as the "delicatessen handler of Mozart" in an appropriately critical review of his complete cycle for DG in the sixties with the Salzburg Mozarteum, reissued. It is not that they are poor; it is that others have so much more elegantly stated this composer's genius. Also, I would discourage the listener from obtaining any performances of the Mozart Piano Concerti conducted by Nikolaus Harnoncourt, regardless of how outstanding his soloist might be. Despite his often creative and innovative thinking which indeed I do respect, Mozart does not benefit from the effects of what is to me a sledgehammer approach, either.

As for the concerti in question enumerated above, I have some personal favorites. They are single recommendations, and all are available currently. For Piano Concerto Nos. 19 and 23, find Brendel and Marriner with the Academy of St. Martin in the Fields on Philips. A nearly perfect entertainment, expertly spun and delivered! You will have no regrets.

For Concerto No. 21, referred to in our home as the "headache" concerto because an aspirin manufacturing company played the second movement of this concerto ad nauseum on the television in the seventies, also known inappropriately as the *Elvira Madigan* concerto, I would encourage the listener to seek out the Gulda/Abbado recording on DG or the Pires/Abbado recording on DG; either will bring much pleasure.

If the listener is interested in older performances, Rudolf Serkin's and Robert Casadesus' recordings of many (but not integral) Mozart Piano Concerti have been reissued in resplendent modern sound on Sony Classical in what I consider to be one of the great gifts of the Gramophone. I learned these performances as a child, and rehearing them some thirty years later I thought would be a disappointment. I am pleased to say I am wrong; the recordings were great in the sixties; they are even better now, and the artistry is beyond reproach, as good as any currently before the public. These two sets, along with Curzon, will go with me to my *Desert Island*.

For the specific concerti referred to, my present recommendations are shown below.

- Piano Concertos Nos. 19, 21,23
    Philips 442 269.2. Brendel, ASMIF, Marriner
- Piano Concerto No. 21
    DG 415 842.2. Gulda, VPO, Abbado
- Piano Concerto No. 21
    DG 439 941.2. Pires, Chamber O Europe, Abbado

Mozart: Die Zauberflote (The Magic Flute)

There has for ever been an insatiable urge to read in a musician's final work a concluding apotheosis, a realization of humanitarian ideals, a reconciled rounding off to life, a return to divine simplicity, a harmonious dying away. And *Die Zauberflote* has not been immune to the critical analysis that is the lot of all last works, and to a search for some transfigured wisdom. The importance of Mozart's last opera, *Die Zauberflote*, has been overestimated.

The facts dictate otherwise: Mozart needed money, and he had to make do. Since magic operas, especially with spectacular stage devices and fireworks, were fashionable and well attended in Vienna, this new work promised to earn him something. Here was a means to achieve solvency, even if it meant a concession to popular taste. And these had been trying times in his own life. Without doubt he was aware of the futility of his own condition (from his point of view) and, psychologically at least, he was in an unstable condition. One may even say that he had given up: he no longer had the inner impulse, the initiative, or the strength to jest like the good old days. To his wife Constanze he wrote, "I mean to take a long rest in your arms." To be sure, Mozart's music in *Die Zauberflote* is for long stretches at its highest level. But it was conceived as an unpretentious entertainment, and is not equal to the pretentious claims made for it later.

The story of *Die Zauberflote* is ridiculous. Its silly combination of morals and magic, Freemasonry and fairy tale, allegory and doggerel is laughable. And Mozart knew how silly it was. "If we make a fiasco I cannot help it, for I never wrote a magic opera in my life." What he did write was the first true German music drama. The German blossoms out in this score with overwhelming conviction. All the purest sentiments of the German mind appear in brave, bold phrases in this serene sweep of lovely melodies and solemn mystic choruses: love and faith and friendship and simple trusting devotion, from Papageno's delicious German songs to the rollicking *Slave Chorus* which suggests nothing so much as a real German holiday, *Mannergesangverein* and all! *Die Zauberflote* is an integral indispensable part of German life, molded into the hearts of Germans from the Danube to the Rhine.

Die Zauberflote has been interpreted as Mozart's fullest exposition of what music and drama mean, and of what they achieve in conjunction as an opera. Music is predestined, drama improvised. Music erects the dizzy vertical chain of being which joins earth to heaven. The opera's magic totems are musical instruments: the golden flute, the silver bells, the wooden panpipes. The three ladies in *Die Zauberflote* who hand over the flute extol the humane ministry of music. Music has the Orphic power to revive the dead; it banishes sorrow, they say, cheers up the mourner, and encourages the old celibate to take a wife. Yet if music is to be an aid to human happiness (*Menschengluck*), it cannot belong exclusively to the virtuosi. The potion must belong to all nature—any sound made by man or beast may qualify as music. Silence, imposed upon humankind as one of its trials, is also brought into music's sonic domain.

The motive of *Die Zauberflote* is the gentler and moral feeling of love. Not sensual abandon, not that violent intensity and impetus of desire, not that maddening perpetual whirl of infatuation, but conjugal love, where the most reverent praise is sung by two characters, Pamina and Papageno, without the slightest erotic interest in each other. Love that means kinship and kindness, love that emanates a human warmth and the blessings of care and companionship, love concerned with with propagation and the constitution of family. Love in this opera is generously parenteral, breathing life to others. The instinct is a law of nature, synonymous with humanity.

Finally, it has been argued that in *Die Zauberflote*, Mozart also expresses the Divine, that through the artist's intuition his religious feeling breaks away from the confines of an individual faith to show us the essence of all faith. *Die Zauberflote* sings of the joyous freedom of the virtuous, and its simple strength, calm beauty and serenity form perhaps the nearest approach of modern art to Greek art. The perfect purity of certain harmonies in this music soars to heights which are hardly even reached by the mystical zeal of the knights of the Grail. In this work, everything is clear and full of light. In the glow of this light Mozart died on December 5, 1791.

Mozart's *Die Zauberflote* (*The Magic Flute*) has been extraordinarily well served in recorded medium since microgroove began. I grew up on performances by Klemperer (with Popp, Frick, Jurinac, Seefried et al.), the monophonic Karajan recording for EMI, and a splendid recording on London conducted by Sir Georg Solti with the Vienna Philharmonic, featuring a soprano named Christina Deutekom in the role of the Queen of the Night. I thought this performance to be nearly beyond reproach until I was introduced to two additional recordings, both of which are currently available.

Now at budget price, a once full-priced digital recording by James Levine and the Vienna Philharmonic was issued which knocked me off my feet. The immediacy of the recording, the spontaneity of the interpretation, and the excellence of the recorded sound made Levine's recording for me a dream come true, and I thought it could not be bettered.

I was wrong, as I often am, and Sir Georg Solti revisited the work with the young soprano Sumi Jo approximately six years ago, again for London Records. This is one of the most exciting performances on disc, and it is also one of the shortest, being at nearly breakneck speed. The performance does not, however, feel rushed, and I believe that Solti has never made a finer operatic recording than this. This recording has received accolades from all corners of the globe, and both the singing and orchestral accompaniment really are outstanding. The Vienna Philharmonic has this work in its blood, and it can rightfully call this music its own!

- Die Zauberflote
    London 433210-2 (2). Vienna PO & State Opera Chorus, Solti

- Die Zauberflote
    RCA 4586-2RG (2). Vienna PO & State Opera Chorus, Levine

A Time for Revolution

It was the age of wisdom, it was the age of foolishness. It was the epoch of belief, it was the epoch of incredulity. It was the season of Light, it was the season of Darkness. It was the spring of hope, it was the winter of despair. In the New World, a rabble of colonists had overthrown an Empire and drafted a Constitution; in the Old World a rabble of citizens had stormed the Bastille and executed a king. And in the midst of them, the guillotine, ever busy and ever worse than useless, was in constant requisition. In short, it was a time for revolution.

It was the philosophers of the age of enlightenment that had forged the watchwords and prepared the ground for this chaotic explosion. The age of revolution (roughly 1770 -1800) took place during a great awakening and marvelous discovery of the human ego which grew into a mighty chorus of self-assertion. And when the bloodletting and the ugliness had come to an end, there emerged a new and undisputedly victorious middle class with expanding expectations of scaling barricades heretofore considered impregnable. Youthful, courageous, ambitious, vigorous and glamorous, and efficiently ruthless, they took for their rallying cry the slogan of Jean Jacques Rousseau, "Myself Alone!" They turned for their inspiration to classical antiquity, to the clean, simple, uncluttered lines of the ancient world, and in the perfection and grandeur of the Greeks and Romans they found the intellectual bath, the secular baptism, that had given the first and unfading tone and tincture to all of the arts.

In this changing milieu of neoclassicism, music understandably reflected the stormy events of the age. With the overthrow of the monarchy and organized religion, music no longer existed for the entertainment of a privileged class of society but served a higher purpose: to arouse patriotism,

69

to serve the people, and ultimately, all humanity. The public at large became the most important patron, and performances now reached a far greater audience than ever before through public concerts for musically informed listeners who paid for their admission. Much of this revolutionary music was destined for outdoor ceremonies and public performances, with mass choruses and large orchestras.

The artist, and specially the musician, found himself enjoying new privileges. Whereas Haydn had been obliged to wear the household livery like any other servant, the unmannerly Beethoven was quite willing to keep an Empress waiting, and he accepted the financial support of his patrons as something that society owed to him as an artist. Certainly he did not show himself overly thankful, and at times he was downright insulting. For, he said, there were and will be thousands of princes, but there was only one Beethoven! Music was the wine that inspired humankind to new acts of creation; it was the link between ordinary mortals and the Supreme Being, and Beethoven considered himself the Bacchus who pressed out this glorious wine for mankind and made them spiritually drunk - his music was the mediator between the life of the spirit and that of the senses.

A significant advance in the music of this age was the technical mastery of the *development* of a musical theme. With Haydn, the emphasis in development had been simplicity. Simplicity was necessary to express the new secular feelings and to replace the abandoned contrapuntal structure, and a clearness was needed to convey in absolute music what had before depended upon words. With Haydn, as the strings uttered the soft hum of woods and meadows, it was an idyllic and lyric utterance that was content to be in a joyous state. Mozart had crowned the secular outburst by deepening its poetry, idealizing its humor, and adding a serious note. With Beethoven, the music passed from the stage of amusement to heroic expression and the articulation of stern messages.

In Beethoven, everything became subordinate to the expression of a great, continuous, homogenous thought or feeling. He dethroned Beauty and set up Feeling. He was the first to combine the dignity of detail with a distinct purpose and a defined kind of feeling. *Meaning* became more important than *Beauty* in itself, and no other form of utterance was so powerful for its expression as music. In his hands, the art of the *development* matured to give life and reality to music, as to all human thought, and through it he achieved the energy and power which could rouse to action. Anyone could make an enchanting melody, but it was when one could develop the tune, and talk with sequence and coherence, that one became master of the magic language. And through his developments, he infused music with feeling and the fullness of the human experience, and of the pure joys that spring from the elemental relations of man to man, and mate to mate. With the symphonies of Beethoven it became certain that the poetry that lies too deep for words does not lie too deep for music, and that the vicissitudes of the soul, from the roughest fun to the loftiest aspiration, could stand by itself in the dramatic and subjective powers of sound, quite apart from the decorative musical structures of which hitherto they had been a mere feature.

In a way, the revolution that took place in music at this time was wrought by the tortured and unyielding spirit of Beethoven. The first musical product of the age of revolution was the *Eroica* Symphony of Beethoven (Symphony No. 3). It was utterly unlike anything that had ever been heard in the world before; nothing before had ever resembled its "grandoiseness, splendioseness and neuroseness." Compared to its effort, its hurry, its excitement, aspiration and exhausting climaxes, everything else seemed platitudinous, puerile and unoriginal. Whereas Haydn had been refined as the most cultivated country gentleman of his day could be, and Mozart had the refinement of nature and the solitude of the soul, Beethoven remained an unlicked cub even when he had grown into a very grizzly bear. His was the most turbulent spirit that ever found expression in pure sound. The impetuous fury of his strength which he could quite easily contain and control and often would not, and the uproariousness of his humor, went beyond anything that had hitherto been found in the works of a composer. He was Defiance Incarnate, and he died as he had lived, challenging God and defying the universe.

Beethoven's younger contemporary, the mysterious Franz Schubert, seemed hardly suited to a revolutionary age, and yet he almost single-handedly developed the romantic German *Lied* or art song. Schubert rarely reached the Olympian mastery of his peer; his music was more delicate, less sombre, softer, but true and sincere, never morbid or weak, but with the magic virtue of lighting on some touch of undreamed beauty that crowned the mystery. If Beethoven was a prophet, Schubert was a seer.

Song was nothing new to the music lovers of the age of revolution. Europeans had a tradition of song that went back to the Middle Ages, and probably even farther back to the beginnings of music itself. Moreover, there were tunes from the popular operas, but all such songs were comparatively stiff and formal things. And so the Revolutionists and their successors, the Romanticists, created a species of song, less artificial than an operatic aria but more sophisticated than a folk song, that was so individual that it has retained its German name to distinguish it from all others. It was called the *lied* (*lieder* in the plural), or art-song, and it became responsible for the whole Romantic ideal in music that was to affect the piano and the orchestra.

The inspiration for the *lieder* was the verses of Schiller and Goethe with their melting, ecstatic descriptions of pastoral scenes and rapturous romance. Here, the rhythm of the spoken word and the natural tones of the human voice were transmuted into sounds that enshrined in poetry and music the common spirit of humanity. The songs were sung in such a way as to interest listeners not only in the music but also in the poem. Each vocal line, like its piano accompaniment, was designed with the utmost care and insight to reflect, amplify and spiritualize the expression of the words. Sometimes, each verse of poetry was sung to the same melody and accompaniment (*strophic* form). At other times, the text was followed as closely as possible, setting each line with its own music, depending on the unity of the mood, style and the sound of the words to make the song a coherent whole (*durchkomponiert*, which meant *through-composed*). The song itself followed the old tripartite form: the first melodic phrase was repeated, the second provided contrast, and the first returned as a conclusion.

Mozart and Beethoven cannot be considered typical composers of German *lieder* yet some of their songs represent characteristically and most beautifully the German art-song in its beginning. It is Franz Schubert, however, who is associated most closely with the *lied*. Beauty of the melodic line, unfailing power of characterization, perfect coordination of the musical form and poetic content, and a magnificent balance of the vocal part with the background of the piano accompaniment are some of the outstanding characteristics of Schubert's art as expressed in his over 600 *lieder* and his song cycles.

Another contemporary composer, Carl Maria von Weber was a revolutionary in a different sort of way—he released German music from the tyranny of Italian domination and from the suzerainty of the French influence on German literature. His music came from the same impulse that had stirred the beginnings of German literature in Herder and Goethe, and he created a new kind of opera which expressed the mysterious relations of the human heart to the strangeness of nature around it. Everything in his music was freshly Teutonic—language, titles, legends, characters. The music that follows are the works of Beethoven and Schubert.

Beethoven: Symphony No 1.

It was at the suggestion of Baron van Sweiten, the patron of Haydn and Mozart, that a virtuoso piano soloist from Bonn, Ludwig van Beethoven (1770 - 1827), began work on his first symphony. Four years later, at the birth of a new century, it was premiered at a concert in Vienna that was held for the composer's benefit. The time, April 2, 1800, seemed auspicious, and the composer, an aspiring man who was rising fast in aristocratic circles, was twenty-nine years old. Mozart had been dead for a few years; Haydn, the acknowledged father of the symphony, had as many more to live. The development of this new composer had been slow; Mozart had already given his forty-first symphony to the world at the age of thirty-one, whereas Beethoven had so far written only two other works for orchestra—his first two piano concertos.

In accordance to the musical manner of the day, the composition followed the established symphonic pattern with its customary four movements. The first movement, which was dedicated to the Baron, was an *Adagio molto* in the old tradition that Haydn had never broken. Though it showed the good breeding of the conservative Viennese court, complete with a minuet in its third movement, Beethoven's contemporaries had reason for alarm when they heard the iconoclastic opening chords, full of mystery and suspense, at its first performance. For, underneath its facade of elegant restraint lurked a prophetic strain, an untamed power and virility, that smelled of a revolutionist! The contemporary press, too, was less than complimentary; one terribly disturbed critic called it "the confused explosions of the outrageous effrontery of a young man." Others felt that there was too much use of the wind instruments and that the minuet seemed too heavy-footed, and a celebrated conductor from Halle, a sentinel of the old regime, even considered the entire opening passage from the last movement as being incompatible with the dignity of symphony concerts.

To those familiar with the power of the *Eroica* or the dramatic passion of the Fifth Symphony, this music is certainly a calmer experience. Its structure is the essence of simplicity—the principal theme of the first movement, though not distinctive by itself, is made more interesting by the skill with which it is treated, and the second movement is full of charm with the soft accompaniment for timpani showing an intimation of the startling effects that the composer was to later produce with this instrument. Nonetheless, it is bland music when compared to the complex developments of the future symphonies. Indeed, Hector Berlioz was to remark contemptuously, "This is not the true Beethoven!" Yet its admirably wrought music, clear and lively, has continued to delight audiences, from its unusually modern beginning, through its sunshiny radiance, to its psychologically powerful climax. And when the *Eroica* came to outrage its first critics, it was his first symphony that they pointed back to as a model symphony!

Unlike the first symphonies of Dvorak, Prokofiev and Shostakovitch, Beethoven's Symphony No. 1 is not a student work. While its orchestration is not as opulent or beefy as later works, this is Beethoven in full bloom, intellectually well developed and yet simply elegant.

In 1962 Herbert von Karajan embarked on his second integral Beethoven Symphony cycle, this time for DGG in Berlin. This cycle has long been favored as one of the best complete cycles of Beethoven's symphonies since the advent of long playing microgroove, and remains a staple of the CD catalog at budget price. Karajan's recording of the First Symphony still fares well in any crowd, and his interpretation remains lean, swift and elegant. It is currently featured in the 87-CD *Beethoven Edition*, issued in 1997 as an anticipatory celebration of the 100th year of DGG. The performance is glorious from start to finish, and remains well recorded. It is, to me, preferable to his four later accounts.

In 1969, the Little Orchestra of London and Leslie Jones recorded the first Beethoven Symphony in a very early Dolby-A noise reduction based recording for Unicorn Records, pressed in the UK both in vinyl and on cassette. This remains to me the *Din* of Beethoven Firsts because of the small scaled forces used, and the utterly propulsive nature of the performance. It is on par with Jones' recording of the Eighth Symphony. If you come upon this recording in a used record store, or can find a copy and import it from the UK, do so, as you will not be disappointed.

The Hungarians Dohnanyi, Szell and Reiner have contributed superb Beethoven Firsts to the lexicon of available recordings. I don't know why it is that Hungarians make such great conductors, but the Cleveland Orchestra under both Dohnanyi and Szell provide us with limpidly clear, exciting renditions of the work approximately thirty years apart. Either will bring great pleasure, as will Reiner's recording, which was originally issued on a two LP set including a fabulous Beethoven Ninth Symphony. Reiner and the Chicago Symphony Orchestra are of pyrotechnic elegance in this performance, and the playing can scarcely be improved upon. The tempi are all on the slightly fast side, and despite using very large orchestral forces, unlike Jones and Marriner, to be discussed below, one would not know from the accuracy of the playing that a full orchestra was being utilized.

For me, the most preferable available modern version of the work remains that of Sir Neville Marriner with the Academy of Saint Martin's-in-the-Fields on Philips. This recording, made in 1971 and first appearing in a four LP box of *The Rise of the Symphony*, was a landmark performance in its day, and it still retains the freshest of sound. The scale of the performance is well nigh perfect, and it is brilliantly punctuated with the most detailed of recorded sound. It certainly is competitive with any modern digital version, of which I have not encountered a better one.

- Symphony Nos. 1, 2
  Philips 432 274-2 PSL. ASMIF, Marriner

Beethoven: Symphony No 2

Scarcely a year had passed since the debut of his first symphony when Beethoven noticed a growing loss in his hearing. His doctor advised him to rest his ears and escape to a retreat away from the noise of

Vienna, and so the composer spent the summer of 1802 at Heiligenstadt, in a lone large house belonging to a peasant, that stood on an eminence from which the Danube and the plain could be seen in the distance. Here, he could take long walks alone in his beloved woods and fields outside the village, or sit for hours in the shade of a favorite tree, communicating with nature, and contemplating his shameful malady. And it was here, in the shadow of the Carpathian mountains, wrapped in the silence of the fields where he could conceal his infirmity, that he composed his second symphony. It was a remarkably witty and exuberant piece, considering the moments when he believed himself to be the most miserable of God's creatures. There were times when Beethoven was aroused to defy his fate, and there were times when his depression brought thoughts of impending doom. And he was in love, which was misery enough for anyone!

This music is all nobility, energy and pride. One can sense the youthful ardor of a noble heart that keeps intact the finest illusions of life, and still believes in immortal glory and self-sacrifice in love. Like its predecessor, the composer tried to make the Second Symphony conform as closely as was possible with the traditional mold. But the music here no longer merely amuses and charms: the minstrel has doffed the guise of an entertainer and has taken the stand of poet and prophet. Perhaps it was taken with reluctance—he could not help the greatness of his words, he could only deliver his best expression. And when the fire appeared, perhaps it came unknown to the prophet himself. There is little question of a dramatic moral force evolving in this music, a kind of hidden truth like the "evidence of things not seen." From the full pause at the start—a sacred silence—to the replacement of the traditional minuet of the third movement by a playful yet happily serene *scherzo,* the music expands to show its own spontaneous quality, an independent utterance, and the growth itself is all of the real Beethoven. The forceful, the lyrical, the fierce —indeed, the introductory music is a masterpiece wherein the most beautiful and unexpected effects follow one another, and the touchingly solemn melody and the bold rhythm set the emotional stage from the outset.

The Second Symphony, the longest symphony to be written at that time, was performed in Vienna in 1803 in a long Beethoven program—the audience listened not only to this symphony but also to the First, then to one of his piano concertos, and finally to his oratorio, *The Mount of Olives*! Needless to say, the work was no more fortunate with the critics than its predecessor, and one learned musicologist dubbed it "a gross monstrosity, an immense wounded snake bleeding to death but unwilling to die."

What goes for Symphony No.1 is almost duplicated with Symphony No. 2 in terms of performance options.

Karl Bohm and the Vienna Philharmonic Orchestra in their Beethoven Bicentennial release captured the Second in a very landlersque way, a leisurely but pointed, beautifully executed performance that could not be better captured by the microphones. This remains to me the most poised and elegant of Beethoven Seconds, but perhaps not the most exciting. Karajan and the 1962 Cycle with the Berlin Philharmonic still comes out on top, in my opinion, for early stereo recordings of the work, in a rather exciting, vibrant reading which was very well miked in its day. Again, later performances still don't have the beautiful sound that Karajan produced with this orchestra at this time.

Again, the Hungarians Dohnanyi and Szell crowd a busy field of contenders for sweepstakes in the Beethoven Second Symphony. Though nearly 30 years apart, Szell's performance is particularly well engineered and performed, and shows the Cleveland Orchestra at its very best form. The last movement of this performance is truly hair trigger perfection, and I have not encountered a better finale than this recording. The percussive aspects of the closing bars have never been captured more effectively before the microphones. Dohnanyi's recording with the same orchestra is equally exciting, but is a little bit more ambiently captured, and I've just heard it very recently. It remains an excellent digital option for those wishing the most recent of recording technology, although I would say in deference to Szell that Dohnanyi's recording does not to me represent an improvement sonically overall. Reiner and the Pittsburg Symphony Orchestra capture the work brilliantly in a 1940's recording recently reissued by Sony Classical (Heritage Series). This is a very virile, exciting performance which is only restricted by its age. Those interested in collecting monophonic recordings that have been brilliantly repackaged need not look further than this excellent recording which is also faced with Mozart symphonies with the same forces.

Again, Sir Neville Marriner and the Academy of Saint Martin's-in-the-Fields remains the paragon of elegance and accuracy in performance, and I would easily recommend Marriner's recording, on the same CD as his First Symphony, as my premier choice in this work, considering configuration as well as excellence of recorded sound.

- Symphony Nos. 1, 2
    Philips 432 274-2PSL. ASMIF, Marriner

Beethoven: Symphony No 3 (Eroica)

The ostensible occasion of this symphony appears to have been the career of Napoleon Bonaparte. When Beethoven was composing his Third Symphony in 1803 and the spring of 1804, he had in mind one of his great living heroes - the young Napoleon. His imagination was fired by the poetic ideas of freedom and equality for, in the French leader's democratic proclamations, he saw the hope of the world. And to capture the new dramatic spirit of the revolutionary and romantic era spawned by Napoleon, he created the most influential single symphony ever written.

The whole understanding of this work depends upon distinguishing the profound joy of the Hero in an universal cause who, in this revel, deserves a clear right to his exultation. Beethoven was in the habit of reading Homer, and in this magnificent musical epic, memories of the *Iliad* play their inevitably beautiful role. It is a song about the Hero in all his various moods. The song of mourning must come too, and come it does, with the highest sense of fitness, in the second movement, where the expression of grief is steadily maintained and in forms so pure and noble as to remain unequaled in all music. But death is an incident of far less importance, a small non-event, compared to the thoughts and deeds of an eventful day. Just as the solemn rites at the grave of their leader were followed by the ancient Greek warriors by a celebration of games, so, too, this music pursues, in its four movements, a curious balance between solemn foreboding and exultant dance, a strange mixture of a cavernous gloom and unreined joy that is the typical feeling of the Hero.

The *Eroica* was also a landmark in Beethoven's own spiritual development and a turning point in his music. Hitherto, he had expressed a young composer's conceptions of a few stock poetic situations. He had "made" and "composed" music to express emotions and experiences that were pretended but not actually experienced. A critic could have objected to his sorrows because they were not genuine sorrows. But in this music, Beethoven was expressing the most profound experience that he had yet passed through himself —his progressing deafness—when his courage and defiance of his fate had been followed by despair. He was expressing what he personally knew when he made the power and heroism of the first movement succeed into the black night of the second. And he was again speaking of what he knew when he made this *Funeral March* to be succeeded by the indomitable uprising of creative energy in the next movement—a turbulent, irrepressible, deathless creative energy that was surging from depths that even he had not suspected.

The whole work was a miraculously realized expression of a supremely important personal experience: it expressed the human spirit, reborn in the light—or rather, the fire—of one man's inner conflict. Though he may have thought Napoleon a hero, his conception of the heroic he had earned himself! From the innermost depth of his being he had cried out the agony of his deafness, and it was answered by the mysterious horn-call of the *Eroica*... "Lazarus, arise!" And it was surely no accident that the "Prometheus" theme dominated the finale of this music. For Beethoven was nothing if not a Promethean figure, reaffirming the power of man to shape his own destiny. Like Robespierre, he sought to *remake* the world in the image of his own transcendent vision.

The story of how the subtitle *Eroica* was legitimately given to it by its composer is well known. In the summer of 1804, Napoleon crowned himself Emperor, and an outraged Beethoven, crushed by the annihilation of his ideals that he believed he had shared with his hero, ripped the title page from his manuscript that he had dedicated to Bonaparte. "Is he then, too, nothing more than an ordinary human being?" he cried. Later, when the symphony was published, it bore a new name: *Sinfonia Eroica, Composed to Celebrate the Memory of a Great Man.* The Napoleon that Beethoven had admired was dead in his mind. Now the symphony transcended all flesh and was dedicated to the spirit. Its first public performance was conducted by Beethoven himself in 1805.

Beethoven's Symphony No. 3 (*Eroica*) was the second work I learned. That may have been ambitious, but I collected nearly two dozen recordings of this work prior to learning a third work in my childhood. Unfortunately, the first performance I learned was probably one of the worst, that of Leonard Bernstein and the New York Philharmonic Orchestra, a devastatingly poorly played, poorly engineered recording. It nevertheless was an athletic, exciting performance, and unfortunately, many performances that I appropriated subsequent to that time were far less compelling. I remember reading Bernard Jacobson's review of the performance in High Fidelity magazine in mid-1964. I literally wept because of how devastating the analysis was, and while I didn't know better, twenty years later I reread the review and agreed completely with this critic's analysis. I don't encourage people to find this recording, despite the excitement it generates.

The Vienna Philharmonic has fared well in this work with both Bohm and Bernstein, the latter in a somewhat comical, angular performance which is hammered out with the kind of precision that Lennie demanded of the Vienna Philharmonic in his reassessment of the Beethoven Symphonies in 1979. If you want to enjoy the work and laugh at the same time, find Bernstein's second performance of the work.

I have come to enjoy my *Eroica* Symphony in a lean, small scaled atmosphere, and thus, two recordings immediately come to mind that are worth finding. One is very poorly played, but is a *Desert Island* reading of great proportion, and the other is one of the best played recordings I have encountered and is a budget disc.

The first of these two recordings, that by the late Hermann Scherchen and the Vienna State Opera Orchestra is available on MCA Classics as part of a 4-CD box of Beethoven Symphonies with several different orchestras. This same performance is also available on a Millennium CD recently reissued. The performance uses a small orchestra force, and is at a lightningly quick tempo. The orchestra falls apart in the third and fourth movements on several occasions, but the performance is spirited, bright eyed and humorous. The tempo of the coda of the finale, let alone other portions of all movements, is almost unplayable, but this exotic reading, which was actually well received when it first appeared, remains a highlight of the LP era.

The second recording, one which readers will readily find, was made available in the early eighties by the Moss Music Group. The Cincinnati Symphony Orchestra with its then music director, Michael Gielen, clearly had studied Hermann Scherchen and his approach to the *Eroica*, and although the performance is by no means a copy of it, it is equally brilliantly conceived and, in this instance, perfectly executed by an extraordinarily well trained orchestra which has become one of the great orchestras of North America. I cannot recommend more highly this budget CD to all listeners, and encourage them to seek it as their *DIN* standard for this work. The EMI remake in 1996 (EMI CDC5 60090-2) is also superb.

Karajan's wonderful 1962 performance of the work remains his greatest to date, and perhaps the best recorded of all five of his commercial performances. It is somewhat more leisurely than Gielen, but extraordinarily elegant and poised. I especially like the first and last movements of this performance.

James Levine and the Metropolitan Opera Orchestra recorded the work for DG in the Manhattan Center a number of years ago. This performance is conceptually much like Toscanini's statement from 1949 on BMG/RCA but it is even more brilliant. The first chords of the work are played with such precision, as are the last two of the finale, as Beethoven had requested, that one sees that the conductor has studied the score and understands it perhaps better than anyone else in the recorded format. The intention is for this to be grand scale Beethoven, and to "blow away" the listener. This is my favorite orchestral conception of the work, but it is unfortunately spoiled by some of the worst engineering flaws that develop, curiously, only in the mid portion of the finale, which leads me to believe that DG is aware of this, and hopefully will be able to resolve the technical imperfections which prevent us from hearing into the orchestra in the closing minutes of the performance. The stage loses depth, and the proscenium appears to be a vertical one in which one can only hear brass, timpani and strings. Curiously, the recording reverts to the kind of sonic depth that unfortunately fails to grace the Toscanini recording mentioned. I certainly hope Levine insists upon re- engineering of the finale or re-records the work prior to its reissue or packaging as part of a complete cycle which would be a very desirable issue from this source.

I could speak all day about desirable performances of the Beethoven Third Symphony, but will merely mention noteworthy performances by name and orchestra. Eugen Jochum and the Amsterdam Concertgebouw Orchestra of Amsterdam on Philips Concert Classics produced a splendid recording in the mid sixties of this work, and it is extraordinarily exciting and atypical of the European tradition in that it is a speedy, virile interpretation. Erich Kleiber and the Vienna Philharmonic recorded the work in the monophonic era for Decca/London, and this remains a superb interpretation as well. The monophonic sound is not a drawback. Carlo Maria Giulini recorded the *Eroica* Symphony in 1977 with the Los Angeles Philharmonic Orchestra in a performance which shows the orchestra to truly be one of the great ensembles of the world. While it is a patrician reading, it is elegantly stated, and shows just how well developed this orchestra can be, given proper leadership. Kubelik's excellent Berlin Philharmonic recording should also not be missed. A classic, large orchestral version, it is lithe, clean and beautifully proportioned.

For original instrument performances, I would encourage the listener to study the performances of Roger Norrington and the London Classical Players for EMI, and John Eliot Gardiner with the Orchestre Romantique et Revolutionnaire for Archive. I tend to lean towards Norrington in this performance because of the finale being more effective, but both performances are A-1 interpretations of the work.

In his valedictory performance as conductor, the late Klaus Tennstedt allowed EMI to issue what may have been his final concert performance of the work, and certainly his final known commercial recording. His *Eroica* Symphony with the London Philharmonic Orchestra is exceptionally well recorded and played, and is of the central European tradition—a deliberate, somewhat slow perform-ance of a grand scale. I don't prefer this approach, but of its kind, there is none better.

I have barely scratched the surface of my *Eroica* collection, but in those mentioned, you will find one to please all tastes.

- Symphony No. 3 (Eroica)
   MMG/VOX Prima MWCD 7147. Cincinnati SO, Gielen
- Symphony No. 3 (Eroica); Overture: Creatures of Prometheus
   EMI Dig. CDC7 49101-2 Classical Players, Norrington
- Symphony No. 3 (Eroica)
   Belart-Karussell 450 037. Berlin Phl., Kubelik

Beethoven: Symphony No 4

The year 1806 began explosively for Vienna with its occupation by Napoleon's troops. For Beethoven, too, the year began explosively with emotional and physical turmoil. His opera *Fidelio* had failed in its first performances, he was working on eight major masterpieces simultaneously, and he was being continually pressed for money because of his own debts and those of his relatives. By the end of the year, he had completed most of his Sonata *Appassionata*, the three *Razumovsky* String Quartets, his Fourth Piano concerto, his Fourth and Fifth Symphonies, and the Violin Concerto—perhaps a reflection of the desperate effort made to assure a position in the world! About the time that he was working on his Fourth Symphony at the summer castle of his patron, Prince Lichnowsky, he was also in love with the Countess Therese von Brunswick, and he had reason to believe that his sentiments were being reciprocated.

Of all his symphonies, the Fourth is the most happy, and ingratiating, and complacent. Gone are the ode and elegy; the music is lively, brisk and cheerful, imbued with a heavenly sweetness. Here is a record of the sheer state of the joy of existence, craved after and highly prized, felt by a sensitive but strong, confident and healthy man. There is something pretty and sweet in this music, like a slender Greek maiden, and it shows Beethoven in a happy mood, taking joy in consciously producing a very lovely and perfect thing.

No one could be so severe as Beethoven and, just a moment after, so jolly. And in the subtle element of humor, there is little doubt again that he stands as one of its chief creative spirits. The woes and littleness of actual things are lost in the broad universal view, and the quality of this all-embracing happiness lies in its bold surmounting of all human ills with its triumphant vigor. Save perhaps for the contemplative introduction, the first movement is full of joy. There is an irresistible tenderness and feeling of peace in the angelic melody, a pure German folk-song, of the second movement, a playful minuet is retained in the third movement, and the gaiety and outpouring of joyous laughter persists to the end in the ceaseless chattering of sparkling notes interrupted by some wild raspy chords.

The work was first heard publicly in 1807 at a concert given for the benefit of the composer, and Beethoven himself conducted the performance.

The Fourth Symphony of Beethoven is perhaps the last Beethoven Symphony I learned, and perhaps may be the most difficult to come to for many a listener, if only because the introduction, as perfect as it is, outlasted my patience when I was about fourteen years old. No doubt the introduction is the most ominous of all Beethoven Symphonies. Suffice to say, there are many superb

"Fourths" on the market. Again, if you have any one of those discussed here, you need not look further.

Carlos Kleiber and the Bayerische Staatsorchester produced a performance in live concert which has been issued on Orfeo, a CD which is as perfect in its immediacy and presentation as Kleiber's appropriately famous recordings of Symphony Nos 5 and 7, to be discussed later. This is a brilliant live performance, with all tempi on the fast side, and the audience participation is nil until the decay of the final note. The actual concert resulted in foot stomping and rhythmic applause, I am told, but we are spared the ovations and audience antics. Find this Fourth; buy it! You will not need another one.

Of studio recordings, the 1962 Herbert von Karajan recording with the Berlin Philharmonic remains a paragon of elegance and stature, and despite it being thirty five years old, it still remains one of the great recordings of the vinyl era. The sound may be a bit dated, but the impact of this Fourth is much the same as with Kleiber, or Kubelik, to be discussed below. It is the well judged tempi which are most apt, and the engineering results in everything being in proper proportion, thanks to the use of a studio-converted church and an outstanding engineer, Otto Gerdes and his associates at the time, Elsa Schiller and Gunter Hermanns. It is possible this will only be available as part of a five-CD box, but the price of this complete cycle is well worth the single performance of the Symphony No. 4 alone. This Karajan performance is not to be confused with the 1958 EMI cycle with Karajan and the Philharmonia, nor the 1975 video, or the 1977 or 1982-5 cycles for DG and Sony.

One would not normally associate the Israel Philharmonic with great Beethoven, nor with the conductor Rafael Kubelik who, only relatively late in his life, recorded all nine symphonies with nine different orchestras for DG. But this performance is unbelievable, from its magical opening moments to the utterly knife-like precision of the final notes of the last movement. The recorded sound is splendid, but a bit angular by modern standards, but in 1976, this was a performance to contend with. Strange as this match of Kubelik and the Israel Philharmonic is, the performance is one of great gramophone significance and is worth your research. The LP and cassette are faced with a fine, somewhat landleresque Beethoven Symphony No. 2 with the Royal Amsterdam Concertgebouw Orchestra recorded in the Gootesaal, Amsterdam. The engineers are the same as in the Beethoven Symphony No. 8 reviewed elsewhere in this book, with Kubelik and the members of the Cleveland Orchestra, but each recorded in the Kubelik cycle sounds very different, as no one location is used for two symphonies. This is a must for lovers of the work.

If you are able to find a taped copy of the Baltimore Symphony Orchestra's performance of Beethoven Symphony No. 4 conducted by its music director, David Zinman, from the early nineties, this is a performance to treasure, much like Carlos Kleiber's own live recording. It may even be more exciting in some ways than Kleiber's studied interpretation.

In conclusion, Carlos Kleiber's live recording on Orfeo is well worth owning, and it should be sought. If you are unable to find it, and still want Kleiber, you may be able to find a Philips Video of his live performance with the Royal Amsterdam Concertgebouw Orchestra, a somewhat less compelling No. 4 which benefits from excellent sound and pointed rhythms.

- Symphony No. 4
    Orfeo C100 841 A, Bayerische Staatsorchester, Kleiber
- Symphony No. 4
    DG 429 036.2GX5 (boxed set), BPO, Herbert von Karajan
- Symphony No. 4
    DG 2535441 or DG 2740155 (boxed set), Israel Philharmonic Orchestra, Rafael Kubelik

Beethoven: Symphony No 5

It remains unknown why Beethoven needed such an emphatic, unmistakable, short, and easily remembered motif for his next symphony—the most awesome of all symphonies, the most humbling even though it would incite us to defy and conquer. The story that is commonly told is the famous remark by Beethoven's companion, Anton Schindler, that the four notes that open the first movement—perhaps the best-known notes in all music—represent "Fate knocking at the door." And out of these four notes, whatever may have been their origin, arises a cosmos of breathtaking proportions and dread significance, overpowering in its force and strength. Never before had music so nakedly and shamelessly, and with such burning rays, exposed the tempests and triumphs of the human soul. Here, revolution became confined within the four walls of a symphony! This ruthless, blazing, awesome music cannot be the utterance of one man's thought or feelings, his secret sorrows, his pent-up anger, or his dreams full of dejection—it is the tormented, cynical, hopeful and, finally, triumphant voice of all mankind, a pitiful and puny cry that bears within it the seed of man's intense humanity and the elements of his final greatness. Listen to it! And you will come under its spell, as mankind has done for more than a hundred years, to find new meanings and no meanings, and sometimes, even in the no meanings, sublime intimations of wonder, bewilderment and delight, harsh humor and unreasoning defiance, hopeless supplication and assured triumph.

His papers reveal that the germ of this music was gestating in the composer's mind since 1800, but it was left, like strong wine, to lie upon the lees before it was presented for the first time at a concert in 1808, a few days before Christmas. The conductor was Beethoven.

In 1975, the musical world was shaken by the appearance of the son of a famous conductor, Eric Kleiber. Son Carlos, in his late forties or early fifties, was virtually an unknown on the shores, and DG had the temerity to issue at full price a thirty seven minute recording of a work that was far over-recorded—the Beethoven Fifth Symphony! This incandescent reading was an immediate hit, and has remained at the top of anyone's short list of Beethoven Fifths since its appearance. Comparisons to even the greatest of Beethovenian interpretations of the period, such as those by Karl Bohm, Eugen Jochum, Herbert von Karajan, Otto Klemperer, just to name several, were not so much pointless as to become tiresome. The inspiration of the performance, the choice of tempi, the hair trigger perfection of the Vienna Philharmonic, and the brilliant engineering of the recording and spontaneity of the rendition, made it a *Desert Island* performance. The recording has earned a place on the shelves of most collectors, and I know few people who feel anything other than great endearment to it as their first choice of a rendition of this work. In my book, it is unsurpassed, and little more needs to be said other than for one or two selected comparisons.

Fritz Reiner and the Chicago Symphony produced an excellent Beethoven Fifth in the late 1950s, one that should be heard, simply to show how brilliant an ensemble the Chicago Symphony was before anybody recognized how fantastic this orchestra was on an international scale. The performance still sounds quite fresh, despite its nearly forty years of age.

George Szell recorded a nearly definitive Beethoven Fifth with the Cleveland Orchestra in the late 1950s, as well, at Severance Hall, Cleveland. This performance has some of the hair trigger brilliance of the Vienna Philharmonic recording with Kleiber, but is somewhat briefer due to a lack of repeats.

Either of these alternative versions are still excellent in my book, and they outclass most Central European orchestral performances of the work quite handily. I know there are long lists of Beethoven Fifths everywhere, but anyone of these is sure to excite.

Kleiber's recording has been on the market at full price for nearly twenty years, and only recently, reissued at mid price in conjunction with the Symphony No. 7, discussed below. Kubelik recorded the nine Beethoven Symphonies from 1973-1976. His Symphony No. 5 with the Boston Symphony Orchestra is a classic, large-scale reading to be considered one of the best of its kind

- Symphony Nos. 5, 7
  DG 447 400-2, VPO, Kleiber

- Symphony Nos. (i) 5, (ii) 7
  Belart-Karussell 450 038-2, (i) BSO, (ii) VPO, Kubelik

- Symphony No. 5, 7; Overtures: Coriolan, Fidelio;
  RCA Red Seal 09026-68976-2. Chicago SO, Reiner

- Symphony Nos. 2, 5
  Sony Classical SBK 47651. Cleveland O, Szell

Beethoven: Symphony No 6 (Pastoral)

That Beethoven should create a great musical work under the inspiration of Nature was inevitable. In the prison of his growing deafness he found happiness outdoors, walking alone in the Vienna woods as he sketched his musical ideas, watching the awakening birds and splashing waterfalls, drunk with the perfume exhaled from the drenched earth and the blooming wild flowers, impregnated by the richer music which flows in all Nature herself, which is specially diffused in the vibrations of light and shade, and the song of the rivers, forests and insects. He was fully alive to the countless lovely and tender things in life, and his reaction to nature was spontaneous, direct and unsophisticated. There is none of the cultured affectation of a "love for nature" in this music; indeed, only a man pure in heart could have written the *Pastoral* symphony. Beethoven's natural world teaches less of man and morality than of its own immortal truth, of the chastity of Creation and the cyclic beauty of God's given world.

Feelings, scenes and events have all had their place in the arts. And *feelings* is the key that pervades this music, an expression, in sound, of the spirit of nature, of the feelings aroused by communication with nature, be it a trip to the countryside or a visit to the brook—the cool freshness of the morning air, the still dew-laden leaves, and the sweet smell of newly turned brown earth. Often, when Beethoven means to give but a touch here and there of realism, the music is transformed from free feeling to a graphic account. Thunder, wind and blinding rain all crash together and lightning flashes, but when the worst is over, we have *feelings* again, expressed in the sentiments of a shepherd's song.

The *Pastoral* symphony was first performed in 1808, in the same program that included the debut of the Fifth Symphony.

I find this work the weakest of all the Beethoven Symphonies from an interest standpoint, although it is an elegant, poised statement of programmatic material pertaining to Beethoven's visits to the countryside. There are really only a few great Pastoral recordings. This is an exceedingly difficult work to pull off both in concert and in commercial recordings.

I would like to dispel a commonly held myth that one of the great recordings of this work is that of Bruno Walter and the Columbia Symphony Orchestra. I find this performance to be heartfelt and a warm personal statement, but little else. It is not well recorded, suffers from overly prominent mid range, tubby timpani and, in the final analysis, really is not well played.

The storm is little more than a May shower; definitely not *Sturm und Drang*. I am stunned that after nearly forty years of existence in the catalog that this performance is still highly regarded. I say this because I want to direct the listener to exciting performances of the work, not deadly ones.

There are three performances that I am compelled to state are of equal importance in my collection, and are equally good, and the listener will simply have to choose one of them and run.

Karl Bohm and the Vienna Philharmonic's performance for DG for the *Beethoven Bicentennial* is one of the great performances I have ever encountered. It is exceptionally well conceived, studied and executed, and I know of no higher compliment than to say that this is an authoritative performance of the score that lacks eccentricity and is delivered with great candor. Its nearly thirty year age does not in any way deter me from giving it a wholehearted recommendation, as the recorded sound is opulent still. The storm is particularly exciting.

For original instrument lovers, the performance by John Eliot Gardiner and the Orchestre Romantique et Revolutionnaire remains a paragon of excellence, and is brilliantly recorded and executed. The storm is particularly violent, and comes across perhaps even better than Karl Bohm's performance.

My final recommendation for this work is that of an underrated conductor who I felt to be thoroughly inadequate when I was younger. However, Rudolf Kempe and the Munich Philharmonic Orchestra (EMI Classics for Pleasure, available in most large record stores and by import from the UK), have managed to capture the essence of this work much as has Karl Bohm with the Vienna Philharmonic, and it is my feeling that this performance is destined for perpetuity in the catalog as well. This is a performance which is striking in its elegance and simplicity, and the recorded sound, not quite as detailed as Bohm's, remains excellent. Readers might remember Rudolf Kempe from seeing him conduct the Munich Philharmonic Orchestra in a memorial for the Israeli hostages killed at the 1972 Olympics in Germany. Kempe himself died shortly after that televised broadcast, and I lament this now, feeling that he was under-recorded and under represented in the catalog.

- Symphony No. 6 (Pastoral) — SCHUBERT: Symphony No 5
  DG 447 433-2 VPO, Bohm

Beethoven: Symphony No 7

In a way, Beethoven's Seventh Symphony is an ideal symphony. There are no pictures or storied explanations here, no meanings to be eked out, just a genuine joy from the beauty and glory of an untitled work of pure rhapsodic music. It refuses definition, and the more a work refuses definition, the greater it is. Each listener understands or receives exactly according to his or her capacity, and each one has a right, without pretense of judicial authority, to tell the other how he or she feels about it. Myriad messages have been read in the Seventh—a peasant wedding, a Bacchic orgy, a democratic revolution, a chivalric ballad, an apotheosis of the dance. There is a bewitching rhythmic spell that shines through this music, touched with boisterousness, and it is not without a mordant bitterness. But it is a bitterness that is never precisely pessimism, and certainly never despair.

Some have called the music of this symphony his love music. If it is, it expresses that exquisite, shy and yet joyful tenderness that only the truly chaste have ever achieved. Even in the most abandoned mood of the *finale*, there is no trace of eroticism or the ecstasy of sexual delirium. Beethoven was a moralist in sexual matters, and this music shows that it was due to no asceticism, to no principles, but to the presence of very strong feelings which could allow nothing inferior in that kind to coexist.

Because of his worsening deafness, Beethoven conducted its first performance in 1813 from manuscript. The tide of war was turning against Napoleon, and the composer held the concert in a large hall at the University of Vienna as a benefit for the Austrian and Bavarian soldiers who had been wounded in the Napoleonic wars. The symphony was received with acclaim, especially its slow second movement which was repeatedly encored by the audience.

Two of the greatest recordings of this work emanated from the early years of stereo recording. They were both the product of Hungarian conductors with American orchestras, and truth to tell, few performances have topped either of these interpretations.

The Chicago Symphony under the direction of Fritz Reiner (RCA LSC-1991) first appeared in one of RCA's earliest stereo recordings. The performance is live, lean and swift, and the playing is beyond reproach. It is a galloping, exciting performance which shows the orchestra to be in top form and is recorded with great clarity. In its current CD incarnation, it comes with an effective recording of the Fifth Symphony and recordings of Beethoven *Overtures* which are also worth collecting.

By contrast, George Szell and the Cleveland Orchestra recorded the work in approximately 1958, and it was released as part of the integral cycle of Beethoven Symphonies produced by the Cleveland Orchestra. This Seventh has a noble first movement interpretation, and beautifully played third and fourth movements. The recording is a little bit more airy than that of Reiner's, and somewhat less frenetic, and the elegance of the work in performance here demonstrates its great Dionysian qualities to extreme.

European counterparts for truly great Seventh Symphonies are not few, but honorable mentions should be accorded Eugen Jochum and his Amsterdam Concertgebouw Orchestra performance for Philips made in the early sixties. This performance has all of the brilliance of Szell with a certain degree of refinement of playing in the central European tradition lacking in the domestic orchestral performances. This extra degree of polish makes the performance all the more exciting.

Herbert von Karajan and the Berlin Philharmonic recorded the Seventh Symphony as part of its integral cycle for DGG in 1962. This was, for most of my childhood, the preeminent performance to own in terms of sound quality and performance which has hardly ever been bettered. Unfortunately, then came Carlos Kleiber!

In 1976, when I was a junior student in undergraduate school, DG introduced its vinyl iteration of Kleiber's third commercial recording, DG 2530 706. The performance about blew me out of the water, and I have yet to encounter a performance of such incandescence and brilliance, either live or in the studio. When all is said and done, there is nothing else to do or say, and owning a copy of the Kleiber Beethoven Seventh in one's possession fairly much eliminates the competition by modern standards. Despite the fact that the performance is now twenty years old, it has been digitally restored and sounds better than it did originally on LP. Fortunately, it is coupled with Kleiber's equally brilliant recording of the Fifth Symphony, which predated the Seventh to production by one calendar year. This is the performance to have if you're looking for one recording. Only Kubelik comes close for elegance in this work, with the same forces.

- Symphony Nos. 5, 7
    DG 447 400-2. VPO, Carlos Kleiber

- Symphony Nos. (i) 5, (ii) 7
    Belart-Karrusell 450 038-2, (i) BSO, (ii) VPO, Kubelik

- Symphony No. 5, 7; Overtures: Coriolan, Fidelio;
    RCA Red Seal 09026-68976-2. Chicago SO, Reiner

Beethoven: Symphony No 8

If we must have a tragic symphony or a *pathetique* one, why not a comic? Humor has as much right as pathos, perhaps a little more! On the face of it, the Eighth symphony is a frankly playful piece—it strikes no depth of profound sympathy, there are no great contrasts of mood, and it teaches no lesson whatever. Yet it continues to charm as an undisturbed epic of merriment, with big views and bold flights, much like the symphonies of the good old days of Haydn where the composer had no business but to give pleasure. Short, playful and Haydnesque, there is no slow movement in this composition—the composer preferred not to inject any contrast to the pervading lightness. The music brushes away the frowns, and cozens the listener gently and cheerily out of sadness to wring a laughter from the tears. After the first public performance of the Eighth Symphony in 1814 in Vienna, a friend remarked to Beethoven that it had received less applause than the Seventh. "That's because its so much better!" growled the composer. And Beethoven meant what he said. For here, in this music, is the vast unbounded laughter of a man who has lived and suffered and, scaling the heights, has reached the summit.

Beethoven's Symphony No. 8 is a happy symphony, written directly after the Dionysian No. 7 and before the monumental No. 9, apparently at a moment of humor and repose. This short work, often grouped with Symphony Nos. 1, 2 and 4 for their relative brevity and somewhat smaller orchestral forces, has the wit and humor of a healthy Beethoven, though he was ravaged by alcoholism, cirrhosis and, questionably debated by some (see Marek's landmark text), syphilis. This symphony is a pistol, and should be played with brio and elan. The three versions listed below, several on CD, others destined for reissue on CD, are a must for the collector of this work.

The performance by Christopher Hogwood and the Ancient Academy of Music is played as if everyone was plugged into a 240 volt line. Tempi are all on the fast side, the playing scrupulously clean and neat, with humor, wit and charm. This 1989 recording is clearly the most modern of this *Desert Island* bunch, with top notch sound, and a wonderful Symphony No. 7 as a bonus. Especially remarkable are the brass in the finale, along with the timpani, which crack in a way which, if you aren't careful, may actually damage your loud speakers if played at too high a level. This performance, at its conclusion, always brings forth gales of laughter in our home because of the splendid articulation of the performance but also the wit and wisdom of the composer shining through so brilliantly. This is a must even for non-original instrument haters, and if you have a CD player which has variable speed control, simply advance the play back speed by 1.5%, and no more sour, chewy, sounding strings will plague your ears. To me, this is nearly a perfect Beethoven No. 8.

Leslie Jones and the Little Orchestra of London, using modern instruments, recorded the Beethoven Symphony Nos 1 and 8 in the early 70s for Unicorn Records using some of the first Dolby-A technology for quieting. This splendid recording, first issued in 1969, brought Leslie Jones to prominence; he is known mainly for his outstanding Haydn *Paris* and *Salomon* Symphonies from the same source, which are no longer available. This Symphony No. 8 is effectively as good as Hogwood in the modern instrument guise, with the same British flair noted by members of the Academy of Ancient Music for Hogwood. The tempi are engaging, the recorded sound excellent, and the Symphony No.1 accompanying this disc is equally fine. Despite their age, these recordings deserve a place on your vinyl shelf, and a letter to Unicorn-Kanchana might see these discs reissued one day on CD.

Again we find Rafael Kubelik in excellent form in the Beethoven Symphony No. 8. On this particular LP, a lumbering but gorgeous Boston Symphony rendition of Symphony No. 5 is also heard. Kubelik was the first conductor to record all nine Beethoven symphonies with nine different orchestras as a single project for DG during Hans Weber's and Heinz Wildhagen's tenure. Both doctorate producers, they along with senior producer Dr. Hans Hirsch had the idea of recording projects such as these (Abbado's first Brahms cycle with four different orchestras) but the idea never quite panned out beyond these two cycles. We're now seeing some DG cycles with multiple orchestras, but not one different orchestra per symphony.

This 8th, recorded in Severance Hall, Cleveland, sounds as if there is one microphone per instrument placed before the players. There is a tad clumsy clarinet contribution at moments, but this performance, especially in the finale, is absolutely beautiful and well proportioned, sounding like Cleveland under Szell without the ponderous retard Szell opts for in the finale which renders his reading noncompetitive in that moment, and puts Szell and his Symphony No. 8 off the short list of great "Eights." The Polygram subsidiary, Belart, has reissued some of Kubelik's Beethoven cycle, but not Nos. 4 or 8 at this time. I don't think that is a long termed issue, however. Try to find Kubelik's entire cycle or this reissue from that cycle. You won't be disappointed.

- Symphony Nos 7, 8
  London 425 692.2, Academy of Ancient Music, Hogwood
- Symphony No. 8
  Unicorn UNS 200. Little O of London, Leslie Jones (LP)
- SymphonyNo. 8
  DG 2535407 or DG 2740 155, Members of the Cleveland O, Kubelik (LP)

Beethoven: Symphony No 9 (Choral)

It was as early as 1793 that the youthful Beethoven aspired to set to music Schiller's *Ode to Joy* as an expression of his own dream of the brotherhood of man. Its incorporation within the framework of a symphony took form in 1817, and the completed work was first performed in 1824. The path to this glory was long and tortuous, and beset with all manners of troubles—numerous lawsuits, and the anxieties brought on by his unworthy nephew Carl whom he had adopted as a son. And though the idea of a symphony with a chorale had long been forming in the master's consciousness, his notebooks tell us of his extraordinary struggle to connect in a natural and logical manner the chorale conclusion with the preceding movements. Schindler has recorded well for us the day when Beethoven—now a suspicious, preoccupied lone wolf among his kind—rushed into the room crying out, "I have it! I have it! Let us sing the song of the immortal Schiller *Freude!*"

The Ninth was his final complete symphony, a Gargantuan masterpiece pregnant with meaning, where he was forced to turn to the human voice to unfold the cosmic thoughts and emotions that surged within him. It was his ultimate expression where he used rhythms and intonations and the words of a poem to drive his thoughts and feelings into our consciousness. The serenity of the slow movement, for example, is a serenity that contains within itself the deepest and most unforgettable sorrow, and yet a sorrow which is transformed by its inclusion in that serenity. Beethoven's Ninth is a masterpiece of modern tone poetry, and every literary man needs complete his culture by listening to it; its performance is a celebration rather than an entertainment.

The symphony was first performed in Vienna on May 7, 1824.

There is no short list of great Beethoven Ninths. I will attempt to condense the list to three or four performances, all of which have brought me great pleasure, one being very new to the catalog, and will likely see domestic release at the time of publication of this book.

The 1963 recording by Herbert von Karajan and the Berlin Philharmonic remains a classic of the gramophone. It is a large orchestral, romantically styled performance, but it is reasonably lean, light of foot, and architecturally well delineated. Karajan did not at this time in his career have the Teutonic heaviness that befalls his later three performances of the work. The first movement is for me one of the most exciting I've ever encountered, and the second movement, likewise, is equally propulsive. This recording is available as part of DG Originals and should not be missed.

In 1972, Sir Georg Solti recorded this work for the first time with the Chicago Symphony Orchestra. This is a very beefy performance with moderate tempi, but the gorgeous recorded sound and opulent engineering as well as superb contributions from Yvonne Minton and Martti Talvela make this bold and brazen performance one of the best all-around versions of the work available. Solti's later recording of the work pales by comparison, even if the voice accompaniment is more polished. I would definitely avoid the later recording, especially because of the more leisurely tempi which Solti adopted for that interpretation. Originally issued on two LP records spread over four sides, one movement to a side, the listener will be in for a tour de force both sonically and spiritually.

Of original instrument versions, I have no greater praise than for that of John Eliot Gardiner whose wonderful recording with Orchestre Romantique et Revolutionnaire is brilliantly projected. The first movement, taken at a lightningly quick pace, is played unbelievably well, and the performance itself is a monument to his excellent leadership and the contribution of superb orchestral and choral forces. A similarly dedicated performance by Sir Roger Norrington and the London Classical Players is available on EMI; I must confess that this is equally as good a performance as Gardiner's but there are some atypical choices of tempi in the performance which I enjoy hearing, but I'm not certain I would want to live with them exclusively. This is particularly notable in the finale.

A performance which appeared in December, 1997 on DG with Giuseppe Sinopoli with the Staatskapelle Dresden is fast becoming one of my favorite interpretations. This performance has all the benefits of Solti with some of the inspiration of Gardiner in one modern orchestral rendition. The recorded sound is sumptuous, and the vocal contribution are beyond reproach.

Unfortunately, I would not want to be without any one of the performances aforementioned, and perhaps another twenty or thirty in the catalog. However, having heard all the available performances currently on the domestic market, I think few of them in the aggregate are any more inspiring than those listed.

- Symphony No. 9 (Choral)
  London 430 438-2LM.Chicago SO, Solti
- Symphony No. 9 (Choral)
  DG Dig 447 074-2 ORR, Gardiner
- Symphony No. 9 (Choral)
  DG Orig 447 401-2, BPO, Karajan

The complete symphonies of Beethoven are available as boxed sets, but few are strong performance-wise throughout each set. I can recommend the following boxed sets as being uniformly outstanding.

- Symphonies Nos. 1-9
    DG Dig 439 900-2 (5). ORR, Gardiner

- Symphonies Nos. 1-9; Overtures: Coriolan; Creatures of Prometheus, Egmont
    EMI CMS5 65184-2 (6). London Classical Players, Norrington

- Symphonies Nos. 1-9
    DG 429 036-2. BPO, Karajan

Beethoven: Overtures

What an unhappy term an "Overture" is! The origin of the word arose from nothing but a dance which was played by an orchestra as an introduction to a scenic piece or dramatic representation. Later, the musical introduction became synonymous *with* the piece rather than illustrating it; when the concert overture culminated in its final apotheosis, there was no need for the curtain to rise: all had been said! One can only marvel at what has come of it in the course of time through the inventive genius of the great masters. Composers have felt obliged, since Beethoven's liberal usage, to give it to their orchestral works for almost any piece written in almost any form.

Beethoven was very attached to the music of his first overture that he composed in 1801 for a ballet called *The Creatures of Prometheus*. It is a piece of Mozartean lightness, an early Beethoven who salutes Prometheus as a teacher of art and science. Many ideas from this score appeared in later works: the German Dances, the slow movement of the Second Symphony, the conclusion of the *Eroica*, and the variations and fugue for piano, later called the *Eroica* variations. The overture is perfect theater music, with its mysterious tremolos and hints of the drama to come, and it sets up exactly the expectant mood for the audience as the curtain rises.

Beethoven's genius also provided Heinrich von Collin's play *Coriolanus* with a noble opening work to set the mood for the tragedy. A victorious Roman patrician Coriolanus—untamable, restless and proud—who had been wrongly impeached and banished from the state, finally comes to his greatest day of reckoning: the very men who had condemned him to ignominy and exile were about to be delivered into his keeping so he might execute the vengeance that he had so long brooded over. But the Romans had a final card to play to ward off his onslaught of their eternal city. They called upon the noblest matrons of Rome headed by the venerable mother of Coriolanus, and his wife Volumnia with their two children, to go to his tent and entreat the great warrior for mercy. The humble pleading of the women, their tears, their grievous sorrow went to the heart of Coriolanus. Vengeance which had seemed so goodly before became now a fruit of bitter taste. Coriolanus succumbs to the prompting of his inner conscience, and returns to his original alliance and to certain death. It is the raging power, nobility and pathetic beauty of this vital scene that is captured in the music.

A tone poem before tone poems were invented, *Coriolanus* prepares the listener for the central struggle of the play. The music begins with sober earnestness, as terrifying chords seemingly arising from an unknown world of spirits fearfully announce a subterranean thunder as the audience tenses for the approaching tragedy. The main theme, representing the troubled and restless figure of Coriolanus, has within it the character of an unease that cannot be stilled, a longing that cannot be satisfied. A second theme suggests in music the personal characteristics of the man himself. The music grows in pathos and brilliance that is well fitted to unfold the high drama in which heroes appear and go down in defeat. The single movement ends quietly in somber tones: as the violins strive in vain to reanimate the hero's former courage and resolution, a doleful bassoon, the diminuendo of a cello, and the brief plucking of a double bass unite to form a tense expectancy of the highest tragic effect.

Beethoven wrote four overtures for his only opera *Fidelio* based upon another French opera *Leonore*, and all of them are mood pieces to prepare the audience for the subject and character of the work that they are about to hear. The story deals with the rescue of a political prisoner, Florestan, by his wife Leonore who dons man's clothes and calls herself Fidelio. In the three *Leonore* overtures, only incidental musical episodes from the main opera are used. When *Fidelio* was first produced, it was preceded by the overture now known as *Leonore 2*. The other two *Leonores* and *Fidelio* were written for subsequent revisions and revivals. Because of its more brilliant exposition and incisive finale, the *Leonore No 3* ranks first in popularity, but some have preferred the second in terms of grandeur of conception and imaginative originality. Which of the four overtures best serves to introduce Beethoven's great opera? Perhaps the ideal *Fidelio* overture will never be heard and never was written.

Beethoven took up the composition of the music for Goethe's play *Egmont* with eagerness and excitement. Not only did he admire Goethe more than anyone else in German life, but the play dealt with a theme that had always kindled a fire in his breast: "liberty against tyranny." The work dealt with the struggle for freedom in the Netherlands from Spanish rule, and in the overture Beethoven produced the most remarkable example of incidental music in history. The thematic material is of a dual character, representing Egmont as a hero and also as a lover of the heroine Clara. The opening chords typify the despair of the oppressed Flemish people. Then the two themes are introduced and developed in a free fantasia fashion. The first phrase brings in the wood winds in an imitative style, with each instrumental entrance suggesting the entrance of a group of people into the freedom struggle. Egmont's doom is foretold by a sad melody from the strings which interrupts the progress of the people. As in the original historical record, Egmont's death is accompanied by brilliant fanfares. Goethe's message, and Beethoven's: Live free or die!

The *Overtures* by Beethoven have rarely been boxed in a complete and comprehensive manner. There are several cycles of complete overtures presently available, notably those by Karajan from the 1960s on DG, Abbado and the Vienna Philharmonic from the early digital era, also on DG, and I believe by Kurt Masur and the Gewandhaus Orchestra, Leipzig. My preference is to select overtures on an individual basis, and there are several recordings which should be sought for this purpose. When properly played, the Beethoven

Overtures are exciting symphonic miniatures, and are indeed perhaps more exciting than some of Beethoven's best symphonic movements.

I would encourage the listener to obtain the Abbado cycle if a complete cycle were required, as its modern sound and excellent performances remain exciting. However, I am of the opinion that one should have the Szell recording of the three *Leonore Overtures* and the *Fidelio Overture* on Sony Classical, as this is an indispensable staple of the repertory. Never mind the age. The playing is superb, and the sound is good even by today's standards. While there is some duplication, I suggest the listener obtain all the Beethoven *Overtures* recorded by Fritz Reiner and the Chicago Symphony, among them, *Coriolan* and *Fidelio*. The Chicago Symphony simply could not be bettered in terms of technique and execution, now or in the past by other conductors, and these brief performances remain a tribute to a great artist and a formerly great orchestra. I would avoid interpretations of the *Overtures* by later conductors of the Chicago Symphony whose approaches tend to be far too beefy and gluttonous, as well as Harnoncourt's complete set.

I have no recommendations for original instrument performances of the Beethoven *Overtures*.

- Leonore Overtures I, II and III; Fidelio Overture; King Stephan Overture
    Sony Classical SBK 63062. Cleveland O, Szell
- Symphony No. 5, 7; Overtures: Coriolan, Fidelio;
    RCA Red Seal 09026-68976-2. Chicago SO, Reiner
- Overtures (complete)
    DG 429 762-2GH2. VPO, Abbado

Beethoven: Piano Sonatas

If mankind had been satisfied with beauty alone, music would scarcely have gone beyond Mozart. Beethoven's melodies are not more beautiful than Mozart's. What distinguishes Beethoven's music from his great predecessor is its emotional content, grappling with emotions that had been hitherto unexpressed. Beethoven started his career composing piano sonatas, and he kept on composing them with ever-surer mastery. The sonatas therefore display a range of compositions, from the gay and polite earlier works to his last and greatest sonata, a majestic farewell to a musical form whose full powers he had been the first to call forth.

The thirty two piano sonatas possess, between them, the breadth and majesty of symphonic thought and the intimacy of chamber music. Taken as a whole, there are sonatas of feeling and sonatas of passion, architectural sonatas that are abstract in spirit, theatrical sonatas that encroach on the territory of the stage, and sonatas that are veritable autobiographical confessions. Together, they are like a vortex of dust set whirling by a wind. Today it is the power of the wind that strikes us. But Beethoven, in the beginning, saw only the dust and the confusion.

It was with his sonata No 8 (*Pathetique*), written a year before his first symphony, that Beethoven subjugated virtuosity to the poetic idea. Not incorrectly did Beethoven call this sonata his *Grande Sonate pathetique*, for it is a truly distinct emotional experience. The powerful introductory chords sound an unfathomable grief, a dramatic pathos that, in its best and worse sense, seems to gush out to the heart's content and gives way to an energetic and defiant melody. There is a page of serenity and repose that passes into an almost lighthearted gaiety. Ever since his companion Schindler narrated that Beethoven had described the "dualism" in this work as a dialogue of conflict between a man and a woman, generations of critics have read the idea of personified conflict in this music. Some have called it a contest between an unhappy man and his Fate; others have found in it the inspiration and poetic meaning of the legend of Hero and Leander. The work is dedicated to Prince Carl von Lichnowsky who had first welcomed the composer under the roof of his Viennese town residence as an unknown and poor lodger with respectable recommendations.

The sonata No 14—the *Moonlight Sonata*—is romantic and dreamy music "*quasi una fantasia,*" as enchanting and as unreal as a fairy tale. Scarcely any sonata has had so much written about it. It is pleasantly romantic to think that this piece, dedicated to the young

Countess Giulietta Guicciardi, is the musical counterpart of Beethoven's famous love letter to the "Immortal Beloved." Although the serenity of the opening music suggests moonlight on the waves (perhaps a moonlit night on the Lake of Lucerne), it is a unique expression of suffering, as insistent as it is outwardly calm, and the rest of the piece tells of a sky heavy with leaden colors that finally breaks out into a storm, a conflict of unprecedented vehemence!

The *Moonlight* paints a gigantic soul picture that, even in its convulsions, preserves its harmony and its natural nobility. The weeping and disheartened soul seen at the commencement of the music is goaded into a fury of passion. A vertiginous whirlwind, expressed in a syncopated, roughly rhymed melodic motive, leads to a fresh pelting of hail that cuts and shakes the soul. Fragments of the motive are used over and over again, haphazardly, until they fall away with ebbing energies, exhausted and defeated—a wasting of the heart's blood. There is a silence—with no more strength to cry out, the man is silent, his breath is cut short.

But as in all ancient tragedies, sorrow is subdued by the strength of the soul. After a moment, the subdued recovers and raises himself. Here is an end to the sobs and the furies. What has been said is said, and the soul is empty. In the final bars of the music nothing is left but majestic strength, mastering, dominating and accepting the torrent.

Sonata No 17 (*Tempest*) is the greatest of the early sonatas. The inquirer who asked Beethoven what his music "meant" usually received an answer according to his folly. Certainly there is more illumination in this case in the composer's advice: "Read Shakespeare's *Tempest*." Here is a mood that is common to both. This music is of the most dramatic kind which, like Prospero, is almost as far beyond tragedy as it is beyond foul weather. The music lends itself to many experiences through the faintly troubled serenity of the second movement with its aerial balance and Elysian peace, and its weary sigh from a breast oppressed with ecstasy that fades slowly into sleep with a sigh of happiness. Here is an energetic and restless character expressed in the first movement, and a rippling and stormy nature in the last. Here is love, grief, combat, the exaltation of living, despairing cries, unconquerable energy and premonitory flashes of somber heroism.

Sonata No 21 (*Waldstein*) is a prodigious virtuoso sonata that reveals a hitherto unknown world of sound, and requires more than just virtuosity to do it full justice. The fingers run and fly over the keyboard even as the mind sleeps and dreams. For, the music flows like clear water as an interior landscape unfolds: the joy of the open air, free flight, the vibrations of Nature, and pious contemplation. Beethoven is in the fields filled with religious emotion, an intoxicating ecstasy in Nature that is controlled by the mind. Here is the Beethoven of fiery tempers and dramatic accent, a mystic spirit that plumbs the profound depths of feeling. Yet it is an exuberant and high-spirited Beethoven that is heard in the final *rondo*—a full-throated hymn to joy, a chorale of a whole people, the joy of humanity at large in the face of the Eternal.

With Sonata No 23 (*Appassionata*: Amorous Passion), Beethoven raised the sonata form to a new level of intensity. Here is a great lament of broken loves, hopes, friendships and ambitions; a grand hymn of passion, of that passion which is born of the never-fulfilled longing for full and resplendent bliss. Not blind fury, not the raging of sensual fevers, but the violent eruption of the afflicted soul thirsting for happiness. In the first movement the work is a night piece, with dismal spectral shadows and soft wailings rising out of the lowest depths, a wild outcry from a soul in anguish as Fate is heard knocking at the door. The second movement forms a contrast with a song of blessed peace and solemn prayerful thoughts: From the depths of sorrow the spiritual eye looks upwards to the serene, forgiving countenance of the Supreme Being. The music rises upwards by degrees so that the final sounds seem as if suspended in heavenly regions. The finale's atmosphere is one of terror. A shrill cry of pain bursts forth suddenly. A howling flood of tones is released and flows wildly and irresistibly through the entire piece, now whispering softly, now roaring loudly. It is music reminiscent of Dante's Inferno!

In a book of this type, it is impossible to annotate notes for each and every piano sonata that Beethoven wrote; the effort would encompass a text larger than this book itself. The sonatas encompass the range of Beethoven's compositorial skills from adolescence to the last years of his life, and depict a wide range of emotions as well as provide for the listener a log of Beethoven's astronomical growth as a composer.

If there were one cycle that I would take to my grave with me, it would be that of Richard Goode which was recently issued on the Nonesuch label. This is an extraordinarily well recorded and documented cycle which is elegant, tasteful, and well presented. While Richard Goode is not a household name to most listeners, I can assure the reader that they will not be disappointed. Mr. Goode's career has blossomed in recent years, and he is of the same stature as any of the more common household names, most of whom have completed outstanding Beethoven Piano Sonata cycles of their own. Among these should be included Alfred Brendel (three times), Wilhelm Kempff (1955 mono, 1960s stereo, with preference to the former), Artur Schnabel, Maurizio Pollini (in preparation), and Ashkenazy (twice), among others.

I cannot recommend an original instrument cycle of the Beethoven Piano Sonatas due to the relatively unpleasant sound of the hammerklavier over sustained periods of time, and I caution the listener not to invest in a complete cycle of the Sonatas for original instrument.

There is one incomplete cycle that requires special mention, notably to recognize the talent of a superb Russian pianist who died all too young. The great Emil Gilels was in the process of completing a Beethoven Sonata cycle at the time of his death in the early eighties. Those performances he did record have been issued in a box by DG, and the listener is encouraged to consider these either as a primary cycle, if those works which are missing are not essential to the intended collection, or as a superb alternative to the principal cycles mentioned above. The playing is inordinately grand, and the recorded sound is superb.

- Piano sonatas Nos 1-32 (complete)
    Elektra Nonesuch/Warner Dig. 7559 79328-2 (10)
    Richard Goode

Beethoven: Piano Concerto No. 5 (Emperor)

One thing is definite: Beethoven did not name his final piano concerto after the all-conquering Emperor Napoleon. Story has it that a French officer in the Vienna audience was so carried away by the music that he proclaimed it "an emperor among concertos." Posterity has agreed with the unknown soldier—it is a fitting climax to Beethoven's concerto style which had evolved from Mozart and Haydn and which sowed the seeds for Liszt and Brahms. It is one of the most original, imaginative, effective and, perhaps, one of the most difficult of piano concertos. It does exact the maximum of technical ability, but it is also music that is sincerely expressive and satisfying in its emotional significance. The music given to the orchestra is of symphonic proportions, but it is intimately bound to the piano, and when it sings, the piano is always the dominating voice.

In connection with the imperious quality of this Concerto, it is worth recalling that at the time of its composition, there was a war with Napoleon going on practically under Beethoven's window, and he frequently had to take refuge in the homes of others. The music opens majestically, with solid chords from the orchestra, in a rhapsodic outburst which warns that something of immense grandeur is about to unfold. And as the music progresses to explore the full splendors of the piano, Beethoven seems to be recalling his past, embodied in the Fifth Symphony, first in the link between the first two movements, and then again at its close. In the final coda, the drum beats out a rhythm reminiscent of the Fifth Symphony while the solo piano begins a mysterious communing with itself that leads downward to a level from which it gathers itself for the last rising scales that bring in the orchestra and end the work. In a composer's evolution, no work is an island! Not often is an audience privileged to hear such a confluence of double genius: master of the orchestra, giant of the pianoforte. And not soon is it likely to forget such a grand experience!

This, the longest and most grand of all Beethovenian concerti, is far from my favorite, but it probably serves as the best introduction to the art form which Beethoven produced. The opulent and protean intentions of this work are perhaps best illustrated by an opulent and protean performance.

When I was training in medical school in Chicago, I had the pleasure to hear the late Chilean pianist, Claudio Arrau, perform the work with the Chicago Symphony under the direction of Carlo Maria Giulini. This performance was broadcast on WFMT-FM and on the Amoco Radio Network both in the Midwest and across the United States of America. The performance was not only exciting, but masterful. Fortunately, only shortly thereafter, Arrau recorded the work on Philips with Sir Colin Davis and the Dresden Staatskapelle, one of the world's great orchestras, and the performance is distinctly similar, stimulating, and much more satisfactory from an aural perspective than the live performance mentioned. This remains a stately interpretation, well played and conjured, and it has its own charm, but not to all tastes.

Other favorite versions of mine include those by Vladimir Ashkenazy with the Chicago Symphony under the baton of Sir Georg Solti. This is a somewhat more animated, robust performance than either of Arrau's interpretations, and despite its twenty five year age, is probably a better interpretation than either of the subsequent ones he has made with different orchestras.

I am also enamored of the performances by pianist Maurizio Pollini, the first with the Vienna Philharmonic Orchestra with Karl Bohm and subsequently, with his close friend Claudio Abbado and the Berlin Philharmonic Orchestra.

For those wishing an original instrument interpretation of the work, my current favorite is that by Robert Levin as soloist with the Orchestre Romantique et Revolutionnaire conducted by John Eliot Gardiner, on Archiv.

- Piano Concerto No 5 (Emperor)
    London 417703-2. Ashkenazy, Chicago SO, Solti
- Piano Concerto No 5 (Emperor)
    Ph. 416 215-2PH. Arrau, Staatskapelle Dresden, Davis
- Piano Concertos Nos 1- 5
    Ph. 456 045-2PH3. Brendel, Chicago SO, Levine

Beethoven: Violin Concerto

The Violin Concerto in D major was written by Beethoven during one of his happiest periods, even though it was completed during the Napoleonic invasion when French soldiers were quartered in the same house as the composer. The Archduke Rudolph, Prince Lobkowitz and Prince Kinsky had joined in a financial arrangement designed to keep Beethoven's genius unembarrassed by the necessities of life so that he could devote himself with single-minded application to produce great and sublime works of art. And in the same year, Beethoven had become engaged to Theresa of Brunswick, perhaps the real "Immortal Beloved." Story has it that the four notes which persist throughout the first movement were suggested to the composer by the nocturnal rappings on a door by a neighbor whose family were sound sleepers, and who commonly mislaid his latch key. Some have called this section "The Drum Stage" because a drum had never been put to such eloquent use before. The Concerto lay neglected for many years since its first presentation which had been played by a soloist without rehearsal resulting in an unsatisfactory performance.

It will be difficult for the average music lover to trace the wonderful underlying structural perfection of the music, not because it is particularly involved, but because the utterly appealing loveliness of the music itself leaves one compelled simply to delight in its colorful charm and beauty. There is something in the voice of the violin that speaks directly to something within the audience, something that defies definition but is existent and recognized by all. Whether the master draws a tenuous isolated thread or a wondrously embroidered fabric of sound floating apart from the orchestra like a disembodied being, or whether he conjures from the frail heart of the violin the most brilliant and passionate utterances that shift delicately in light and color, it is a tone that not only blazes and burns with the fervor of the composer's song but also envelopes the listener in a mystic and glorifying glow that radiates from its intrinsic beauty and delicacy. Notice, too, the five quiet taps on the timpani at the very top of the first movement—they are a structural component of the movement, and the rhythm of these five notes recurs throughout the work.

Next to the Brahms, Mendelssohn and Tchaikovsky violin concerti, the Beethoven Concerto stands as one of the great monuments to the instrument, and no less a monument is the interpretation by Jascha Heifetz with Charles Munch and the Boston Symphony. This recording was made contemporaneously with the other "great" violin concerti which Heifetz recorded in stereo for RCA, and the sound afforded from Symphony Hall in Boston with the splendid orchestra and a spirited accompanist that Munch was, is well nigh undeniable. The performance has the brilliance of anything made by Reiner or Szell during this era, and Heifetz plays like an angel, as always. Particularly impressive are the first and last movements, and standing against those that are forty years newer, this recording still has a pride of place on my shelves.

There are probably fifty other outstanding recordings of the work available, but another more modern performance which stands alone is by the young German violinist, Anne-Sophie Mutter. In her recording with the Berlin Philharmonic Orchestra under the direction of Herbert von Karajan, she excels with brilliant playing and benefits from the most sympathetic of accompaniments from Karajan and his players, and this performance has a certain degree of poise and charm which, while not lacking in the Heifetz recording, is less in evidence. Karajan certainly was the person in control here, but the Mutter recording has stood the test of time and has recently been reissued by DG. Mutter re-recorded the work in digital sound for Sony Video in what is a rather technically beautiful production by Telemondial. Those with a Laser Disc player or VHS video cassette player would do well to obtain this performance in video because of the overall beauty of the production which remains stunning to this day. This is a slightly more mature reading than the original DG Mutter recording, and is equally desirable.

A final, excellent interpretation is by Itzhak Perlman with Carlo Maria Giulini and the Philharmonia Orchestra recorded for EMI in the early eighties. This is also, strangely enough, a performance which is available on Laser Disc, but it is somewhat saccharine in its presentation and the tempi are rather priestly as is often the case with Giulini's interpretations. This concept is further validated by listening to a more recent recording of this concerto with Giulini and Salvatore Accardo with the La Scala Philharmonic on Sony Classical, which is a gorgeous, well rounded performance but becomes tiresome due to its patrician approach.

A final interesting oddity is Beethoven Opus 61a, the Beethoven Violin Concerto as played on the piano! Peter Serkin first recorded this work with Seiji Ozawa and the Philharmonia Orchestra for RCA in the seventies, and later, a more stimulating performance by pianist/conductor Daniel Barenboim appeared on DG. The latter recording has recently been reissued on DG Galleria, and is absolutely worth hearing.

- Violin concerto in D; - MENDELSSOHN: Violin Concerto
  RCA 09026 68980-2. Heifetz, BSO, Munch
- Violin concerto in D; - BRAHMS: Violin Concerto
  DG 457 861 GX2, Anne Sophie Mutter, BPO, Karajan

Schubert: Symphony No 5

Franz Schubert (1797 - 1828) is the most popular and the most mysterious of the great masters. His music is always mystically charming and speaks direct to the feelings. We do not knit our brows in listening to him nor do we wonder at his meaning. We sit content in quiet ecstasy, much like children listening to entrancing fairy tales.

His music is a faithful reflection of the warm, genial, lovable, guileless nature that was his. The mystery lies in the total want of clues into the machinery of his creations, and one is still baffled by the causes, inheritances, traditions and influences, broad and narrow, personal and national, that might have inspired his works. Like Mozart, his output was untiring and spontaneous, often impulsive. He did not need outward objects or stories for his romanticism, nor the heroic or the epic for his fancy. He did not chisel out his utterances; they came without searching. Though Schubert, in his moments, mounted higher than any, they were usually mere moments, not continuous thought. Perhaps if he had lived longer—he passed away at the age of thirty one—he might have breathed the broad human sympathy that comes only from the Hero who has struggled and conquered, and looks on in sympathy.

None of his symphonies are more magically inspired than his Fifth Symphony. Throughout this piece, there is not a single dark thought to cloud the exquisite sunniness and pure lyricism of its music. From its vivacious opening that follows a momentary hush of introduction, through its captivating meditations and unforgettable melodies to its spirited and happy finish, the mood is one of exalted cheerfulness. Schubert composed this work in 1816 for an amateur orchestral group that used to meet at the home of one of the violinists, and the probable reason for the omission of drums and trumpets from this work—it has been called the "Symphony without drums and trumpets"—is that there *were* none in this nonprofessional group. Schubert was nineteen when he composed this work.

This work is a gorgeously lyrical tour of Schubert's world of ideas and dreams. It is, at once, one of the easiest symphonies to get to know, much like Prokofiev's *Classical Symphony* and Bizet's *Symphony in C*.

The work has been well served since the beginning of long playing records, and one of the best reissues I have come across is that of Fritz Reiner's Chicago Symphony recording from the late 1950s. It is a songful, lyrical performance, with Reiner actually smiling for a change. The orchestral response is stellar, and the recorded sound, even by today's standards, is excellent. There is a superb British import of Dietrich Fischer Dieskau conducting the New Philharmonia Orchestra made at Abbey Road Studios in February, 1973. This recording was produced by Klemperer's producer, Suvi Raj Grubb, who was a gifted contributer to the EMI legacy of recordings. What is unique about this performance is that Mr. Fischer-Dieskau is himself a baritone, and has recorded the complete Schubert *Lieder* on more than one occasion. His insight into Schubert the composer is probably more profound than most conductors, and the performance he delivers, along with an excellent interpretation of the 8th Symphony, is a gift from Heaven. This record must be imported, but it is absolutely worth every penny. Moreover, it is a budget priced disc. Other great recordings of Schubert's Symphony No. 5 include those by Abbado, Sir Thomas Beecham, Karl Bohm, Carlo Maria Giulini (Chicago Symphony Orchestra version), Carlos Kleiber, and the late Istvan Kertesz.

- Symphony No. 5
  Royal Classics 6454, NPO, Fischer Dieskau
- Symphony No 5 - BEETHOVEN: Symphony No. 6 (Pastoral)
  DG 447 433-2 VPO, Bohm
- Symphony No. 5 - BRAHMS: Symphony No 3
  RCA 09026 61793-2 Chicago SO, Reiner

Schubert: Symphony No 8 (Unfinished)

Schubert lived in an age which, in music, philosophy and poetry, has been given the name "Romantic." There was a sense of mystic depth and meaning that filled German poetry in his time, that expressed not so much a German national feeling as a certain national mission, or message, of the Germans to the world through their words and music. And Schubert, with all his personal genius, came to voice in song this unuttered national German feeling. He wrote his symphonies in the manner of his national folk-songs; indeed, many of his symphonies were dependent on his German folk-songs (*Lieder*), and in them he expressed feelings which had strong relations to the spirit of his age.

The *Unfinished Symphony* is equally remarkable whether viewed in the whole literature of music, or merely in the group of Schubert's works. It is not, as might be inferred, his last unfinished work, for it was written six years before the end of his short career. He left it unfinished with only two movements, along with other unfinished works, during a period of unparalleled artistic struggles in his brief life. It is, however, together with his Ninth symphony, absolutely his highest level. In language of inexpressible beauty, it explores the most mysterious regions of the human soul and heart. There is an intensity of passionate emotion, a degree of spiritual exaltation, and a completely satisfying and wholly expressive message in this music. Why this work was not performed until thirty seven years after the death of the composer has remained a mystery—it is the one that is the most performed today.

This work, in two movements, simply lacks a third and fourth movement, and has been known as the "Unfinished Symphony." There are many interesting performances of this work, and it is difficult for me to find any truly unique performances as compared to the other Schubert symphonies, if only because I am not as enamored of it as I am of the Fifth and the Ninth Symphonies.

Carlos Kleiber and the Vienna Philharmonic have a stellar recording on DG, which is coupled with a splendid and fashionable version of the Schubert's Third Symphony, a youthful work. It is a light, airy performance which has guts where needed. The VPO and Kleiber don't miss a note. Likewise, Giuseppe Sinopoli recorded the *Unfinished Symphony* early in his career with the Philharmonia Orchestra for DG, and this performance still is an excellent, if somewhat idiosyncratic, clearly elucidated interpretation. It is paired with a splendid version of Mendelssohn's Fourth Symphony (the *Italian*), and is not bettered in sound or interpretation by Kleiber. Other excellent performances of the work include the Berlin Philharmonic recording by Karl Bohm, and Claudio Abbado with the Chamber Orchestra of Europe.

Historically, the first DG recording by Herbert von Karajan is also excellent, and is one of the most rational, conventional performances he committed to disc. It also benefits from excellent recorded sound, which is not always the case with later Karajan recordings. I would avoid Karajan's later EMI remake, as well as Bohm's Vienna Philharmonic remake of the *Unfinished Symphony* which was made late in the conductor's life.

More recent releases of the complete Schubert Symphonies have included performances by Nikolaus Harnoncourt and the Chamber Orchestra of Europe. Compared to the almost simultaneously released (within a year) Abbado cycle of the Schubert Symphonies with the very same ensemble, I find Harnoncourt's contribution to be insensitive and, to me, seems a sledgehammer approach to Schubert even though the playing of the Chamber Orchestra of Europe is very good. Abbado's is utterly elegant by comparison. I don't believe the Eighth Symphony would dramatically benefit from original instrument interpretation, but I have no doubt that major contributors in this aspect of the repertory will make their presence known in due time.

- Symphony Nos. 3, 8
  DG Originals 449 745-2GOR. VPO, Kleiber

Schubert: Symphony No 9 (Great)

In March, 1828, Schubert began his Ninth symphony. In November, Schubert was dead. It was a year of glorious production, almost as if the young composer knew that he had not much longer to live, and that he must write in a feverish burst of activity if he was to give voice to all the music that was still within him. And it is, in every way, in the unity and large scale of its design and in the unflagging intensity of its breadth and depth, a symbolic and directly eloquent expression of this great heroic struggle of his final year. The strange, prophetic and portentous utterance proclaimed by the horns at its opening, one of the most unforgettable experiences in music, seem like a great fanfare, a prelude to his departure. More than any other work, this long symphony reveals something of the Schubert that might have been, with its unabated flow of wondrous melodies, its compelling vigor and vitality, its overflowing inspiration, and a superb grandeur imbued with new and mighty forces.

Some have seen in this music a panorama of the composer's life in Vienna, the bright and flowery city where he loved and toiled— sparkling today, gloomy tomorrow—with its lovely women and public pageantry, its great Cathedral and the silvery Danube spreading slowly over verdant plains towards the distant silhouette of the lofty Alps. Listen to it, and you will hear life in every vein, coloring down to the finest gradation, with meaning everywhere, and in the whole you will find a suffusing romanticism such as no other work by Schubert has made known to the world.

The manuscript was picked up by Schumann in a bundle of papers that were in the possession of Schubert's brother whom he visited many years after the death of the composer. A copy was dispatched to Felix Mendelssohn who performed it at a memorable concert in Leipzig in 1839.

This major symphonic work, Schubert's last completed symphony, approaches the enormity of any large-scaled Beethoven or Brahms symphony. It is for me a valedictory work, a proud and shining example of what Franz Schubert left as a legacy.

I first learned of this work in 1969 when I was presented as a gift the Herbert von Karajan performance by the Berlin Philharmonic, his first in stereo. Unfortunately, it was not as well received by the British as it was elsewhere. It is a heavyweight performance, in some ways slightly militaristically performed, and it excels in demonstrating Schubert's gifts as well as that of the Berlin Philharmonic better than any other performance that I have encountered. From the moment of the opening French horn until the percussive ending with filament brass, this performance is well nigh perfect in execution. The tempi are all appropriate, if slightly on the fast side, and the ardent presentation of the First Movement, the lyrical beauty and turbulence of the Second Movement, the jaunty dance rhythms of the Third Movement, and the proud, inflected string work of the Fourth Movement, along with a well miked timpanist, make this performance well nigh perfect.

This is a perfect example of my belief that the performance one is first exposed to seems so often the only "correct" performance. In my case, I will add that there are outstanding recordings of this work by Abbado, using new critical editions of the score with the Chamber Orchestra of Europe, by Kurt Masur and the Leipzig Gewandhaus Orchestra, Giuseppe Sinopoli and the Dresden Staatskapelle, and William Steinberg and the Boston Symphony at budget price. In response to those individuals who would attest to the excellence of Bruno Walter's recording from 1960, I would say that it is uncompetitive and lifeless compared to any of the others. I have no idea how this recording reached such critical acclaim, as it is not well played, barely adequately recorded, and quite mundane. I don't believe that this work benefits from original instrument performances, although there are versions by several conductors, notably Mackerras.

- Symphony Nos. 8, 9
    DG 423219-2, BPO, Karajan

- Symphony Nos. 8, 9
    DG 437 689-2GH. Staatskapelle Dresden, Sinopoli

Schubert: Piano Quintet (Trout)

In the last decade of his tragically short life, Schubert lived freely in a quiet unpretentious circle of adoring friends. He was affectionately nicknamed *Schwammerl* ("Tubby"); with little money and no permanent income, he was often compelled to share with them their clothes, food and living space. And in return, this shy and sensitive little man with a warm heart and an innocent mind regaled them with a flow of melodies in his beautiful chamber music—spontaneous, incessant and irrepressible, leading often to excessive diffuseness. For their celebrations and parties he wrote his marches for hands and his waltzes; together they consoled him for the lack of family life, and these so-called Schubertiads or gathering of friends around their master were the joy of his sad life.

The *Trout* quintet he composed for his host while passing through the small town of Steyr during a walking tour of upper Austria. A piece suitable for *haus musick* was requested, but with two stipulations: the instrumentation should be the same as a quaint Hummel quintet which was the host's favorite, and the piece should include a variation movement based upon the theme of Schubert's song *Die Forelle* (*The Trout*)—another favorite of the host. And so was born the *Trout* quintet for which the composer played the piano part completely from memory during its first house performance.

This is the first piece of chamber music which I learned as a child, and I must confess that even if it is a "light" Schubert, it is nevertheless inspired and joyous music making all at once.

I possess no fewer than fifteen recordings of this work, all of which are joyous, and any of which I could easily recommend. One of the earliest recordings to which I was exposed was that of a performance by Peter Serkin early in his career with Alexander Schneider as first violinist on Vanguard. This disc has been reissued, and despite its thirty five year age, sports excellent sound and a spry performance.

Not far behind this is the one by Peter's father, Rudolf Serkin, recorded at Marlboro, Vermont at approximately the same time. This is equally spirited an interpretation but is characteristically different from start to finish. It is definitely worth hearing.

The Beaux Arts Trio with pianist Menahem Pressler have recorded an excellent performance of the work for Philips, at mid price. This is a soulful performance which is not at all flashy, but yields great dividends in enjoyment because of its elegance. Finally, Alfred Brendel has recorded the work twice for Philips, once with the Cleveland Quartet and once with several performing soloists who clearly must be his social friends. Both performances are worthy, inspired renditions, and I would encourage the listener to seek either of them if available.

- Piano Quintet in A (Trout)
    Ph. 434 146-2. Beaux Arts Trio (Menahem Pressler, piano)
- Piano Quintet in A (Trout)
    Ph. 446 001-2. PH. Brendel and friends

Romanticism

The historical basis for the outburst of Romanticism lies buried in the great liberation of the common man that followed the age of revolution. A deeper religious conviction, the flood of new ideas regarding liberty and human rights that poured out of the French Revolution, and the success and enlargement of America as a republic were undoubtedly the forces working underneath the surface. The Romantic period (roughly 1800 -1850) was a time of great turbulence when men and women were becoming aware of their own individuality, and were asking deeply troubling questions that the abstract and rational formulas of the preceding age of elegance could not answer. In all classes and trades, young people's brains were in a state of fermentation. They smelled regeneration, liberty and novelty, and they wanted to have their share of it. And more than any other great period in the history of ideas, Romanticism was not a clear age or school born in a given city, but a specific temperament nurtured in a number of human hearts and minds that stormed cultural barricades and consolidated its conquests of the arts.

The Romantic temperament was a fragile and anxious one, imbued with a delicacy of spirit and a soft epicene vulnerability that was frequently and easily broken on the rack of human life. Yearning was an especially cultivated Romantic pastime that provided the impetus for action, but since the yearner had no clear notion of what one was after, it often expressed itself as an inchoate dissatisfaction with one's lot, and a sense of uncertainty hung about one's undertakings. The therapeutic or redemptive function of Nature was a recurrent Romantic theme. Conceived in a peculiar relation to the self, it displaced both God and society in their cosmology, and became the means through which the self realized itself. And the Romantics were great depressives, coming to grief in love, strung on dope and dying young. Even when they did not die young, they exhausted their artistic capabilities early in life.

The very essence of Romanticism was extremism. In music, painting and literature, the Romantic inclined simultaneously to the minute and the monumental, to the self and to universal history, to a microscopic examination of the nuances of individual emotion with loving exactitude and to the telescopic scanning of the whole historical panorama with the boldest possible strokes. Romanticism encompassed both the poetic work of Wordsworth and the conceptual work of Hegel. Common qualities of the heart and mind—a common sensibility—inspired these seemingly dissimilar, though contemporary, cultural enterprises. In the first, human psychology was the focus, and real events served as the occasion for its representation. In the second, the matter examined was historical reality, and psychology was explored as it reflected this reality. Both reflected the spirit of the age.

Although the spirit for the Romantic explosion was kindled all over Europe, the cup fermented most and overflowed in Paris. Sparks from the flame of revolution flew into all the domains of intellectual and practical life. At the head of the younger generation stood the romantic battering ram, Victor Hugo. Ingres, Delacroix and David invented dramas of color and transplanted romance to canvas. On the stage reigned the genius of cheerful play, Rossini. In the concert hall, Berlioz—ardent, struggling, full of ideas and inventions—was already holding the door-latch in his hand, Malibran sang and revolutionized the opera and, in a single night, Paganini, when he appeared on the podium of the hall of the Grand Opera, unconsciously transformed Liszt who, as if touched by a magic wand, transformed the whole art of piano playing.

The Romantic era was far from being a man's world and, from its beginning, brilliant women gave to it a good part of its character and direction: the Bronte sisters, who wrote intensely and passionately of all shades of love; Margaret Fuller, whose intellect men found frightening; Mary Wollstonecraft, who was sixteen when she ran away with the young poet Shelley, eighteen when they were married, nineteen when she wrote *Frankenstein,* and twenty five when Shelley drowned at sea; Lola Montez who, after affairs with Liszt, Dumas and Ludwig I of Bavaria, stormed gold-rush California; and Madame de Stael, whom even Napoleon found a formidable adversary. Together, they stressed imagination and emotion, the variety and contrasts of human experience, and the unique vision and value of each human being.

The epoch of Romantic music that followed the age of revolution was the greatest period of color and colorful fantasy. Never had the world experienced such a glittering array of colors as arose from the Romantic orchestra. Growing ever larger, it employed more instruments in increasingly artistic combinations to disperse its colors and spread them out upon broad tonal canvases. Whereas the classical style expressed the ideas and scenes which caused emotions, the Romantic school expressed the feelings and emotions *themselves* in sound. One by one, the characteristic forms of the architecture of music that had been created in the age of elegance began to melt and flow in the heat of the modern passion. Lyric music gave way to declamations, and diatonic harmony to chromatic harmony. Melodies were expanded and spun out, and motifs became programmatic.

The music of the Romantic period captured the spirit of the times. The Romantics depicted lovely summer nights punctuated by glow worms flashing through meadows that shone silvery in the moonlight, gray mists rising from the fields, and even foreign countries. It was the Romantic tone with its magic powers that described the air and sun, and the colors and the atmosphere of foreign landscapes. But they knew little of heavy clouds massing for a storm, or of thunder and lightning. Mendelssohn let the elves and goblins dance in Shakespeare's magic forest with the moon throwing its light upon trees and bushes. The wind whistled across the gray North Sea around Fingal's Cave, and the Italian sun shone down upon brightly garbed couples dancing a tarantella. In the music of Berlioz, will-o-the-wisps scampered across the moors, sylphs danced, and hosts of witches flocked to the Blocksberg.

Even the symphony of the Romanticists became something else than what a Beethoven symphony had been. The Classical symphony had come forth from a spiritual unity, and the facility for creating great artistic and musical forms hinged on just such a unity and philosophy. But in the nineteenth century, this force of cohesion and organization began to weaken, and the more the contrasts and conflicts that created a rift in life, the weaker grew the forces that had shaped the great pattern of the symphony. Beethoven's music had culminated in great emotions, in the glorification of man, love, freedom, humanity and the adoration of God; his melodies were clean and noble and possessed of ethical sentiment. In Romantic music, the evolution of ideas was replaced by a portrayal of moods, the fantastic took the place of the lucid, and sensuous forces became strengthened even as the spiritual and idealistic powers declined. The frescoes of Berlioz, bold and subjective as Byron's poems, glowed in color like the paintings of Delacroix, and the tragic symphonic poems of Franz Liszt, with their grand dramatic gestures, had nothing in common with the spirit of Beethoven. They belonged to the world of painting and theater, not of philosophy.

The two great Mendelssohn symphonies, the *Scottish* and the *Italian*, were impressive landscapes seen though the eyes of an educated wanderer who always carried his sketchbook and who, with a light hand, sketched all the peculiarities of a strange landscape. Drawing the gray mists and the wind-blown waves of the Hebrides, he was as much the painter as when he reproduced the colorful dabs and speckles, with dancing colors and sparkling lights, of *A Midsummer Night's Dream*. These were realistic landscape paintings that were no longer the scenery of Beethoven. Schumann's symphonies were romantic stories filled with wanderlust, with spring magic and recollections of youthful dreams, with choruses sounding from the church tower and fanciful love singing its songs in all forms of nature—in the magic of a forest and on dewy meadows, and in the flowers and breezes of Spring.

There is an astounding wealth of Romantic piano music in sketches and nature scenes, in rhapsodic avowals and personal confessions, in whimsical notions and witticisms. The miniature forms of the piano poem took the place of the broadly constructed sonatas as the main creations of the Romantic imagination: impromptus, dances, *moments musicaux*, ballades, scherzos and preludes abounded.

Operas reflect the intellectual climate of their age. Whereas the opera in the age of elegance held the everyday reality of domestic and social concerns at the heart of its creative imagination—the world of things and relationships, of alienation and reconciliation and gestures—the very essence of Romanticism was extremism. Romantic composers found in the opera an ideal genre for one of their basic tenets, namely, the union of the arts as a total conception encompassing music, drama, and the visual arts. Hitherto, they claimed, music had tried to make itself the dramatic focus and had failed. Its only salvation lay in a balanced collaboration with poetry that invoked a merging of verbal and musical language. Composers went further afield for their plots, experimenting in medieval chivalry, Eastern romance, fairyland, sentimentality and horrors. The librettos and the music written for them became more intense and vehement, sentimental comedy developed into romantic drama, and melodrama was invented.

Simultaneously, there was a musical development that was purely technical, a tendency to treat operatic ensembles as if they were instrumental symphonies with a great deal of formal repetition of phrases, and a huge piling up of voices and instruments towards the end. Vocal melodies came to be conditioned as much by a sense of the words as by the demands of musical inspiration. The chorus was replaced by the orchestra which was much better at the subtle emphasis of emotional situations on stage. And at the center of this massive unification stood an intense subjectivity—the drama of the self stood at the heart of most Romantic operatic creations.

The story of Italian music in the Romantic period is essentially the story of opera, and the story of Italian Romantic opera is essentially the story of the music of four great men: Rossini, Bellini, Donizetti, and Verdi. The creator of the German Romantic opera was Carl Maria von Weber who took off where Mozart had left off, and spent all his career fighting off the hegemony of Italian opera in Germany. From Weber a direct road led to the towering personality of Wagner who overshadowed the whole opera production of his time, and exerted an unparalleled influence on the musical life of his world.

Classicism in music had stood for the perfect and regular development of beauty in the formal terms connected with Greek art. Romanticism, which displaced form to get play for feeling, allied itself with the Gothic and the Celtic genius. Mendelssohn's gentle melancholia and Schumann's dreamy sadness constituted the borderline at which the German Romantics in music penetrated the dark tragic tone and the hard belligerent timbre of the classical symphony. Existence became once more mysterious. Perhaps Romanticism may be best summed up as "the right to hope that mystery carries with it."

Berlioz: Symphonie fantastique

Gustav Mahler used to preach that if a composer could say what he had to say in words, he should not bother trying to say it in music. Program music was created to imitate a sound, usually in the world of nature or an animal sound, or portray a picture or scene or a mood, or narrate a story or an idea. However, music can seldom be a picture of something only and nothing else, and even if it were to paint a perfect picture with all its details, it would really do nothing—one could catch it much better in a painting or in words. Some composers have refused to have their work narrowed or whittled down to answer a picture or story. A title, by absorbing attention and creating false interest in an *a priori* arbitrary significance, prevents a pure enjoyment of the emotional or the beautiful by natural perception. Generally, there is a real loss in the apparent gain to eke out music with a "meaning."

We must be careful not to accept any story or description about a piece of music except when it is given by the composer himself. There is no doubt, however, that in some cases, a particular story may be easier to catch in sound if it is specifically defined. And for Hector Berlioz (1803 - 1869) who defied convention and tradition, music did not exist except for the telling of stories. Writing for large masses and incorporating even larger orchestras, he was seized with the passion of painting pictured designs with his orchestral palette, and he reveled in the sensations of startling instrumental effects to portray the events of his story. And yet there was a serious nobility, a heroic reach, in his art so that when we are on the point of condemning him as a scene painter, we suddenly come upon a stretch of pure musical beauty that could only flow from the unconscious rapture of a true poet.

All his life, Berlioz was dominated and tormented by a morbid craving for love. But his love was never the strong, clear-eyed passion of a man who has faced the realities, the charms and the defects of the woman he loves; his was that of a youth that lives in dreams. And in the autobiographical *Symphonie fantastique* he told the tale of a young dejected artist whose ineffectual draught brings not death, but the strangest of desires for his beloved. In a fit of rage he kills her and is condemned to the gallows, and he dreams the full cup of last agonies. The symphony was born out of Berlioz's own unrequited love for the Irish actress who later became his wife. Fantasic is right! Not only is this the first program symphony, it is also one of the few symphonies to claim a sequel: *Lelio* or *The Return to Life*.

This lengthy and complicated work has been well served since the dawn of long-playing microgroove, and different interpretations have been released over time. Both original instrument and modern instrument versions are available, and both of these should be listened to because the rather heavy orchestration, in less than an optimal recording, can obscure the part writing of this most intricate work. Original instrument versions of this work do not, for me, serve as the end-all of interpretations. However, they should be part of a serious collector's compendium of recordings.

The listener is encouraged to consult performances by John Eliot Gardiner and the Orchestre Romantique et Revolutionnaire on Philips, and that of Sir Roger Norrington on EMI, for their academic interpretations played on original instruments. For me, there are many good recordings of the *Symphonie Fantastique*, including those by Abbado, Boulez (often considered one of the greater interpretations), all three of the recordings by Sir Colin Davis, Charles Munch's recording with the Boston Symphony, Muti's recording with the Philadelphia Orchestra, and Sir Georg Solti's two recordings for London Records. There is also an excellent, provincial recording by Charles Dutoit and the Orchestre Symphonique de Montreal, on London. All of these depict the work in a rather Gallic style, and all have much to say about the imagery that Belioz wished to illustrate.

There are two recordings in my mind, strange bedfellows though they may be, that better depict the work in modern instrumentation than any that I have encountered elsewhere. They are indeed strange bedfellows, and are from conductors whom I normally do not prefer in basic repertory. One is Seiji Ozawa's, in his 1973 recording with the Boston Symphony Orchestra (his first was taped in Toronto for CBS). This performance takes the inherent, brilliant beauty of the

Boston Symphony and its hall, and melds it to the excellence of the Charles Munch recording of approximately fifteen years earlier. It is clear from listening to both performances that the orchestra is not only the same ensemble, but the interpretation has changed little. Perhaps this is because of lack of inventiveness on Ozawa's part, or perhaps Ozawa has clearly listened to Munch. Regardless, this is an elegant, light-of-foot but intellectually heavyweight recording which should be heard.

Herbert von Karajan recorded the *Symphonie fantastique* in 1964, and it was destroyed by the critics, appropriately. It was a leaden, low voltage reading which lacked any subtlety or elegance, and it was deadly from the get go. The performance is still available. However, in 1975, Karajan re-recorded the work with the Berlin Philharmonic, and the results were rather stunning. This is both an extraordinarily heavyweight recording with massive forces, and an incredibly pungent percussion section. The recording literally explodes from the sound system, and the impact of the recording is beyond expectations. Karajan used to like a very murky recorded sound, shrouded in mist and fog. This recording, engineered by Gunter Hermanns supervised by Hans Weber and produced by Dr. Hans Hirsch, is so meticulously characterized that literally every instrumental part can be heard in proper perspective. This includes the rather deeply positioned but dramatically well heard woodwinds, individual members of the string section, both left and right, and the percussion, which is nothing short of unbelievable. The impact of the *March to the Scaffolds* shows the hair-trigger perfection of the Berlin Philharmonic, as it outshines in this instance virtually any performance by any orchestra I have encountered. The performance is not a rapid one, but it does not linger or plod. It is indeed a far cry from Karajan's unacceptable effort of eleven years earlier.

The partnership of Michael Tilson Thomas and the San Francisco Symphony has been widely admired since its inception, and from the foundations of a good American orchestra we now have a superb ensemble of musicians which sounds remarkably like the fine traditional Central European orchestra. Maestro Tilson Thomas's new recording of the *Symphonie fantastique* is a performance that sits midway between Ozawa and Karajan in terms of lightness of touch and heft (brute force); it is elegantly spun and masterfully captured in Davies Hall in San Francisco by Bertelsmann Music Group engineers. It goes straight to the top of any short list of this work. Those looking for a performance witrh the best characteristics of both Ozawa and Karajan in clearly the most modern of sound need look no further.

- Symphonie fantastique; Excerpts from Lelio
  BMG/RCA 09026 68930-2, San Francisco Symphony,
  Tilson Thomas

- Symphonie fantastique
  DG 415 325-2GH. BPO, Karajan

- Symphonie fantastique
  DG 431 169-2GGA. BSO, Ozawa

Berlioz: Overtures

"I have taken up music where Beethoven left it," said Hector Berlioz when he was twenty five years old. Posterity has come to recognize some justice in the claim. Yet no musician was more ridiculously criticized, more scoffed at, and more insulted in his own country and for the greater part of his career. With a passion for color and movement equal to Delacroix, he was already dreaming of monstrous orchestral works as a fiery young warrior of eighteen, under the influence of all that was vivid and sensual and highly colored in the life around him. But the new musician had not only to make his bricks to his own pattern, he also had peculiar difficulty finding his straw. Berlioz' real greatness is better perceived when one looks at him sympathetically in relation to the music of his epoch, and nowhere are his intoxicating and exciting instrumental coloring, his extraordinary discoveries of orchestral tones, and his inventions of nuances better revealed than in his Overtures.

One of his earliest overtures, *Les Francs-Juges*, contains a melody that Berlioz had written when he was twelve. It was not the only one—the other boyhood tune that he was to use in later years is the familiar theme that introduces the first movement of the *Symphonie fantastique*, and the *idee fixe* in the same work. *Les Francs-Juges* is a youthful work, but not immature: an opera based upon a story of secret "vigilantes" in late medieval Germany. Villainy menaces purity—the former intrigues in the first busy theme while the latter resists with its cool upright second theme which caps the music heroically. In the *Waverly* Overture, based upon Sir Walter Scott's novel, "dreams of love and Lady's charms give place to honor and to arms." Dreams of love are heard first, probed by the cellos; these give place to honor and arms. Oddly, there is no hint of a Scotch atmosphere. *Les Francs-Juges* was presented by the young composer together with *Waverly* in a unique one-man show or festival—an event that had hitherto been unattempted by any musician in France! And no one was more astonished by the brilliant colors and tones and the subtle expressions of thought in the music than the composer himself when he heard it for the first time. A story has it that at the overture to *Les Francs-Juges*, he wept and tore his hair and fell sobbing on the kettledrums!

The music for *King Lear* and *Rob Roy* were completed almost together when the composer was recovering from an ineffectual suicide attempt after a romantic crisis in his life. Berlioz claims to have composed the former just four weeks after he had read the play; the latter he sketched after Scott's novel. *King Lear* is a loosely scoped realization of the Shakespearean tragedy that can be a musical trap: one may forget to hear the bold music by looking raptly for the characters! But his most extraordinary work, standing above all like a wonderful isle where a temple of pure art is set up, was *Romeo et Juliette*. Here is music of light grace and vibrating passion, magnificent in its wonderful clearness and simplicity and its apt expression of ideas. In its immortal love scenes, he expressed his feelings with an exquisite delicacy and an almost girlish purity that have remained unsurpassed in the annals of beautiful music.

Berlioz was perennially in love with love, and he continuously lost himself in visions and sentimental shadows. And in the music of *Romeo et Juliette*, he poured out the story of his life—a life that was a prey to love and melancholy, doomed to a wringing of the heart and awful loneliness, a life lived in a hollow world among worries that chilled the blood, a life that was distasteful and that offered no solace to its very end. There was a terrible *mal de l'isolement* which pursued him all his life, vividly and minutely. He was doomed to suffering and, what was worse, to make others suffer.

The overture from the opera *Benvenuto Cellini* shows Berlioz' spontaneity of melodic invention. In a work that takes less than ten minutes to play, there are five melodies of admirable richness and originality, all of them plastic and expressive of personality, varied in form, working up by degrees to a climax, and then finishing with strong effect. A whirling-dervish opening limns Cellini's iconoclastic temperament in this tumultuous music. The opera was a failure, but the composer took the thematic material and built it into the popular *Roman Carnival Overture.* Simple in its contrast of love song and dance (a beautiful love song sung by a *cor anglais* alternates with the *saltarello*, a wild Italian dance), its melodies capture the scene and spirit of swarming and merry crowds enjoying a colorful and gay carnival. Unmindful of the insistent carnival noises are a pair of lovers—a delicious Berliozian musical moment. The two themes are developed together, but the dance figure eventually dominates, the lovers cede to the fun, and the music expands in all directions to come to a powerful close.

In the overture to the opera *Beatrice and Benedict*, adapted from Shakespeare's *Much Ado about Nothing*, wit is in perpetual contrast with the humor of gentle sadness. A trim potpourri of tunes sets up the music with caprice and dash, opposing a flirtatious first theme to a lyrical second one. The music skims lightly over the conflict between sweet purity and Calibanism, and uses grotesque and airy figures to half-conceal the purblindness of evil. The instrumentation is pure filigree work, tonal bubbles which act like champagne to paint a drama of make-believe.

Unfortunately, there is relatively little in the way of comprehensive recordings of the Berlioz *Overtures* currently in print. Fortunately, the two recordings that I am familiar with are outstanding, and either will suffice for a basic collection.

Sir Colin Davis and the London Symphony Orchestra recorded the *Overtures* as an early part of their complete Berlioz cycle, and this now nearly thirty year old recording for Philips still shines brilliantly in the lexicon of recorded performances for truly *Desert Island* status. I listen to this disc perhaps only once every five years, but it continues to bring great pleasure. There is not one overture that lacks panache, flare, and excitement. This recording was made before Sir Colin became very "careful" when recording, and it does not lack for spontaneity.

A more recent recording, in digital sound, from the Montreal Symphony Orchestra with Charles Dutoit is perhaps somewhat more refined, a bit more polished, but almost equally exciting as those by Sir Colin Davis. Being a recent release, it benefits from the attributes of digital sound and truly impeccable playing by North America's greatest French orchestra. Again, either recording will bring great pleasure to the listener, and I would encourage the listener to audition both, if at all possible, before purchasing. These really are significant disparate interpretations, sound notwithstanding, but are both highly worthy.

- Overtures
    Ph. 416 432-2. LSO, Colin Davis
- Overtures
    London 452 480-2LH. Orchestre Symphonique de Montreal, Dutoit

Mendelssohn: Symphony No 3 (Scotch)

"Felix" (the happy one) was a well-chosen name for Mendelssohn (1809 - 1847), and in his music he consistently revealed his real self—the cheerful, contented and successful man that he was. He was, in his own impetuous, light and often lovely style, superficial if you like, but always his own unique self, composing in an idiom invented by himself, not following a school and not founding one. He lived in an apparently perennial youth, always very impressionable, and he never lost his sense of wonder and delight. And it comes as no surprise that the beginnings of a symphony were already brewing in his head when he walked, at the mysterious hour of twilight, through the Palace of Holyrood during his trip to Scotland in 1829. Here, Queen Mary had lived and loved, and here, before the ivy-encrusted alter of the broken and mouldering, roofless chapel, she had been crowned Queen of the Scots.

It has been suggested that the mind would be far more open to the enrapturing beauty of this music if the listener were to cast aside the impressions created by its descriptive subtitle. After all, pictures need no illustration. There is little of the wild sounds of bagpipes or fiery epic in this wonderful wealth of fine thought and charming melodies. It is not deeply-felt music, but the sounds and songs have refined surface beauties. The Scottish tunes are heard through a German mind, and if the romance of rough scenes and dread danger be detected, it is more akin to German poetry. The symphony was first performed in Berlin in 1842, with the composer conducting.

This is an absolutely joyous work. In a recent PBS program, Peter Ustinov narrated the circumstances under which the work was written and how Mendelssohn's impressions were expressed in the various movements. I suggest the reader attempt to locate a copy of this video program, for it is truly excellent. Contributions in the video by the Leipzig Gewandhous Orchestra under the baton of Kurt Masur aid immeasurably in illustrating what Ustinov is discussing.

A pivotal Mendelssohn Third Symphony was released in the late fifties by Peter Maag and the London Symphony Orchestra, and it has hardly been bettered since its appearance. Contributions by Abbado, Flor, Solti, Maazel, Sanderling and Karajan have also been made, notably Karajan's version which is indeed one of his best recordings of all time. I particularly enjoy the brilliance of the Berlin Philharmonic in this work, even though it is not particularly light of hand. Abbado's original London Symphony recording for London, and his remake with the same orchestra for DG are both excellent.

Original instrument versions by Norrington and Bruggen are also available, and each of them has nice touches which make them both worthy of hearing, if not owning. On the other hand, I find Harnon-court's contributions to this piece of the musical lexicon to be heavy handed and obtuse at times, no matter what the reviews have said about this particular work.

- Symphony No. 3 (Scottish)
  DG 429 664-2 (Boxed set). BPO, Karajan
- Symphony No. 3 (Scottish)
  DG 427 810-2GDC. LSO, Abbado
- Symphony No. 3 (Scottish)
  London 443 578-2. LSO, Maag

Mendelssohn: Symphony No 4 (Italian)

There is a story that a respectable composer once gave a very strange recipe for a symphony: "Get your themes and fit them in the estab-lished molds." In other words, be original with your tunes and melodies, but in form, follow the strict guidelines of tradition! And no one followed this recipe more closely than Mendelssohn. Felix Mendelssohn made no advance in the outline of the symphony over Haydn. His power lay in his mastery of the many-voiced palette of instrumental colors that seemed to be bred in his very fiber. He was in little touch with the great and stirring spiritual and intellectual discoveries of his time. He was driven to find emotional content in scenic description or historic sentiment, and in his celebration of the picturesque and the material, he was a poet in the highest degree. And in his wonderful expression of local color, he was more affected by outward stimuli than by feelings. In a word, Mendelssohn was the orthodox gentleman-musician of his century.

There is no technical lack nor want of detailed beauty in his Fourth Symphony. In its enchanting beauty, its poetic charm, and brilliantly pure melodies there is nothing lacking; the real trouble is the want of profound feeling of the content of its message, or a motive purpose strong enough to sustain a clear thread throughout. Men-delssohn was twenty one years old when he had passed through Italy on his way home from England in 1831, and in this music he expressed his enchantment for the ideal land of beauty, joy and art that had held Germans captive through the works of Goethe. It is a pure German expression of delight, a highly poetic and beautiful utterance of the German idea of Italy. There is evidence that the brilliant *Saltarello* finale was inspired by a carnival in Rome. The symphony was composed two years after his Italian tour, but was first performed posthumously in Leipzig in 1849.

This sunny work, depicting the experience of Mendelssohn on holiday in Italy, is really that of a German composer interpreting the life and times of an Italian. If performed in the wrong idiom, it is a disaster. The performance must be earthy but light, and it must move without labor. Unfortunately, most grand orchestral performances do labor, and therefore, the list of optimal performances is indeed relatively short.

Sir Georg Solti, early in his career, performed a particularly light-of- foot, mean-spirited version of the Italian Symphony with the Israel Philharmonic Orchestra, currently available on London Weekend Classics. It is excellent, and it is the first performance that I learned. It has been out of the catalog for all too long. Another outstanding performance, also dating from that time frame of the late 1950s, is that by George Szell and the Cleveland Orchestra, which is accompanied by music to *A Midsummer Night's Dream* by Mendelssohn. The performance is particularly fleeting and intricate, and adequately captured in early stereo sound. Another relatively early recording by Claudio Abbado is that of his Italian Symphony with the London Symphony Orchestra, which Abbado re-recorded for DG in digital sound during his tenure as music director of that orchestra. The original recording, for London Records, has been reissued with his performance of the Scottish Symphony, and both of them make a very nice CD. I tend to prefer the newer recording for its improved sound. Interestingly, Abbado has re-recorded the Symphony a third time, using as its packaged partner the same incidental music to *A Midsummer Night's Dream*. I think the most recent performance is clearly the best, as the Berlin Philharmonic knows this work well, and had recorded it previously with von Karajan in what is probably too heavy handed a performance, although well played.

Frans Bruggen and the Orchestra of the Eighteenth Century has recorded the work in original instrument form for Philips, and I think this a wonderful, live version that is particularly transparent. The work does in some ways benefit from original instrumentation, although I don't think I would want to live with this form alone.

- Symphony No. 4; Overture: A Midsummer Night's Dream
  Sony MYK37760. Cleveland O, Szell
- Symphony No. 4; Overture: A Midsummer Night's Dream
  Sony Classical SK 62826. BPO, Abbado

Mendelssohn: Violin Concerto in E minor

This is the sort of work that, all by itself, justifies a composer's life. Mendelssohn's Violin Concerto in E minor is probably the most popular of all violin concertos, and with good reason. Aside from its eloquent and superbly violinistic melodies that are full of vitality, it was a boldly innovative work for its time, a light but highly polished masterpiece that exerted considerable influence on subsequent violin concertos of the Romantic period. It was as perfect as it could be—in classical poise, melodic suavity, refined romantic feeling and emotional breadth and daring, it was an epitome of Mendelssohn's style. Finesse, cultivated taste, an unerring sense of the appropriate, and a gallant *savoir-faire* were the characteristics expressed in this piece by Mendelssohn—the gentleman *par excellence* of Romanticism in music. The beautiful tone and the melodic line of the solo instrument can be traced throughout the music; the violin stands out like a moving, vividly colored silhouette against the pastel shades of the orchestra.

Never before in a violin concerto had a soloist made his first entry before the orchestra had outlined the themes. In this work, the violin itself sings out the first tune with fine feminine grace and freedom as the music begins, dispensing with the usual orchestral introduction. There is a faint touch of melancholy in the second tune, and then the violin takes off from a marvelous cadenza to exploit the full limits of its acrobatics. The tones of the instrument are crystal clear and fully extended: deep and full, or glittering and ethereal, flying high or lingering, as solid as a Gothic ornament in stone and as gossamer and delicate as filigree lace. The feminine character of the music can still be felt in the exceedingly beautiful *berceuse*-like melody of the second movement, with a rhythm reminiscent of a cradle song. The searching eloquence of the opening of the finale makes it the most magical passage in the whole concerto. How vigorous and vital, and varied and colorful a violin can be is explored in the final movement. The tones dance as lightly as a will-o'-the-wisp, ethereal, mysterious and luminous, hanging imminent for a moment like a pale star, or singing with a quivering warmth and passion that seems to emanate straight from the heart. The music ends in an unsurpassingly powerful and brilliant climax.

Mendelssohn wrote two violin concertos, so do not inadvertently select the concerto written in a different key thinking it is the "principal" Mendelssohn Violin Concerto—it is not. The other concerto is an earlier, and unfortunately far less interesting work, although it is worthy in its own right.

I was introduced to this work by the Jascha Heifetz performance made for RCA with the Boston Symphony Orchestra under the direction of Charles Munch. This still remains a staple of my diet, and may be, at least for me, the greatest recording of the work made to date. However, I am looking forward to Maxim Vengerov's anticipated Teldec recording of the work.

Another performance which has been particularly impressive to me is that by the Italian violinist Uto Ughi, under the baton of Georges Pretre for RCA (RCA RO 70111). Ughi seems to have an intuitive knack for this work which exceeds my expectations each time I hear the performance. It may be necessary to import this recording from Canada or the UK as I have not seen it domestically, but it is worth seeking due to the overt joy that it produces upon hearing. I think it is a more gratifying reading than any other modern stereo version

I've encountered, despite the excellence of some two dozen record-ings in the catalog.

Honorable mention should be given to Joshua Bell, Gil Shaham, Kyung Wha Chung and Nathan Milstein (his DG performance), as all of these artists have contributed, quite frankly, A+ performances to the recorded lexicon of Mendelssohn's Violin Concerto in E minor.

- Violin Concerto in E minor—TCHAIKOVSKY:Violin concerto; Serenade
  RCA 09026 61743. Heifetz, Boston SO, Munch

Mendelssohn: Overtures

Nothing worried Schumann more than his inability to decide which among the overtures of Mendelssohn was the loveliest. These are works of such delicate structure that the most boorish criticism will approach them timidly and make an obeisance before them. Original, and exquisitely happy, they are radiant with pure light, absolutely without shadow! And of none is this more true than the blooming and youthful overture to Shakespeare's *A Midsummer Night's Dream*. The music is not involved with the action or the love relations of the four young people. Rather, it accompanies the fairy motifs of the play, and its shimmering strings and whispering wood winds capture the unforgettable magic of a green forest night bathed in the sweet warmth and drowsiness of midsummer. The music is charming and witty—from the first entrance of Puck and the elves, the jesting and chattering of instruments, to the exquisitely beautiful fairy music, "in grove or green, By fountain clear, or spangled star-like sheen,"—it is filled with delicacy and quaint humor. There is also the familiar wedding march—the first march that Mendelssohn wrote—with its joyous pomp and lively rhythm, and the inevitable note of sadness that seems inexplicably to touch every bridal with smothered misgiv-ing.

The overture inspired by Goethe's twin poems *A Calm Sea* and *A Prosperous Voyage* was written two years later, and has the same imaginativeness as the earlier music. There is a chilling stillness and

138

serenity in the slow introduction that depicts a becalmed sea underneath a stuporous sky, with a suggestion of surging movement and breadth. The cheerful final section, dealing with the triumphant arrival of the ship to shore with trumpet fanfares, also ends in an unexpected quiet stillness.

It was an auspicious moment when the composer visited The Hebrides and sketched the opening of his masterpiece, *The Hebrides Overture* (*Fingal's Cave*). The entire piece, with its shifting rhythms, ceaseless motion, and color-flecked orchestration conveys a uniquely vivid and spacious musical image of the sea. Salt spray and sea gulls, nature in peace and fury, are palpably portrayed here as best as music can paint it.

It is not necessary to know the tale of the romance between the proud and knightly Lusignan and the seductive and yielding Melusine—half fish, half woman—to understand the music of *The Fair Melusine*. The overture murmurs of old legends, beginning with an enchanting water-like motif, somewhat cold and mute on the surface but ebbing and flowing underneath with such effect that one seems to be carried from the battleground of violent passions to the sublime, earth-embracing ocean. The watery waves rise into the embraces of the lovers, now covering them, now separating them. The tender and enduring melody of Melusine lingers in the music, reminiscent of a tune from primeval times.

Contrasts are far more obvious in the *Ruy Blas* overture, written six years later. A grandiose introduction, an agitated and furious main theme, and a more lyrical second subject are introduced very effectively against an incisively violent rhythmic background. Mendelssohn himself had little love for the tragedy that Victor Hugo had written about a Spanish nobleman's valet who loved a queen, and there is little in the music that can be called tragic. But there are several moments of vivid dramatic suspense and vigorous, full-blooded melodrama, a carousel of brave and base natures, court intrigue, disguise, blackmail and poison that well deserves the music's popularity.

Felix Mendelssohn was a brilliant young composer, artist and intellectual giant, who died all too young in his early thirties. Having visited his grave site in Berlin, along with other members of the Mendelssohn clan, I have some sense that he felt as if he belonged to the community, and standing at his graveside at Hallesches Tor, I could literally hear many of his symphonic works, including several overtures, in my mind, knowing from where they came.

There are only several comprehensive recordings of the Mendelssohn Overtures, my favorite being that of Claudio Abbado and the London Symphony Orchestra for DG. In short, these are well edited, selected and performed, and are blessed with excellent sound. Another DG recording is with the London Symphony Orchestra and Gabriel Chmura, which may only be available on deleted LP and MC. Chmura, little known in this country, delivered some rousing performances in his program, and I suggest that the reader seek out a used copy of this recording, although it will be difficult to find.

Finally, there is a recording on BMG/RCA with Klaus Peter Flor and the Bamberger Symphoniker of a program of Mendelssohn Overtures which if not spellbinding in their excellence, are more than ably played and recorded by this young originally East German talent. Flor considers himself to be a Mendelssohn specialist and BMG has marketed him as such. As good as his performances are, I don't think they hold a candle to Abbado or Chmura, but I mention his recordings here because they may well be the most readily available in many locations.

- Overtures
    DG 423104-2GH. LSO, Abbado
- Overtures
    DG 423 025-2GMF. LSO, Chmura

Schumann: Symphony No 1 (Spring)

Robert Schumann (1810 - 1856) has never ostentatiously summoned a body of followers. He has been a comet without a tail, but for all that, one of the most remarkable comets in the firmament of the arts. His worshippers have always been the single and lonely ones that carry in them something of the character of the sensitive mimosa. There is an intimate quality in Schumann's art—to meet in quiet comprehension of the master during a mysterious tête-à-tête at a piano, *that* is genuinely Schumannesque.

Schumann referred to his first symphony by the descriptive title of *Spring*. He might have called it the *Clara Schumann Symphony*. For, this music does not convey the song of birds or the flowing of brooks in the countryside, but the springtime that the composer found in his heart after emerging from the winter of his courtship of Clara Weick whom he had known since she had been a child of only thirteen years. He had triumphed over all the legal, moral and emotional obstacles that old Weick had placed before him in his opposition to the marriage of his daughter! There are no deep premeditated qualities in this work. It is simply unpremeditated joy, the exhilarating sunshine of happiness that comes with marriage, and it is to be enjoyed without any anxious searching for latent philosophies. In it, he poured his feelings, consciously or otherwise, for his wife—from the contentment of the purest kind expressed in the opening song of the violins as spring's clarion blows o'er the dreaming earth, to the *Finale* which expresses the simple spirit of a man who has dropped his last care and is at peace with the world. In springtime, it must be so!

The First Symphony was sketched out in four days in 1840, the year of his honeymoon with Clara. Tradition has it that the music was written with a steel pen that the composer had found on Beethoven's grave in Vienna. It was performed the following year at Leipzig in a concert conducted by his good friend Felix Mendelssohn who showed unselfish care and consummate mastery to make it a success. Clara, already a popular soloist, played the piano works of different composers, including her husband, at the same concert.

It has often been said that Schumann's orchestration leaves much to be desired, and that his music is difficult to perform. I'm convinced, as are many musicologists and musicians, that this really isn't true. If one just lets the music play on its own, things go awfully well.

The list of excellent Schumann's First Symphony is not short, including athletic performances by Bernstein, thoughtful and contemplative interpretations by Szell and Sinopoli, two Kubelik Cycles, and a rather rhetorical Furtwangleresque interpretation by Barenboim with the Chicago Symphony. The Szell performance, as part of a complete cycle, has been considered by many to be one of the pinnacles of his career, and it is delightful to have that performance reissued on Sony Masterworks Heritage. Levine's recordings with the Philadelphia Orchestra have been reissued on RCA and these are far to be preferred to his later Berlin Philharmonic accounts. Levine's is one of my favorite performances of all time, along with the original Berlin Philharmonic performances under Kubelik. Sir Georg Solti gave us an excellent, highly charged performance with the Vienna Philharmonic from London in excellent analog sound many years ago, and it still is a preferred version. Kurt Masur and Wolfgang Sawallisch have provided outstanding versions with the London Philharmonic Orchestra and the Dresden Staatskapelle respectively, and either of these make very good central European versions.

My preferred choice comes from the Cleveland Orchestra, not with George Szell, but with his successor, Christoph von Dohnanyi, a performance of great, keen insight, ample clarity, and elegance. It is rhythmically pointed and charged, and is delineated beautifully. This performance is well nigh perfect in my mind, and betters that of Szell in terms of recorded sound and lucidity.

- Symphony Nos. 1 (Spring), 2-4
  London 452214-2 (2). Cleveland O, C. von Dohnanyi

Schumann: Symphony No 2

Schumann was one of the first masters to be born and bred in a social class whose main function was not the service of another. He was also the first of the great composers not to have the distinction of

142

being a child prodigy. Education and culture had their own rightful place in his youth, and he became steeped early in the reflective art of poetry, especially the German verse of the poet Richter. Indeed, one might almost say: Who does not know Richter, does not know Schumann. Under this influence he lived, breathed, listened and spoke unconsciously, and developed that strong introspective quality that characterized his nature. He received in verse and gave out in sound. His taste for meditation was hard to abandon, and he preferred to explore hidden recesses of thought and special sentiment—national, legendary or local—rather than to utter naive bursts of untitled feeling. If he had lived into a vigorous middle age, he would probably have matured into the highest poetic composer.

Although his music reflected the ideals and thought of contemporary German poetry, pervaded with the spirit of German legend, it was the emotional significance of the words that he mirrored in his music, following up the emotional thread wherever it might lead him. He seldom set out deliberately to translate a certain subject into music; he was the first to admit that he always wrote the title of a work *after* its composition. The Second Symphony, his longest one, is one such piece. It has no title or association, so that the listener is not inclined in any particular direction. It does not paint objects, and it is not at all philosophical. But it is typical of Schumann in its peculiar subjectivity, a very personal expression of feelings and subjective emotions where the music is turned away from its supposed vocation of mere beauty to become a most powerful utterance of high feelings of deep intensity.

Hardly four years had passed since his happy marriage to Clara when Schumann began to suffer greatly from nervousness, depression and loss of memory that culminated in a nervous breakdown. It was during his convalescence at Dresden that he began work on this piece; years later, he was to remark that this music reminded him "of a dark time." But the sickness of body and soul had made the eyes of his mind unusually bright. The first movement, perhaps, reflects his bitterness and struggle to beat the pain and suffering of his disease. But there is none of the invalid thereafter. The music becomes buoyant and exhilarating, though never reckless, occasionally relieved by moments of genuine tenderness, to end in a dramatic expression of power and courage, as if one were triumphantly beginning the battle of life again. The first version of this symphony was performed in Leipzig under the direction of Felix Mendelssohn.

The Second Symphony suffers from no lack of contenders for the *Desert Island* award, and the contenders are virtually the same as those mentioned earlier for his First Symphony.

A notably romantic and rhetorical performance by Barenboim is unforgettable, but it is not rhythmically pointed nor architecturally extraordinarily clean. Solti's recording with the Vienna Philharmonic, unfortunately, was not well engineered, and despite its explosive nature, can't be considered seriously because of the recorded sound. Otherwise, it would be at the top of any list.

Riccardo Chailly and the Concertgebouw Orchestra give a splendid version on London Records, recently recorded, that is far less anemic and pallid than Haitink with the same orchestra recorded approximately ten years before. Indeed, none of the Schumann symphonies that have been recorded by Haitink are competitive, despite the beauty of the playing and the excellence of the recorded sound. Chailly is a contender for a very bucolic but inspired performance. Leonard Bernstein's recording with the Vienna Philharmonic is unforgettable for its *sforzandi*, but this does little to save a very willful performance from being nothing more than a caricature of the work.

The performance I learned the work on was that of Dietrich Fischer-Dieskau and the Bamberger Symphoniker on a now unavailable BASF LP. Fischer-Dieskau's handling of the lyrical aspects of the work are extraordinary, and the recorded sound, even today, holds up very well. If one can find this record, buy it, beg it or steal it! You will not be sorry. Unfortunately, he does not appear to have plans to re-record this in digital sound in the new medium.

The most compelling performances I have encountered of this work are the outstanding version by the Berlin Philharmonic and Herbert von Karajan recorded in 1972, and that of James Levine and the Philadelphia Orchestra recorded in 1978. The two are distinctly similar interpretations, and either one, if one can find them, will bring great pleasure. At this time I believe they are both part of integral cycles of all four Schumann Symphonies.

- Symphony Nos 1-4
   DG 429 672-2GSE2 (2), BPO, Karajan
- Symphony Nos. 1-4
   RCA 74321-20294-2 (2). Phil O, Levine

Schumann: Symphony No 3 (Rhenische)

In 1850, Schumann moved with his beloved Clara and their children to the city of Dusseldorf by the Rhine. Before the end of the year, he had visited Cologne twice, and within the ruins of its famous Cathedral, amidst the mysterious shadows of its lofty, slender Gothic pillars grouped like trees in an ancient forest, he had witnessed a majestic ceremony of the crowning of a cardinal. The same year he put his impressions of the joyous simplicity and the fresh naturalness of Rhenish folk life and the countryside, and his awesome experiences at the Cologne Cathedral, into music. It became his Third Symphony, and he dubbed it the *Rhenische* symphony.

But there is no need to know anything of the Rhine land to enjoy this music. Whether one knows the title or not, the words are not the symphony itself—they are only meant to suggest. The music speaks not of localities but of memories and aspirations which belong to us all. In any case, it has an undeniable persuasive charm, from the strong and rugged melody at its beginning to the majestic solemnity of the trombones in the *Cathedral* scene. Here is music teeming with the typical ideal life of the German, the stirring roaring spirit fearless of the cynical world, firm with a manly tread, and with some rough humor too. Here is good comfortable German romanticism, both airy and earthy, and the more you have of it, the better you feel! The symphony was first performed in Dusseldorf in 1851 where Schumann himself conducted from manuscript.

This somewhat programmatic work in five movements is, to me, the most dramatic and foreboding of the Schumann symphonies, and I love it dearly. One of my earliest exposures was again to the recording on a long-deleted BASF LP, with Dietrich Fischer-Dieskau conducting the Bamberger Symphoniker. The performance is lyrical, beautifully conceived, and permanently etched in my mind as what the work should sound like. The recorded sound itself is somewhat boxy, especially compared to the Second Symphony, but if you can find this recording, either on LP or cassette, make it your own. You won't need any other. In the absence of the Fischer- Dieskau recording, however, there are a number of excellent versions, including Szell in the Cleveland Orchestra as part of his integral cycle, and Dohnanyi and the Cleveland Orchestra as part of his integral cycle.

There is a very interesting original instrument version with Roger Norrington and the London Classical Players on EMI, but I fear that this will be supplanted by an even more interesting performance soon to be released by Archiv that is conducted by John Eliot Gardiner and the Orchestre Revolutionnaire et Romantique. Reports of his performances in live concert were stellar, and those searching for an unvarnished view of this work in original instrument form would do well to await it.

My favorite performance of the *Rhenische* Symphony in currently available recordings remains the most willful of all time, and it depicts the rapids of the Rhine River to perfection. This is Leonard Bernstein's final recording of the work, with the Vienna Philharmonic Orchestra, recorded in the mid 1980s. It is available as part of a two CD box of all four symphonies at mid price, or if found individually, it is paired with an excellent version of the Schumann's *Piano Concerto* with Justus Frantz at the keyboard. This is an excellent version of the work, and should not be missed.

- Symphony Nos. 3 (Rhenische); 1-2, 4
    DG 453 049 GTA2 (2).VPO, Bernstein
- Symphony Nos. 3 (Rhenische); 1-2, 4
    London 452214-2 (2). Cleveland O, C. von Dohnanyi

Schumann: Symphony No 4

The Fourth Symphony, chronologically, was not Schumann's last symphony. Soon after his marriage to Clara, and after the completion of the First, another work was being wrought in the depths of his soul. Heaven had been disposed kindly towards him, he could not have been happier than during its composition and, on Clara's birthday in the fall of 1841, when the ink had barely dried on the final note, he presented her with the completed score. It was also the day on which they christened their first child, Marie.

The work was premiered in Leipzig together with a composition by Liszt for two pianos in which the Schumanns were the soloists. The Schumanns created a sensation with their playing, and the enthusiasm of the audience for their virtuosity was such that it utterly eclipsed their appreciation of the new symphony! Discouraged by the poor reception at this first performance, he laid it aside for ten years. A drastically revised and re-orchestrated version was performed with more success at Dusseldorf in 1853 at which Schumann himself was the conductor. Little did he then suspect what Fate had in store for him—his health continued to deteriorate, in 1854 he attempted to commit suicide by throwing himself into the Rhine, and he spent the rest of his life thereafter in an insane asylum near Bonn where he died in Clara's arms in 1856.

This symphony is Schumann's great lyric poem for orchestra. It is more poetic than any of his other symphonies, and its romantic and melodious qualities, together with its intensity and power, have endeared it to generations of audiences. It is not a spectacular work—Brahms, himself, had always preferred the original scoring—but it possesses an insight and sincerity that has remained eminently satisfying.

This valedictory Schumann Symphony, a cyclical work, returning to the same theme as the first movement in the finale, is one of my favorite pieces of all time. It has been beautifully served on record since the long playing records era, with outstanding performances by Karajan in monophonic sound for DG, followed by an early stereo account with the Staatskapelle Dresden as part of the Salzburg Festival, and then in later performances in his 1972 cycle with the Berlin Philharmonic and in a live performance with the Vienna Philharmonic. Any of these would please any critic of the work.

Again, Szell, Sinopoli, Kubelik, and Levine have outstanding versions, any of which would please even the most critical of listeners. Of conventional versions, Dohnanyi and the Cleveland Orchestra stands out for its coolness of temperament and deliberate delivery, a performance which is well nigh perfect from start to finish. It is beautifully punctuated with tympani, and always impresses me. The Vienna Philharmonic recording with Leonard Bernstein, and the Chicago Symphony Orchestra performance with Daniel Barenboim are both somewhat willful, the latter being played in the rhetorical, 19th Century style, much as Furtwangler did in his excellent monophonic recording for DG with the Berlin Philharmonic in the 1950s. Again, any of these would please those interested in somewhat wayward interpretations. As relatively buttoned-down a performance as Dohnanyi's is, I suppose it is the most livable of the excellent performances, and suffers from no eccentricities of character. To that end, it is my first choice on a very long list of loved performances.

- Symphony Nos 3, 4
    London 421643-2. Cleveland O, von Dohnnyi

Chopin: Piano Works

"Hats off, gentlemen—a genius!" With these prophetic words, Robert Schumann announced to the world an unknown young Polish composer who had just written his second piece for the piano. Frederick Chopin (1810 - 1849) knew that his strength lay in the piano, and to it he turned as the best medium to sing his thoughts. He persuaded rather than commanded the instrument, and drew from it secrets that no one else had realized it possessed. He did not need an orchestral army to lead the spirit of Beethoven into the concert hall—he was great in small things! And in his 169 exquisitely perfect small piano pieces, he poured out his intense imagination and deep poetic vein, his effeminately tender lyrics and heroic passion, in music that could stab the heart or display a whimsical lightness that was almost boyish in its exuberance.

The many facets of his personality he expressed in an elastic variety of musical forms, like a jeweler putting a different jewel in an old setting. His productions were not all alike; the trunk was indeed the same, but the fruits were the most divers in savor and form. He used the *ballade*, where the development of the music gave it the character of a musical narrative, to tell the story of his unhappy love affair with Maria Wodzinksa. They were his most poetic works, alternating between intense fervor and brooding melancholy, quivering with the deepest emotions, full of sighs, sobs, groans and the transports of passion. In his *polonaises* and *mazurkas* he spoke on a grander scale with a nationalistic ardor for the soul of his native Poland, where he had been born but which he had not seen since the age of twenty. These works were like guns buried in flowers; in them he revealed his oddity and morbid eccentricity, even his wildness and hate. Yet so throbbing a life flowed in them that they seemed to have been actually improvised in the ballroom! And his impassioned *impromptus* were so overflowing with boldness, love and contempt that they may well be compared to a poem by Byron.

His *etudes* (studies) he transformed from a naked technical exercise to an esthetic art form. Varied in color, sentiment, mood and atmosphere, inexhaustible in their musical imagination, they combined, at times, poetry with high feeling that was both fascinating and a trifle frightening. He loved the night and its starry mysteries, and in his *nocturnes* ("pieces for the night"), he displayed the night side of his soul, and breathed a serene beauty and nobility suggestive of moonlight and a comforting darkness, or whisperings at dusk—a gentle introspection like the tranquil musings of a remorseful lyric poet. His *rondos* were lovely, romantic and graceful—he who does not yet know Chopin had best make his acquaintance with these compositions! His *scherzi* possessed a restless driving energy, an inner demon of discontent, that was not allowed to rest. But it was in his charming and magnetic *waltzes* that he excelled as the sensitive and frail child of the luxurious Paris *salons*. They were *salon* pieces of the noblest sort, thoroughly aristocratic to the tips of his fingers, and if they were played for dancers, half of the ladies should be young countesses! But in the glitter and whirl and swing of the dance lay a more melancholy mood, a more personal sentiment.

His *preludes* he composed at Palma, on the island of Majorca, where he lived with the extravagant and romantic novelist Georges Sand, an arresting personality with an almost masculine assertiveness, who rode horses astride, wore trousers, and smoked cigars. When the skies were gray and the frosty winds howled at night in a dismal and terrifying manner, and the plaster fell off the walls from the cold, Chopin shivered and coughed while Georges Sand built the fire and smoked! In his *preludes* he dreamed of idyllic far-off lands with glowing skies and gorgeous flowers, the sound of children's laughter and the distant strum of a guitar, and the song of birds among the damp leafage. Others were dreary and sad, and wrung the heart while they charmed the ear, and in some he called to the mind's eye visions of dead monks, and the songs of their funeral chants which had obsessed him.

Chopin, the supreme poet of the piano, died of tuberculosis in 1850, surrounded by friends, pupils and the women who loved him. Conspicuously missing was Georges Sand, though they had mutually sworn that he should die only in her arms.

Chopin's output was so enormous and legendary that it is impossible to summarize his works on several recommendable CDs.

Recent compilations of a variety of his works by Mikhail Pletnev (on DG 453 456-2GH), Alexander Brailowsky on a Sony Classical imported CD from the Netherlands, and Richard Goode on Nonesuch are particularly enjoyable. An older recording of Ashkenazy's own personal favorite Chopin piano music is available on a 2 CD box from London, perhaps the best overall recommendation for variety of Chopin's output.

A comprehensive recording of Chopin for piano was compiled by BMG/RCA with the incomparable Artur Rubinstein, some recordings of which are monophonic, but all are utterly worthwhile.

150

Michelangeli, the reclusive Italian pianist who died just a few years ago, had a retrospective of his pianistic output including Chopin reissued on DG not long ago which is highly recommendable even if just a bit quixotic. He was a rare diamond on the keyboard, even if difficult to work with in the studio. Stories abound that he recorded certain works at 2 or 3 AM in order to avoid adventitious noise from civilization outdoors, and one possibly apocryphal story is told of his disappointment with a particular concert and at the intermission he could not be found to complete the evening program. It was rumored that he had boarded a plane and was gone before it was truly recognized that this had occurred.

For those looking for the *Nocturnes* only, I would encourage the listener to find Maria Joao Pires new recordings on a 2 CD box from DG; they are splendid (DG 447 096-2GH2). Ivan Moravec recorded the *Preludes* for Supraphon as did Martha Argerich for DG; the approaches are so contrasted that the listener is encouraged to study each.

This leaves precisely 90% or more of the Chopin oeuvre unrepresented by these pages. If it were up to me, the novitiate listener would best be served by Goode's recording for Nonesuch or Ashkenazy's 'collection of favorites.'

- "Favorite Piano Works"
  Decca Double 444 830-2 (2). Vladimir Ashkenazy
- Preludes
  Supraphon SU3165-2111. Ivan Moravec
- Preludes
  DG 431 584-2 GCE. Argerich
- Nocturnes
  DG 447 096-2 GH2. Maria Joao Pires

Liszt: Symphonic Poems

It was Franz Liszt (1811 - 1886) who hit upon the form which came to be known as the symphonic poem—far inferior to the symphony, but more adequate for its special poetic intent. It was music impressed with more and more of that poetry which, if one may believe those who have felt, loved and suffered strongly, defied the analysis and definite expression of the human languages. It had no other object than to incorporate the feelings, spirituality and thoughts that had compelled a composer to create his work. All exclusively musical considerations, though they were not to be neglected, were considered subordinate to the action of a given subject—the return, change, modification and modulation of musical motives were conditioned by their relation to the poetic idea.

The symphonic poem, as exemplified in the works of Liszt, consisted of one long movement easily divisible into sections. Often, the structure of the poem was in two parts with contrasting moods: as in *Prometheus* (mourning and transfiguration), in *Tasso* (lament and triumph), and in *Mazeppa* (martyrdom and victory). The composition could be based upon a number of themes, and there may occur any number of changes of key and tempo. Repetition of themes, and their development through theme metamorphosis, were important features whereby a theme was presented in successively different shapes, bearing always a recognizable relationship to its original shape but undergoing changes of rhythm, melody and harmony which gave it an entirely different aspect. Since such a loose form did not permit any way of predicting what would occur in a composition, a written program was generally supplied by the composer to allow listeners to enhance their enjoyment.

Liszt wrote twelve symphonic poems. And in them he devoted the full riches of his cultural interests, and sheltered all great poetry and all great thoughts from Dante and Tasso to Lamartine and Goethe. Yet they have not won the place which he claimed for them—for, a man can hardly be so impressionable as Liszt and yet be sturdy enough to be original!

Liszt was enough of a romantic to know that in his work *Les Preludes*, the images of man pitted against Fate, symbolizing love, human aspirations, nature and immortality must, of necessity be vague, rather than follow a story. However, he did preface this symphonic poem with his own free and rhapsodic program which reads: "What is life but a series of preludes to that unknown song whose initial solemn note is tolled by death? The enchanted dawn of every life is love; but where is the destiny on whose first delicious joys some storm does not break?.... And what soul thus sorely bruised, when the tempest rolls away, seeks not to rest its memories in the calm of pastoral life?... but when the trumpet gives the signal, he hastens to danger's post... that in the struggle he may once more regain full confidence in himself and in his powers." Here, then, are the contrasting pastoral and warlike elements that dwell loosely in this continuous piece of music—intimations of immortality, an idealization of love, the slings and arrows of outrageous fortune, a longing for the healing balm of pastoral solitude, and the triumphant return to battle.

In *Orpheus*, Liszt felt an understandable kinship with the Greek musician of the legend. The orchestra is played like a gigantic lyre, with the harp ubiquitous, soothing a savage beast. A basic theme can be recognized throughout the work that develops tension out of its own urgency. The music ends in a haunting series of chords uttered by the wood winds.

Mazeppa was inspired by a Victor Hugo poem that tells the ordeal of the ghastly ride and rescue of the Asiatic hero who is tied naked to a wild horse that races over plains and hills until the animal succumbs from fatigue. The horse devours space in the music, but all interest is concentrated on the man who thinks and suffers. Rushing strings introduce the first theme descriptive of Mazeppa himself, given out by trombones, cello and double basses. The breakneck ride is reproduced with vividness and power. The music expands to unfold the limitless immensity of the boundless steppes, and the man feels conquered by a thousand details of this vast expanse, and the more so because he is unable to see them. Brilliant sonorities and powerful dynamics are contrasted with passages of poignancy suggesting the hero's suffering. The animal falters and falls to the cries of a thousand birds of prey expressed in the moaning strings and a solo bassoon and horn. Then a thrill sparks the lower strings, trumpets blare a brash gypsy fanfare, and the hero is found and rescued. The work ends on a note of tranquillity.

Duality portrayed in contrasting themes are common in the symphonic poems. The two themes in *Prometheus* alternate: one threatening misfortune, the other promising glory (*Malheur et gloire!* Misfortune and glory!). Prometheus' misfortune was his punishment for stealing fire from the Gods for humankind; his glory was the knowledge and power of fire that he brought to man. And the tonal portrait of the Italian poet *Tasso: Lamento e trianfo* emphasizes the duality of the hero's suffering and triumph—the genius who was misjudged during his life is surrounded after death by a halo that destroys his enemies.

These orchestral tour de forces are rarely recorded comprehensively, and there are certainly preferred individual performances of many of them, such as *Tasso*, for which I encourage the listener to seek out Solti's amazing interpretation on London. Masur has also recorded the work for EMI and the result is somewhat more bucolic a statement than Solti's.

As for *Les Preludes*, if this is what the listener is searching for specifically, Muti's excellent Philadelphia Orchestra recording for EMI, a deleted performance by Mehta and the Vienna Philharmonic on London, and again Solti's interpretation with the London Philharmonic are all worthy competitors in this field.

For me, one of the most interesting performances of *Les Preludes* comes from pianist Leslie Howard, on Hyperion. His traversal of Liszt's piano music and some of the orchestral works as transcribed by Liszt for piano are truly revelatory, and the elegance and panache of Liszt somehow comes over to me far more satisfyingly on piano than it does with full orchestra.

For those looking for the complete Symphonic Poems, fortunately there are excellent renditions which are understated and elegant, which often help out these rather garish works. The typically unassuming and often myelophthisic conductor Bernard Haitink and the London Philharmonic Orchestra have, on four CDs, recorded all the Symphonic Poems in what is currently the only complete set available. We are fortunate to have this set in the discography.

- Symphonic Poems, Vol 1 and 2
  Ph.Duo 438 751-2; 438 754-2. LPO, Bernard Haitink

Rossini: Overtures

An overture without a melody is like a novel without a hero. Whereas other composers saw melody as but a link in a chain, Gioachino Rossini (1792 - 1868) made of the single link a perfect and complete art form, capable of expressing the noblest sentiments of the human heart and life. Melody is concise, simple in structure, symmetrical and organic—a living germ. It comes into existence by a supreme act of creation, it may be amplified and set in rich decorations, but it is complete in itself.

Perhaps the composer was obeying a social force when he founded the melodic school of opera. After the storms and bloodshed of the Napoleonic wars, calmness, repose and oblivion were needed in public life. Rossini brought to his music the qualities best fitted to charm society, to entertain it, and to lull it into pleasant dreams. He was captivating and exhilarating; he was imposing to the last degree in his splendid moments; he was clever, and full of fun; his practicality was largely due to good sense; and he did not settle down to offering the public frivolous work until it had snubbed him for taking himself more seriously. *Guilleme Tell*, *Semirade*, *The Barber of Seville* are words that conjure memories of melody and little else; but how rich, how dignified, how delicious is the feast! Audiences have never failed to hear each melody with delight, each a gem complete and polished, bringing alive the natural scenes and brilliant comedy of the situations.

Any enumeration of Rossini's innovations lose their significance because they have become so universally adapted—his expansion of the power of melody to a high pitch to gain color and intensity, his enlargement of the resources of the orchestra, his unmistakable sympathy with the trend of Romantic literature, his application of crescendo and diminuendo as orchestral effects, his efforts to invest the drums and brasses with new and special values. And all this becomes even more significant when one considers his exceptional disadvantages in respect to the illiteracy, the Bohemianism, the ignorance, narrowness and squalor of his environment during childhood.

In November, 1815, Rossini went to Rome where, in less than two weeks, he wrote his masterpiece *The Barber of Seville*, based upon the play by Beaumarchaise. Thus began a triumphant new era in Italian opera buffa. Genius flashes and flames on every page, the Promethean fire descends upon every tune. The music is bright and fresh and spontaneous from beginning to end, sparkling and effervescent like bubbles in champagne. Enter Figaro, the quick-witted barber—perhaps Beaumarchaise himself! Figaro here, Figaro there, Figaro everywhere! It has been said that, in his time, the Figaro solos that pattered to the gay lilt of Rossini's orchestra passed from mouth to mouth as far as Polynesia, and the natives of the Southern seas hummed it as they cooked their breakfast of shell fish!

Semiramide, a characteristically Italian operatic version of Voltaire's *Semiramis*, is an admirable example of the decorative and melodious style of Rossini. Some have called it his finest overture. The music dazzles with its trills, its variations, and the incredible flexibilities of its intertwining sonorities. It opens softly, then gathers momentum like an onrushing river beneath an Asiatic sun to end in one of the most stirring climaxes in all music.

The wit of the *Barber* speaks in more sober accents in *William Tell*. The tunefulness and brilliance are here in abundance, but they strike a deeper note. There is dignity, a loftiness of expression, a picturesqueness, and a feeling for the portrayal of true patriotism that are entirely different from, and on a higher level than, anything else that he ever wrote. The overture is one of the most famous in the entire realm of opera. And with this opera at the age of thirty seven, Rossini brought to a close his career as a dramatic composer. The success of *William Tell*, added to the results of a prudent marriage and the friendship of the Rothschilds who looked after his savings for him, secured his future pecuniarily.

But Rossini still lives. Laughter and truth can never be far separated from each other. No matter how wildly humankind may wander among mysticisms and myths in the paths of tragic arts, the moment the Barber's general profile advances upon the operatic stage we are in the region of common sense and beauty. For art, when it is sufficiently truthful to become immortal, is always founded on common sense, and common sense Rossini had in a remarkable degree.

There are two basic camps to recordings of the Rossini *Overtures* —old and new.

The reader is encouraged to seek out performances by Fritz Reiner and the Chicago Symphony Orchestra on RCA, Tullio Serafin and the Rome Opera Orchestra on DG, and Szell with the Cleveland Orchestra on a now deleted Columbia (CBS) LP and MC. These three recordings demonstrate the epitome of great orchestral playing from approximately thirty to forty years ago, and yet the stereo sound is still eminently satisfying. Reiner's orchestra plays at unbelievable tempi, and yet, the performances cohere as if by magic. The great strengths of the Reiner recording include perhaps the definite *William Tell* Overture and, with Szell, a virtually definite *La Gazza Ladra*.

There are multiple modern contemporary recordings, including those by Marriner, Abbado, and Chailly. Marriner's can be ruled out of the court immediately because his 4-LP, now 3-CD box of the complete Rossini *Overtures* is hardly Italianate, and the performances lack idiomatic expression. They are, however, beautifully played and recorded, so anybody looking for the comprehensive collection of Rossini *Overtures* might consider this box. Riccardo Chailly has recorded the complete Rossini Overtures with the Teatro Communale di Bologna recently for Decca, and I believe this recording is available as a 2-CD performance on London. If not, it should be imported. This is a truly authentic response to the Marriner recording mentioned earlier, and will bring great pleasure.

However, the best remains for last, with recommendations for Abbado's DG recording of the Rossini *Overtures* made in 1975 being my primary recommendation. These are well nigh perfect interpretations, and I can recommend them without hesitation. Despite their analog sound, they spring to life. Recordings of *La*

Cenerentola and *Il Barbieri di Siviglia* are from the actual Abbado recordings of the complete operas, and the rest of the overtures are from studio performances made to complete this program of Rossini *Overtures*. Abbado also recorded Rossini *Overtures* during an interval when he briefly was between long termed contracts, but he did these for RCA. This disc is available at budget price, but there is some duplication of material between the DG recording with the London Symphony Orchestra and this RCA recording with LSO. The opera overture *Elizabeth, Queen of England* sounds awfully similar, if not identical, to Rossini's overture *Il Barbieri di Siviglia*. Finally, Abbado re-recorded the Rossini *Overtures* recently, in digital sound using the Chamber Orchestra of Europe, in truly polished performances which I can also recommend. They are not to me quite as exciting as the LSO recordings, but they are indeed excellent.

Finally, the Orpheus Chamber Orchestra, conductor-less, has recorded the Rossini *Overtures* for DG in a truly blazing program which is spirited and shows great adherence to score markings and remains truly *echt* in its authenticity. I can also recommend this recording highly.

- Overtures
    DG 419 869-2. LSO, Abbado
- Overtures
    DG 415 363-2 GH.Orpheus Chamber Orch
- Overtures
    RCA 60387-2 RG. Chicago SO, Reiner

Puccini: La Boheme

In the Romantic world, Puccini's love melody is a universal melody. It is more strained and intensive; when the violins sing and the harps ripple and the tenor voice rises, the air is filled with a fine perfume like a parlor full of dandies. In *La Boheme*, all the characters are desperately young, all the action is between cold and warmth. It is an opera of innocence; no one is evil, and triviality inscribes at the very heart of what is noble. Moments of sweetness, moments of peace, lightning flashes of mischief and happiness, the infinite grace of a joy dispensed for the representation of suffering—*La Boheme* moves from sadness to gaiety, from youth living its happiest days to a hint of the agony of approaching age. And through the joyful raindrops of real gaiety, death approaches. A very young woman loses her life, from too much flame wasted when everywhere is cold. Life slips away quietly on tiptoe while all around everything is swirling and whirling. Very young people bustle around her, fragile and ephemeral, powerless and fickle, exquisitely caring and tender but incapable of mastering a too harsh reality. *La Boheme* confronts youth with the infinity they seek; *La Boheme* is natural death.

For me, there is only one *La Boheme*, and I'm sure that many opera lovers will agree, but others will probably frown. Due to Pavarotti's exclusive contract with the Decca Recording Company of the UK, Karajan had to switch labels to make this recording. Mirella Freni and Pavarotti make this a splendid event, one of the true gramophone classics and, not unlike Kleiber's Beethoven or Mravinsky's Tchaikovsky, this is the only *Boheme* that you will need. When all is said and done, there is nothing else to do or say.

- La Boheme
    Decca 421 049-2. Freni, Pavarotti, Chorus of the Deutsche Opera, BPO, Karajan

Sibelius: Symphony No 2

Jean Sibelius composed his Second Symphony in Rappalo, Italy, in a room overlooking a beautiful garden of camellias, roses, almond trees, cypresses and palms. And this pastoral setting is reflected in the music, though with suggestions of tragic foreboding. From the beginning, the music of Sibelius had its roots in his native soil, and it was natural that it looked to the Slavic countries for its models. Both by instinct and conviction, he combined the physical hardihood of his country's native tradition with the intellectual strength of its awakened nationalism. Slavic in mood and expression with a tendency to overstate drama and yield to exaggerated emotions, it is dramatic, moving and tragic, often overwhelming in its sentiments and climactic surges. Here are unbridled feelings and brute force expressed in overlavish colors and effects, and images of fjord and crag and the gray unfriendly sea, of sparse covered meadows and acrid salt marshes.

The first movement paints in music the peaceful pastoral life of Finland in its time of contentment and freedom. The second is intensely patriotic, charged with high feeling against any form of oppression. In the third movement, the awakening of national consciousness is portrayed, and the finale is an expression of the composer's hope for the future deliverance of the motherland. The Finns themselves regarded the last movement as symbolizing the triumph of their national aspirations. Certainly the wide expressive range of this entire music, from its pastoral opening to its victorious conclusion, makes it one of the greatest of the Sibelius symphonies.

The Second Symphony was composed in 1901, and performed in Helsinki the following year.

The craggy naturalistic tendencies of the orchestration of this Finnish composer, one of the greatest of the turn of the century, is perhaps best depicted by this single symphonic work. It is certainly the most approachable of all the seven Sibelius symphonies, and the first one that I learned at a very young age. It, too, has been extraordinarily well served in recorded format.

Some will say that Karajan's final recording of this work for EMI is too stern, controlled and manipulated to be valid, but I find its icy temperament to be emotionally fulfilling and enthralling. The recorded sound is opulent, even if it is from the early digital era, and although the tempi are indeed on the slower side, the orchestral playing is of such splendor that the recording cannot be considered anything less than a highly significant contribution of Karajan's output. It is indeed more enticing than his original stereo recording of the work for EMI from the late fifties (with the Philharmonia Orchestra, not the Berlin Philharmonic).

Vladimir Ashkenazy, not unlike his recording of the Rachmaninoff Symphonies, succeeds again with Sibelius. He has recorded an integral cycle of the Sibelius Symphonies with the Philharmonia Orchestra in the eighties, and it has been considered among the best available. The recording of Symphony No. 2 in this cycle is lush, verdant, and almost bucolic rather than "tundraesque" in character, and is a dramatic reading.

Ashkenazy had another opportunity in the nineties to re-record this work with the Boston Symphony Orchestra in Symphony Hall, Boston, and this recording yet again outdoes the already excellent Philharmonia performance. This is the preferred performance of the two Ashkenazy readings which I have encountered, especially as it contains an excellent interpretation of *Finlandia* along with another short work by Sibelius. While the Philharmonia-Ashkenazy Sibelius Symphony No. 2 is available at mid price, I would go for the gold and spend the additional money on the Boston Symphony version. In particular, the last movement is a stunner, and it's clear that the orchestra is enjoying its time with Ashkenazy.

Sir Simon Rattle has recorded the Second symphony for EMI in a truly remarkable performance which also deserves pride of place on one's shelves. I must confess that his Sibelius cycle may go closer to the heart of the composer's intentions that Ashkenazy's, and the architecture of the works may be somewhat better delineated. The recorded sound from EMI, however, although excellent, is not quite in the same league as the Decca/London sound afforded to Ashkenazy.

My ultimate favorite of this work dates from the mid sixties, and is a performance by the Concertgebouw Orchestra of Amsterdam with George Szell. This is currently available at mid price, and is a splendid reading which does not suffer sonically despite its greater than 30 year age. If there were one performance I was to live with, it would be this one, and I would have no regrets about its less than optimal recorded sound.

- Symphony No 2
    Ph. 420 771-2. Concertgebouw Orchestra, Szell
- Symphony No 2
    London 436 566 2LH. BSO, Ashkenazy

A Time to be Free

The three decades between 1848 and 1878 were decisive in the history of European nationalism. Under the influence of German Romanticism, Russian Slavic nationalism rejected individual liberty as its foundation. Instead, it favored a perfect national community based upon a transfigured national past with ancient traditions and beliefs in which an individual could be fully himself only as an integral member of the nation. It stressed the belief that every individual was determined by an organic national or ancestral past that was fundamentally unaltered and unalterable. The national past set the model, and the concept of a unique personality was transferred from the individual to the nation. Men, said the German poet Herder, were the products of their national communities, shaped by traditions and wrought by the language of their ancestors. The folk soul (*Volksgeist*) manifested itself not in the sophisticated poetry and music of the courts but in the anonymous folk poetry and folk songs of the race. There was a divine dignity about the lowest in the human rank, whether racial or individual. Vague and semi mystical concepts of folk culture and folk music now came to the fore, and music became a distinctive way of measuring a country's cultural vitality. National pride became related to and was expressed in a nationalistic music.

The national idea in music springs from the songs of the people that outlive the passing of generations, and can bring comfort, heal sorrow, and make for a better understanding and brotherhood among the "folk." What is the most beautiful and meaningful in song lingers on over the ages, so that the tunes eventually emerge from the crucible of time as a wonderful symbol of the spirit of a people rather than of the individuals who gave them birth. And the material elements, the abundant rhythm and rich colors of individual and varied folk-songs become only a means by which the national temper is expressed.

In itself there is nothing special about a national idea that needs to be enshrined in music. A true national celebration must above all be spontaneous. Even then it can have no sanction in art unless it utters as a primal motive the resistance of the masses to suppression that is the elemental pulse of free life itself. The oppressed of a nation represent a universal type, their wrongs are the wrongs of all, and so their lament has a worldwide appeal. And it is from the lowest classes that the rich spring of folk-song arises upon which all music is reared. Music is the feeling of the pure joys and profound sorrows that spring from elemental relations, and the fullness of the human experience. Herein lies the nobility of the common people and their song. And in as much as nationalistic music is founded upon the folk-songs of a country, it is necessary, first of all, to know the conditions that made such songs possible.

Russia, hardly a part of Asia except in spirit, had to wait for a long time before her own national musical life became awakened. The fifteen hundred miles that separated the heart of Russia from the progressive art and culture of Italy and Germany should have at most required decades rather than the centuries that Russia took to embark on its modern journey. Perhaps the delay was due to the fact that the European Renaissance and the Reformation had bypassed the Russian nation, and the country's traditional attitudes toward learning, with its proverbial indifference and the natural limitations of its resources, had precluded the emergence of a native champion to shorten the period of darkness and disturb the ways of the Orthodox Church. Indeed, it was not until the fall of the Romanovs that musical instruments or women's voices were even admitted in the Church.

The direct inspiration for much of Russia's nationalistic music was the exiled poet Pushkin. In an extraordinary short life of thirty seven years that was filled with romantic passions, political reversals and literary triumphs, this brilliant Slav plunged his Motherland into the riches of her own culture. His legacy of poetic material drawn from the fairy tales, historic epics and folk songs of the Russian people was enormous: from his pen flowed such charming and imaginative works as *Ruslan and Ludmilla, Eugene Onenin, Boris Gudounov, Rusalka, The Golden Cockeral* and many others that endless Russian composers are still drawing upon for their inspiration. One can no more separate Pushkin from Russian music than a tree from its roots.

The nationalistic music of Russia literally began in 1804 with the birth of Mikhail Glinka. But it was Balkirev who attracted around him, almost by a mesmeric force, that motley group of young geniuses who astonished the musical world by their dazzling color, their barbaric extravagance, and their gorgeous pictures that expressed the spirit of the Russian people. Together they formed the Mighty Five, *Moguchaya Kuchka* ("the mighty little heap"), fanatically conscious of the freshness and beauty of the music of their nation, and determined to express it in exuberant defiance of all conservative opposition. For, aristocratic Russia was still in the habit of importing its amusements, and it was the Italian operas and French operetta that absorbed the court of Catherine I. None of the Five had gone to a conservatory of music because there *was* none in Russia; all of them had been trained for occupations outside music. Cesar Cui was a world authority on military fortifications; Borodin was a professor of chemistry who would have lived on in the annals of chemistry even if he had contributed nothing to music. Moussorgsky was an alcoholic officer in the Preobrazhensky regiment, and Rimsky Korsakov was an officer in the Russian navy. And their direct combined legacy has included Scriabin, Glazounov, Stravinsky, Rachmaninoff, Prokofiev and Shostakovich!

The national idea in music is not everywhere equal. It reflects the environment as well as the heredity of various nations. Perhaps, it may also be a question of the quantity of the outward message and of the intensity of the suppression of the people. The songs of the North are intuitively more rugged and heroic than the songs of the South. Some national songs, like the Bohemian, lend themselves only awkwardly to the larger forms. At other times, the bigger burden of a greater national message unconsciously seeks a larger means of expression as in a symphony or an opera.

Of all the Slavic nations, Bohemia has the most cheerful and light-hearted folk songs. The polka, for example, originated in Bohemia. As the Poles are Slavs, Polish nationalistic music is to a certain extent imbued with the melancholy that is native to the Slavic nature. But their melancholy is of a poetic nature rather than a tragic character. And as a proud and free people, their music reflects a more heroic and determined character than that of Russia. The stately *polonaise*, which was the ceremonious court dance of ancient Poland, and the charming *mazurka*, the dance of the people, are part of their legacy.

The characteristic of Scandinavian songs is their elemental strength, a native ruggedness that is expressive of a sadness that is characterized not so much by the human emotion of sorrow as by that mystical and awesome feeling which comes from being alone with wild nature. The tunes are angular rather than graceful, with a wintry sweetness, and the music is filled with sweet poignant yearnings so reminiscent of their brief but blooming summers.

"The people invent; the composers only arrange." The music that follows captures the spirit of the people, a people struggling to be free, bearing the imprint of deep and virile ideas that are markedly national.

Tchaikovsky: Orchestral Works

To sympathize fully with the spirit of the nationalistic music of Russia, both composer and audience must be thoroughly familiar with the nature of the Russian landscape: from the waste of the steppes to the loneliness of summer, from the barbaric extravagance of the aristocracy to the sublime patience of the poor common people. There should also be a knowledge of Russian literature: of the epileptic tales of Dostoyevsky, the passion of Pushkin and the irony of Gogol, and the novels of Turgenieff and Tolstoi in which mysticism and realism are strangely blended. And nowhere was the unrest, the fatalism, and the vague aspirations towards a brighter and freer Russia more fully echoed than in the art of Tchaikovsky (1840 - 1893). Tchaikovsky was a Russian in the fullest meaning of the word. His melodies and harmonies of folk-song came from the countryside where he grew up, and since his earliest childhood he had been impressed by the indescribable beauty of Russian folk music. And from this source sprang his passionate love for the Russian character in all its aspects.

In 1887 Russia was at war, and Tchaikovsky, responsive to the temper of the times, composed the barbaric *Marche Slav*. It had an immense success and, being a stirring expression of the emotions that were then dominant in Russia, it was regarded by some as prophetic of the triumph of the Slavonic cause. Here is pure patriotic music, complete with the angry pounding of drums summoning a call to battle, the wailing chant of an oppressed people, the defiance expressed through a Serbian folk tune, the exultatative music of anticipated triumph displayed in a joyous dance and, finally, the strains of the Russian national anthem. The Serbian folk air is one that is customarily sung to the words: "Come, glittering sun, You do not shine the same." The *Marche* ends in a dashing and magnificent fanfare.

The *1812 Overture* commemorated the burning of the city of Moscow that broke the back of Napoleon and accelerated his eventual defeat. Here are resounding brass, rolling drums, challenging fanfare, thundering cannons, and jubilant church bells pealing out a mighty rejoicing. Russian folk tunes alternate with the French *Marseillaise* in whirling masses of tone, the music begins with the Russian hymn "God preserve Thy people" sounded with antiphonal majesty by the brass, and ends with the Russian national anthem, amidst the rolling of drums and the joyful reverberation of cathedral bells.

No less patriotic is the *Andante Cantabile* from his string quartet. The story goes that one day, while the composer was at work, he heard a plasterer singing beneath the window a sad and beautiful song which he could not dismiss from his thoughts. This song, mournful and tender, was an old tune loved by the Russian peasants, and it became the substance of the slow movement of Tchaikovsky's quartet. The entire movement is played with muted strings, producing a veiled and mystic tone. The mood is tenderly wistful, especially in the plucked cello piece in the middle section. "Never in the whole course of my life was I so proud of my creative power as when Leo Tolstoi, sitting by my side, listened to my *Andante Cantabile* while the tears streamed down his face." It is difficult to listen to this exceptionally beautiful piece without being similarly moved.

The *1812 Overture* has been performed in a number of iterations, that for orchestra alone, orchestra with chorus, orchestra with Carillons, orchestra with chorus and Carillons, and perhaps in other versions unknown to me. I like my *1812 Overture* performed with all the bells and whistles pulled, played at a high volume so that everybody can hear it down the street!

There are two compelling performances with orchestra, chorus and Carillons that are particularly persuasive. Sir Colin Davis and the Boston Symphony Orchestra recorded the work for Philips in the pre-digital era, and the results are still glorious today. The dynamic range of the recording is sufficiently broad to articulate Tchaikovsky's intentions amply clearly, and the choral accompaniment is outstanding from the start of the work to the finish. A similar performance by Neeme Jarvi and the Gothenberg Symphony Orchestra has been recorded by DG, and this performance, which benefits from slightly better sound that Davis, is available on DG.

Outstanding orchestral versions of the work include that of Fritz Reiner and the Chicago Symphony Orchestra, Zubin Mehta's Los Angeles Philharmonic Orchestra recording for London, and Daniel Barenboim's performance with the Chicago Symphony Orchestra for DG.

Of historical interest is a rather impressive reissued performance of the work by Antal Dorati with the Minneapolis Symphony Orchestra on a Mercury Living Presence CD which includes some of the first attempts to document cannons in the long playing medium. This recording has a slightly constricted dynamic range but, at over thirty years of age, it is admirable in its depiction of the battle scene. Other works on this disc are also worthy of a rehearing.

There are probably two dozen versions of the *1812 Overture* which are also excellent, two dozen of which are middling, and several which probably use artificial cannons that are outrageous, one being Karajan's 1966 version with the Berlin Philharmonic which is positively hilarious. The repetitive electronic cannon brings tears to my eyes with gales of laughter! How he thought this effective is beyond me! The reader is encouraged to audition these aforementioned performances as all will bring pleasure.

As for *Marche Slav*, this is a work which is close to my heart as I learned it at a very young age, perhaps the second or third work that I actually managed to master in my single digit years. The first performance I was exposed to was that of Eugene Ormandy and the Philadelphia Orchestra which later became an inadequate performance for a variety of reasons.

Currently, my two favorite recordings are that by Zubin Mehta and the Los Angeles Philharmonic and the Chicago Symphony Orchestra with Daniel Barenboim. What I like particularly about Barenboim's performance is that he fails to retard at the conclusion of the work which keeps the momentum of the performance going, and the recorded sound of this performance is particularly splendid.

Of more than historical interest is an outstanding performance by Fritz Reiner made for RCA close to the same time as Reiner's own *1812 Overture*. This is an exceptional performance which demonstrates the outstanding playing ability of the Chicago Symphony at the time and, despite its age, should not be missed by the interested listener.

Performances of the *1812 Overture* are often paired with *Marche Slav*, and if you're able to find a performance of the *Overture* with which you are satisfied, it more than likely will be faced with an equally satisfying performance of *Marche Slav*. These are short war horses for orchestra which are great for children to learn because of their brevity and their wit, but they are mainstays of the basic repertoire for adults to learn as well.

- (I) 1812 overture; (ii) Romeo and Juliet (fantasy overture); (iii) Serenade for strings in C
      DG Dig 439 468-2 (I) Gothenburg SO, Jarvi (ii) Phil O, Sinopoli (iii) Orpheus CO
- Marche Slav; 1812 overture; Capriccio italien
      DG 400 035. Chicago SO, Barenboim

Dvorak: Slavonic Dances

Dvorak's first set of *Slavonic Dances* injected a breath of fresh country air into the drawing rooms of Europe. Like Byron, the composer awoke to find himself famous and be able to look back upon the times of darkness and disappointment as a man looks back upon his dreams. Their quick and unexpected popularity resulted from them being at the right time at the right place. Nationalism was beginning to sweep the Slavic spirit, and the *Slavonic Dances* came as a distinct revelation. They seemed to spring directly from the soul of the people and capture the Slavic character in every musical phrase—the stormy high spirited moods, the whimsical merriment, the charm, the touch of coquetry, and the ardent tenderness of the lyrical passages. It is absurd to listen to this music indoors—this is open-air music, to be played with good wine and hearty food in the congenial company of village folk, with the hills and forests all around.

Indirectly, it was Brahms who precipitated Dvorak (1841 - 1904) to fame by recommending his music to the publisher Simrock. The Bohemian composer was commissioned to write a set of *Slavonic*

Dances in the style of Brahm's popular *Hungarian Dances*, and he composed them for piano duet but scored them at the same time for orchestra. Unlike Brahms who had been guilty of "stealing" his melodies for his arrangements, Dvorak's tunes were original and his orchestration individual, with a heavenly naturalness surging through them. The music is alive in every part with new detail and coloring, and fascinating melodies and harmony. He created a large variety of moods while still retaining their elemental quality, from the terrific vitality of the *furiants* and the wistful music of the gypsies to the charm of the *sousedska,* one of the most delightful of all dances. Moreover, he was not particularly concerned about keeping strictly to one type of dance within a single piece: the seventh dance, for example, begins in the style of a Moravian *tetka*; when it becomes more agitated it resembles a galloping *kvapik*, and it also contains elements of the *skocna* and *vrtak*.

Whereas the first set of *Slavonic Dances*, comprising dances native to Bohemia, is almost strictly Czech in style, the second set is Slavonic in a more broader sense, with a feeling that is predominantly Yugoslav or Little Russian.

The Slavonic Dances by Dvorak are major contenders in the orchestra repertory, and one of the earliest works I recommend new listeners to learn. Each dance is anywhere from 3 to 8 minutes, and the vitality and infectiousness of the rhythms cannot be denied. There are excellent recordings available of these works combined on single CDs by Previn and the Vienna Philharmonic, Antal Dorati and the London Symphony, Kubelik and the Bavarian Radio Symphony Orchestra, Istvan Kertesz and the Israel Philharmonic Orchestra and, most notably, George Szell and the Cleveland Orchestra. There are incomplete versions of equal repute by Fritz Reiner and the Vienna Philharmonic on London, one of his few appearances on that label. While Previn has the finest sound of all, performances by Kubelik and Szell top my list for all time favorites, especially as they are highly idiomatic interpretations.

- Slavonic Dances
  Sony SBK 48161. Cleveland O, Szell

- Slavonic Dances
  DG Originals 457 712-2GOR. Bavarian SO, Kubelik

Mussorgsky: Pictures at an Exhibition

Modest Mussorgsky (1839 - 1881) was an unfinished musician, a composer of great instinct rather than polish, and he remained voluntarily ignorant of the principles of his art. His music was uneven and angular with rough, bizarre and inexplicable harmonies, harsh measures and disagreeable exaggerations; his genius was audacious and original. But he loved and understood the Russian people—good and bad, wise and foolish—with his whole heart, and in this love he found his inspiration. The Russian landscape and the Russian people revealed themselves to Mussorgsky as they had done to Tolstoi, and Russian humility and Russian compassion struck him as Dostoevsky had been touched. Like them, he displayed devotion to the wretched, to the poor and to the criminal, all of them as creatures of God. The human experiences in Russian peasant huts and fields inspired him, and in every simple conversation he found a revelation into the peasant soul, true though artless, as in the song of the poor idiot begging for the love of a pretty girl, and in the expressions of the peasants trudging through the snow as laughing, singing country girls run playfully towards them. And in the fanatical hate that he felt against everything formal and technical, as against the intellectuals in art, there was something of the great hate that filled Tolstoi—a hate against all forms of civilization that barred the way to God. Mussorgsky was a Russian of the common Russians.

He did not sing of love, the habitual theme for songs, but of people in their profound misery, of the joys and sorrows of children, and of life and its petty absurdities. He carried polemics and satire into music. He was original through the variety, truth and depth of the sentiment that he expressed, in the wealth of his shading, in the light pleasantry, almost farce, of his comedy, and in the gaiety and even in the tragedy of his humor. His choruses were not the conventional groups of the past but of real people, a multitude of living and impassioned beings. His popular scenes were truthful, animated, highly colored and intense, with a natural inclination towards violence and brutality. But bizarre and formless as his music often was, it had a force of expression and a dramatic accent of which no one could deny the intensity and, when happily inspired, it produced a profound and lasting impression.

Musically, the *Pictures at an Exhibition* show the composer at his most characteristic. It is a musical record of a visit to a posthumous exhibition of the paintings of his artist friend Viktor Hartmann, and the piece describes his reaction to each of the artist's compositions. The darting, pausing, limping gnome (*gnomus*) and the heavy lumbering ox cart (*bydlo*) are more vivid than those which work out musical stylizations of realistic sound: the squabbling children in the Tuileries garden, and the chatter of women in Limoges market. *Baba-Yaga* describes the most striking creation of Russian folk lore—a tall and bony, hideous old woman with an excessively long nose and disheveled hair who lives in a cottage standing on fowl's legs, and who travels abroad in an iron mortar that she propels with a pestle. The double portrait of the two Jews, one fat and pompous, the other whining and begging, deserves a place beside the best of song caricatures; it is perhaps the *ne plus ultra* of instrumental characterization. The *Heroes Gate at Kiev* makes an imposing crown to this work. The music, which evokes a gigantic procession through the gate, with brilliantly colorful pageantry and chanting, is typically Mussorgskian in its middle: pealing bells seem to fling their wild harmonies from stately Byzantine turrets, and the splendid and powerful music rises spaciously to a cosmic intensity as sonorous brass and tolling percussion joyfully reach a deafening climax.

This work, not unlike the Brahms' *St. Antoni Variations*, comes in two versions—piano and orchestra. Fortunately or unfortunately, the orchestral version comes in a series of different orchestrations, of which we will concern ourselves here principally with the Ravel orchestration.

173

I learned the work on the piano version, and have always had a special place in my heart for Vladimir Ashkenazy's original recording of the work for London made in 1967. This is a brilliant performance, recorded with close-in sound, and remains a highly competitive version. At the same time, the epitome version of the work is probably the performance by Sviatslov Richter recorded in Sophia, Bulgaria during the month of February, 1958, when seemingly everybody in the audience had an upper respiratory infection. Nevertheless, the playing is transcendental, and the tempi chosen for the conclusion of the Great Gate of Kiev are stunningly quick. This recording, I believe, may only be available as part of a Richter retrospective, but the listing below is a single CD which may still be available.

Other outstanding performances of the work include Ashkenazy's second traversal of the work for piano, Lazar Berman's performance for DG, Alfred Brendel's performance for Philips, Barry Douglas' performance for RCA, Mikhail Pletnev's performance for Virgin, and Ivo Pogorelich's recording for DG.

Concerning the orchestral versions available using Ravel's score, it is difficult to choose one single performance. Even in monophonic sound, the recording by Rafael Kubelik and the Chicago Symphony on Mercury Living Presence CD remains a tribute to the all too brief association of Kubelik with this august body of musicians.

Subsequent to Kubelik, the conductor Fritz Reiner recorded what may be considered the epitome orchestral version of the piece with the Chicago Symphony for RCA. Bud Herseth rings out the opening promenade theme on his trumpet in such a way that he seems to say, "This work is ours." This may be the case, as the Chicago Symphony has recorded the work subsequently with Solti, Giulini, and Jarvi. It seems to me, however, that each successive performance following Reiner led on to a downhill course, albeit very slowly. Giulini's performance is truly outstanding, Solti's is very good, but Jarvi's should not have been recorded. It is not that it is bad; it is simply that there are many better. Other performances of the work include Claudio Abbado's two performances, one with the London Symphony Orchestra which I prefer, and his later recording with the

Berlin Philharmonic which probably is equally good but doesn't captivate me quite as well.

Herbert von Karajan recorded the work in 1966 with the Berlin Philharmonic, and his remake in the late eighties is nowhere near as compelling. This is one of Karajan's better efforts on disc, and probably should be heard. The Philadelphia Orchestra recorded the work with Riccardo Muti for EMI in a very exciting, race to the finish performance, in 1979. The excellent analog sound and brilliant dynamic range of the recording make it a highly competitive version.

Finally, Guiseppe Sinopoli has recorded the work with the New York Philharmonic in excellent digital sound for DG. Comparing this performance to earlier attempts by the new York Philharmonic, including those by Bernstein and Mehta, it appears that the vast majority of the orchestral body has been replaced by retirement and attrition, and the New York Philharmonic in this recording sounds like a truly fine ensemble which it has not for many years. The recorded sound, further, is brilliant.

Alternative orchestral versions of the work are numerous, but I would like simply to mention that Stokowski's interpretation on London Phase Four is probably not worth hearing. It is vulgar and tasteless. The pianist, Vladimir Ashkenazy orchestrated the work himself and it is paired with his second keyboard version of the work on London. I am not enamored of this performance.

By comparison, however, a performing orchestral version of the work by Sergei Gortschakov and Leo Funtek as interpreted by the Toronto Symphony Orchestra under the leadership of Jukka-Pekka Saraste for Finlandia Records is extremely interesting, and is delivered in truly outstanding sound. Those looking for an alternative version of the work would best be served by this monumental performance which is recorded in some of the very best sound I have encountered.

- Pictures at an Exhibition (piano version)
  London 425 045-2LM. Askenazy

- Pictures at an Exhibition (piano version)
  Philips 420 774-2. Richter

- Pictures at an Exhibition (arr. Ravel)
  RCA RCD1-5407. Chicago SO, Reiner
- Pictures at an Exhibition (arr. Ravel)
  DG 429 785-2. NYPO, Sinopoli
- Pictures at an Exhibition (Gortschakov & Funtek)
  Finlandia 0630-14911-2. Toronto SO, Saraste

Rimsky-Korsakov: Scheherazade

The honor to have composed the first Russian symphony goes to Nicolai Rimsky-Korsakov (1844 - 1908). But the composer was fully cognizant of the strong and weak sides of his remarkable talent. He lacked the imagination, warmth and passion necessary for broad, original and firmly defined orchestral works, and he therefore avoided music drama that was founded on real or historical subjects. But he was a musical colorist and landscape painter, the Degas of music, and his landscapes were delightfully attractive. And so he turned to themes of fantasy and fairy land, bearing the imprint of his Russian nationality. He loved nature and the Russian legends that nature inspired. He was inclined to the song form and had an intimate knowledge of folk songs which he employed in his works with indisputable originality, and in which he found his most felicitous and melodious inspiration.

Scheherezade is a four-movement suite inspired by the *Arabian Nights* in which the fair, sensual and fawning storyteller spins many marvels and tales of adventure. It is a keen work in Oriental musical bravura with strange tonalities and skillfully blended orchestral color. A pedagogue might stray aside sadly in his judgment of this work that requires the imagination of the listener to be in sympathy with the imagination of the composer for a full enjoyment. For, this symphonic poem provokes swooning thoughts such as come to partakers of the leaves and flowers of cannabis and the poppy; here are stupefying perfumes of frankincense and sandal wood. The melody of this music is wild, melancholy and exotic, a droning such as falls from the lips of white-bearded and turbaned men garrulous in the sun; and then again there is the reckless chatter of the babbler in the market place, drunk with unmixed wine.

Here is music where Orientalism runs riot—the billowing sea peopled with fantastical monsters, the beating of drums and the calls of the wood winds, dances that heat the blood to a boiling fever, and the intoxication of bare flesh whirling to maddening rhythms. The music tells of Sinbad the explorer, and of the incredible adventures of the Kalandar Prince who spent a mad evening with a porter and three ladies of Baghdad. And then there is Scheherazade, the wily narrator, who too is merely a gossamer shape in a dream. She fades away, and her soul dies on a high note exhaled by a wondering violin.

I must confess to have never enjoyed this work! Perhaps it is too programmatic for me, and too repetitive. Truthfully, I find it an annoyance, and yet I admit that it is one of the great works for large orchestra that has ever been written, and the orchestration is a work of genius. The composer began as an officer in the Russian army and wrote music as an avocation; he ended up a renowned professor of music who produced some illustrious students.

To my mind, there are three great recordings of this work, and no matter how good the ne'er do wells, if you have one of these three, you need no other. Don't miss Fritz Reiner's excellent recording in early stereophonic sound with the Chicago Symphony. It is absolutely worth its mid-price status despite being nearly forty years old. The late Russian conductor, Kiril Kondrashin, recorded the work for Philips, and this compelling performance is perhaps more intelligible than Reiner's, but certainly not more elegant. The best recorded of the three, and equally as well stated and depicted is that by Sir Charles Mackerras on Telarc, a domestic label which produces recordings of exceedingly high engineering refinement, if not always of equally compelling performances. This is one of Telarc's greatest efforts and most successful recordings.

If the listener is in the mood for a performance which best demonstrates the attributes of a stereo system, then the Mackerras is one of the great recordings of the CD era for this purpose.

- Scheherezade; Capriccio espanol
  Telarc Dig CD 80208. LSO, Sir Charles Mackerras

Smetana: Ma Vlast

Nationalistic feelings first stirred in Bohemia shortly after the French Revolution, but no strong political movements were developed until the revolutions of 1830 and 1848. Friedrich Smetana (1824 - 1884) was the first to channel Bohemian nationalistic aspirations into music, and he alone was responsible for establishing a broadly based Czech style which embraced far more than the basic elements of Czech art music and folk song. He did not rely on specific folk-songs. He sought his own national style—his musical individuality grew up intimately with his love of the soil—that blended with the true life of his people and their songs and legends. And this very individuality made him not only great among his own compatriots, but great among modern composers. He preserved the proper relations between music and art—the ever flowing melody in the orchestra should never interrupt nor disturb the dramatic sense which, in turn, should display a consistent physiognomy. The use of music was to characterize the dramatic events and their individualization through the *leit-motive.* The charm of Smetana to the outside world lies in the fact that while the national character remains the foundation of his thought, he knew how to clothe national Bohemian music in modern and high forms, and at the same time remain truly original: always himself, always Smetana.

Like Beethoven, Smetana suffered from deafness, and in 1874 he was obliged to give up his activity as a conductor. Money was needed for consulting foreign medical specialists, and to gain the means Smetana gave a concert in which he performed two symphonic poems, *Vysehrad* and *Vltava.* These pieces soon became part of a cycle of nationalistic symphonic poems bearing the general title of *Mein Vaterland* or *Ma vlast,* dedicated to the city of Prague.

The first of these, *Vysehrad,* bears the inscription on the score, "In a condition of ear suffering." The bard is reminded of the sight of the fortress Vysehrad, of the songs of the legendary singer Lumir, and he sees the palace in its former glory with its assemblage of knights and he hears the triumphant song of the warriors. And then he sees the decline of the ancient glory. There are wars and battles, the noble hall falls into ruin and decay, and Vysehrad now stands deserted and forsaken—a mere picture of its past glory. And yet, the echo of the lyre of Lumir is still heard amidst the ruins.

The second piece, *Vltava* (*The Moldeau*) bears the inscription: "In complete deafness." The symphonic poem tells of two springs which, gushing forth in the shade of a Bohemian forest, unite and form the Moldeau river. The river, a mighty stream, flows through thick woods and open countryside. In its quiet waters are reflected many a fortress and castle, witnesses to a splendid bygone age of chivalry, solitary guardians of a vanished martial fame that is no more. The sound of horns in a joyful chase is heard in the music, and peasants dance their merry dances in wedding festivities. And at night, when the moon shines, water nymphs prance beside the silver waters under star-cool skies.

Sara, the third, takes its title from a valley, north of Prague, which was named after one of the noblest mythical Bohemian amazons. The fourth bears the title *From Bohemia's Fields and Groves*; the fifth, *Tabor,* the stronghold from which the Taborites took their name, introduces their famous war chant. The final piece is *Blank,* named after the mountain on which the warriors are supposed to sleep until they shall be called to fight again for their country's freedom.

The Moldau is one of six movements of a large orchestra work written to depict the composer's homeland; the aggregate work, *Ma Vlast* (better known to those who love the work as My Blast) is not always compelling and exciting, but this single movement is perhaps one of the greater fifteen minutes of Smetana's fifteen minutes of fame, per the artist Andy Warhol.

The Moldau is exceedingly well served on record, but my favorite performances are by Hungarian conductors, Szell on Sony Classical, and Dohnanyi on London, the latter quite a recent release. Other outstanding issues include each of the four performances of the work that Rafael Kubelik made during his lifetime, with my favorite being that which he performed with the Boston Symphony Orchestra for DG in 1972. This is readily available on DG at mid price.

Of interest to the listener may well be the most unusual perform-ance of the work released to date. The conductor, Sir Roger Nor-rington, has committed to disc a complete *Ma Vlast* using original instruments and his outstanding band, the London Classical Players. This, too, is as equally exciting as either Szell or Dohnanyi, and is in brilliant recorded sound.

Any of the performances enumerated above should please. Most are accompanied by other parts of the cycle of *Ma Vlast*, so when looking only for the *Moldau*, be certain to look under the heading of Smetana's *Ma Vlast* at your local purveyor.

- The Moldau (From Ma Vlast)
  Decca Dig 444 867-2. Cleveland O, Dohnanyi
- The Moldau (From Ma Vlast)
  Virgin Veritas CDC 72435 4530128. London Classical Players, Norrington

Grieg: Peer Gynt Suite No 1

Music has always been a cultivated art in Scandinavia. The finding of relics of ancient musical instruments such as the *Lur* in the peat bogs of Denmark is evidence for early instrumental music in the region. But it was the legends, traditions, folk-songs, scenery, and the freedom of gesture and motion characteristic of the peasant life of his native Norway that Edvard Grieg (1843 - 1907) imbued into a new world of vivid, picturesque and lively nationalistic music. Natu-ral beauty filled him perpetually with a self-renewing sense of wonder—wonder at the skylines of birch, pine and fir, vistas of near-vertical mountainside, vast awesome forests, streams, waterfalls and moss-grown stone. And in his native folk-music, the sad and somber songs and the lively dances, instinctive as it was with the life-spirit of the Norwegian countryside and its peasantry, he discovered a whole new vehicle for color and atmosphere to evoke the mood and capture the soul of a natural scene. Grieg became the first nature mystic in music. "In his eyes," said a visitor of Grieg, "one catches a glimpse of Norway."

Grieg was a miniaturist. He learned to depict, not grossly, but fastidiously and subtly; his music became suggestion rather than categorical statement of fact. He painted his orchestral colors in fragile tints rather than with flaming colors. Like the man himself, the sounds are gentle, tender and delicate. And his lines fall in easy places: to paint the midnight sun, to gaze upon the tiniest petals of beautiful wild flowers, and to create the sweet sounds of an evening wind in the trees. Here and there, a touch of the wild barbarity of a Viking warrior makes itself felt by a certain robustness, abruptness and ruggedness in harmonic changes, and in rhythms so irregular as to be almost without rhythm. But the passion is seldom very deep or fierce. Of course, it is not contended that the beauties of Grieg's music lie all on the surface, but they are scattered so thickly there that no one averse to diving deep need do so.

In his allegorical poetic drama *Peer Gynt*, (Pare Yoont is about as near as you can get to it in English), Henrik Ibsen drew on Norse folk legend to create a story of a rough Norwegian lad who worries his mother and all his older friends by his fantastic talk and his wild dream of adventures. Six years after its premiere, Ibsen revised his play and asked Grieg to write the incidental music for it. For, *Peer Gynt* is a masterpiece of Norwegian literature, a fantastic drama in rhymed verse, full of scenes that can haunt a composer and compel him to give them musical expression. And the more Grieg saturated his mind with the poem, the more clearly he saw it as a work of much witchery, deeply permeated with the Norwegian spirit. And so began a collaboration between Norway's greatest playwright and its leading composer to firmly establish that country's fame to a full-scale artistic nationalism, as well as give it a place in the mainstream of world culture. Soon after its first performance, Grieg divided his score into two orchestral suites, the first of which is his most popular symphonic work.

The music of the movement, *Morning*, is breathtaking, and exquisitely transmutes into sound the sensation, light and color of a natural phenomenon—the first glimmerings of sunrise over high mountain peaks. The sun mounts in the sky, birds trill, and soft breezes come in from the sea. The orchestra, shaped and finished as by a master craftsman, is remarkably evocative of those clear but mysteriously melancholic mornings that are such features of the enchanting but all too fleeting Scandinavian summer. The lovely melody has suggestions of yodelling in the mountains and of cow-bells. It is difficult to explain why the reedy sound of an oboe against the ruffled silkiness of a sustained string triad can be so captivating! The silvery ripple of flutes playing with a clarinet, while a solo horn has the melody, creates an atmosphere of unmatched beauty, and then gentle horn fanfares, sounding further and further away into the distance over trilling flutes and oboes, recall a huntsman's call.

For the rest, Aase's death music is deeply pathetic and can move a listener who knows nothing of Peer Gynt, Anitra's dance which begins like a waltz is charming, and the Dovregubben orgy is a riotous piece of weird fun.

This music, while it is indeed no doubt great, does not strike me as being of the stature of many other composers referenced in this text, but saying so is not to belittle Grieg's efforts. I feel his Piano Concerto and vocal music are far more compelling. However, *Peer Gynt* is a work well worth learning, and I would suggest that the listener obtain the complete incidental music, and simply not the *Suite* for orchestra to *Peer Gynt*.

To that end, I have only one recommendation for this work, and that is the recording on DG of Neeme Jarvi and the Gothenburg Symphony Orchestra, which was originally issued in a complete box of the complete orchestral and vocal music of the composer. If one purchases the complete set of the works of Grieg, one will also learn the true protean nature of this relatively under-applauded composer.

- Peer Gynt (Incidental Music)
  DG Dig 423 079-2. Gothenburg SO, Jarvi

Sibelius: Symphonic Poems

Few great composers have equaled Sibelius (1865 - 1957) in terms of longevity. When he was born, Berlioz was still alive and Liszt was in his prime. During his long life, he passed through the "contemporary" music of Tchaikovsky, Dvorak and Brahms. When he died in 1957, the language of music had become unbelievably transformed. Throughout his life, Sibelius expressed a profound fascination for the folk lore of his native Scandinavia. And nowhere did his discoveries of the grand landscape of Finnish mythology become more articulated than in his symphonic poems. They spanned the whole of his creative career, from the full-blooded romanticism of his youthful years in *En Saga* (meaning, *A Saga*) to the monumental *Tapiola* of the great master.

In *En Saga*, rich in melody and full of strange and savage orchestral color, he set the stage for the atmosphere of a Nordic saga. The music comes fresh from pagan soil, untainted by long or refined culture. There is no story in this piece, no great demands on the powers of concentration or comprehension; just an evocation of a magical atmosphere in majestic sound that leaves the listeners free to supply its tale from their own fantasy.

On the other hand, the *Four Legends* each have a tale to tell that is inspired by Finland's epic poem, the *Kalevala*. *The Swan of Tuonela*, the black guardian of the portals to the Finnish underworld, floats with icy serenity along the dark and rapid waters that surround the land of death, singing her lonely song. The haunting melody is chanted expressively by an English horn, and the whole music unfolds the brooding, evil beauty of this magnificent scene. Inspiration runs high in the story of *Lemminkainen*, the typical hero of Nordic mythology, and the *Maidens of the Island*. Here is music both passionate and tender, rhythmic and dance-like, as the young hero frolics with the lonely maidens while their husbands are away at war, but is forced to leave upon their return. Their parting is indeed sweet sorrow, and he departs to the repeated farewells of grieving wood winds emulating the cries of the cranes and geese that had flocked the fairy island. In a companion story, *Lemminkainen in Tuonela*, our hero is killed just as he is on the point of shooting the black Swan. Trembling strings surge forward insistently with an irrepressible magnetic force as the black waters of the River of Death sweep the hero's dead body to the realm of Tuonela. The music is unbearably beautiful and awe-inspiring, evoking powerfully the dark and sombre colors of the legend.

Even if Sibelius had written nothing else, the felicitous and atmospheric tone picture of *Tapiola* would have indicted him into the hall of the great masters. Here is an elaborate network of magical sounds transformed into the most exquisite hues and tints of the ancient and mysterious, bestial landscape of Tapiola, kingdom of the forest god Tapio. Here is an unexplored and unpeopled land of unending sunless forests where dusky trees stand widespread in the gloom, and wood-sprites weave magic secrets and savage dreams. Massive brass play imaginatively with wood winds and strings to create the variety of moods, color and sounds, and the terror and majesty of the vast forests. Yet underneath this immense loneliness there is a longing for human contact.

There are few comprehensive compilations of the major Sibelius tone poems; most are available individually tacked onto the conclusion of a Sibelius symphony on CD or are associated with the violin concerto in a similar manner. I grew up with one superb compilation showcasing the Orchestre de la Suisse Romande under the baton of Horst Stein, known for his appearances at the Wagner Bayreuth Festival and for a rather excellent cycle of the Beethoven Piano Concerti with Fredrich Gulda, released only at budget price in the USA on London Stereo Treasury. Stein is capable of extracting such exacting performances that one would be convinced that this was a rather tight Vienna Philharmonic or Chicago Symphony performance, but indeed, the source is an orchestra not normally associated with the composer Sibelius. These four poetic works jump to life with vibrant playing, truly superb acoustics and engaging readings from a far under-recorded, almost unknown group of musicians. Find this disc, and you will care for no one else's *Finlandia*, no matter how well played. The other works are all in state of the art appearance, and have never sounded more brilliant, despite the analog sound of almost twenty years ago.

If Horst Stein's recordings are not available, one could then consider *Finlandia* as performed by Vladimir Ashkenazy and the Boston Symphony Orchestra on London, and the other principal Tone Poems as conducted by Sir Colin Davis on his new BMG or former Philips Symphony Cycles. Herbert von Karajan's Sibelius tryptiques on DG are also excellent, as are Sir Simon Rattle's on EMI. Any of these will please, but Stein's recording is unique.

There is also a new compilation of Sibelius tone poems on the Finlandia label, conducted by the highly capable and dynamic conductor Andrew Davis.

- Tone Poems
  London 4176972DC. Orchestre de la Suisse Romande, Horst Stein
- Tone Poems
  Finlandia 0630-15242-2. Royal Stockholm Philh, Andrew Davis

Verdi: Aida

Giuseppe Verdi (1813 - 1901) set the world to music. His operas encompass the theocratic ancient Egypt of *Aida* and the bigoted Babylon of *Nabucco*, the imperial Spain of *Don Carlos* and the licentious Italian Renaissance of *Rigoletto*, the provincial German courts of *Luisa Miller* and the contemporary Parisian demimonde of *La Traviata*. Like Shakespeare, Verdi heard everyone at once and lavished music luxuriously on all people alike.

Tragedy was to affect profoundly this man and his music. Verdi had scarcely begun his career when an unknown disease carried off his wife and two children. For a moment the heart of the master failed him. But he had his life to live and his work to do, and his genius drove him on. Italy was groaning under Austrian misrule, and love of country, if not of life, was strong in him. And with his music, as Garibaldi did with his armies, he determined to set the Italian nationalistic spirit free. He made his music the life source of his people, their means of salvation. To sing is a symptom of vital courage as when Aida taunts Amneris by declaring herself equal in rank. The voice which is the body's proud possession also serves as a conduit for the spirit, and Verdi bestowed it upon his countrymen as their means of spiritual redress.

With his second opera *I Lombardi*, Verdi launched his patriotic campaign against the Austrian censor. And Verdi all but had the operatic battlefield to himself—Rossini had retired, Donizetti was dying, and Bellini had already died, pitifully young. The libretto did not treat directly of Italy's wrongs, but it had verses susceptible of patriotic interpretation, and even the presence of the police could not silence the tumultuous demonstration by an audience whose heart had been stirred, in a simple and eloquent way, when the chorus began the broad and stately hymn to liberty, "O God of all nations."

Aida is an opera for the ages that never ceases to captivate. From the confines of the desert, conveyed from memory to memory, across the thousands of years separating us from it, this struggle between the two heroines comes down to us, vibrant and alive.

A Nubian chieftain's daughter who is now enslaved in Egypt, the young Aida is handmaiden to the Princess Amneris from whom she has hidden her own noble origins. The two women discover themselves to be rivals in love of the hero, Radames, who is appointed to lead the Egyptians against the African hordes commanded by Aida's father Amonosro. Radames returns home victorious with Amonosro in chains. Here are all the ingredients for high drama in the tumult in Aida's heart: devoted to her father, fearful for her lover, and the slave of her rival in whose power she must live. The code of classical heroism is brutalized in Radames when military honor overrides personal loyalty. Aida's crisis comes when, bullied by the captured Amonasro, she is made to betray her lover rather than her country. Opposite the strong, savage and fair Amneris, replete with the violence, dignity and anger of an Egyptian princess, is Aida—black, weak and gentle, a slave. The Egyptian is condemned to live as an authoritarian queen, and the Nubian woman is condemned to die. The first one finds herself back with her animal-headed Egyptian Gods, the second carries out her death, locked alive in a stone crypt with her lover.

There are no monasteries here to retire to; truth must take refuge in fugitive vocal asides. Aida's is the still small voice of personal affection, trying to make itself heard through cohorts of opposition, reduced eventually to ineffectual pleading. Ultimately, in this world of sound and fury that signifies nothing, the only vocal integrity lies in silence. Aida is self-protectively mute, prevented from owning to her identity. A weight impends above everyone, finally made visible when a huge stone slab is lowered to seal the lovers alive in their tomb. And in the end, this grandest of operas ends almost in a whimper, in the last suffocated duet of the dying lovers and the muffled interjections of Amneris, now a figure shrouded in black, kneeling upon the stone that seals the vault, imploring the Gods to give her adored one peace.

There are many outstanding recordings of *Aida*, but one stands out in my opinion, for its contributions by cast, chorus and orchestra alike. The Abbado recording meets all of my requirements for this proverbial, classic operatic work, and is depicted in a dramatic, emotional but yet unaffected interpretation. Great laud is owed to Abbado for a reading which is so unaffected that I feel that the listener is exposed simply to Verdi, and Verdi alone without manipulation or histrionics.

Another classic recording of the work is by Karajan and the Vienna Philharmonic from a much earlier vintage, and while the sound is by no means in the Abbado class, it, too, can be highly recommended, especially as it comes from a period in that conductor's past which was decidedly free of eccentricity.

- Aida
  DG 410092. La Scala O and Chorus, Abbado

The Age of Opulence

The nineteenth century—bustling, working and pushing—came to an end with a triumphant shout. And what an opulent era (1870-1900) it had been! The departing spirit had much reason to be satisfied for it had accomplished much: the lot of the working class had been improved with industrialization, middle-class prosperity had boomed, a multitude of inventions had made life more comfortable, and strange and shiny machines held out new hope for a better world. Splendor was all around, all that glittered did indeed seem like gold, and it was a marvelous time to be alive.

Everything had to be big to be good! There was a military elegance and picturesque glamour in court life, public buildings were decorated with fat symbolic friezes and supported by bloated columns, and ladies and gentlemen posed gracefully as they strolled through international expositions of science and industry, drove in elegant coaches through the *Bois* or around the *Ringstrasse*, took the waters at Baden Baden, and glittered in gowns of taffeta and tulle in opulent boxes at the opera. Cast-iron columns, the steam engine, wood-pulp paper, synthetic dyes, fertilizers, celluloid and silk substitutes, anesthesia and antisepsis, all seemed poised to change man's life. Socialism, nationalism, scientism and realism—these were the watchwords of the age of opulence.

It was an age of excruciating duality. On the one hand, the new writers of *La Belle Epoche* raised the voice of conscience to create a greater awareness of social conditions through their social dramas and social novels. On the other, the poets of *The Gay Nineties* journeyed through half-closed lids into a dream world, putting on not only rose-colored glasses (*couleur de rose*) but glasses tinted blue and purple as well. Fantasy flourished, and the "symbolists" and "decadents," or whatever they were

189

called, splashed color luxuriously onto verse to create a luscious imagery and play with love—love transient and insubstantial, love frankly erotic with the charm of the physical unlaced with self-conscious provocation. Vice was made virtue, be it only a paper vice under a paper moon. Gustav Klimt painted pictures and ceiling designs in which modern colors were blended with Byzantine gold; passion gleamed seductively from the dark eyes of beautiful women whose nude bodies were coiled around one another like snakes. And music strove to evoke the same artfully colored luster, the same decorative glamour, and the same erotic heat.

All this newness, this desire for experimentation, this curiosity to reach a hitherto closed world, this delving into the subconscious strata of the mind, and this love of color was absorbed into the music of the opulent era. To the testimony of words was added the audible evidence of sound. Classic romanticism was still strong: the mighty sonorities of the symphonies of Brahms expressing emotions mastered and carefully directed belonged, with all their newness, to the tradition. But others spoke a new language influenced by the world around them as expressed in Mahler's First Symphony, in the seemingly inexhaustible melodies of the ballets and symphonies of Tchaikovsky, in the sophisticated wit of Offenbach's operas, the ebullience and unforced gaiety of the waltzes of the swarthy Johann Strauss, and in the lavish, free-flowing decorative music of Camille Saint Saens. And above them all, Richard Wagner gave a totally new dimension to music drama when he combined song and an expanded orchestra to tell complex stories in dazzling edifices of sound. Wagner portrayed in large pictures all the phenomena of nature: the Rhine flowed broad and majestic, storms raged, a rainbow formed an arched bridge above the clouds, the moon threw its silver rays upon the gabled roofs of Nuremberg, and flower beds glittered when the Good Friday sun shone down upon them.

Johann Strauss the Younger : Waltzes

Nowhere was the pleasure and ease, the splendor and the luxury, of the age of opulence better evoked than in the grace and delicacy of the waltz. Here was beauty without heaviness, levity without vulgarity, gaiety without frivolity, and a strange mixture of exuberant musical richness and popular simplicity that charmed the hours of youth and renewed the youth of old. And in Vienna, where the waltz was a narcotic more potent than alcohol, the undisputed arch-magician and Waltz-King, Johann Strauss the Younger (1825 - 1899), reigned over an orchestra that gushed out his melodies through an instrumental choir of two hundred spirited musicians who drove his audience to passions bordering on mad fury.

Weber, Schubert and Beethoven had all belonged to the waltz genealogy, and Haydn and Mozart as well. Gifted minstrels had contributed to its rhythmic improvisation, but it was with Strauss that the waltz reached its magical blend of sentiment, brilliance, abandon, glitter and nostalgia. To a romantic city thirsting for gay life and seeking escape from a gnawing conviction of emptiness, the waltz provided a perfect salve. And nineteenth century Vienna waltzed feverishly.

In a way, the waltz was at once the clue to the Viennese temper and the city's rich history. In its lush flow was mirrored the melancholy sparkle of carnivals and cafe life, and in its entrancing spell the festive and pleasure-loving Viennese discovered their own ripe voluptuous love of life. From the Landler and folk dances of Bavaria and Bohemia, from city and countryside, from cafe and wine shop came the elements that coalesced into this new and great anthem: the Waltz.

The *Beautiful Blue Danube* is a series of short waltzes composed after the traditional Viennese fashion of combining many short, contrasting movements of similar type and meter. The well-known theme of the first of the eight waltzes in the series is said to have come to the composer at a concert where he heard someone quote the first lines of a poem on the river: "River so blue, So blue and bright." Fascinated by the rhythm of the words, he jotted the theme on his

191

stiff white cuff. And the alluring tune, which has brightened countless faces with its opening bar, would have been lost in the laundry forever had it not been for the sharp observation of his wife. It was first performed by a male chorus to accompany a political poem recited at an unsuccessful concert to uplift the spirits after the Austrian defeat by the Prussians. A purely orchestral version was put together the following year at the Paris World Exhibition. And the city went mad! It was performed every night, the Prince of Wales whistled it to his mother Queen Victoria, fish from the beautiful blue Danube was served at banquets, and the tune marched triumphantly through Europe into America. As long as the *Beautiful Blue Danube* lives, Vienna must linger in the hearts of humankind.

Unlike many waltzes that begin in a rather hesitant way, unlike some other waltzes that seem to float nebulously into the present from afar, *Voices of Spring* plunges right into a fast tempo to celebrate the joy which reflects the reappearance of sunshine and flowers that bathe the parks and gardens of Vienna at the birth of the new season. The *Emperor Waltz* was written in support of Franz Josef on the occasion of the fortieth anniversary celebration of the Emperor's reign that had remained strong despite the Anti-Hapsburgh revolution of 1848. The Hapsburgs have not endured; the waltz, their royal tribute, has. In the *Artist's Life*, we experience the grace and light-heartedness of an artist's life; *Vienna Blood*, perhaps better translated as Viennese Heart or The Spirit of Vienna, is a later work, and it captures the dreamy, heavy-lidded sensuality so typical of that city.
When Strauss died in 1899, something of Vienna died with him. He was buried at the side of Brahms and Schubert.

There are a litany of excellent recordings of the Strauss Waltzes in the catalogs, most of which are at least enjoyable if not good. At one time, the conductor Robert Stoltz undertook the responsibility to document the entire Strauss family output, and I'm not quite sure if this job was completed or not, but for many years, his recordings, currently not on CD in their entirety, were considered a staple for waltz lovers.

The then concertmaster of the Vienna Philharmonic, Willi Bosk-ovsky, took baton in hand and led the Vienna Philharmonic in a number of recordings of famous Strauss Family Waltzes, culminating in his 1979 recording for Decca/London which was that company's premier digital recording on two LPs.

Since that time, it seems to have been the job of major recording companies to document the Vienna Philharmonic's New Year's Day concert on an annual basis, often playing the very same works annually with different conductors and the same orchestra. I can't say that these are innovative programs, but any one of the 1979-1998 New Year's Day Concerts with the Vienna Philharmonic would make an excellent assortment of music by the Strauss Family, although in recent years, some conductors have selected works by other compos-ers.

If one is looking specifically for Strauss Family Waltzes, there is an outstanding budget disc by Karl Bohm and the Vienna Philhar-monic of some six waltzes which is utterly gorgeous from start to finish. I can say no more than to indicate that I'd be very happy with this collection, and it's more than enough Strauss for me.

For those seeking some more depth and a greater number of waltzes to demonstrate diversity, DG has reissued several LP releases by Herbert von Karajan and the Berlin Philharmonic Orchestra on DG Originals of some truly excellent Strauss Family Waltzes which demonstrate the pinnacle of playing by this august body of musicians. Karajan's Strauss is a bit more "slick" than Bohm's which is almost painfully Viennese, but either should provide you with great pleasure. Boskovsky's rather comprehensive collection on London (six CDs) is superb.

Several domestic orchestras have attempted Strauss programs, and while they are exquisitely well played (notably the Chicago Symphony Orchestra's recording with Barenboim and the Boston Pops with Arthur Fiedler), I think that these have to be ruled out of court because they really aren't *echt*.

- Waltzes
  DG Musikfest 423 681-2 GMF. VPO, Bohm

- Waltzes
  DG Originals 449 768-2 GOR. BPO, Karajan
- Waltzes
  London 455 254-2 LC6 (6). VPO, Boskovsky

Bruckner: Symphony No 4 (Romantic)

The question of Anton Bruckner's (1824 - 1896) place in the annals of music can hardly be said to be settled although he has left nine symphonies. Whatever may be the final answer to the question of the greatness of Bruckner's symphonies, there is no doubt that he had his full share of technical profundity and a striking mastery of melodious weaving. He certainly shows a freedom, ease and mastery in the symphonic manner and a sure control in the interweaving of his themes, even in his use of dual themes where the point lies in neither of the two motives but in the interplay of both. At times this complexity is almost marvelous in the clear simplicity of the concerted whole. Bruckner is here the schoolmaster, and his music is a splendid substrate and object lesson for future musicians. Some have called his early music *Gebrauchsmusik*, music written with devotion by a professional craftsman in the only idiom known to him, which was the Classical style. The one distinct drawback in Bruckner's symphonies, as some have pointed out, is a lack of the intrinsic beauty of the melodic ideas, and an absence of the strain of pathos that sings from the heart. For, of what gain is music that is impressive in its workmanship but denies the special charm of constant tuneful flow?

In the Fourth Symphony (*Romantic),* the main music is played on the wood winds. It is a symphony of wood winds where the forest horn is sovereign—a call of horns begins the work, awakening a widening world of echoes with a murmuring maze of lesser notes. The special quality in this music lies in the interweaving of its tapestry in which the horn blasts are but an interlude. In the *Andante*, the charm is less in the tune than in the delicate changing shades of harmony and tone colors. One is ever surprised in the gentlest of ways by which a horn enters among the whispering strings, or by the shock of a loud sudden blare. But one cannot be consoled for the want of a heartfelt melody.

The *Scherzo* is a kind of hunting piece (Bruckner at one time called it *The Hunting of the Hare*), full of the sparkle, color and romance of bugles and horns—a spirited fanfare broken by hushed phrases on the strings or wood winds, reminiscent of an elf-like mystic dance played on the softened call of trumpets. The *Trio* sings apart in a soft voice like a simple ballad between the gay revels, at times like a dance melody during the Huntsmen's meal. The *Finale* is conceived in mystical retrospect over mysterious murmuring strings, with long sustained notes in the wood winds and horn mingled in a soft carrilon of horns and trumpets. And in such mystic musings the music ends, slowly drawn out in a profoundly moving hymn, triumphant for its own sake. Here lies Bruckner's true poetic abode rather than in the passion and ecstasy of romance into which he was being vainly lured.

I came to Bruckner as a late teenager always erroneously presuming that his music and that of the music of Gustav Mahler were remarkably similar. Boy, did I get a wrong number! Bruckner speaks to me in a way that Mahler does not, in a somewhat ecclesiastical manner with broad brush strokes rather than somewhat hysterical gesticulating utterances.

I came to learn the Fourth Symphony first, while at camp one summer, in Otto Klemperer's performance on Angel S-36235, and I thought this to be the way the work should sound until many years later. It was recently reissued on EMI CD, and again at super budget prices on a label which has appropriated many elderly EMI recordings.

In 1973, the conductor Daniel Barenboim embarked on a complete Bruckner Symphony cycle with the Chicago Symphony Orchestra, with the first sessions occurring in the Medinah Temple in downtown Chicago. This was DG's first recording in the Midwest, and the recording had a protean dynamic range and perhaps even better than some of the London recordings of the era (with Solti) that demonstrated the peak abilities of this orchestra in terms of how loudly it could play. Loudness, however, in and of itself, was not an issue—this performance glows from beginning to end, and if it is slightly quirky, it is still a grand statement and perhaps my favorite recording of this work despite having heard at least thirty others since the recording was issued as DG 2530 336. Fortunately, the performance has been reissued.

Other excellent recordings of the Bruckner Fourth Symphony (Romantic) include that by Eugen Jochum and the Berlin Philharmonic Orchestra for DG, Martin Sieghart and the Bruckner Orchestra of Linz for Camerata, and twice by Gunter Wand and the Norddeutscher Rundfunk for BMG/RCA. Another interesting and worthy performance is by Wolfgang Sawallisch and the Philadelphia Orchestra for EMI.

Bruckner wrote symphonies which were edited in several editions, and because of this, some conductors have chosen to take alternative edition approaches to the performances of certain movements. The listener is encouraged to obtain Eliahu Inbal's recording of the Bruckner Fourth Symphony with the Frankfurt Radio Symphony Orchestra for Teldec. In particular, the third movement uses a different version which really is almost unrecognizable to those who know the Haas and Nowak scores. This is an interesting aside for those who develop a taste for Bruckner symphonies.

- Symphony Nos 4 (Romantic); 7
    DG 453 100-2 GTA2. Chicago SO, Barenboim

Bruckner: Symphony No 7

When Bruckner was working on his Seventh symphony, Richard Wagner, his idol, fell gravely ill. "I came home and was very sad. I thought to myself, it is impossible that the Master can live for a long time, and the *Adagio* came into my head." Bruckner's fears were well founded. Wagner passed away just as the final bars of the slow movement were being completed. As part of his tribute, Bruckner used the Wagnerian Bayreuth tuba that had been created by the

Master for his music-dramas, and composed a quartet in the slow movement to contrast the dark and smoky side of the tuba with the mellowness of horns and the brilliance of trombones and trumpets. From then on, the Wagner tuba was to remain an integral part of the later Bruckner symphonies.

The music of the Seventh symphony is mighty and massive; it is the composer's *magnum opus*, the least overbearing and his most consistently inspired work, and the one in which his aspiration towards grandoiseness and sublimity came closest to realization. But it is not easy to assimilate this work, nor is there any way to develop an appreciation of it except by repeated hearings.

The slow (*Adagio*) movement is among the most stirring pieces in the annals of music. It is a funeral march blending majesty with sorrow, the grief of a noble heart speaking of pain with restraint, touched with an otherworldly radiance. The voice of the composer's grieving, of his tenderness and exalting praise speaks out from this noble and impassioned elegy with subjugating eloquence and beauty—in the music of this sorrow, there is a curious intimation of immortality. A cymbal crash signals the climax. The first and fourth movements sound triumphant without forcing the issue, and the *scherzo* contrasts earthy jaunty rhythms with a touching lyrical introspection.

The symphony was performed at a concert dedicated to bid farewell to "the Master." Many years later, its funereal music was played once again for the several hundred persons who had gathered in the Karlkirche in Vienna to bid another master, Anton Bruckner, a last farewell.

I will assert at the start that my favorite recording of the Seventh Symphony presently is that by Giuseppe Sinopoli and the Staatskapelle Dresden for DG. This is for me a monumental recording, captured in brilliant sound and played with a limpid clarity and anatomical dissection that has not been duplicated in my experience.

Other excellent performances of the Seventh Symphony include those of Claudio Abbado and the Vienna Philharmonic, Karl Bohm and the Vienna Philharmonic, Riccardo Chailly and the Berlin Radio Symphony Orchestra, Kurt Eichorn and the Bruckner Orchestra of Linz on Camerata, and Daniel Barenboim and the Chicago Symphony Orchestra on DG. Forget Szell's version of Bruckner's *Symphony No 7* from the Salzburg Festival on Sony Classical; despite his unusually fine Bruckner Symphony Nos 3 and 8 with the Cleveland Orchestra from studio performances, this recording is not of the same caliber.

I find the second movement of the symphony to be of the most eloquent statements in music, and it is particularly known for having been played on official German radio as the Germans fled France, and then again at the death of Adolph Hitler. Those who know their history will probably recognize the work from newsreels of the time.

Because the Barenboim Fourth and Seventh Bruckner Symphonies have been reissued as a 2-CD set on DG very recently, they also become the overall recommendable choices because of ease of obtaining the performances, let alone their general excellence. However, the listener should not fail to find the Seventh Symphony with Sinopoli as well.

- Symphony No. 7
    DG Dig 435 786-2. Dresden State O, Sinopoli
- Symphony Nos 7; 4 (Romantic)
    DG 453 100-2 GTA2. Chicago SO, Barenboim

Brahms: Symphony No 1

Its majestic architectural design, rich poetic ideas, earnest elevated spirit, rugged pathos, and its virile, concentrated, defiant energy have made critics call the first symphony of Johannes Brahms (1833 - 1897) "Beethoven's Tenth Symphony!" And there may be much truth in this, for Brahms was the true inheritor of Beethoven's symphonic crown. Some have called it his *Pathetique* symphony, reading in its stormy opening the emotional struggle that the composer faced between his love and admiration for Robert Schumann and his unadmitted love for Schumann's wife Clara. Movement after movement, it struggles upward in a titanic striving to overcome a monumental grief, and it ends in an exuberant paean of triumphant joy. It is the last movement that is the apex of this work—here is mystery and suspense, drama and majesty, at its best! This is music of immense strength and musing tenderness, molded in the great line with epic sweeps, and noble and moving in its own way.

Music ran in his veins naturally. Generations of his ancestors had earned their daily bread through playing musical instruments, and the young composer was fortunate to garner the interest of the great Franz Liszt, and then find an enthusiastic propagandist of his music in Schumann. The first outlines of a symphony were sketched by Brahms in 1855 after he had heard a moving performance of Beethoven's Ninth Symphony. The composer had already reached maturity when he completed it twenty years later. Brahms himself conducted the work in Mannheim in 1876; its first performance had actually taken place a few days earlier where Brahms had sat in the audience.

The Brahms Symphonies have fared well on recorded media. There are many excellent integral Brahms cycles including fine performances of Symphony No. 1 by Szell, Karajan (1964), Solti, Sanderling, and Abbado, simply to name a few.

Ever since Toscanini's pioneering monophonic audio and video recording of the First Symphony, the work has been considered an imposing figure in the recorded literature, and the better it is captured by the microphones, the more dynamic and imperious a work it appears to be. There are indeed so many good performances of the work that a performance, to be seriously considered as a contender for a *Desert Island* status must really say something substantively different than those that have preceded it. To that end, I have limited my references to two outstanding recordings: one, a middle of the road interpretation which does everything just about perfectly, and another which has a story unto itself.

Khristoph von Dohnanyi and the Cleveland Orchestra recorded a Brahms cycle for the Teldec label approximately a decade ago. This cycle contains many excellent performances, but the performance of the First Symphony is truly exceptional, and is pinned on an excellent pedal point with superb tympanic punctuation and brilliantly captured contributions from strings and brass alike. The performance is at tempo, and everything moves along efficiently, with some gravity, but without being ponderous. The performance ends in a jubilant fourth movement, and upon its conclusion, one wants to hear the recording again from the beginning. This performance incorporates most of the outstanding characteristics of many of its predecessors, clearly showing that Dohnanyi had studied not only the score, but the work of other major conductors and their orchestras. This is a Brahms Symphony No. 1 for all time, and it actually outperforms in many respects the outstanding version that Szell made with the same orchestra more than twenty years earlier. It shows the Cleveland Orchestra to have matured into an even better ensemble than Szell had, and certainly, the recording venue is vastly improved from what Severance Hall was, at least to the engineers, long ago.

In 1977, the conductor James Levine was scheduled to record Brahm's Symphony No. 3 at the Medinah Temple in Chicago. The recording went rather flawlessly and there was over an hour of available studio time at the disposition of the conductor. Producer Thomas Z. Shepard agreed that there was sufficient time, if all went well, to record the Brahms First Symphony, which had been previously played and rehearsed for concerts at that time. The scores were distributed, and in essentially one take, with very little editing, a complete performance of the First Brahms Symphony with the Chicago Symphony was committed to tape. In the original LP jacket liner notes, Shepard related the events, and a rather remarkable recording was produced. Levine's performance of the First Symphony has not been duplicated since in terms of intensity, excitement or the nearly crazed abandon with which the performance is dispatched. This is truly an unforgettable event, and it has the spontaneity of a live performance. Truth to tell, I've listened to the performance very carefully since its appearance in 1977, and I have failed to hear the edits referred to by Mr. Shepard in his description of the event. This is normally a relatively easy task, especially with headphones.

The performance begins with a blaze of brass and tympani, but not imperiously like Toscanini, but in its own way unique. This is followed by a relaxed second movement, and an optimistic third movement which is delivered to a finale of Herculean proportions, one that ends at a tempo of such a frenetic speed that one would think the orchestra could not hold together. However, everything coheres to a tee, and the final chords of the piece demonstrate the hair- trigger perfection with which this orchestra is frequently associated, especially with conductors such as Abbado and Solti. Compared to the Solti recording of the same work, produced at roughly the same time, this is an incandescent performance whereas Solti's is merely excellent. The recorded sound may not be quite as well delineated as one would expect for the time, let alone today, but this is still an excellent stereo analog version of the recording, and it takes pride of place on my shelves. It is lamentable that James Levine's re-recording of the work with the Vienna Philharmonic (DG) has yet to be released in the United States since is only a close approximation of the spontaneity and brilliance of the Chicago Symphony rendition. The sound afforded on the Vienna Philharmonic remake is infinitely superior. As this is a budget issue, this version of the First Symphony is easy for all to obtain. Unfortunately, it is accompanied by a lackluster *Academic Festival Overture* with Leonard Slatkin and the St. Louis Symphony, and a horrific performance of the *Variations on a Theme of Haydn* with the Philadelphia Orchestra conducted by its then music director, Eugene Ormandy.

- (i) Symphony No. 1; (ii) Variations on a Theme of Haydn; (iii) Academic Festival Overture
  BMG-RCA 09026-61715-2, (i) Chicago SO, Levine;
  (ii) Philadelphia O, Ormandy; (iii) St. Loius SO, Slatkin

- Symphony No.1
  Teldec 8.43479.Cleveland O, Christoph von Dohnanyi

Brahms: Symphony No 2

It has been said that in a purely Romantic period there can be little of final truth. Romanticism, with its singing of separate beauties and its predominance of pure feeling, is like entering a garden of unknown boundary and contents in which one can wander in reckless enjoyment. There is little place for the order, form and limits of a classical symphony in this garden. Johannes Brahms grew up in an age when the spirit of the Romanticists was crying its most complete utterance. But the youth was not afraid to stand out, strangely cold, against the moderns, and in his natural reaction to it—romantic rebellion from Romanticism—he brought back classicism. Though Brahms absorbed the spirit of the Romanticists, he gave it a new dress of form. He grasped thoroughly and mastered the classical style from its outset, and blended the Romantic spirit with the depth of Bach's style and the structural freedom and boldness of Beethoven.

The Second Symphony allows a reading of a new master purely and absolutely from his work. Here is a blended feeling of simplicity and novelty—the expression is all new for his time, but the sentiment is of all time. The very melody in the beginning of this work is of direct and unaffected simplicity, a German song of ancient Teutonic feelings and utterance, with none of the vehement contrasts of Romanticism. Yet it seems to come forth from Romantic caves and dells, enlightened by the revelation of time in its conventional sentiment. Brahms composed this lyric and sunny work in the virginal countryside around the tiny village of Portschach on Lake Worth where "melodies are so plentiful that you have to take care not to crush any underfoot." Some have called it his *Pastoral* symphony, even a "serenade," inspired by the warm geniality and placid beauty of its plentiful melodies and idyllic moods, suffused, as it were, with warm winds and sunshine playing on summer waters. He called it playfully his little *sinfonia*, his favorite one, and he would break through his usual reserve as regards his own music to speak of it with warmth and enthusiasm. This cheerful and delightful work, with its pastoral freshness and rhythmic caprice, was performed on the last day of the year 1877.

The Second Symphony has no shortage of outstanding available performances, some more exciting than others. The work has a dreamy quality, and actually begins with a lullaby which is known to most people of the Western world. In addition to the excellent in-cycle performances by Abbado (Berlin Philharmonic), Szell (Cleveland Orchestra) and a rather spikey but exciting performance by Kertesz with the Vienna Philharmonic (one of his earliest recordings), there is an outstanding version by Eugen Jochum and the London Philharmonic on EMI. This has an extraordinarily wide dynamic range, and is a rather rapid performance recorded during the Indian Summer of this outstanding conductor. It ought to be heard, especially at budget price.

Of versions on original instrument, Sir Roger Norrington's performance on EMI is pressed with an excellent performance of the *Tragic Overture*, and the performance stands out as a significant addition to the lexicon of the Second Symphony.

My own personal all-time favorite is that by Claudio Abbado and the Berlin Philharmonic performed in 1972, long before his complete cycle with the same orchestra. This performance has an extraordinarily large dynamic space surrounding it, and though it lacks definition in the low frequencies, the beauty of the performance, and the gilded playing and the airiness of the acoustic make it a rather exotic interpretation. This is not a tough performance, but rather, an elegant one which is light of hand. It certainly fits the mood of the work, and currently, I believe, it is only now on a deleted LP (DG 2530 125). The recording was also later reissued on DG Resonance LP and cassette. The 1989 remake is also fine.

If I were left with but one choice of this work that is currently available, I would have to carry to my *Desert Island* the live performance by the Vienna Philharmonic and Carlos Kleiber, which is offered with a rather good performance of the Mozart Symphony No.36 (Linz). The Kleiber version is much like Abbado's interpretation, but it is a bit less ethereal and a bit beefier. Audience participation does not hurt this performance and, for the most part, contribution from them is negligible until the end of the work. This is a work to cherish and to love, and the performance is successful in communicating both the contemplative and rosy emotions that Brahms wished to express in this work.

- Symphony No. 2
    Ph.Video VHS 070 161-3. VPO, Kleiber
- Symphony No. 2
    DG 427 643-2. BPO, Abbado $$$
- Symphony No. 2; Symphony Nos 1, 3; Tragic Overture; Academic Festival Overture
    EMI Double Forte CDFB 72435 61515 2. LPO, Jochum

Brahms: Symphony No 3

Johannes Brahms was not fortunate with his audience. The coldness with which his symphonies were received was not merely the traditional Viennese reluctance to accept something new; it was inexperience to respond to music conceived on so gigantic a scale, so broad in outline yet so exquisite in detail. And his Third Symphony, with its subtlety and poise, its mellow warmth and its autumnal richness, fell upon uncomprehending ears. Yet this glorious music, quivering in parts with a romantic twilight, has been interpreted, at one time or another, as a musical picture of Hero and Leander, or Iago and Desdemona—the eternal struggle between good and evil. Clara Schumann saw it as a forest idyll! Some have called it Brahm's *Eroica,* a heroic work, in tribute to its dominant heroic mood, virile conflicts, supreme wisdom and its serene resignation. Unlike the preceding work, humor is wanting in this symphony—from the two chords, loud and long, that open the music, it is overcast with somber clouds and burdened with stern gloom.

There is a story that, at the time that he was working on this symphony, the fifty year old Brahms was in the grip of a midsummer passion with a much younger woman, Hermine Speiss. But to the twenty six year old *contralto*, the composer was merely a figure of worship, and her only true interest in the world was the art song (*Lieder*). Brahms composed this work in Weisbaden, where Hermine lived. The symphony was first performed in 1883, and though the professional critics were bitter in their descriptions, the eloquence of the music itself proved too powerful, and an enthusiastic audience made the concert a success.

The Third Symphony has fared very well on record, especially from the 1960s onward. It goes without saying that this is a biographical statement in certain respects as Roger Norrington has noted publicly, and contains themes which have personal and collegial references throughout. Again, the same contenders who have recorded complete cycles have yielded generous fruits of their efforts, including individuals such as Kertesz (Vienna Philharmonic Orchestra), Karajan (Berlin Philharmonic:1964), and Szell (Cleveland Orchestra). One of the great recordings produced by Bruno Walter and the Columbia Symphony was for CBS. Walter's recording of the Third Symphony, now on Sony Classical, is one of the great glories of the gramophone, and it should be heard by all those learning the Third Symphony.

With the advent of recordings played on original instrument, there have been contributions by Roger Norrington and the London Classical Players which are notable. I consider this a supreme version, and especially interesting because of his own personal insights into the work as well as the contribution of a relatively down sized orchestra in the performance of the symphony. Using modern instruments, but using the style of the original Meiningen performances, Sir Charles Mackerras and the Scottish Chamber Orchestra have performed the Third Symphony for Telarc Records, and this is a stimulating alternative to modern instrumentation and the peculiarities of original instrumentation. This also is a recording that should be heard.

For my money, a thoroughly modern instrument version is still my preferred vehicle for this symphony, and it would have to be that of James Levine with the Vienna Philharmonic Orchestra. It is, if anything, a highly charged Brahms which is not going to be to everyone's liking. This is a blatant performance, and it screams the word Brahms all over the stage from start to finish. The extraordinarily high dynamic range of the recording helps with the impact of the outstanding, hair-trigger perfect playing of the Vienna Philharmonic. The recording is complimented by an excellent performance of the *Tragic Overture*, a work which I have rarely enjoyed as much as in this recording, along with the *Alto Rhapsody* sung beautifully by Anne Sofie Von Otter.

An alternative to this performance, somewhat more musical and less blatant, is the outstanding performance by the Berlin Philharmonic and Claudio Abbado, recorded shortly after his appointment as conductor of the Berlin Philharmonic in 1990. This recording is coupled with the *Tragic Overture* in a somewhat more demure performance, along with the *Schicksalied*.

- Symphony No. 3
  DG 439887-2, VPO, James Levine

Brahms: Symphony No 4

There is a rare blend of sorrow and understanding, an autumnal warmth and inner strength, that comes to the fore in the last works of any great artist. In Brahms, these qualities became developed relatively early, and came to be expressed in the works of the entire final decade of his life. And this is unexplained, for Fortune had smiled favorably as she recorded the life of the composer—placid, happy and successful, untouched by misery or poverty. In a way, this piece stands apart from all his other symphonies because it is the most subjective and is a remarkable revelation of the composer's personality, and of the resignation and the profound understanding that his own earnest nature and the passage of years had brought to his crusty exterior. As the years went by, he was forever seeking more difficult problems to solve, and yet his works became simpler, more clear of idea and conciseness. Gone are the storm and stress of the First Symphony, the drama and action that had inspired his earlier pages. Something has replaced these things in the Fourth Symphony, something wiser and more precious. Some have called it a bitter and pessimistic piece that drips with melancholy like a yew tree, but pessimism is not despair. And if this be an expression of resignation, it is the resignation of strength and faith, of an awareness of the other side of life, of the indestructibility of thought and beauty.

Brahms is the musician's poet. After one has suffered with Beethoven, fought with Wagner, loved with Chopin, and made his experience of the world with Liszt, one turns from them all with a sigh of relief and seeks his spirit in Brahms. For Brahms opens the door to a world outside itself. Little of the turmoil of modern life echoes in his music; the stream of personal experience seems to flow past his door, observed but unexplored. And in his last symphony, Brahms delineates the world and the compelling impulses of mankind. This is indeed a building made without hands, built of love, strength, holy passion and character, of mountains, seas, the sun and freedom. Like a true poetic spirit, the music reveals all this in conflict, in the struggle of life and death.

The Fourth Symphony was composed in the chilly Alpine village of Murzzuschlag where the springs were short and the cherries never ripened for eating because of the cold. The manuscript was nearly burned in a fire that broke out in the composer's house, but was fortunately saved by one of his friends. Its first performance was in Meiningen in 1885; the Vienna concert, where it was played on March 7, 1897 was Brahms last public appearance—a few weeks later, on April 3, he passed away from cancer at the age of sixty four.

The Fourth is perhaps the most fateful of all the four symphonies, and a good performance of the work has to imbue the listener with a sense both of resounding grace and pathos. Not unlike the other symphonies, there have been many outstanding recordings in the course of this century, notably by such conductors as Victor deSabata, Giulini (Chicago Symphony), Barbirolli (Vienna Philharmonic), Abbado (London Symphony Orchestra), Solti (Chicago Symphony) and others who have performed complete cycles.

For a Brahms Fourth Symphony to be competitive, not unlike the other symphonies, an interpretation really must again say more than just what a competent or even excellent performance of the notes has to say. To that end, having listened to four or five dozen performances in the course of my studies, I would assert that there are several versions which take pride of place on my shelves.

One such version is on LP only, that of recording engineer Otto Gerdes who is also a fine musician in his own right. Maestro Gerdes performed the Brahms Fourth Symphony and the Wagner *Prelude* to *Die Meistersinger von Nurnburg* with the Berlin Philharmonic in 1969. The purpose of this recording was unclear, perhaps being a valedictory gift to Mr. Gerdes upon retirement from DGG. The performance is fateful, unique in both dynamics and shading, and the tempi are all on the very clipped side. The recorded sound has great depth, but not great dynamic range. If you can find this recording, I highly recommend you appropriate it, copy it and save the vinyl LP from further exposure. I doubt that this recording will ever see the light of day on CD, if only because of its relative exoticity. The catalog number DG139 423 is permanently etched in my mind, along with the following performance, also on the same label.

Carlos Kleiber, the quixotic, heroic and inimitable conductor who appears publicly only when it is time for him to commit a new work to the microphones, produced a Brahms Fourth Symphony in the early 1980s with the Vienna Philharmonic Orchestra which is Herculean in its presentation, and yet has all the nuances of an extraordinarily sentient interpretation. This performance is correct from start to finish, and must apologize to no other performance for any shortcomings. When all is said and done, there is nothing else to do or say but to find this recording and commit it to memory. It is that good, and few have approached its excellence. It is entirely different from Gerdes' rendition, and neither should be compared to each other.

- Symphony No. 4
     DG400 037-2GH, VPO, Kleiber
- Symphony No. 4; Variations on a Theme from Haydn
     London 430 440-2LM, LSO, Solti

Brahms: Piano Concertos

A heavy responsibility had fallen upon the shoulders of Johannes Brahms when he was barely twenty. Robert Schumann had announced him to the world as "the highest ideal expression of his time ... burst upon us, fully equipped, like Minerva from the brain of Jupiter." Others had predicted that he would be "the most considerable musician of his age." The youth was clearly in a spot; the adulation, as expected, had aroused distrust in some quarters, resentment in others, and a few were frankly skeptical. With battle lines thus formed, a great symphony seemed justified. And so Brahms buckled down to a project that began as a symphony, became a sonata, and ended as a much revised first piano concerto.

It goes without saying that a work created in such an unusual way does not conform to the ordinary conception of a solo piano concerto. The piano and the orchestra are treated as equally important, and though the solo part is anything but easy, it is not a piece of ostentatious virtuosity. There is a certain plastic fullness and massiveness of orchestral color that harmonizes most happily with the passion and melancholy of the music.

The music plunges at once into the speech of high tragedy. Here is Brahms of the most virile and dramatic themes, marked by conflicts and passions. Here, too, perhaps, is the composer's inner turmoil in hearing of Schumann's attempted suicide. And this sorrow overflows into the second movement where two beautiful themes are developed with deep feeling: one for muted strings, and the second for clarinets. The manuscript of the second movement bore the inscription: *Benedictus qui venit in nomine Domini*. Though Brahms was in the habit of addressing Schumann as *Domine*, it is more likely that the "blessed person" who came "in the name of the Lord" was Clara Schumann. For, in connection with this music, Brahms had written to Clara: "I am also painting a lovely portrait of you; it is to be the *Adagio*." The closing *Rondo* pulsates with an animal spirit, but after the cadenza, a feeling of contemplative beauty returns.

The second piano concerto was begun two decades later on his return from his first Italian journey. The music expresses a wonderfully balanced serenity—the tragic and violent mood and the demoniac passion of the first concerto has vanished. Here is the ripe and mellow speech of a mature man who is given less to rebellion and defiant action and more to reflection. The Italian sun, the tranquillity of the Italian countryside, and the gentle beauty of the Italian spring turning to summer suffuses the opening music. In the second movement, a cogent theme announced by the piano is followed by a contrasting sweet melody for strings. A cello opens the next movement with a melody of unsurpassed beauty, gentle and reflective, speaking of other worlds far removed from the fret and frenzy of mundane existence. The music ends in a bouquet of light hearted gypsy melodies—now permeated with romantic ardor, now wildly abandoned.

Since early stereo, Brahms' Piano Concerto No. 1 has been extraordinarily well served on disc. Two of the earliest stereo recordings I encountered were by Rubinstein with Reiner and the Chicago Symphony, and the Leon Fleisher/George Szell recording with the Cleveland Orchestra. The Rubinstein/Reiner recording was actually released on LP in mono, and only in the last decade did it appear in a stereo iteration on MC and ultimately, CD. The performance is a brilliant one, with the Chicago Symphony showing typical hair trigger perfection playing even as far back as 1955! Rubinstein may have been considered by many to be a showman of the keyboard, but indeed, he was an extraordinarily hefty intellect, and his performance shows this to be the case. The recorded sound by today's standards is thin and nasal, but much can be heard.

I wish the same thing could be said about the Fleisher/Szell recording, as it, too, is an extraordinarily spirited performance with the best of orchestral playing. The sound, however, is thin, two dimensional, and lacks detail. The piano can be heard reasonably well; the strings are given prominence in favor of the rest of the orchestra. This is all too evident in the finale, where I am convinced that I have to actually think the parts that simply cannot be heard. The performance, nevertheless, is a golden one, and those who wish to hear Leon Fleischer at the peak of his playing power should consider this recording.

Pride of place on my shelves is another Szell recording, this time with Clifford Curzon, and the London Symphony Orchestra, that yielded one of the greatest Brahms First Piano Concertos ever to appear on record. This performance has remained in the catalog since its first issue in 1962, and the sound is still quite robust and hearty. Honorable mention should be given to Rudolph Serkin with George Szell and the Cleveland Orchestra in that orchestra's remake of the work from 1968.

The pianist, Krystian Zimerman, recorded the work with the Vienna Philharmonic and Leonard Bernstein in a rather romantic, athletic version of the performance which is a live recording for DG. This performance, dating from 1984, is splendid, but it is, as with many of Bernstein's later recordings, somewhat willful.

Alfred Brendel has recorded the work twice, once in a currently unavailable performance with Hans Schmidt-Isserstedt for Philips, and again, with Claudio Abbado and the Berlin Philharmonic Orchestra, in a somewhat more forthcoming, stout performance which approximates the greatness of the recording that I consider my *Desert Island* preference. Brendel and Abbado certainly have the modern sound sweepstakes for this work at this present time, although I believe that Abbado and Pollini will soon issue perhaps an exciting performance very shortly with the Berlin Philharmonic, again for DG.

In 1972, the great Russian pianist, Emil Gilels, recorded both Brahms Piano Concerti for DG with the venerable conductor, Eugen Jochum. Although this is a patrician, somewhat Teutonic performance, the playing of the Berlin Philharmonic is beyond belief, and Gilels develops the most voluptuous piano sound that I have encountered in this work at any time. His playing is also beyond reproach. My initial reaction to this performance at first hearing was that it was too slow in the aggregate. I tend to like fast performances of virtually everything. I have come to moderate that somewhat hasty viewpoint, and have determined that perhaps other performances that I have enjoyed might be too brisk. The recorded sound is still miraculous.

The opening note is reminiscent of what Andre Previn said was his reaction to conducting the Chicago Symphony; "It is as if you were standing behind the Concorde (at take off)." This is a robust recording, and it has been reissued at mid price. Do not miss this performance!

The sweepstakes for the Brahms *Piano Concerto No. 2* are very similar to that of the first Concerto. Fleischer and Szell have a superb Second Concerto on Sony Classical, but again, much like the First Concerto, it is an antique sonically. There is another Chicago Symphony performance of the same vintage (1961), this time with entirely different forces, including the Russian pianist, Sviatoslav Richter, and conductor, Erich Leinsdorf, who was substituting for conductor Fritz Reiner who was indisposed presumably from a severe bronchitis which ultimately caused Reiner's demise. This is a splendid Brahms Second Piano Concerto, and the work has never been better played than this. The recorded sound is resplendent compared to the Fleischer recording and it belongs on everyone's shelves.

Serkin and Szell have an excellent recording of the work as performed in January, 1966 for then Columbia Masterworks, now Sony Classical. Claudio Abbado and Alfred Brendel have recorded a superb Brahms Second Piano Concerto for Philips, which again, tops the list of best engineered recordings of this work currently available. Stephen Kovacevich recorded the Second Brahms Piano Concerto with Wolfgang Sawallisch and the London Philharmonic Orchestra shortly after his outstanding performance of the First Piano Concerto, and this interpretation, which I have seen in concert, is a highly desirable one which lacks for nothing. It is inspired, but the dynamic range of the recording, even by standards of 1972, is somewhat narrow. It is for that reason that I am unable to recommend his otherwise outstanding performance of the First Piano Concerto.

As great as Emil Gilels' 1972 recording of the Second Brahms Piano Concerto is, and as much as I feel it is on my short list of favorite performances, a new recording by Murizio Pollini with Claudio Abbado and the Berlin Philharmonic for DG now takes first position on my shelves. This is a well nigh perfect reading insofar as interpretation goes, and it has been well received throughout the world. This performance will not disappoint you!

- Piano concerto Nos. 1-2; Fantasias, Op. 116
    DG 447 446-2. Gilels, BPO, Jochum
- Piano concerto Nos. 1-2;—FRANCK: Symphonic Variations;—
    LITOLFF: Scherzo
    London 425 082-2 Curzon, LSO, Szell
- Piano concerto No. 2
    BMG/RCA 07863 56518-2. Richter, Chicago SO, Leinsdorf
- Piano concerto No. 2
    DG 453 505-2-. Pollini, BPO, Abbado
- Piano concerto No. 2
    BMG/RCA 07863 56518-2. Richter, Chicago SO, Leinsdorf
- Piano concerto No. 1
    EMI Dig CDC7 54578-2, Kovacevich, LPO, Sawallisch

Brahms: Violin Concerto

Johannes Brahms composed only one violin concerto, but in it he reconciled the two opposite sides of his creative mind—the lyrical songwriter and the constructive symphonist. For this Concerto is a song for the violin on a symphonic scale, undisciplined with a fiery spirit of independence, with its lyrical outpouring of charming melodies balanced by rugged grandeur and violinistic virtuosity. Warm, expansive and robust, the tunes grow and blossom like opening flowers in a richly stocked garden, perhaps the result of the idyllic surroundings where this work was created—at Portschach-am-see, a beautiful spot in the southern Austrian Alps. In this masterpiece, Brahms is a musical sensualist with intellectual affectations, an ornamentalist without ornateness, florid without excess, whose arabesques have the dignity and fervor of pure lyric speech. Perhaps not since Chopin have the possibilities of decorative figuration developed so rich a yield of poetic loveliness as in this magnificent music.

Brahms first composed the Concerto in four movements, but later cut out the middle movements and rewrote the *Adagio*. The music opens with a traditional introduction by the orchestra that announces the first theme, peaceful and subdued, in the bassoons, horns and lower strings, then in the oboe and strings, and finally by the full orchestra. A second theme follows, the violin comes in with a kind of breathless passage, and the themes are developed broadly but personally in a manner not unlike a Platonic dialogue, with poetry added. Somewhere a storm breaks out in the orchestra, and the entire music is charged with electricity. Here is music inspired by a dreamy romanticism rising to joyous energy. The second slow movement has an astonishing quality of unadulterated beauty. It is a delicate and imaginative study in the decoration of an exquisite single melody, pastoral in character with dreamy arabesques, said to be based upon a Bohemian folk-song singing of an autumnal evening. The decoration does not alter, but develops the melody musically into a glorious pattern. The gentle dreams of the slow movement are blown away by a single gust from the wood winds in the finale. The violin picks up an exciting Hungarian gypsy melody and rhythm with charming effect and breathtaking virtuosity. The music ends in a march-like theme with suitable military suggestions by the orchestra.

For me, the Brahms *Violin Concerto* is the epitome violin concerto, much as Mozart's piano concerti are for me the epitome compositions for this type of work.

It is not surprising that Jascha Heifetz and Fritz Reiner with the Chicago Symphony have delivered what has long been considered the standard bearer of performances for this work. I have the same sort of respect for this performance as I do for Heifetz' version of the Tchaikovsky Violin Concerto in D.

Another great performance, perhaps even more technically exciting that Heifetz, is that by Gidon Kremer with the Vienna Philharmonic Orchestra conducted by Leonard Bernstein. This performance has the brio of a live recording, and indeed is available on video. The playing is impeccable, but Kremer really takes a bite out of this work, and delivers what is for me the best of the three performances he has recorded, including one very recently which was perhaps more mature but much less compelling with the Contcertegebouw Orchestra of Amsterdam with Harnoncourt.

The then teen-aged violinist, Anne Sophie Mutter, recorded the work for DG with the Berlin Philharmonic Orchestra under the baton of Herbert von Karajan in approximately 1982. This is a soulful performance, somewhat more lyrical than either Kremer or Heifetz, but truly overwhelming in the guttural tone that she obtains from her instrument. I would not want to be without this recording, or Kremer's, especially in the era of excellent recorded sound, as both have a concussive effect upon me equivalent to that of the San Andreas Fault! Mutter recently re-recorded the Brahms Violin Concerto with the New York Philharmonic under the direction of Kurt Masur. This is an unusually personal statement, a somewhat romantic interpretation, with able-bodied accompaniment by Masur. It does not displace my particular soft spot for the original Mutter recording, which I would take any day over this newcomer. No doubt Mutter is perhaps more dazzling technically than she was as a teenager, and no doubt the sound is more realistic from a concert hall setting, but the performance does not have the same kind of incandescence as the original teenage version.

Finally, I suggest to the reader that imminent recordings by Gil Shaham and Maxim Vengerov (for DG and Teldec respectively) be listened to very carefully, as it is possible that this entire hierarchy of recommendations could be toppled by either of these amazing musicians. This is a staple of the classical repertory, and perhaps the greatest violin concerto written. It is a work to learn and love.

- Violin concerto in D
    DG 445 595-2 GMA Kremer, VPO, Bernstein
- Violin concerto in D
    DG 439 007-2 GHS Mutter, BPO, Karajan
- (i) Violin concerto in D; (ii)- BEETHOVEN: Violin Concerto
    RCA 09026-61742-2. Heifetz, (ii) BSO, Munch (i) Chicago
    SO, Reiner

Brahms: Orchestral Works

The compositions for orchestra belong mainly to the mature period of Brahm's art. A story has it that Brahms was shown an interesting work by a well-known biographer of Haydn that Haydn had written for the band of Prince Esterhazy's troops. Some have attributed this piece to Pleyl. Its second movement, entitled *Chorale St Antonii*, was based upon an old Burgenland pilgrim chant, and Brahms used this irresistible little melody as the theme for the *Variations on a Theme of Haydn*. This was Brahm's first ambitious work that was exclusively for orchestra, and it was the one that convinced him that he was ripe for a major symphonic assignment.

The theme is voiced by the wood winds, following which come eight variations in which the theme is only passingly suggested. But so wide and flexible are the moods and feeling with which the theme is varied, that one is tempted to give a special place to the *Haydn Variations* among the whole of the master's orchestral compositions. Here is music that is fluid, supple and graceful (Variation 1), often sensuous (Variation 2), now graceful and delicate (Variation 6), now of a poignant beauty (Variation 8). The music ends with a restatement of the theme in a dramatic climax.

The *Haydn Variations* also exist in a two-piano arrangement made by Brahms which the composer frequently played with Clara Schumann. It is believed that the orchestral version preceded the two-piano one.

As an expression of gratitude for being awarded the degree of Doctor of Philosophy by the University of Breslau, Brahms wrote the *Academic Festival Overture* to capture the spirit of the occasion. It is the lively occasional composition of a genius—to take it too seriously would not be fair to the composer. It is a very jolly potpourri of student songs, reminiscent of beer-mugs and mischief and the harmless ragging of the guileless freshman, of the mystery of youth in its full athletic dignity, and the spirit of Alma Mater. The music ends in a rousing finish to a tune that every German student presumably knew—the famous *Gaudemus Igitur*.

216

An apt companion to the jolly *Academic Festival Overture* is the *Tragic Overture*. Here is tragic music of Greek nobility and spaciousness—Brahms' most profound ruminating music. Two major themes are developed along epic lines: the one reflective of a great and brooding sorrow, the other providing an antidote of optimism.

These three shorter works are symphonic miniatures and, with the exception of the *Tragic Overture*, are very easy to warm to. The *Variations on a Theme of Haydn* actually has two separate opus numbers in the catalog. Opus 56A begins with a brief chorale and ends with an *Andante* as the finale, and in between these two sections are eight glorious variations.

Virtually all conductors who have recorded the Brahms Symphonies as an integral set have recorded these *Variations*, and strangely, one of my favorites of all time comes from a source which in my mind has never truly been considered a great Brahmsian interpreter.

The conductor Sir Georg Solti recorded the symphonies and the *Haydn Variations* in 1979 for London. His performance is beefy, big and bouncy, let alone exciting. The orchestra plays beautifully for Solti, and the performance shines brightly. It is a happy performance, not a heart on sleeve interpretation, and I cannot recommend it more highly.

In 1973, the conductor Istvan Kertesz died suddenly while swimming in the Dead Sea near Tel Aviv, Israel. His performance of the *Haydn Variations* was incomplete at the time, but the members of the Vienna Philharmonic, with whom he recorded the work, elected to complete the performance conductorless, by performing the *Andante* finale as a tribute to him. The performance was a loving and spirited one, not as punchy as Solti's, but somewhat more lyrical and beautiful. The sound is not at all dated, and the interpretation is sound. This performance is available as part of a 2-CD box that includes the *Serenade No. 2* as well as the First and Second Symphonies, and makes an exceptional purchase. The recordings of the Symphonies are variable in terms of sound, with the Second Symphony dating from 1967.

The second catalog listing, Opus 56B, is a four-hand piano rendition of the work, and has been well served since the advent of stereo LP. My first exposure to this version of the work came from an Odyssey (Columbia Masterworks) recording with Robert Gold and Alan Fizdale at the keyboard. I was stunned to hear this work performed in this manner; it was the first time I had ever heard what I consider to be a purely orchestral work scored for piano and, since that time, I have searched wherever I can for piano versions of orchestrally scored music. Gold and Fizdale more or less held the sweepstakes for this work until about a decade ago when pianists Murray Perahia and Sir Georg Solti recorded the work for CBS Masterworks, now Sony Classical. I believe this was Sir Georg's second appearance as a professional pianist in stereo, and the performance is wonderful from start to finish. Accompanying this work is the Bartok *Sonata for Two Pianos and Percussion* which rounds out an extraordinarily desirable disc.

The *Academic Festival Overture* is reminiscent of the scene of a graduation from the university. One can picture the academic regalia being worn by the graduates and professors as they line up for Commencement ceremonies. It is a work of rapt glee and happiness, tinged with a small amount of wistfulness. Its brevity is an act of genius. My single favorite interpretation of the work remains an older Sony Classical disc with Bruno Walter conducting the Columbia Symphony Orchestra, made in Los Angeles in 1960, in the Indian Summer of Bruno Walter's life.

What is so unique about this recording is the slight retard that Walter makes just before the entry of the theme *Gaudemus Iquitur* which is played at tempo. The retard and cymbal crash are so blatant that it would have made Brahms laugh and applaud.

Since Walter's time, there have been innumerable excellent performances of the work, but none more enjoyable. My favorite in modern sound is that of Eugen Jochum and the London Philharmonic Orchestra for EMI, but Claudio Abbado and the Berlin Philharmonic have also recorded an outstanding version twice. Why Karajan, a great interpreter of Brahms, failed to record the work is beyond me. I understand he never performed it publicly, either.

Not unlike Schumann's *Manfred Overture*, the Brahms' *Tragic Overture* can be a deadly work to listen to if not conducted with guts and foresight. I have a closet full of performances which are utterly deadly, and yet these are from some of the most renowned musicians. Why this is so is something I will never understand, but there is only one performance in the catalog which has brought me truly any pleasure in thirty five years of listening.

In anticipation of the Brahms Centennial, the conductor James Levine recorded all four Brahms Symphonies in a rather neat, well played package with the Vienna Philharmonic, and included in this cycle was a performance of the *Tragic Overture*, among one or two other shorter Brahms orchestral and vocal works. This is a hammered performance, one which clearly shows the conductor in sympathy with my sentiments about how dreary this work can be. Fortunately for the listener, you will not be obligated to buy the entire box of symphonies to obtain this performance. In fact, as of the printing of this book, the Levine Brahms cycle is not available in North America. However, as a single issue, the Brahms Symphony No. 3 and the *Tragic Overture* and *Alto Rhapodie* from this integral set is available, and this itself is a *Desert Island* CD. The Third Symphony and the *Alto Rhapsodie* are given outstanding performances all told. I regret to say that inasmuch as there are probably thirty other performances of the *Tragic Overture,* I cannot recommend any of them to the listener besides this one. The difference is really very dramatic between this interpretation and those of all others.

- Variations on a Theme of Haydn (St. Antoni Variations);
  Symphony No 4
    London 430 440-2LM. CSO, Solti

- Variations on a Theme of Haydn;
    London 448 197-2LF2. VPO, Kerterz

- Variations on a Theme of Haydn (arr. for 4-hands piano);
  —BARTOK: Sonata for two pianos and percussion
    Sony MK42685. Perahia, CSO, Solti

- Academic Festival Overture
    Sony MK42021. Columbia SO, Walter

- Academic Festival Overture
  EMI 7243 5 69515 2 5. LPO, Jochum

- Tragic Overture; Symphony No. 3; Alto Rhapsodie
  DG 439 887-2GH VPO, Levine

Mahler: Symphony No 1 (Titan)

Gustav Mahler (1860 - 1911) emerged from the mantle of Beethoven and his own teacher Bruckner, and like them he sought to give an intellectual content to his symphonies. His music is rich in philosophic and metaphysical implications. He was possessed by a passion for greatness and, in their scope, his symphonies were to transcend those that had been written before. He desired nothing less than to give musical scope to the "complete man" and, on occasion, even he was overwhelmed by some of his own inspirations. He looked upon his First Symphony, which he called a symphonic poem misleadingly subtitled *Titan*, as an adventure of the soul that issued from his heart like a mountain stream. The merry first two movements are but a prelude, and the parody of the third movement is an intermezzo. They are all just a preparation for the fourth movement which is expanded mightily, and gives the appearance of being the aim and meaning of the music. Mahler provided subtitles as clues to his intentions, but it is doubtful whether they greatly help in their understanding.

The music opens with a delightful, expectant open-air feeling of Nature awakening at the early hours of dawn, and leads into an Austrian peasant dance. Then follows a long Huntsman's funeral march set to the tune of the nursery rhyme *Frere Jacques*, curiously Semitic, expressing the cry of a deeply wounded heart in the uncannily oppressive and ironically closed atmosphere of a funeral. And from it springs precipitately, like a flash of lightning from a somber cloud, the final music that ends in alternating moods of nervous excitement and true serenity, without the climactic stress of traditional triumph, yet none the less joyous in essence.

The beginnings of this work can be traced to his seventeenth year; Mahler was twenty nine when he conducted this work for the first time in Budapest in 1889. The entire score was revised in 1893.

Mahler was known for writing incurably long and complicated symphonies which had emotions varying from one extreme to the next. Mahler himself was probably a hypochondriac, and had a myriad medical problems including rheumatic heart disease which threatened him from about the Sixth Symphony onwards. That personal tragedy, in addition to the death of a newborn daughter, set the stage for the content of his later works.

The First Symphony depicts birth and an introduction to nature, and it is one of the shorter symphonies along with No. 4. There are many outstanding records of Mahler's Symphony No. 1, so many, indeed, that the list is truly long. Historically, one would consider performances by Jascha Horenstein and the London Symphony Orchestra on Unicorn CD. In good stereo, it still could be of great interest because Horenstein was familiar with Mahler. This performance is still a class act, and should be considered for those interested in hearing the work from the horse's mouth. Another individual who was familiar with Mahler as a person was Bruno Walter whose Columbia Symphony recording for CBS is still in the gramophone catalog and has been reproduced on CD very well. It tends to be somewhat bass and midrange heavy, as were most recordings of that period due to problems in equalization of play back of orchestral music through stereo systems of the time. Both recordings capture the essence of Mahler's intentions very well, and both are entirely satisfactory renditions.

Problems arise when comparing these two excellent interpretations with modern recordings with even greater orchestras, benefiting from the acoustics of better venues, and in some cases, the presence of audiences. Claudio Abbado has recorded the work twice, once with the Chicago Symphony and once with the Berlin Philharmonic. Both are digital recordings. The Berlin recording is the more recent, and the audience is present. Abbado uses Leonard Bernstein's Stinger in the final note of the performance, which brings the audience to its feet, perhaps in shock! I'd buy this recording just for the last note. But the Chicago Symphony recording is particularly delicate and endearing to me, as I watched it go to tape in the 1980s in Chicago.

Another live performance, by Leonard Bernstein and the Royal Amsterdam Concertgebouw Orchestra, is perhaps the most labile that I have encountered, perhaps getting us closer to the composer's true emotional state with respect to the work. The performance has many inventive niceties which improve greatly upon his earlier rendition with the New York Philharmonic. I can't recommend this performance too highly, despite its flaying hysteria.

James Levine and the London Symphony have made an excellent recording for RCA with the LSO, as has Zubin Mehta with the Israel Philharmonic for London Records. Mehta's remakes for Sony and later Teldec are much less satisfying for reasons which are unclear to me. Seiji Ozawa and the Boston Symphony have made an excellent performance for DG, and the CD includes the peculiar "Blumine" movement which normally is not included in the recordings, respecting Mahler's request. This is a competitive performance whereas Ozawa's redo for Philips is a an insensitive, perfunctory reading of the score suggesting not the slightest understanding of Mahler's intentions socially, spiritually or ethnically.

If there were one performance that I would have to take to a *Desert Island*, however, it would be the one that I learned first—that of Rafael Kubelik conducting the Bavarian Radio Symphony Orchestra. This performance dates from 1968 and, even at budget price, has the freshness and brilliance of a recording made yesterday. It may lack the stinger on the last note of the final movement, but the performance is an endearing one, and its scale is not so huge as to be overwhelming. As seen in perspective with the other nine symphonies, perhaps Kubelik had a better sense of proportion of the work when compared to later works.

- Symphony No. 1 (Titan)
    DG Originals 449 735-2 GOR. Bavarian RadioSO, Kubelik
- Symphony No. 1 (Titan)
    DG 427 303-2 GH. Royal Amsterdam Concertgebouw O, Bernstein

Mahler: Symphony No 2 (Resurrection)

Mahler continued his intellectual and philosophic expressions into the Second Symphony. It is a passionate inquiry into the "why" of human existence, probing into the meaning of human suffering. The problem of death had special significance to the composer. The First Symphony already contained thoughts about death, and the dirge sounded sneering and grotesque in the third movement while the soul wept. The Second Symphony he devoted completely to the question of life and death, the terrors of the Last Judgment, and the eternal bliss of resurrection. It was his mystery play of the Hereafter out of which the song of the bird of death resounded. There is a scant interruption provided by a buoyant and charming folk song, a pastoral, that breaks the momentous rumbling of his discontent. Then the music ends in a climax of shattering power and grandeur sung by voices and orchestra—a reaffirmation of life!

The idea for this triumphant conclusion came to him at a memorial service for his friend and mentor Hans von Bulow. As he sat in the church amidst a thousand people, his mood and thoughts of the departed one were exactly the same as that of the symphony on which he was then constantly occupied. Just at that moment, the chorus near the organ intoned a chorale, and suddenly, like a thunderbolt, everything seemed to stand clear and vivid before his soul. What he had experienced he then shaped into sound in the ecstatic finale of this symphony, his monument more enduring than brass, expressing an intimation of that immortality that most humans seem to yearn for.

The first three movements of the Second Symphony were performed for the first time in a concert conducted by Richard Strauss in 1895. Mahler, himself, conducted the full score a few months later in Berlin.

The *Resurrection* Symphony is the first of Mahler's to use a chorus, subsequently also used in Symphony Nos. 3 and 8. This is indeed a work depicting a religious event, and holds true to form in terms of content and progression. The work is an enormous one, and the dynamic range required to reproduce it is extraordinary.

Early recordings such as those by Klemperer with the Philharmonia for EMI, and Bernstein with the New York Philharmonic, only tell part of the story—they are handicapped by the limitations inherent in engineering at the time, although these performances certainly are important historically and should be heard by the avid listener. It's very difficult to pick one *Resurrection* Symphony that meets all criteria for an optimal performance. Indeed, in writing this portion of each chapter of this book, I have been well aware that no individual will necessarily agree with me as to my own selections. But that is not the point of the book.

I am particularly enamored of Claudio Abbado's first *Resurrection* Symphony recording with the Chicago Symphony, with Carol Neblett and Marilyn Horne. This recording was made in the Medinah Temple in Chicago in February, 1976, and represented the culmination of a number of concerts and prior performances with the orchestra. It is a meticulously crafted, beautifully executed recording, which exceeds Abbado's later live performance with the Vienna Philharmonic, also on DG. Zubin Mehta made an excellent recording with the Vienna Philharmonic of the Resurrection Symphony in the early 1970s, a record which disappeared from the shelves and only was recently resurrected on CD, no pun intended. This performance includes Christa Ludwig, who is acutely familiar with the work, and Ileana Cotrubas, both of whom make this exceptionally well engineered recording utterly delightful. Sir Georg Solti and the Chicago Symphony have bettered Abbado's interpretation only sonically, because the contributions of Mira Zakai and Isobel Buchanan don't compare to those made by Abbado's soloists. The dynamic range of this recording is truly astounding, and if you're looking for a performance to blow you away, this is perhaps the one to have, because Solti's rapt control of his orchestra is unparalleled in this work. Sir Simon Rattle's recording of the work for EMI is an outstanding example of the best of EMI engineering, a commodity which, in my opinion, is often in the dog house. I would say at the outset that this is one of my favorite *Resurrection* Symphonies, as it is sane, sober, and fails to verge on the hysterical. It is exceptionally well documented, and I prize it highly. A rather willful performance by Hermann Scherchen and the Vienna State Opera Orchestra and Vienna Academy Chorus is available on Theorema CD and it is a studio recording. The first release was in 1958, and there are some subtle cuts in the performance, but overall, the performance, which is taken at a variety of tempi, is both compelling and memorable. Individuals looking for an alternative version of the work should consider Scherchen's interpretation. Educated historians will tout Klemperer's early and final versions of the *Resurrection*. I find these unsatisfactory readings for personal reasons, the most important of which was his general inability to effect coherent playing from large orchestral and choral forces late in his life.

My own personal favorite is also a willful performance, but is anatomically dissected in such a linear, clean manner by the well known psychiatrist-conductor Giuseppe Sinopoli, that its excellence is undeniable. The separation of the mere brass parts is so direct and impressive that the final peroration in the last movement reaches celestial heights. I have not encountered such a well dissected, painstakingly crafted performance in many years, and I fear that the criticisms this recording has received over time are unjustified. If you want to learn the work well the first time, and learn a performance which really does depict the work accurately, I suggest that you find Sinopoli on DG.

- Symphony No. 2
  DG 415 959.2GH2. Philharmonia Orchestra, Sinopoli
- Symphony No. 2; 4
  DG 453 037-2 GTA2. Chicago SO, Abbado

Tchaikovsky: Symphony No 4

It is perhaps curious that before Tchaikovsky, there are no tragedies among the classic symphonies. In poetry and drama, the tragic seems to be a natural medium for the expression of bold flights and deep questions. Symphonies, on the other hand, seem to end merrily—there is always a *scherzo* to break the funeral march! The gospel of despair is surely very near the limit of the musical realm. With Peter Ilyich Tchaikovsky (1840 - 1893) came a composer, a neurotic pessimist *par excellence,* not of heroic strength and will but of weakness and terror, easily insulted and injured.

There is a consistent sadness, blended with a tense passion, throughout the Fourth Symphony. "I am extremely lonely," wrote the composer, "I do not make friends easily... all winter I was constantly unhappy, sometimes on the verge of despair. I longed for death." There is no haven in life. The waves drive us hither and thither, alternating between grim truth and fleeting dreams of happiness, until the sea engulfs us. And so the music pursues a restless and fitful course, mourning the past but wanting the courage to start a new life. Even the reckless and hectic rejoicing at the conclusion of the work is interrupted by a sardonic proclamation of Fate. Rejoice in the happiness of others, the music seems to say, and you can still live—though the ending is brilliant, it is akin to despair.

The Fourth Symphony was written in 1877, immediately after Tchaikovsky's disastrous marriage and nervous breakdown that led to a convalescence abroad. It was also the warmest period of his strange relationship with the woman he never met, Mme. von Meck, to whom the work is dedicated. At her request, he wrote for her private use a program to the music, but there is no need to read it to experience the feeling in this music.

The Fourth Symphony is a rather happy statement compared to the Fifth and Sixth Symphonies, and it has been gloriously represented in stereo sound throughout the history of long playing microgroove.

There are numerous great performances, and to simply list then all would take several pages. I would say categorically that the Abbado recording with the Vienna Philharmonic for DG is a stellar analog recording which has few flaws, if any. It is a joyous reading, well captured by the microphones. When Zubin Mehta recorded for the first time with the Los Angeles Philharmonic at Royce Hall in

Los Angeles, the Fourth Symphony was amongst the first three albums released. This version must still stand high on anybody's list; it is expertly played and nicely recorded. If you can find it on LP, or if reissued on CD, it would be well worth one's effort to possess it. Loren Maazel recorded the work for a complete Tchaikovsky Cycle for London in the early sixties, and this Fourth also is excellent, having been well captured by London engineers. Mariss Jansons, a protege of Mravinski, recorded all six Tchaikovsky Symphonies with the Oslo Philharmonic Orchestra for Chandos in the last decade. All his readings are outstanding, and his Fourth is no exception. These are exceptionally well performed, groomed and clean performances, and lack the heart-on-sleeve hysteria of many North American and British orchestral interpretations, especially those of Bernstein, Ormandy, and Rostropovitch.

One of the most outstanding recordings available of this work is that by George Szell and the London Symphony Orchestra which is currently available on a London Historical CD that also includes the incidental music to Beethoven's *Egmont*, to me a most strange bedfellow. Regardless, the history behind this recording is interesting. The recording was made in the 1960s and George Szell refused to allow its release due to what he considered to be technical imperfections which did not meet his standards. He actually indicated that it would be released only over his dead body. And that's precisely what London Records did! When George Szell died in 1971, the record appeared rather quickly on Decca Ace of Diamonds, and ultimately was released at full price in the United States, only to be reissued on CD a few years ago. This performance, like the one described in the next paragraph, really says everything there is to be said about this work.

Yevgeny Mravinsky and his Leningrad Philharmonic Orchestra top my list of optimal performances. Their recording of the Fourth is, from the beginning, unbelievable. When all is said and done, there is nothing else to do or say. Find this recording, even though you'll have to buy it in association with his Fifth and Sixth Symphonies, which is certainly not an undesirable prospect. Still at full price despite its thirty five years of age, the performances are unforgettable, and really continue to impress as if they were made yesterday.

- Symphony Nos. 4, 5, 6
    DG419 745-2 GH2, Leningrad PO, Mravinsky
- Symphony No. 4
    London 425 972-2 LM. London SO, Szell

Tchaikovsky: Symphony No 5

When Tchaikovsky was composing his Fifth symphony, now acknowledged by some to be his greatest, he lamented to his brother that his old creative urge had begun to wane. Had he already "played himself out" as a composer? Had he no more music in him? Always self-depreciating, he sensed a patchiness and "manufacturedness" in this work. Posterity has proved him wrong, but all the public acclamation could do nothing to solve the personal problems of the composer's private life. And as he had done in its predecessor, Tchaikovsky sang once again a brave song of the struggle of Man with Fate.

The same introspective and melancholic self-pity pervades this music, beginning with a gloomy and mysterious opening theme, weary and foreboding, that suggests the leaden, deliberate tread of life. The tune grows to a high point of pathos—nay, anguish—before it melts into an unfailing flow of lesser melodies. There is a vein of the demonic throughout this piece. The demon is half external Fate in the Greek sense and half internal temper, a dreadful reminder of certain great temptations to which all men are subject, and to which some fall. Even the waltz in this music is never really happy; there is always a suggestion of impending fate that gives it an eerie, ghostly character. And though the music rises to a bold and vigorous self-confidence at its end—a change from clouds to sunshine, from defeat to triumph—the end is almost sullen; a tear seems to hang at the edge of the mournful and weary smile.

Tchaikovsky himself conducted its first performance in St. Petersburg in 1888.

The Fifth Symphony is a particularly beloved work, and reveals complex human emotions from both extremes. It is particularly well served in stereo. I grew up on the Abbado/London Symphony Orchestra recording on DG, now reissued on CD. This is an invigorating performance, but it has somewhat blunted acoustics, and is somewhat mid-range in prominence. This is the performance that sounds optimal to me based on my exposure, but there are several other recordings which merit perhaps even closer scrutiny.

George Szell's recording with the Cleveland Orchestra for Sony Classical is a pillar point of the recorded lexicon of the Fifths, and it is expertly played and well recorded despite its senescence. It should be heard. A more recent version by Abbado and the Berlin Philharmonic for Sony Classical improves upon Abbado's earlier London Symphony efforts, and it is brilliantly recorded. Remarkably, it is also a live performance from the Philharmonic made in the mid 1990s. To me it lacks some of the warmth of the 1971 DG recording, as technically outstanding as it is.

There are other outstanding Fifths which could be seriously considered, including an imported RCA recording by Gunter Wand and the North German Radio Symphony Orchestra, a performance which heretofore has not been available in North America. It is a stunning reading, somewhat opulent and deliberate in delivery, and it is somewhat unusual to hear Tchaikovsky from this perspective—but why? Wand is a gifted musician who has been all too late in his life to be "discovered" by the public, although he has been producing outstanding concerts and recorded performances for a very, very long time. Curiously, this Tchaikovsky Fifth is accompanied by a well performed Mozart Symphony No. 40, the only combination of this sort I have encountered in the catalog.

Sir Georg Solti and the Chicago Symphony have recorded the Fifth on two occasions. The first version is eminently more satisfying, and has incredible attack and bite, demonstrating the Chicago brass and hair-trigger perfection of execution, especially in the first movement. This performance is one of my favorites, and is available on a mid-priced CD. Despite its twenty year age, it is an exceptional performance. Zubin Mehta and the Israel Philharmonic recorded the Fifth relatively early in his conducting career. Mehta then re-recorded it with the Los Angeles Philharmonic as part of his complete cycle of Tchaikovsky Symphonies. Regardless, the earlier version with the Israel Philharmonic is an incisive, exciting performance, and if you can find it, either on LP or on reissued CD, it is well worth investigating.

Finally, my *Desert Island* performance is that of Yevgeny Mravinsky and the Leningrad Philharmonic Orchestra, on DG. This performance was recorded in 1961, and probably has not been bettered in terms of idiomatic accuracy. Certainly, the warbling Russian brass is somewhat annoying on first hearing, but the performance tingles with the brilliance and excitement of a most electrifying live performance conceivable, and the orchestral accompaniment is absolutely beyond reproach. This performance is so idiomatically different than most conventional performances that it, if anything, must serve as a counterpoint performance to any that one might have in their collection.

- Symphony Nos.4, 5,6
  DG 419 745.2GH2 Leningrad PO, Mravinsky

Tchaikovsky: Symphony No 6 (Pathetique)

In Tchaikovsky, says Ernest Newman, the blend of East and West is the very essence of the man and his art. On the one side, he seems to trace his descent from the most modern of pessimists who stands aghast at the spectacle of the insignificance of the individual in this complex world. On the other hand, there is a strong Oriental strain expressed in the turbulent rhythms, the love of gorgeous color for its own sake, and the occasional naiveté of design. It is the crossing of these two spirits that makes his music. A phrase of such profound melancholy, of such speechless anguish or despair that one could believe it to have come straight from the heart of the most refined and sensitive modern is followed, almost without warning, by a swirl of primeval passion that takes us back a thousand years in ancestry. And nowhere is this union of the East and the West in music so profoundly symbolized than in his *Pathetique* Symphony.

That the *Symphonie pathetique* remains Tchaikovsky's enduring masterpiece is unquestioned. It is an openhearted human document of immense pathos and tragedy, showing at once a profound humanity and a native tenderness with a tortured sensibility. Some may be overwhelmed by its agonizing misery and suffering, its intolerable sadness, its terrifying march, and its unusual ending—the music ends in a dirge! Here is a song about the bitter grief of life, the attempts to overcome it by forced and unreal gaiety, the vigorous and manly struggle against despair, and finally, surrender and death. Working with no extraneous material, with nothing more than the ordinary forms and colors of orchestral music, Tchaikovsky succeeds in creating one of the most poignant dramas of struggle, defeat and despair that even literature can point to. The *Pathetique* is genuinely Russian—in its exquisite sadness, its philosophical hopelessness of outlook, and its amalgam of Oriental fatalism with an Occidental logic of expression. On the other hand, its immense popularity could be an eloquent commentary on what the general public seems to find in this music— a reflection, perhaps magnified and dramatized, of their own unhappiness and frustration, their own spiritual hunger and bewilderment, that is combined with a purely emotional sense of vague comfort. And the fact that it survives, that it is widely listened to and loved, proves *a priori* that, however tinged it may be with personal melancholy, it is not ultimately pessimistic or destructive in effect.

This symphony was Tchaikovsky's swan song, his musical farewell to the world. For, this time, Tchaikovsky had indeed "played himself out!" Nine days after its first performance which he conducted on October 28, 1893, he died suddenly, giving rise to widely circulated speculations that have never ceased to fascinate his biographers.

The Sixth is a brooding work, also demonstrating the range of human emotion from rapt glee to the depths of irreconcilable depression. This work was Tchaikovsky's own personal expression of his grief at the hands of life, and there have been many academic arguments as to precisely what that grief was. Never mind that argument at the moment; the work is far more important.

There have been many excellent early stereo recordings of the Sixth, including those by Dimitri Mitripoulos and the New York Philharmonic on CBS, Carlo Maria Giulini and the Philharmonia Orchestra on EMI, and Fritz Reiner and the Chicago Symphony on RCA. Any of these are truly excellent basic performances, most of which are available at mid or budget price now. Another excellent Sixth was that by Paul Kletzki and the Philharmonia Orchestra on EMI.

Due to the demands of the score, more recent versions will have greater sonic impact, especially to wide ranging stereo systems. Again, performances which leave greatest impact would be those I would want to live with, and Mravinski and the Leningrad Philharmonic Orchestra say just about as much as there is to say on the subject in their 1961 recording for DG. The performance is at once witty and brilliantly conceived. It totters to a rousing conclusion of the March (Third Movement) and plumbs the depths of depression in the finale. I can't be without this recording, although there are several that are sonically more satisfying.

Solti has recorded an excellent *Pathetique* Symphony for London with the Chicago Symphony as has, surprisingly, Seiji Ozawa and the Boston Symphony for Erato. Even Herbert von Karajan's 1976 recording for DG shows up with about the best played March that I have encountered. The Berlin Philharmonic simply can't be bettered when it comes to accuracy of execution, even when compared to orchestras as well rehearsed and as fine as Cleveland or Chicago. This is a stimulating, evocative performance, regardless of whether or not one is enamored of Herbert Von Karajan as a conductor.

In recent years, the Russian conductor, Mikhail Pletnev has emerged on the scene with an orchestra of his own design—the Russian National Orchestra. One of its first recordings for Virgin was a brilliant *Pathetique* Symphony, and even after a remake with the same orchestra for another label, DG, the original performance still shines brilliantly. If it were one recording I was to live with the rest of my life, regardless of the excellence of Mravinski's, it would be this one. It says it all, probably better than anybody else.

- Symphony No. 6; Marche slav
    Virgin/EMI VC7 59661-2. Russian Nat. O, Pletnev
- Symphony Nos.4, 5, 6
    DG 419 745.2GH2 Leningrad PO, Mravinsky
- Symphony Nos.4, 5, 6
    DG 453 088-2GTA2. BPO, Karajan

Tchaikovsky: Piano Concerto No 1

Few more inspiring tunes can be found anywhere in music than in the opening theme of Tchaikovsky's Piano Concerto No. 1. It is too bad that people are so busy with Tchaikovsky the pessimist that one forgets Tchaikovsky the artist. For, this music is plentifully abundant with phrases of rare grace, and a fresh and original charm in its melodic invention and its rhythmic vigor.

Tchaikovsky considered the concerto form much as a duel, rather than a duet, between David and Goliath with David the victor. On the one hand, there is the orchestra with its power and inexhaustible variety of color, and on the other is the small but highly mettled piano which comes off victorious in the hands of a gifted artist. Alas! It was this very attitude that precluded the composer from writing in this genre successfully in later life when the strain of a fuller experience with the world and an increasing incapacity to make a success of his personal life descended upon him and his music. And so by the waters of Babylon the neurotically captive Tchaikovsky sat down and wept as he grew older! Whereas the sense of despair and anguish that consumed his later life could be admirably channeled into the symphonic form, he was unable to bestride once more that high-mettled piano and come off victorious in the hands of a gifted soloist. For, in a concerto, the soloist can never afford to admit defeat, and Tchaikovsky could no longer believe in the biblical and make David victorious! And though the composer was to write two more works for piano and orchestra, neither of them were truly successful because the composer's heart and spirit were not in them. The First Concerto, revised in 1889, stands unrivaled in its sheer brilliance and grandeur and in the variety and intensity of its color, and for the commanding breadth of its conception.

The ideas in this music are so original, so noble and so powerful, and the details so interesting that though there are many of them, they do not impair the clarity and unity of the work. This is particularly true of the introduction with its now-familiar chords from the piano ringing clear and powerful even against the concerted might of the orchestra. The grandiloquence of the first movement contrasts colorfully with the utter grace and almost pastoral simplicity of the second. The first movement introduces the "blind beggar tune" that the composer had heard the blind Ukrainian beggars sing at a fair in Kamenka, all with exactly the same melody and the same refrain. In the superbly lyrical and gloriously beautiful slow movement, Tchaikovsky made use of an old waltz-like French *chansonette* that his brother Anatol had sung and whistled in their youth. It is played merrily by the strings while the piano brilliantly figures above it, and it creates an amusingly frivolous and scurrying central portion of a movement that acts as a crown to the whole work. The third movement is a rondo whose theme and rhythm suggests some wild and vigorous Cossack dance that springs from the orchestra almost like an animated being into which further life and vivacity are breathed by the keyboard. The music ends in a powerful climax that sweeps in both the piano and the orchestra.

Living in Southern California, this work has all but been destroyed for me by the relentless repetition of the opening theme of the first movement as the introduction to the 8 o'clock evening program on a local radio station. Even though only the first twelve bars or so of the work are heard, I don't care to hear this work again! Nevertheless, it is one of the dozen great piano concerti in existence, and the novitiate should learn the work, if only for its brilliant second and third movements.

I don't think anybody has better stated the concerto than the South American pianist Martha Argerich. She recorded the work for DG with her then husband and the Royal Philharmonic in 1971, and it has subsequently been issued by Philips as a live performance with Kyril Kondrashin and the Concertgebouw Orchestra of Amsterdam. Most recently she returned to the work with her professional colleague, Claudio Abbado, with the Berlin Philharmonic in a live performance which is every bit as exciting as the original recording she made over twenty five years ago. This venerable pianist has had a career both on stage and in recording which is well nigh infallible, and if I were to live with one recording, despite the innumerable excellent recordings, it would probably be the most recent of her efforts with Abbado in Berlin. I need not really say much more about Argerich and her Tchaikovsky.

Without insulting the bulk of professional pianistic musicians on this planet, I should at least mention the outstanding recording by Van Cliburn, also conducted by Kondrashin, recorded by RCA in the late fifties, which brought this then young American artist to fame after his winning of the Tchaikovsky Competition in Moscow. The Russian pianist Yevgeny Kissin has made a brilliant recording of the work with Karajan and the Berlin Philharmonic, and despite his being hampered by Karajan's stern rule, the performance is a successful, if not highly enjoyable one. Kissin's technical brilliance cannot be denied. The British pianist, Peter Donohoe, recorded the work for EMI with Rudolf Barshai and the Bournemouth Symphony Orchestra during the mid digital period, and this is a memorable version. If you have the opportunity to pick up this recording as a boxed set with the Second and Third Tchaikovsky Piano Concerti, all the more worthwhile this investment would be. Another excellent alternative would be that of pianist Jerome Lowenthal in his commanding performance with Sergui Commissiona at the podium with the London Symphony Orchestra on Arabesque. This is a mid-priced recording, and really is outstanding. Why Lowenthal has not had a truly rapturous international career defies logic, but it may be his own choice.

By default I have been unable to mention probably fifty to sixty good to excellent performances of this work by virtue of its popularity, and I regret this, but I would tell you that any of the performances that I have mentioned will please you.

- (i) Piano Concerto No. 1; (ii) Violin concerto
  DG 439 420-2 (i) Argerich, RPO, Dutoit (ii) Milstein, VPO, Abbado (1971)
- Piano Concerto No. 1;
  DG 449 816-2 GH Argerich, BPO, Abbado (1994)

Tchaikovsky: Violin Concerto

It is a wonder that this violin concerto has survived at all. The work seems to have progressed easily with little of the soul-searching, turmoil, exaltation and despair that so often accompanied the composer's bigger creations. However, it remained unperformed for two years because it was considered to be technically too difficult, and when the "unplayable" Concerto was finally played, an influential section of the Viennese press attacked it mercilessly. The echoes of these scathing reviews further embittered Tchaikovsky's already gloomy disposition, and it is not surprising to learn that one particular review haunted him till the day he died, that by Eduard Hanslick who was Europe's uncrowned ruler of musical destinies.

The Violin Concerto itself is certainly proof of the composer's return to the joys of living from the depths of mental despair. He had come from Italy to Clarens in Switzerland in high spirits; life was rose-colored again and, with his brother Modeste and a visiting Russian violinist Josef Kotek, they played a lot of music pieces, including Lalo's *Symphonic Espagnole*. The freshness, lightness, piquant rhythms and the beautifully and admirably harmonized melodies of this work gave him great pleasure, and inspired him to write a violin concerto in which the Spanish element is certainly not lacking. The Concerto bubbles over with the *joie de vivre* which the composer was experiencing at the time.

The plan of the first movement sprang suddenly in the composer's head and quickly settled into its mold. It begins with a brief orchestral introduction that has little to do with the thematic material to follow except in setting the lyrical scene. The music works up for the soloist's entry, but without any dramatic tension so that the violin is able to very quickly settle down comfortably for the main theme. The charming lyricism of the two main themes is matched by the orchestral accompaniment. The slow movement had been originally conceived to be a meditation, but this was replaced on the suggestion of the composer's brother. The present slow movement begins with an introduction by the wood winds which sets a nostalgic atmosphere with a Spanish flavor for the thoroughly Slavic melody, and the music never moves outside the lyric vein of song. A second melody, though still nostalgic, brings in a ray of consolation. Whatever its prototypes, it is one of the most characteristic melodies that Tchaikovsky ever composed, beautifully decorated on its reappearance as it merges into a delightful anticipation of the first theme of the finale. The orchestra at once sets the rhythm of the well-known Russian dance, the *trepak*, in the rondo-like finale. The music, developed from two folk like melodies, is typically Russian in tune and rhythm, and sets the stage for the superb orchestral and soloist brilliance that follows. The work builds up at a brisk pace to a crashing climax.

There are no fewer than sixty good recordings of this work, and three of them spring to mind as highly respectable, modern interpretations worthy of owning right off the bat.

Jascha Heifetz and Fritz Reiner with the Chicago Symphony recorded what may be for most a quasi-definitive interpretation which has stood the test of time—forty years! This is a truly chiseled, drilled performance with spectacular orchestral ensemble and pyrotechnical soloist contribution. It should not be missed.

In 1973, the great violinist Nathan Milstein, who seemed to improve as he aged, recorded the work (also the Mendelssohn Concerto) with Claudio Abbado. The performance is currently in the catalogs on DG Galleria. It shows the nearly seventy year old soloist to be in extraordinary playing condition, and the performance is vibrant and virile. It is far better than a recording made in the late monophonic era by the same soloist with which I was utterly bored as a child. One would think that the reverse would have been true in terms of cogent excitement, but shortly until he injured his hand, Milstein was an exceptional musician who seemed far more impressive as a senior than he was at the ostensible peak of his career.

Unfortunately, with the passage of time, competition increases and delivery of performances by Ubermenschen can occur. Violinist Maxim Vengerov with Claudio Abbado and the Berlin Philharmonic Orchestra have recorded the Concerto for Teldec. For me, while it does not displace Jascha Heifetz's performance of the work on which I was raised, it now is at the top of my list for recommended versions because of the dynamic recorded sound and the utterly impeccable playing. Mr. Vengerov may well be the preeminent violinist of this generation, although recordings by Shaham, Mutter and others are highly comparable.

Don't miss Vengerov's—it is a performance which will take the curl out of your hair.

- Violin concerto in D
    Teldec/Warner Dig. 4509 90881. Vengerov, BPO, Abbado

Tchaikovsky: Ballet Music

The year 1877 seemed to mark the turning point in Tchaikovsky's life. In that year he made his disastrous marriage, and in that year also Fate first knocked at his door. And it was from this time onwards that he began to seek escape in the never-never world of ballets. Ballet music in Russia was not considered to be more derogatory to the dignity of a composer than opera, and the Russian audience had become as keen a judge of one as of the other. Tchaikovsky's genius for ballet music was original, but this was not appreciated at the time of their early performances because of their appalling productions. Moreover, his scores were of too substantial a nature for the ballet-going public who were used to a much more frivolous accompaniment to the dancing. And some of his tunes were even considered to be not "sufficiently danceable!"

Tchaikovsky's ballets are three in number. They all belong to the domain of fairyland which is always a happy background for a ballet. Here all is brightness and life itself—music made for flying toes and gracefully postured lovely bodies; in a word, dance music in its most authentic and beautiful form. The first ballet, *Swan Lake*, is typical of the fairy tales that the Russians had loved to see illustrated by a *ballet d'action*. The music is graceful and attractive, and the score brims with typical Tchaikovskian melodies. Probably for the first time in ballet music a scheme of *leit-motives* is used, two of the principal subjects being the tremulous theme of the swans in flight and the hauntingly wistful theme of Odette herself, assigned to an oboe against soft strings and harp arpeggios. *Sleeping Beauty* is based upon the well-known and well-worn fairy tale. Few ballet scores are so suitable in mood and style for the action that they accompany. The music is a great advance on that of *Swan Lake*, though not deeper than the subject demands, and is melodious in the best sense of the word, fantastic and brightly colored. It consists of thirty numbers, many of which are gems of dance music. The suite is laid down as a prologue and three acts. In it, Tchaikovsky proves as always that musical material of no great profundity can, by skillful treatment through an orchestra's limitless resources, be developed into music of intense and permanent interest. Its successor is familiar to every music lover: the charming *Casse-Noisette* or *The Nutcracker*, derived from Dumas's version of a play by E.T.A. Hoffmann. Not a word, not a whisper of the composer's usual melancholy can be found in it—here is music of brilliance, vitality and a barbaric richness of tonal color and exotic rhythm that is really captivating. It is almost superfluous to point out how delightful these pieces are—as long as the *Casse-Noisette* suite holds sway, the fame of the composer will for ever be kept green.

Those that say that Tchaikovsky could not compose a tune or develop thematic information from that tune are utterly wrong. Tchaikovsky's ballet music is perhaps the greatest and most popular music he wrote, maybe even greater than his symphonic output.

Regardless, these extraordinarily popular works have been reduced to half hour "sampler plates" for the diet of those who are not interested in hearing the entire ballet.

The cellist/conductor, Mstislav Rostropovich, appears for the first and only time as conductor in a single CD of this music for DG Galleria in truly resplendent recordings made in the early eighties with the Berlin Philharmonic. Since their appearance, they have been hailed as well nigh definitive interpretations insofar as elegance of playing, polish, and freedom from eccentricity and a "heart on sleeve approach." I know of no greater performances of the Ballet Suites than these and, as they are currently available, I have no frank desire to recommend any other performances, especially as these are at mid price and excellent analog sound. The listener simply cannot go wrong with these performances.

Those looking for modern performances of the complete ballets would be well served by Mackerras' excellent traversal of the *Nutcracker* for Telarc, Seiji Ozawa's performance of the complete *Swan Lake* for DG, and Jon Lanchberry's recording of *Sleeping Beauty* for EMI, amongst the many performances of these works available in complete editions.

- Nutcracker: suite; Sleeping Beauty: suite; Swan Lake: suite
  DG 449 726-2. BPO, Rostropovitch

- Nutcracker: suite; Sleeping Beauty: suite; Swan Lake: suite
  London 443 555-2 LH. Orchestre Symphonique de Montreal, Dutoit

Dvorak: Symphonies (Nos. 7, 8, 9)

Great men are simple. The heart of the great Bohemian musical genius Antonin Dvorak (1841 - 1904) was that of a child, jovial and kindly with an almost schoolgirl modesty. He had three passions: composing, living in the country, and caring for his pigeons. And his music fed on the life and nature that surrounded him—the highways and forests, the songs of the peasants, and the fiddlers at the fairs and weddings. There is a peculiar wistfulness in his music that seems to come not only from the man but from the entire human race. For Dvorak is the most eminent folk musician. He shows great delight, sympathy and freedom in reveling among the simple tones and rhythms of popular utterance, rearing on them in poetic spontaneity, yet with the balance and restraint of a trained master.

Some have called his Symphony No. 7 one of the greatest and purest example of the symphonic art-form since Beethoven. Dvorak himself strove to convince the world at large that a great composer, not a mere musician, could indeed come out of Bohemia. "Everywhere I go, I think of nothing else but this work, which must be such as to shake the world." It is a powerfully tragic piece marked by grave, even austere, themes, dark harmonies and shrill climaxes. Above a drum roll, the lower strings and horns open the music of the stormy first movement. The work came at a time when Dvorak's mind was deeply troubled: the loss of his mother still lingered in his mind, and his conscious was rebelling against the pressures that were being exerted upon him to compose in accordance with the very German ideals that his country was trying to overthrow. There is a deliberate avoidance of the warmest registers of the strings and an abundant employment of the wood winds and horns. The tragic mood is defined in the haunting lyricism of the second movement as the first violins and cellos sing an impassioned and sad melody, strange in its sincerity and profound grandeur. The beautiful things in this music are not mere delights; they are depths. A restless *Scherzo*, with its infectious rhythms, seems to describe an idyllic sun-warmed landscape, and then reality returns in the last movement as new themes appear, and the music ends forcefully in a splendid affirmation that resolves tragedy into triumph.

Misleadingly baptized the *English Symphony* because it was first published by an English company, Symphony No 8 is the most nationalistic of all his symphonies. Folk melodies come and go in rhapsodic continuity, and the rich yet simple harmonies make it perhaps the plainest of his mature symphonies. The music opens with a masterly contrast between church and the countryside: an eccelesiastical sounding Slavonic theme contrasts with a simple pastoral melody that is articulated high up on the flutes, resembling the warbling of the composer's beloved pigeons. The slow second movement is a little tone poem on Czech country life. A touch of pathos in the opening music gives way to lovely bird sounds, then follows the village band—cymbals and all—whose robust playing rises to a sudden moment in drama which as quickly subsides, leaving the birds calling quietly in the garden. It is not difficult to understand this beautifully elegiac movement. Here is absolute music, plumbing the depths of sorrowful expression. A pleasantly melancholic *dumka* follows, with delightfully naive transparent melodies that seem to look at one with the eyes of a child, and then the music ends noisily, with the same childlike pleasure, to the blare of trumpet calls, goading the listener to hurry along and not miss the fun!

It has remained a much debated issue of how far Dvorak's "American" symphony (Symphony No. 9) is based upon characteristic Bohemian folk lore or upon African music, and further, whether African American music can fairly be regarded as American folk song. The charm and strength of any folk music lies in its spontaneous simplicity, not in its distinctive national quality. It is here that the musician, like Antaeus, touches Mother Earth and renews his strength. And when Dvorak suddenly shifts in the midst of his *New World* fantasy into a touch of Bohemian song, there is no real loss. It is all relevant in the broad sense of folk feeling that does not look too closely at geographical bounds or national prejudice. The music blends his love of genuine Bohemian melodies with his newfound enthusiasm for Negro spirituals, the plantation songs of Stephen Foster, and the songs of the North American Indians, and through it all he expresses his great sympathy for the oppressed colored people. It is as if a poet from a distant land is, at the same time and in the same tone, uttering his longing for his own country and expressing the pathos and the romance of the new. What distinguishes Dvorak's symphony is not merely Bohemian melody or even Negro spiritual, but a genuine folk feeling in the widest meaning.

Upon hearing his last symphony (*From the New World*) that was composed during his sojourn in Iowa, one is left with a feeling of disappointment that the expectations suggested earlier in the music have not been fulfilled. It is an eminently symphonic symphony that makes extensive use of the characteristic symphonic devise of cyclic repetition and development to give an organic cohesiveness to the movements of a large work. For example, the first theme of the first movement recurs in the three subsequent movements, and the finale contains references to nearly every important theme that has gone before. The slow second movement (*Largo*) is one of the most beautiful and haunting pieces of music ever written. Introduced by an English Horn, there is a helpless quality about this theme, in contrast to a vivacious but ghostly variation that appears in the flutes and oboes and is then taken up by the rest of the orchestra. It has been said that Dvorak was especially influenced by the woodland funeral of Minnehaha in Longfellow's *Song of Hiawatha* when he wrote this movement. The permanent hold that this symphony has gained lies in its intrinsic art and sincere sentiment; it has little to do with its nominal title or purpose.

Unfortunately, the Dvorak Symphony No. 9 is so popular as an introduction to legitimate music that it is overplayed, and it overshadows the other great symphonic literature written by this composer who is generally known to have written happy, rather than downtrodden, depressive music. I find the 9th the weakest and least interesting of the final four Dvorak Symphonies; I derive the least pleasure from it compared to Symphony Nos 6-8, no matter how great the work truly is.

The listener is encouraged to learn all nine symphonies. Superb integral cycles of all the works are available from Kertesz on London Records, Kubelik on DG, and Rowicki on Philips, all at mid-price. Kubelik's are the most opulent and Slavic in character but feature the Berlin Philharmonic's polished playing. The Kertesz recordings are a bit more hamische, a bit ragged around the edges and may have more native character, and Rowicki falls somewhere in the middle. If one would choose optimal performances from these three cycles, I would recommend Rowicki for No. 6, the most Brahmsian of all Dvorak Symphonies, Kertesz for No. 7, Kubelik or Kertesz for No.

8 and without question, Kubelik's incredible No. 9 from DG which is fortunately available separately paired with his excellent No. 8.

Symphony No. 6 fares superbly with Dohnanyi and the Cleveland Orchestra (full priced), one of the few single disc performances of the work available outside of the boxed sets of all nine Symphonies. Rowicki, Kertesz and Kubelik are the other major competition, and all are mid-priced. I can't recommend Dohnanyi too highly even though Rowicki's performance is closest to my heart. If you are able to find an old LP or reissued CD of Karel Ancerl's performance of Symphony No. 6 with the Czech Philharmonic on Supraphon, you will also not be disappointed—a wonderful interpretation, nicely recorded.

Single issues are a tall subject. For Symphony No.7, a dark, imposing somewhat mysterious work with a wild finale, I would recommend that the listener try to find Carlos Paita's unacceptably poorly played version on Lodia CD-782. This performance was probably made without rehearsal, and features a nonexistent orchestra (probably because of embarrassment to identify themselves). But the two last movements have a spirit which is indefatigable, and the playing, especially of the finale, is a once in a lifetime experience that should be heard. Never mind that the trio of the third movement falls flat on its face, and that the orchestra is half a beat off from left to right. No other performance has the impact that this one does. It is out of print but may be available in used record stores.

Paita is a music lover turned conductor. I don't know anything of his training. He made some hideous recordings for London Phase Four Stereo in the seventies, some of which were reissued on Lodia (he is the only conductor I know of who has recorded for this label—it may be his own). His personal history is a tragic one, having lost his wife and children in a horrible car crash. His music making is slightly less horrible, but now and then he delivers an act of genius. Despite the flaws of this performance, it is worth researching.

On to more significant Symphony No. 7s! The Amsterdam Concertgebouw and Sir Colin Davis have an outstanding No. 7 paired with a great No. 8 on Philips Silver Line Classics; they are middle of the road, sane, safe recordings that are extremely well engineered.

George Szell and the Cleveland Orchestra had a fine No. 7 on an older CBS Odyssey recording which is extremely refined and Slavic in character which I believe is not available on CD. But pride of place of modern recordings for me goes to both Maazel and the Vienna Philharmonic on DG as well as Christoph von Dohnanyi and the Cleveland Orchestra for the modern sound and outstanding interpretations these two artists have rendered with their truly great ensembles. Another excellent No. 7 is a new recording by Chung and the Vienna Philharmonic for DG which may now just be available in the USA.

The No. 8 is my favorite of the last three Dvorak Symphonies; it is a work I learned early in my childhood, probably at age 11 when Rafael Kubelik's splendid performance appeared on DG 139 181. Only after nearly three decades have I heard a performance of equal elegance and refinement in very similar recorded sound—that of James Levine and the Staatskapelle Dresden for DG, which is paired with a good but not equivalently outstanding Dvorak No. 9. Levine clearly has listened to Kubelik. He hasn't copied him, but the rendition is so similar and so gratifying that I encourage the listener to seek out this performance. It is a smiling, jovial rendition which more than aptly plumbs the depths of this musical study. Dohnanyi and the Cleveland Orchestra for London, and Claudio Abbado and the Berlin Philharmonic for Sony Classical, also present excellent statements in opulent sound; of these two, I feel Dohnanyi is the preferable performance, especially because of the mesmerizing way the conductor handles the second movement.

Symphony No. 9! Hmmmm! There are probably forty superb recordings, beginning with Reiner and the Chicago Symphony on BMG/RCA (mid-price), Kondrashin and the Vienna Philharmonic for London Records (also mid-priced), Kertesz' original Vienna Philharmonic recording for London (budget price)—NOT the performance from his complete cycle from the London Symphony Orchestra (mid-priced), Kubelik on DG as mentioned earlier as my principal recommendation, Solti and the Chicago Symphony on London, and either Cleveland Orchestra recording with Szell (now over thirty years old on Sony Classical) or Dohnanyi and the Cleveland Orchestra.

Finally, there are two 2-CD sets of the last three Dvorak Symphonies if the reader wishes to exclude No. 6. Both are at mid price. Dohnanyi's excellent Cleveland series is available this way, as is a traversal by Carlo Maria Giulini for EMI with the Philharmonia Orchestra and the London Philharmonic Orchestra. These EMI recordings show Giulini in great form, before the "great slow down" which now yields the most priestly of interpretations. A "servant" to music, I would say, is an understatement about his reverence for composers' intentions. They are great interpretations; they are not quite as trenchant and dogged as Dvorak can be played, but will bring much pleasure.

- Symphony No. 6
  London 430 204-2 LH. Cleveland O, Dohnanyi
- Symphony No. 7
  LODIA LO-CD 782. Philharmonic SO, Paita
- (i) Symphony No. 7; 8 (ii) 9 (New World); (i) Symphonic variations Op. 78
  Philips Duo 438 347-2 (i) LSO (ii) Concg. O, Sir Colin Davis
- Symphony No. 8
  DG 447 754-2. Staatskapelle Dresden O, Levine
- (i) Symphony No. 9;(ii) Slavonic dances Nos. 1, 3 and 7/ Op 4611; 3 & 7; 10 and 15 Op.72/2 & 7
  DG 439 436-2 (i) BPO, (ii) Bav. RSO, Kubelik

Saint Saens: Symphony No. 3 (Organ)

Few composers of the age of opulence were as marvelously diversified as Camille Saint Saens (1835 - 1921). He had been, with somewhat unequal success, a poet, dramatist, mathematician, naturalist, philosopher, critic and musician, and his music was as varied as his mind. A classicist by education, he readily expended himself in capricious fancies, imparting a charm and brilliance to the most ordinary things. Some of his music, like *Proserpine* and *Ascanio*, was superficial, thin and cramped, without much depth or force. But when he had the whole orchestra at his disposal, the situation changed. Saint Saens wrote five symphonies; its magical instrumentation, soft richness, supple and elegant architecture, and the sparkling diversity of its instrumentation makes his Symphony No. 3 one of the most important of French symphonies.

Two new elements added to the orchestral resources enhance this novel masterpiece: the piano is employed as an orchestral instrument with passages for two and four hands, and the organ is introduced resolutely to produce special effects through its sustained tones and its sudden and magnificent reinforcements of the orchestra's sonority. Another most remarkable characteristic of the score is that it grows, in its entirety, out of the expansion and transformation of a single fundamental theme which serves as a center for the four movements, and about which the accessory musical ideas orbit.

The main theme, uneasy and sorrowful as first presented by a string quartet, enters into the most diverse instrumental combinations. It mingles with the reverie of the *Adagio*, sometimes passing from instrument group to instrument group, and sometimes veiled beneath variations. It is metamorphosed to take part in the fanciful *Scherzo*, and again spreads out in flights and showers of brilliant orchestral tone colors. Then the *finale* commences, and a new change of rhythm converts the original tune into a chant. It is divided and broken up into fragments and then brought together and gradually broadened out, while the vibrant blasts of the brass appear to acclaim its triumph.

The symphony was composed for members of the London Philharmonic Orchestra in 1886, and performed by them under the baton of the composer.

The Saint-Saens Symphony No.3 (Organ) is one of the great showpieces for high fidelity systems, and itself is a wonderfully joyous work which recently was featured in the full length motion picture *Babe* in a variety of incarnations, not all particularly tasteful. Nevertheless, the work is a classic of the gramophone, and has fared well in recording since its earliest stereo iteration which is still in the catalog, that of the Boston Symphony Orchestra with conductor Charles Munch.

While most conductors performing the work have indeed listened to Munch's pioneering recording, it is by now so far outdated sonically that no matter what anybody tells you, it is not competitive. Far too little of the score comes through in this recording to make it a worthwhile purchase, unless for historically purposes exclusively. I know many people will argue this with me, but then they should make comparisons to those listed below.

Charles Dutoit and the Montreal Symphony Orchestra have performed this work for London in a truly splendid recording captured at the St. Eustache Cathedral, and the ambiance of the recording, the depth of the dynamic range, and the playing of the Montreal Symphony are beyond reproach. This is truly a Gallic reading, but is of a stature normally expected of international orchestras, not simply good French orchestras. I cannot too highly encourage the listener to seek out this excellent recording.

There is a somewhat curious performance by the Chicago Symphony Orchestra and Daniel Barenboim in which the recording of the organ is synchronized from the Cathedrale de Chartres, outside Paris. The organist, Gaston Litaize, was provided a copy of the recorded performance minus organ, and dubbed in his synchronized playing to a second set of DG microphones in the Cathedral and the amalgam was issued as DG 2530 639 in 1976. This performance is somewhat more spontaneous than Dutoit, a bit more ragged around the edges, but is extraordinarily effective and should be heard as well. It remains my single favorite recording from the standpoint of sheer excitement.

There are other recordings of the work by James Levine and the Berlin Philharmonic with organist, Simon Preston, which, despite several glitches in the closing bars, yield outstanding results, and playing of a superior orchestral body. This, like Dutoit and Barenboim, is a fairly natural-sounding recording.

For those who must shake the roof beams, one will have to obtain the old CBS/Sony recording by the Philadelphia Orchestra and conductor Eugene Ormandy. His tasteless performance demonstrates organist E. Power Biggs as if each pipe of the organ had a microphone unto itself, and the pedal point in the second portion of the first half of the work as well as the second half of the second portion of the work are incredibly well captured despite the sterile orchestral interpretation. For those wishing really to hear 24 Hz and 36 Hz tone generations, this performance is for you! But not for your neighbors! Be certain that you have a woofer that is at least 16" in diameter to reproduce this recording accurately. It will have a greater effect upon canines down your block than sending a signal down the street by playing *Tannhauser* at full volume!

I know I've left out a good two dozen outstanding recordings of the work, but these are my favorites. Any of them will please, including the Ormandy which should be used for demonstration of amplifier output only. It will bring a smile to your face.

- Symphony No. 3 (Organ)
     London 410201-2. Hurford, Montreal SO, Dutoit

- Symphony No. 3 (Organ)
     DG 415 847-2 GGA. Litaize, Chicago SO, Barenboim

Bizet: Orchestral Works

In 1872, the French dramatist Daudet asked George Bizet (1838 - 1875) to write some music to accompany his forthcoming play *The Woman of Arles* (*L'Arlesienne*). The plot cleverly spun two contrasting webs. In the first, a forthright young man falls in love with a beautiful woman from Arles. When she proves unworthy, he tries to forget her but, in spite of his childhood sweetheart who truly loves him, he loses control of his emotions and puts an end to his troubles by throwing himself from the loft of a farmhouse, crushing his skull on the stones below. Contrasted to this is the other tender love story of an old shepherd and his wife who, in spite of difficulties and years of involuntary separation, remain true to each other.

The lovely region of Provence, in which the city of Arles is nestled, is rich in lore and medieval song. In the Middle Ages, troubadours had passed through this land enriching its simple life with their ballads and legends. In later times, bands of gypsies roamed its countryside, playing and singing their quaint songs and lively folk-airs. It was from the rhythms and tunes of this rich and ancient heritage that Bizet composed his twenty seven engaging and melodious short music pictures—some are very short—to enhance the meaning or charm of some individual incidents in the three-act play.

The play was a failure, but a few months later, an orchestral conductor selected five of its music pieces and played them at a concert. Thus was born the first *L'Arlesienne Suite*. Later, others selected other numbers and the second *Suite* came into being. Some have called it Bizet's finest music.

It can be fairly said that Georges Bizet's great fame rests securely on only one work: his great opera *Carmen*. To it he brought his full creative style, his marvelous melodic gift, his flair for brilliant orchestration, and his fine dramatic instinct. And through it he proved his right to be considered a great composer. Bizet worked painstakingly at the score—the *Habenara* was revised fifteen times, and the *Toreador Song*, that has never lost its power to elicit an ovation, was interpolated as an afterthought!

The music in *Carmen* is not authentically Spanish, and Bizet never meant it to be. He utilized Spanish folk material only to give the work its local color. He was trying to recreate the mood and atmosphere of Spain by using Spanish rhythms and tone colors, but his style of composition is French to the core. *Carmen*, despite its background and setting, its wild and strange exotism and its irresistibly voluptuous and fierce gypsy flavor, is a French and not a Spanish opera. But it is the most Mozartian opera since Mozart in which enchanting musical invention goes hand in hand, almost without a break, with dramatic veracity and psychological characterization. Here are beautiful melodies, expressive harmonies, and exquisite orchestral colors all concentrated, in a heightened form, in a single masterpiece.

The music of the overture is of the simplest and the most innocent kind. It begins with the animated theme of the entry of the bullfighters, on to this is tacked the refrain of the *Toreador Song*, another nonchalant key-leap brings a repetition of the arena music, and then enters Carmen,—is it the actual woman, or the Fate of which she is the embodiment? The music ends, or rather remains suspended, arrestingly, questioningly, in the upper air.

Sentimental legends die hard, and that of Bizet's untimely death having being brought about by the "failure" of his opera still survives in some quarters. Bizet passed away three months after the opening performance of *Carmen*.

The delightful suites from *L'Arlesienne* and *Carmen*, the latter from Bizet's most famous opera, have fared extraordinarily well in the recorded format since the beginning of the industry. The suites are usually offered together, and the combination provides a rather good auditory picture of Bizet's orchestral output and of some of the great highlights from his operatic masterpiece, *Carmen*. These are highly gallic, characteristic works of this outstanding composer whose music is revered in the opera house. Actually, Bizet wrote several operas, including the *Pearl Fishers*, and both it and *Carmen* are splendidly valuable assets to the operatic literature.

Herbert von Karajan recorded these works relatively early in the stereo era for EMI with the Philharmonia Orchestra at a time in Karajan's career where he had not suffered the egocentric need to mold and shape phrases according to his desires, and these recordings retain a freshness and vitality rarely heard in later Karajan perform-ances. The recordings are light, fresh and unfussy, and they do not have the Teutonic heaviness that imbued much of his work, and they remain a testament to his artistry. At budget price, they are a veritable steal!

Claudio Abbado and the London Symphony have recorded these works in genuinely exciting, hair trigger perfect performances on DG. These really must be heard, because the playing is of an order of magnitude greater than the Philharmonia from several decades be-fore. Charles Dutoit has recorded the same works with the Orchestre Symphonique de Montreal in what is perhaps the best recorded sound available, and these cannot be recommended too highly as well. They are highly polished, idiomatic performances played by an orchestra which has the music in its blood.

Not long ago the young conductor, Myun-Whun Chung, recorded these works in highly idiomatic performances and excellent sound with the Orchestre de la Bastille during his tenure as music director of this excellent opera company. I recently heard these performances not realizing that the record actually had been issued, and I found them to be very exciting, virile and imaginative performances. This record is very good value for the money, and contains quite a lot of music. Next to Abbado, which benefits from more polished playing, it would be my second choice. Finally, Sir Thomas Beecham on an old EMI release has recorded the Symphony in C along with the two *Arlesienne Suites* using the French National Radio Orchestra and the Royal Philharmonic Orchestra, and these gallic readings, although somewhat sloppily played, have great swagger and charm of their own.

Igor Markevitch and the Orchestre des Concerts Lamoureux, now on Belart-Karussell (formerly on Philips Classics, 1959), have compiled all four works in a super budget CD available by import, and these are highly idiomatic readings in still excellent sound. The immediacy of the recording is shocking despite its age and, in some respects, it is the most exciting of all performances that I have heard.

Any of these recordings will bring great pleasure, and one need not look further despite the numerous versions on the market.

- Arlesienne Suites 1 & 2; Carmen Suites 1 & 2
  DG 423 472-2 GGA. LSO, Abbado

Wagner: Die Meistersinger von Nurnberg

In the little town of Nuremberg, Richard Wagner (1813 - 1883) created an idyllic microcosm of German society—indeed, of the social order in its entirety as he conceived it, a vision of the union of political, economic and artistic values. A society that did not honor and cultivate art was doomed: it inevitably grew oppressive and finally collapsed under its own weight. The singing contest in Reformation Nuremberg provides the backdrop for a robust bourgeois world of cobblers, goldsmiths and town clerks, united in the cultivation of prosperity and art. They are all artists, poets, businessmen and, of course, Master singers, who produce not only songs but shoes, and who consider the latter just as worthy of their creative energies as the former. The vitality of one could not be considered in isolation from that of the other: art and society are intimately linked; social well-being and artistic excellence are mutually dependent.

This most popular of German music dramas is a philosophical comedy. At the emotional heart of it lies a romantic sacrifice, and that sacrifice is the source of the music that moves us. It is a romantic triangle between the old and the young, and the heroism of the older member of the triangle provides the drama with its finest moments. And from this polarity arises the events in the drama that mark a moment of personal reckoning—dignified, insightful, generous and vulnerable age expressed in nuanced and deeply beautiful music, and insensitive, preening, empty-headed youth, entranced by surface glamour. The relationship between Hans Sachs and Eva is utterly chaste, but we know all along that it is one that has no future.

The music of *Die Meistersinger* is ingenuous, but transparent and unsubtle, representing the fact that it is painting masses and types rather than individuals. The whole essence of the music lies in its simple characterization and simple storytelling. There is no great fateful principle running through it that can be symbolized in short orchestral figures and flashed in the music at desired moments. There are two main *motifs* in the music. The first is the assertive theme of the Master singers—bold, strong, downright and inflexible—representing tradition with its indurated ideas and immovable prejudices, albeit with its solid worth. And then there is a pastoral theme, the theme of Awakening Love, representing change and regeneration, the new blood and freshness of the avant garde that is necessary to transfuse every existing culture. And as the music progresses, the two themes weave together—the old order changes yielding place to new, and the old school and the new wave make their peace.

Wagner's principal comic opera is one of the most approachable of all of his works. The music is joyous, easy to appreciate, and is so tuneful that it's very hard to forget it. From the opening of the overture to Act I until the closing scene, there really isn't a moment of Dullsville. It is also my single favorite work, and of the Prelude to Act I of *Die Meistersinger von Nurnberg* I have some forty recordings of the overture alone.

The work has been well served in the recording studio since the early 1950s. One of the great Hans Sachs was a man named Paul Schoffler, who made a number of recordings of this work. Hans Sachs is supposed to sound like a mature adult mentor, and indeed, in his 1951 recording with Hans Knappertsbusch and the Vienna Philharmonic, he comes across justly so. This is my favorite recording of all time, even though it's selfish to do so from borderline variable Decca monophonic sound, with clear changes in pitch noted between the overture and the opening of Act I, as they were clearly recorded on different dates. This is known because a collection of Wagner Overtures with Knappertsbusch is available on Japanese Decca (The King Record Company), all of which are matched to each other quite nicely. The clarity of the orchestral playing, the resolute intent and purpose of all the vocal contributions make this a delightful performance, one which Wagner more than likely would have approved of, especially with respect to tempi. We know that Wagner would have performed his opera rather quickly, and Knappertsbusch is probably the quickest of all performances recorded subsequent to that time.

There are also excellent performances in monophonic sound from Von Karajan and Kempe, both on EMI. Another recording by Keilberth has also crossed my desk, a stable reading, but a noncommittal one. Rafael Kubelik recorded a performance, presumably for DG with Hans Hotter, but the performance was never issued commercially for some unknown reasons (presumably an artistic ban) until about a half a decade ago, at which time it appeared on several labels, Calig and Myto. It makes an excellent reposing version for those who wish a bit less relentless an interpretation. The performance has been exceptionally well received, and one wonders why it remained an obscurity from its recording date of 1967.

In 1975, Jochum recorded the work for DG with the German Opera Company of Berlin, with Dietrich Fischer-Dieskau in the role of Sachs. It is not so much his contribution which concerned the critics, or me—in fact, I felt his contribution to be excellent, although some found him to be "immature-sounding." What bothered me the most is the performance sounded as if it was recorded from under a wet blanket.

Sir Georg Solti recorded the work with Norman Bailey as Sachs in a performance which was both praised and criticized by opera lovers around the world. The recorded sound was staggeringly good, however, and the performance was most agreeable to me, and brought me a great deal of pleasure. It was not as well received in the USA. I was stunned to learn that Solti decided to re-record his only Wagner opera because he wasn't satisfied with his first *Meistersinger*, and his remake, from live concerts in 1996 in Chicago, issued in celebration of his fiftieth year with the Decca Recording Company, while it certainly has an excellent cast, suffers from changes which have occurred with the Chicago Symphony as a consequence of changes in its music director. The orchestra now sounds much unlike it did for Solti for nearly two decades; the performance seems drenched in a syrupy, Schlagoberic confection which is pasty and heavy. The somewhat flat stage presence doesn't help matters, as this is a live studio rendition without stage depth. Unfortunately, as much as Solti felt this to be a valedictory statement, it is far from that in my book. Barenboimisms abound, and the performance to me is soporific despite Solti's best intentions. Prior to the issue of Solti's second recording, a new performance with Wolfgang Sawallisch was issued on EMI, a rather stentorian version which lacks excitement despite Sawallisch's excellence as a musician.

I realize these are rather nonspecific comments about a monumental work, but I have identified with this work since approximately age five, and feel that it is part of me. There is going to be no ideal *Meistersinger*. Too many factors are involved to have an optimal version with all contingencies handled desirably. Where one performance excels with orchestral playing and engineering, the same will suffer with sub optimal voices. Wherein one excels with voices, it will be an elder recording from the monophonic era.

If I had to recommend a single version for audio playback only, I would suggest you find the Solti recording with the Vienna Philharmonic now, because it's liable to go out of print. It is to me the most roundly satisfying of all versions, and if this were not available, then Kubelik's excellent version on Myto or Calig—the performance is the same in either case.

I very much enjoy a recording with the Bayreuth Festspiele under the conductor Horst Stein, with this performance being available on video. For those who wish to learn the work with visual assistance, this would be my recommendation.

- Die Meistersinger Von Nurnberg
  Decca 417 497-2 VPO, Solti
- Die Meistersinger Von Nurnberg
  Philips Video VHS 070 413-3. (2). Bayreuth
  Festspiele/Stein

Wagner: Overtures

The appearance of Richard Wagner upon the horizon of opera was a phenomenon, a movement in himself who spanned and grasped in his mighty fist a whole world of expression. He was a transcendent genius, a sparkling spirit of flame, worthy to wear a double crown of fire and gold. For a generation he was decried by many, and extravagantly worshipped by others, neither of whom understood him.

A Wagnerian program was not just going back to Greek tragedy that had sought to combine poetry, drama, mime, costumes, dance, song and instrumental music to illuminate human experience to the depths and in universal terms. Since that time, Shakespeare had developed poetic drama beyond anything the Greeks could have conceived, and Beethoven had evolved the expressive powers of music beyond the limits of speech altogether. Wagner combined the achievements of Shakespeare and Beethoven into a single art form, something that, on the analogy of poetic drama, could be called music drama.

Whereas traditional drama depicted, for the most part, personal relationships, such as what goes on outside and *between* people, their chief concern about what when on *inside* them was limited to motive. Music drama, on the other hand, was predominantly about the insides of people—not in the chain of motives bringing about cause and effect, but in their emotions. It explored and articulated the ultimate reality of experience that went on in the heart and soul. Music became a uniquely expressive means to express the inner reality in all its fullness, unfettered by the limitations of speech. Wagner's music was an emotionalizing of the intellect, and the combination of poetry and symphony provided the takeoff point. To listen to Wagner's music simply as great music is to miss all this.

Wagner was quick enough to appreciate that an ideological synthesis of the arts in which all the arts were of equal importance would be at odds with the reality of the situation. For, the arts are of widely differing expressive potential, and even an ideally realized synthesis would feature some arts more prominently than others. And music, being able to penetrate to the innermost core of things in a way none others can, would play a star role. Music has a special power to move and even to disturb, and this has something to do with bringing what has been unconscious to consciousness.

The essential gift is the power to produce themes that are beautiful and memorable in themselves, and to work these with natural energy and seeming spontaneity into large-scale structures that constitute aesthetic objects in themselves, beautiful in a different sort of way. Wagner's music is like an endless melody, always going from somewhere to somewhere else in a bold and purposeful way. The themes are unique for their unusual conciseness, often only two or three bars, but are so distinctive in their personality that they have only glancingly to be hinted in some remote context to get the full reference at once. Each of his works remains a sound-world of its own, distinct and distinguishable from the others, and everything about it acquires its being within that world. There is a *Tristan* world, a *Meistersinger* world, a *Parsifal* world, a world of *The Ring*—they are wholly separate, each with its unique musical cosmic dimensions.

The music of Wagner is a wonderful experience: no doubt about it! It is the magnet that draws people to Wagner. Hardly anybody has the slightest idea of what it all means the first time, but before long the music begins to stir within you, and disturb you and haunt you with a growing urgency and a desperate desire to go back to it again. Only a piece of the true Wagnerian kind can combine, in one stroke, a dramatic effect, a scenic effect, and a musical effect, the total result being a popular effect, the value of which has been proven for over a hundred years by the roar of excitement that never fails to burst forth as the curtains close in.

The Overture to *The Flying Dutchman* is a marvelous piece of marine painting in which the strife of the natural elements in the sea and sky accompanies the agonizing of a lost soul, the ancient tormented mariner, who is ultimately redeemed by the pure love, loyalty and compassion of the maiden Senta. There are two leading themes. The first typifies the Curse and the wandering mariner's yearnings for rest and eternal oblivion. It is eerie and full of spiritual hunger, wailed out by the brass with a furious accompaniment for strings, like the waves of a rising sea. The second elemental theme is an exquisite flowing melody, the message of Redemption, associated with the personality of Senta. The apotheosis is reflected in the close of the Overture, when Senta's tender theme becomes a song of victory.

The Overture to *Tannhauser* is of symphonic proportions. The music of sacred and profane love in an earthly garden of paradise unfolds as the Overture progresses: magic apparitions at nightfall, rosy mists, intoxicating perfumes, the bewitching gyrations of a wanton and voluptuous dance typify the sensual and spiritual elements. The manly figure of Tannhauser, the Minstrel of Love, approaches in the enchanted twilight. He hears a voice, tremulously sweet, like the call of sirens, and a female form of indescribable beauty, Venus herself, rises before him. The music breaks out into a rapturous love-paean, there follows a bacchanal with wild mirth and wilder dances, then a half-regretful, half-voluptuous awesome murmur to mark that the unholy spell has worked. The Overture concludes in a curious pulsating figure for strings—the pulses of life that throb and leap for joy in this song of salvation.

The Prelude to *Lohengrin* depicts the Vision of the Holy Grail. It appears in the diaphanous blue of the heavens, growing in brightness until it throws out an overpowering radiance at the moment when the sacred Cup is revealed to the faithful; then fades once more into azure space with its host of attending angels. There is a magic formula in the music, a mysterious initiation that prepares our souls for strange and unearthly experiences to follow.

To understand Wagner, one must be either a fanatic or a philosopher. To enjoy *Tristan,* it is only necessary to have had one serious love affair. All the merely romantic love scenes ever turned into music seem pallid beside *Tristan.* For, here is an ocean of sentiment, immensely German, and yet universal in its appeal to human sympathy. *Tristan und Isolde* is the most miraculous love drama ever written. It celebrates the supreme union of Love and Death, and the *Prelude* expresses the human passion and the dizzy swooning of the lovers into the abyss of night and death. It unfolds several of the main themes of the drama. The principle of these is the melody, slow and suffering, which from its duality seems to typify the lovers and their mutual passion. Next comes a theme generally known as *The Love Glance* which occurs when Isolde and Tristan first meet on the ship. The song of Tristan's yearning and the death-motive follow, and finally the theme associated with the love potion and the declaration of their love. The music rises to an ecstatic climax, and then gradually subsides as though in utter weariness. Love, baffled in life, seeks its ultimate fulfillment in nonexistence.

The term *Bleeding Chunks* was posited by a conductor nearly a century ago to identify orchestral music from Wagner's operas which made good concert repertory. Indeed some have had to be transformed or rewritten just slightly so as to have even a semblance of a conclusion, as many of the overtures simply slide right into a chorus of an opening act or scene. I am troubled about providing single recommendations here as I have, for one reason or another, collected virtually every recording since the dawn of stereo recording of the basic Wagnerian repertory, and there isn't a single disc I would want to be without—even the worst of them all, Carlos Paita's unacceptable traversal of some of Wagner's most beautiful orchestral music. So I shall not list *Desert Island* recommendations singly at the conclusion of this section, but rather, list preferred recordings with their catalog numbers throughout the course of this narrative.

As for the overture to *Tannhauser,* my all time favorite is the 1962 VPO recording by Solti for London; it is a driven performance, especially the closing bars, a guttural one, and will produce brow-sweat for any listener committed to paying some attention to Solti's efforts to communicate his interpretation. It is available on London Weekend Classics (430 136.2) and is worth owning, despite some thin sound compared to the present. Listed just below this would have to be the engineer Otto Gerdes' recording of the work for DG reissued on 413 849.2, which is an absolutely fabulous, lightning quick reading which seems to be a bit soulless at first; rehearing will change your mind. It is absolutely fabulous from start to finish.

Karajan tells the story of how Wagner developed the theme of the overture from hearing a klaxon of a fire brigade wagon heading to the home of a woman who had been baking; her house burned to the ground. As Wagner returned from one of his daily walks, he heard the woman weeping. The amalgam of these two auditory images allegedly created the overture; this may be apocryphal, but it is indeed plausible. If sound is an issue, and the sound of these images may well be heard in the performances, then Karajan's Berlin Philharmonic recording on DG 413 754.2 or his Vienna Philharmonic remake on DG 423 613.2 are worthy competition. A third excellent recording is by that of the Oslo Philharmonic and Mariss Jansons on budget EMI Digital, EMI 5 59848-2. Superb playing from a most unexpected source.

Lohengrin has not been bettered for either Preludes to Act I or III since Karl Bohm (413 733-2) and the Vienna Philharmonic on DG. Kubelik comes in a close second in a very old DG recording on 453 290-2GGA of Act I, which is complemented by a fine *Siegfried Idyll* and a leisurely *Meistersinger*. Horst Stein has a superb *Lohengrin* Act III on Belart Karussell 450 025-2, which is available only by import.

The Vienna Philharmonic plays its heart out for him in an excellent Wagner program.

As for the *Siegfried Idyll* itself, I'd have to go with Karajan and the Berlin Philharmonic recording made in the seventies if it were available packaged independent of his Bruckner Symphony No. 8. But if that were not the case, then I'd opt for Karajan's redo with the Vienna Philharmonic for DG 423 613 or Marriner's outstanding version for Argo, which is currently out of print. Another fine *Siegfried Idyll* is with the Orpheus Chamber Orchestra (without conductor) on DG 431 680-2, a highly worthy competitor with somewhat less dense forces than those mentioned above. It is much like Kubelik's excellent 1963 version for DG reissued on Galleria, mentioned earlier. One more recommendation: Levine and the Berlin Philharmonic recorded a superb *Siegfried Idyll* in 1992 for DG (435 883-2)—another recording not to miss! The rest of the program however is music of Schoenberg and Strauss, all highly worthy music of a slightly later date.

Music from *Gotterdammerung* and *Siegfried* make a simple recommendation because there are really only two on single CDs that are worthy. Reiner's pioneering stereo recording of Wagner's Orchestral Music, originally issued on LSC-2441 and recently reissued on BMG/RCA at budget price contains about the finest hour of Wagnerian orchestral playing that there is to be found anywhere. It begins with wonderful performances of the First and Third Act (in amalgamated segments) from *Die Meistersinger von Nurnburg*, but the *Gotterdammerung* and *Siegfried* are of such a majestic power that they put the listener into a trance despite their nearly forty year old sound. This is a record not to be missed. The conductor George Szell has a program from Wagner's *Ring* which encompasses some of this music equally effectively in terms of playing, but the recorded sound is a bit more metallic and nasal despite its overall brilliance. Either make great recommendations for first time listeners, and are inexpensive. I might add here that Jansons and the Oslo orchestra on the digital EMI reissue mentioned above score highly on the list of preferences in this specific musical literature, as well. Jansons, Szell, and Levine have wonderful *Walkurenritten*, for those looking for that work alone.

Tristan und Isolde, with its *Prelude* and *Liebestod*, represents to me about the most erotic twenty minutes of musical literature. I greatly prefer Furtwangler on EMI (from the complete opera) and Kleiber (from his complete opera recording) but it is inherently unreasonable to collect this short work by purchasing a 4 CD box. Jessye Norman and Herbert von Karajan have said it about as well as anyone on their live DG recording with the Vienna Philharmonic (DG 423 613 2) with voice; Karajan's DG recording with the Berlin Philharmonic without voice (413 754 2) and is, in some ways, an even more evocative performance than the one with Norman. I can't say why, but it brings me to tears, perhaps because of the playing of the BPO which is absolutely beyond one's wildest dreams. This disc, by the way, has a truly "complete" performance of the Prelude to Act III of *Die Meistersinger* which is only six minutes long and this is the true prelude, not what Reiner and Paray have medleyed for their recordings (which may be more interesting to many). The playing here shows the Berlin brass to be what I think they are: the greatest in the world, even compared to Chicago.

Rienzi is an overture little known even by some Wagnerites, let alone the opera. Bohm on DG, Solti on London and Levine on DG have all stated it very well, and it is worth knowing.

Compact selections of *The Ring* abound today. Those looking for a *Ring Without Words* would be well served by Lorin Maazel's excellent one hour traversal on Telarc in resplendent digital sound. Levine's one hour tour, with voice, with the Metropolitan Opera Orchestra, is equally enchanting and displays this opera company in top form, no matter what the critics may have said about the *Ring* cycle as a whole. Levine has also recorded 2 CDs with the MET Orchestra of the *bleeding chunks* without voice (separate from the *Ring* cycle) of which Volume II is one of the finest 72 1/4 minutes of music I have encountered from DG at any time. I am less impressed by the first disc due to a stodgy *Die Meistersinger* Prelude which seems a poor man's copy of Reiner's performance, with the exact same playing time of 9'54". Alas! What that performance could have been!

If one is looking for Wagner's *bleeding chunks* in conveniently packaged ways, there are two choices to consider: Boult's 2 CD set in analog sound from EMI which is jovial, well played but a bit loose of hand compared to the Germanic idiom the music is written for. For those who want *echt* performances which may not scintillate so well as some of the others mentioned, a 2 CD EMI digital reissue with Klaus Tennstedt and the Berlin Philharmonic will have to do—and it is a fine effort, even if the tempi are just a bit leisurely for my taste. Finally, a good representation of the *bleeding chunks* on one CD is available from Jansons on the single EMI Digital reissued CD mentioned earlier. Bruno Walter's 2 CD reissue of his Wagner recordings is to me a disappointment save for his *Siegfried Idyll*. The performances are freewheeling, seeming to be as if they are on a greased railroad track, going nowhere. The *Meistersinger* is kinetic and yet never gets off the ground, especially in the string section in the conclusion of the work. Tubby timpani and a prominent midrange spoil these recordings no matter how good an equalizer one has in one's amplification system; avoid it unless you love Walter or the *Siegfried Idyll*.

While we're on the topic of avoiding, stay away from Dorati and Paray on two separate Mercury Living Presence recordings; Mr. Sforzando (Dorati) and Mr. Paray really are out of idiom here even though reasonably well recorded. Paray recorded something called a *Die Meistersinger Suite* which resembles Reiner's "*Act III Prelude*" to *Die Meistersinger*; but it comes off poorly in the end and it has some bizarre cuts which surprise the experienced listener. This is not a recording to learn the music from. Better to label it, "Don't do it this way!" Likewise, Bernstein's Wagner Concert for Sony Classical is nearly an abortion. It is a willful recording and unimpressive, and the sound from Avery Fisher Hall is nasal and abominable.

One other conductor to forget in this repertory: Barenboim. He has recorded the *Meistersinger* Prelude thrice in digital sound, once in Paris, once in Berlin and once in Chicago, among other Wagner-based programs. His conception is like Schlagobers; cream piled high, lush, mushy sound, lacking detail. One is swept up in the panache of golden sound, but this is to me, and perhaps only to me, superficial. The latest effort with the Chicago Symphony Orchestra is wonderfully engineered, but incomparable to the same music in Solti's recordings and Reiner's recordings with the same orchestra from years past.

Also, forget the new Thielemann recording with Philadelphia for DG; despite great sound the interpretations are Teutonic and the tempi are in the aggregate too slow; Thielemann discussed the issue of tempo in a self-written treatise on DG's Web Site several months ago. Why a young conductor wishes to emulate a practice which has long gone out of vogue in order to sound like conductors of yesteryear is something I do not understand—yet! I will confess to liking his *Lohengrin Prelude*, but *Desert Island* material it is not!.

With all this said, I turn to my single favorite work, the *Prelude to Act I of Die Meistersinger von Nurnberg,* of which I have some forty recordings of the overture alone. Unfortunately the finest performance for my money is part of the complete opera, the 1951 Hans Knappertsbusch recording for London, with Paul Schoffler as Hans Sachs (440 057-2), the most elegant, shapely and sensuous Meistersinger of the lot, despite monophonic sound. He knew the work better than almost anyone. Another outstanding monophonic recording was made by Karajan as the recently inaugurated conductor of the Berlin Philharmonic in 1957, initially issued as Angel 35482, and reissued in 1990 as EMI 7 63321 2. This somewhat militant performance is extremely well played and balanced, and the recorded sound, presumably overseen by Walter Legge, is outstanding. The performance is perfectly proportioned. Reiner's 1959 account is another superb interpretation worth owning, despite early stereo sound. It is at a good tempo, and brilliantly laid out by Lewis Layton and Richard Mohr, Reiner's engineers in Orchestra Hall, Chicago. Kubelik's performance for DG Galleria makes an excellent reposed version for those who wish a bit less relentless an interpretation.

In 1969 the recording engineer Otto Gerdes was given the opportunity of recording a Brahms Symphony No. 4 for DG and he elected to include a stunning performance of the *Meistersinger Prelude*, Act

I, for DG 139 423, now out of print. But geez! Do I hope it appears on DG Originals before that series is concluded as it is the finest stereo *Meistersinger* Prelude to Act I that I have encountered. The playing is of hairpin accuracy and there is no heart on sleeve approach to this romantic music. It is just the music, played full bore. I regret the recording appeared in the catalog for only several years; I still possess several copies of the LP in key locations around my own home and that of my childhood residence.

Karajan recorded a superb *Meistersinger Prelude* in stereo for EMI in 1975 which is lush, verdant and very sexy, but it is just a bit too big. Efforts by Jansons (EMI), Chailly (London), Davis (Philips Concert Classics), Bohm (DG), Norrington (using period forces, quite the fastest Meistersinger on record, approximating Wagner's recommended tempo of just under 8 minutes) and Szell are all worthy competitors in this field, but if it were up to me and I had to live with one modern performance presently in the catalog and not part of the entire opera itself, it would have to be either Reiner (with the added bonus of an outstanding Act III presentation) or Jansons, if only because they are so satisfying overall. I prefer moments of others' more. The *Desert Island* awards still go, however, to Knappertsbusch, Karajan (mono EMI), and Gerdes (DG) because each is so well nigh perfect. I'm still searching for the perfect *Meistersinger Prelude to Act I*; I guess it will have to be the one I hear in my head. Is there someone there ready to let me take on this challenge?

Impressionism

The two decades preceding World War I saw the origin or development of significant forces that were a prelude for far-reaching changes to come in the arts and the sciences, and in industry and technology. Automobiles and primitive flying machines, the phonograph and the photograph, Sigmund Freud and Albert Einstein, workmen's compensation and inheritance taxes, with all their promises of good and evil, seemed poised to change every aspect of the human condition. In the prevailing mood of the *fin de siecle*, the door to the twentieth century seemed to open on boundless avenues of advancement, and a general atmosphere of tradition pervaded the official circles of the Hapsburg monarchy in Europe and the Victorian one in England.

But there were dissenters to this chorus of affirmation. For, underneath this monumental facade of order and confidence that chose to ignore, or pretended not to see, those aspects of life that were shocking or untidy lurked a hidden malaise—the wasting infection of conformism and traditionalism. Unrest was in the air; there was a subdued grumbling underneath the surface. *Fin de siecle* was everything that was sickly, everything that was opaque and unintelligible and new to the times. *Fin de siecle* was socialism and anarchy, and the rising hysteria of life. Foresight, in such times, was indeed a rare gift, but those who had eyes to see saw a frightening future. The world was steadily moving with unresisting force towards the awful cataclysm of world war.

The public dissenters of the day were the creative artists and, as always, Paris became the center of the dissenters' activities. The city's tradition of tolerance towards unconventional behavior made it a magnet for the avant-garde. In prose and poetry, in illustrations and paintings, the dissenters expressed their intuitive disgust for tradition by cultivating intensely the qualities of artifice and affectation, perversity and self-consciousness. Great names abounded: Emile Zola and Baudelaire, Mallarme, Verlaine and Arthur Rimbaud. The vogue was not confined to France—the most famous exponents in England were those two precocious exquisites, Oscar Wilde and Aubrey Beardsley, and in Vienna, Gustav Klimt combined erotic realism with abstraction to achieve dazzling effects that still have the capacity to shock.

The dissenters prized sensibility—the ability to have a creative, if fleeting, response to what they saw, heard or felt. The immediate *impression* was more important to them than form or meaning. A school of French painters headed by Claude Monet had attempted to depict such transitory responses, and snare in paint and canvas the elusive purity of an immediate sensuous experience. They had been christened *Impressionists* by a derisive art critic, and the name had stuck.

The Impressionists rejected all emphasis on form and beauty. They focused instead on atmosphere, on subtle nuances and changing colors and the experience resulting from all this, which *then* suggested form. They did not try to render reality as it stood, but rather the individual's sensations in the face of this reality. They were not interested so much in an object itself as in the intangible aura with which the object was suffused—dust particles, rain, mist, even light, speed and movement. Eventually, what had begun as an instinctive revolt against conformism evolved into an aesthetic dogma.

The dreamlike atmosphere of Impressionist art, a natural consequence of the tendency to shroud shapes in mist and blur their outlines, linked the movement intuitively with one of the contemporary trends in literature, notably Symbolism. The Symbolists' professed aims were vagueness and imprecision, their fields of exploration the fantasy and the dream. And music offered an almost perfect analogy for the elusiveness and evanescence of such a poetic experience. The dazzling and unexpected harmonies in sound seemed to parallal the shifting lights and colors of the painters and poets.

The Impressionist *par excellence* in music was Claude Debussy. It was his Impressionist artist's fantasy that shaped his new music—music that caused the forms to disappear, that veiled outlines in mist, and let the colors swing and sway. Music transformed itself into a flowing and heaving, into a dim medium, into a dusky nervous vibration. The big lines crumbled, and large constructions were replaced by short, repetitious motifs.

The soul of Debussy that vibrated with every motion of the air, every change of the light and with every shadow, set all music in motion with its dreams alone. But the prime of impressionistic art was short-lived. Two years before Debussy died, the German guns had already begun to bombard Paris. But as short as was the era of Debussy, that strong was his influence. Maurice Ravel's initial stimulus came from Debussy who also had a profound influence on his other fellow-countrymen: D'Indy, Roussel and Paul Dukas. One of the greatest post-Impressionistic composers of the English musical renaissance at the turn of the century was Delius, and his influence upon English musicians of the next generation was rivaled only by Vaughan Williams. Both were great mystics and visionaries, imbued with an insatiable love of the countryside, and of nature in all her immensity and unfathomableness. And it is very probable that it was the remarkably impressionistic sequences in the latter's music that was the model for Gustav Holst's *The Planets,* often called the greatest piece of Impressionistic orchestral music ever written. Debussy was acquainted with Albeniz personally and with his music, and it was while in Paris that Albeniz produced the twelve "impressions" for the piano collectively entitled *Iberia.* And it was after his Paris sojourn that the Spaniard Manual de Falla produced his most famous postimpressionist pieces. Debussy's music became widely known in Italy during the first decade of this century, and it was impossible for Puccini and Respighi to remain unresponsive. Stravinsky's lifelong Francophilia is too well known to need much elaboration—his first experiences of Debussy's music were to prove unforgettable.

Debussy: Orchestral Works

The works of Claude Achille Debussy (1862 - 1918) tell the story of Impressionism in music. It is preoccupied, above all, with sensations and atmosphere, the personal perceptions of that intangible aura that interposes and suffuses between object and self, and depicts reality in a far more effective way than any conscious attempt to depict "realistically." And in his obsession to express the immediacy of feelings and impact, to transfer his sense-impressions directly from his sensibilities to the listener, he was impelled to make changes in music that reformed the traditional formulae. Dramatic action was sacrificed to the long exploration of inner feeling. There is a natural-ness, spontaneity and uninhibitedness in his music which always seems to be in a state of near-dissolution, wrapped in a relaxed, fluid and constantly changing incorporeal atmosphere.

Debussy was the first true Impressionist in music, and *Printemps* was one of his first Impressions of nature. It is a work in a very special color, covering a great range of feelings, its subject being the slow and arduous birth of things in nature, like the opening calyx of a flower, their gradual blossoming, and finally the joy of being born into a new life. The music shimmers and sparkles, and a spontaneous lyrical impulse governs its development, noticeably piecemeal, into a mosaic-like overall design. Hushed rolling cymbals, tinkling harps, and a small choir singing wordlessly with closed lips hint at the awe-inspiring nature of the miracle being celebrated.

A new vagueness and fluidity of expression was consolidated in the *Prelude a l'Apres-midi d'un Faune*, a succession of impressions through which a faun's sensual desires and dreams move in the afternoon heat. Here, for the first time, is explored in musical terms that strange intangible twilight borderland between dream and reality, sleeping and waking, the fleeting qualities of memory, and the myriad sensations of forgotten dreams. From out of the orchestra rise seduc-tive tones, the flutes sing delicate passages, and harp tones are blended with a sure hand. The tones glisten like silk and sparkle like light in crystal glasses. All is air, sun, tinted clouds and trembling light. One is inclined to dream when a flute, clarinet and oboe improvise freely, the horns call as from a distance, and little bells ring. The music appears to swim in the light, a frail web of tones turns into fragrance, and the rocks and wood of the landscape float in space like so many colored apparitions. There are no threads of logical discourse here, just a freely sensuous, narcotizing flow of sounds, exotic in contour, breathing the air of another planet, destroying the time-sense, inducing an oriental passivity on our subconscious minds, inviting us to ask ourselves whether, in fact, we have heard it or not in the afternoon heat of a Virgilian sun.

Water was to ever evoke an Impressionistic response in Debussy—ripples, eddies and whirlpools in water, and water gurgling in a stream. And in his third of the *Nocturnes*, *Sirenes*, he paints a dreamy water-piece of sea music, the placid rhythmic motion of the waves, the changing moods of the moonlit *Jeux de vagues* with the indefinable subtleties of their murmurs and shadows, expressed in the shimmering tremolos and long flowing wordless chorus for the female voices.

Debussy spoke often of his great love for the sea, and the endless memories it aroused in him, and he captured the timeless quality and spirit of the sea and its waters in *La Mer*, perhaps the finest creation of mystery in music. Here is a powerful sound portrait of that brooding Leviathan of the deep, from the calm breaking of dawn over its waters to the turbulent storm-drama that ends the music.

Debussy's orchestral output was not generous, but everything he did was elegant and utterly spellbinding. There are several *Desert Island* performances of Debussy's orchestral classics. This music has been recorded notably by Boulez and Dutoit in nearly complete synopses of his output. For those searching for excellent interpretations, I would encourage the listener to investigate either. However, individual performances by specific musicians may be even more enlightening than either Boulez or Dutoit. Be aware that Boulez has recorded this music twice, once for CBS/Sony and once for DG. I prefer the former performances, but the recorded sound is not quite as apt as the more recent versions recorded by DG. Dutoit's recordings are in stunning digital sound, recorded at St. Eustus Church in Montreal. These recordings are living attestation to the fact that the Orchestre Symphonique de Montreal is the greatest of French orchestras.

While it might be said that Monteux and the London Symphony have perhaps made the greatest recording of *Afternoon of the Faun*, I would counter by saying that anyone holding this perception should listen to Michael Tilson Thomas and the Boston Symphony on a 1972 recording made by DG in Symphony Hall, Boston. Nothing more needs to be said. Monteux is great, Tilson Thomas is mesmerizing!

In 1971, using the same forces, Claudio Abbado recorded Debussy's *Three Nocturnes*. This recording won numerous major awards, and fortunately, has been reissued by DG since its LP appearance. To me, the recording has the ambiance of a live performance but has the best qualities of a studio production, and this may be one of Abbado's greatest recordings. It is presently available only at full price on DG but is well worth it, because the record also includes the *Daphnis et Chloe Suite* No. 2 and *Pavane*, both by Ravel, not to speak of the Scriabin *Poem d Extase*. This makes for a very generous playing time, and the performances of each work are state of the art and the state of proper concept. Even though Jean Martinon recorded the complete orchestral works by Debussy, they are not competitive due to lack luster orchestral playing.

Bernard Haitink and the Royal Contcertgebouw Orchestra of Amsterdam have made a stellar collection of the orchestral music of Debussy. The highlight of this cycle is Haitink's performance of *Jeux* as well as the *Three Nocturnes*. Haitink verges on the anemic and pallid, and in Debussy, this helps to enhance the elegance of the composer's intentions.

- Three Nocturnes;- RAVEL: Daphnis and Chloe, Pavane
  DG 415 370-2. BSO, Abbado
- Orchestral Music
  DG 435 766-2. Cleveland O, Boulez (Additional release to be recorded in 1998-99)

Holst: The Planets

For many years, the life of Gustav Holst (1874 - 1934) had been a curious one. An early admiration for Grieg had given way to a prolonged bout of Wagnerian worship, then came his discovery of folk-song, followed by a consuming interest in oriental philosophy, mysticism and the occult. And so it comes as no surprise that when this suite appeared in 1917 (before the discovery of the planet Pluto), nothing so radical in nature had existed in English music. The music was suggested by the astrological significance of the planets, not through any connections with the deities of classical mythology bearing the same names.

Some have called this music the most remarkable piece of pure orchestral Impressionism ever written. For much of the time, shafts and flashes of orchestral color, in which the harp and celesta feature prominently, dart backwards and forwards in a thousand different directions at once and in daring opposition, so that their very fleetingness and insubstantiality impress more forcefully upon the senses. There is more sensual sound here than in any other piece of Holst's music. Although there is no thematic link between the movements, they form a series of contrasting frescoes that gain in decorating effect by being placed next to each other.

In the first movement, *Mars*, Holst takes a long last lingering look at his early Wagnerian infatuation. A single note is played by the strings and percussion, bassoons and horns bring forth an aggressive figure, and wars rage in the brass. The organ adds its might to a great climax. Then, with *Venus,* the second movement, intimations of Impressionism begin to set in. Swaying chords for horn and wood winds with two harps, celesta and *glockenspiel* exploit the familiar lusciousness of Impressionistic sound. The texture becomes even more elaborate as the movement progresses in ethereal delicacy to end in a transparency of color that brings it fully into the Impressionistic orbit. In *Saturn*, flutes and harps toll a knell for the passing of youth, communicating a dull ache, a quiet deadly despair. Harps chime softly over muted strings, the sense of ecstasy grows imperceptibly as tubular bells sound in the distance over a harp and horn rising to a brilliant radiance, and then the chimes dissolve in the ineffable serenity of an immeasurable stillness. In *Uranus*, the magic occurs largely in the lower sections of the orchestra, with basses, tubas and bassoons having important roles. A distressing slide on the organ, followed immediately by a suppression of all instruments, suggests horror and black magic.

But it is in *Neptune* that the music reaches the awe-inspiring acme of the Impressionist world. The sounds and color are transparent to the point of insubstantiality, the thematic content is minimal. The only reality in this limitless vista of time and space is sound, quasi-incorporeal sound, that reflects no earthly preoccupation, that registers and reacts to no human emotions, but ebbs and flows with ever-widening ripples between the strings, two harps and celesta until a distant, unseen choir of sexless and spiritualized women's voices is heard. The wordless voices seem to express a non-humanity; not the reckless, resplendent non humanity of mountain peaks or ocean swell, but a concept that reaches far beyond either of these. The music ends in a dissolution of the orchestral voices until the choir is left alone, their voices swaying backwards and forwards in the circumambient air until it, too, is lost to all human perception.

The Planets was written just prior to the outbreak of World War I, and therefore does not include a salute to the planet Pluto which was undiscovered at publication. The work is a traversal of the allegorical significance of each of the planets of our solar system, and is scored for large orchestra. This is truly an outstanding orchestral showpiece, often used to demonstrate high fidelity equipment.

The Planets has been resoundingly well served since the composer's time, with the first performance being on wax cylinders recorded by EMI. That recording is currently available on CD, and is rather an interesting historical perspective on the work. Each individual movement had to be performed quickly in order to fit onto the correct number of sides for duplication. Unfortunately, this resulted in some rather frantic, scurried playing, with less than optimal outcomes.

The work received a rather unusual performance using Wagnerian tubas by Herbert von Karajan in 1962 with the Vienna Philharmonic, which has also recently been reissued on CD. It is a frightening performance, not particularly well miked or engineered, but is an interesting statement. Karajan's later performance with the Berlin Philharmonic is unsatisfactory on multiple grounds—principally poor orchestral ensemble and questionably sage engineering.

In the early 1970s two recordings were made by directly competitive companies, DG and London. Both were made in the United States of America. The first was by William Steinberg and the Boston Symphony, and the second was by Zubin Mehta with the Los Angeles Philharmonic. These are diametrically opposed performances. Steinberg's is a sonic gestalt; the sound is global, all-encompassing, and reflects the brilliant sheen of the Boston Symphony as recorded in Symphony Hall. The performance is elegant, somewhat fast overall, and gives the overall impression of a live performance due to the ambiance surrounding the orchestra. I find this an indispensable addition to my collection, and I am pleased that it has been restored to CD. This shows the sheer genius of William Steinberg, a former cellist of the Berlin Philharmonic under Furtwangler, who came to America to avoid oppression. Steinberg was one of the great conductors of our time, and it still amazes me that he was considered a stodgy old man in Boston where his live performances, many of which I have saved on tape from FM broadcasts, are still memorable, notably his Beethoven and Brahms Symphonies. This record is a tribute to Steinberg's contribution to the development of the Boston Symphony. Two recordings by the Boston Symphony have been made since that time for Philips, one by Seiji Ozawa and the other by John Williams (Boston Pops); neither of these compare even remotely favorably to Steinberg in any respect.

Zubin Mehta's first interpretation of *The Planets*, recorded in Royce Hall on the campus of the University of California, Los Angeles, is the equivalent of a "plugged in" engineering marvel. It would almost be possible to assert that this recording used one microphone per instrument, but we know that cannot be possible. The immediacy of the recording, despite its twenty five year age, far exceeds Mehta's remake with the New York Philharmonic, and the level of playing shows the orchestra, only about nine years after Mehta took helm of the ensemble, to be a competitive orchestra of international excellence. This is a deliberate performance, well played and executed, and so well miked that one can hear the resin on the bows of the stringed instruments and the fingers moving up and down the stringed instruments. Splendid contributions are made by the organist in *Uranus,* and by Roger Bobo, the tubist, in both *Uranus* and *Mars.* The pedal point capturing of the organ in *Saturn* is most atmospheric rather than a glassy sheen in Steinberg (interesting in its own way), and the choral contribution in *Neptune* is ethereal in its presence.

There have been many contributions to the recorded lexicon of *The Planets* by other conductors such as Gardiner and the Philharmonia, Levine with the Chicago Symphony, Solti with the London Philharmonic, and Sir Charles Mackerras on Virgin, let alone several recordings by Sir Adrian Boult who knew Holst personally and brought the work to prominence. I would say these are all excellent interpretations, some with sound approaching that of Zubin Mehta's first traversal. I would also say, categorically, that I would not want to be without Steinberg or Mehta. As good as the others are, these two performances are indispensable.

- The Planets
    DG 439 446-2. BSO, Steinberg
- The Planets
    Decca 433620-2. LAPO, Zubin Mehta

Vaughan Williams: Symphony No. 2 (London)

When Claude Monet, whose painting *Impression: Rising Sun* caused a hostile critic to coin the term *Impressionism,* sought refuge in London, he found the city with the Thames and its mists and fogs a new and quickening source of inspiration that resulted in no fewer than ninety paintings. And it was this same simple perspective of a river, with its waters reflecting the changing light and color of an inconstant sky, and the mists, smokes and fogs as prevalent even today about the wharves at Greenwich, that inspired Ralph Vaughan William's (1872 - 1958) Symphony No. 2, the *London*.

The opening of the *London* Symphony is the precise equivalent of Monet's paintings of that great city. As the violas emerge slowly over sustained violin chords, the city comes to life gradually and haltingly from beneath a pall of an early-morning mist over the waters of the river. Eventually a massive chord-complex towers above the striking of Big Ben and splits up into rhythms of ever decreasing size, heaving backwards and forwards like the surge of waters. The slow second movement evokes a veiled and phantom world, a pattern of delicate tones and silhouettes, incorporeal yet purely sensual. Here is music that admirably reflects the mood, perhaps, of Old Battersea Bridge, where neither form nor color is defined, but tones predominate with their all-pervasive grayness. In the third movement, people and events flurry by in a sequence consistently nebulous, fragmentary and ill-defined; this is the London of the unending murmuring streets, of the stirring shadow and the amber-lighted gloom. The all-pervasive element is mist; there emerges at one point a merry company at a public house, but in the concluding bars the darkness deepens so as to blot out all traces of human activity. A tragic march follows, and then the music resumes a rippling figure of the Thames at night. Big Ben sounds through the rising river mist, muted horns, trumpets and cornets hover from afar in the night air, and all becomes enveloped impenetrably once again in obscurity.

Ralph Vaughan Williams, along with his compatriot, Sir Edward Elgar, were two of the great nationalistic British composers living at the turn of the century. Vaughan Williams was known for his legion output of symphonic literature, of which this symphony is perhaps the most typical, and perhaps best known.

Vaughan Williams has been served very well in the stereo era, both by Andre Previn and Sir Adrian Boult. My single favorite performance is the later recording of the work by Andre Previn on EMI, which is an opulent recording that captures the spirit and intensity of the work as few others do. Certainly, there are more recent recordings, perhaps ones with more florid detail and sound, but none more moving than the one that comes from Previn's second cycle.

By comparison, Sir Adrian Boult's interpretation is somewhat more personalized, perhaps depicting sentiments unique to a conductor who has lived in England all his life. I treasure this recording, as well, but usually turn to it second to the Previn.

Either of these recordings should bring much pleasure, but I would opt for Previn as a first choice.

- A London Symphony; (i) Concerto accademico;
  The Wasps, overture
  RCA GD 90501. LSO, Previn; (i) with James Boswell

Ravel: Orchestral Works

When Maurice Ravel (1875 - 1937), late in life, heard a recording of Debussy's *Prelude a L'Apres-midi d'un Faune*, he turned to a friend with tears in his eyes and said: "It was when I first heard that many years ago that I realized what music was." And, in fact, this piece was the beginning of all his music. Though the initial stimulus came from Debussy, he evolved his own personal brand of Impressionism that some have even called "post-Impressionist." His orchestra was much less scent and cloud than Debussy; his fantasy was clear, bright, intelligent and witty. Ravel's originality lay in the compromise he effected between a studied vagueness and sensuousness on the one hand, and the clean hard contours of pragmatism and logical classicism on the other. For example, his themes are real melodies, not motivic fragments, however subtly they may be embedded or fused with a sensuous accompanying texture. Ravel's mother was a Basque, and he was actually born in a province in the Pyrenees from which her family came. Hence it is no surprise that the exotic element in Spanish music—the mystery of a Spanish twilight charged with sweet scents and sensuous yearnings, and the provocative ecstasies and flaming colors of Spanish dances— brought him permanently under its sway.

278

His first Impressionistic work, *Jeux d'Eau*, inaugurated a quasi-renaissance in piano music because it was the first piece to exploit to the full the illusory and evocative properties of the piano. All the familiar characteristics of Impressionistic water music are assembled here, from billowing waves of rippling arpeggios to magnificent descending arcs of melody. In *La Valse*, he portrayed the waltz as motion and rhythm, complete with the atmosphere of the ballroom, the chandeliers, the sparkle in the big mirrors, the glossiness of the brown inlaid floors, whirling crowds, luxury, girandoles, uniforms, diamonds, white satin gowns, naked shoulders, and the hot wave of sensuality and motion in three-quarter time. *Bolero* is a solid construction, not just Spanish color display.

His *Rapsodie Espagnole*, one of the most distinguished examples of French musical Hispanicism, penetrated the Spanish folk-spirit, harnessing the free idiom of popular dances with an almost Lisztian flamboyance. It is divided into four sections, played continuously. Every detail tells—and the most sensitive of one's sensitivities responds to the whole, not to the parts. In the most provocative first movement, the *Prelude a la nuit*, there is no blurring of contours despite its *pointilliste* sonority. There is something acrid yet sweet in the sounds of the muted strings as they express the lassitude of a hot evening. And as the hard light of day fades, the loveliness and loneliness of darkness sets in with a growing warmth and an anticipation of promised ecstasy. All the perfumes of the night, all the feverish poetry breathed near midnight is mingled here in the shimmering whirling rhythm. There are languorous chimings, and the movement ends in the lingering sweetness of a celesta.

The hushed and exalted *Daphnis et Chloe*, Ravel's great masterpiece, has virtually no rivals in the Impressionistic orchestral field in the richness and diversity of its music that is part of its perennial fascination. The wordless chorus—Debussy's beloved invention—opens the music to evoke the luminous calm of a clear spring afternoon. This choral rhythm dominates the *danse religieuse* and, after swelling to a climax, the music is lulled by voices to a rapt dreamlike conclusion. In the same way, the voices join the orchestra lost in contemplation of Daphnis and Chloe enfolded in each other's arms, and swathe them in a golden aureole of sound. The nymphs' slow mysterious dance after the brigands have abducted Chloe is introduced by some shimmeringly tremulous, weirdly muted high strings to suggest the unreal light which envelopes the landscape. But the most impressionistic of all is the celebrated dawn scene where a cello melody of enormous span grows out of a shimmering void composed of opalescent wood winds, sensitively blurred. Piccolo bird-song and shepherd's flutes weave in their arabesques, and as the wordless chorus enters, the Impressionistic cup is filled to overflowing.

Ravel was one of the great orchestrators of all time, and his music has been exceptionally well held in recordings for years. Performances of Ravel's music are often marketed as integral sets of the complete works and, somewhat more occasionally, as sample palettes of his work. Among the truly great "sampler" discs are Reiner's notable performances of *Rapsodie Espagnole, Valses Nobles et Sentimentales, Alborada del Gracioso,* and *Pavane for a Dead Princess,* recorded in 1956-1957. This is one of Reiner's great recordings, and should not be missed.

George Szell recorded a partial compendium of the music of Ravel which is one of the glories of the Cleveland Orchestra lexicon of recorded music, including the Suite No. 2 from *Daphnis et Chloe,* and the *Pavane for a Dead Princess.* This particular *Daphnis* uses no chorus, so the orchestration is exquisitely clear.

A historical recording of *Daphnis et Chloe, Pavane for a Dead Princess,* and *Rapsodie Espagnole* appears on the London Historic label, conducted by Pierre Monteux with the London Symphony Orchestra. This recording is one of the great products of the gramophone era, and should be heard in association with another album by Pierre Monteux conducting the London Symphony Orchestra in Ravel's *Bolero, La Valse* and *Ma mere l'oye (My Mother Goose).* These two records perhaps best summarize Monteux's delicate and glorious contribution to recorded literature, and these also should not be missed.

Also, historically, the French conductor Charles Munch and the Boston Symphony recorded most of these works for RCA in the late 50s, and they are now available at mid price. The same engineers that provided recorded sound for Fritz Reiner and the Chicago Symphony also produced Munch's recordings, and I can't recommend too highly their excellence.

While there are multiple excellent contributors to the current literature in the music of Ravel, two stand out as *Desert Island* performances. I select modern recordings if only because Ravel's orchestration is so opulent that it is captured by modern sound in a way which is utterly shattering. The conductor Pierre Boulez has recorded a compendium of Ravel's orchestral works for Sony Classical, many of which were noted above by name, using various orchestras including the Cleveland Orchestra and the New York Philharmonic. These recordings are clinically accurate, seemingly unemotional, and lack some of the hysteria produced by others, none of whom are named here. Boulez had the fortune to re-record much of this literature for DG in the mid 1990s, and these re-recordings, to me, if equally sober, are more illuminating and they are, for me, the great recordings to own. He has given us *Ma Mere l'Oye*, *Rapsodie Espagnole*, *Alborada del Gracioso*, *Bolero* and *Une Barque Sur L'Ocean*, in addition to a complete *Daphnis* and a superb *La Valse*. I am hopeful that more will come from this source prior to Boulez' ultimate retirement, as he is in his 70s.

A third excellent contributor is the Italian conductor Claudio Abbado who has provided a nearly completely survey of the orchestral music of Ravel using the London Symphony Orchestra, of which he was principal conductor in the 1980s. Abbado's acumen is unsurpassed, and his performances demonstrate great joy and exercise no caution.

Rarely have I come across a recording by Seiji Ozawa that I have truly enjoyed, but his outstanding traversal of the orchestral music of Ravel with the Boston Symphony, currently at mid price, is worth hearing, although the performances aren't quite in the same league as those of Boulez, Abbado, and my final recommendation, Charles Dutoit and the Orchestre Symphonique de Montreal. On four CDs,

Dutoit manages to give us shimmering sound, outstanding images, and performances which have the heart and soul of what they themselves consider to be the only great French orchestra located on North American soil.

Finally, there is one *Desert Island* classic of Ravel's *Daphnis et Chloe Suite No. 2* and *Pavane for a Dead Princess*—the recording by the Boston Symphony Orchestra with Claudio Abbado, made in 1971. This recording has won numerous awards, and it should be heard, if not snatched up at the record stores at the moment you see it.

You won't go wrong with any of the modern versions recommended, or any of the historical versions, but to hear Ravel in proper perspective, the newer recordings are far preferable.

- Orchestral Works
  Sony SM3K 45842 (3). Cleveland O; NYPO, Pierre Boulez
- Orchestral Works
  DG 439 859-2 GH; 447 057-2 GH. BPO, Boulez (Additional releases of piano concerti recorded in 1997, and orchestral music to be recorded in 1998-99 with the Cleveland O are pending)
- Orchestral Works
  London 421 458-2LH, or London 400 055-2LH, or London 410 010-2LH. Montreal SO with Ch., Dutoit
- Daphnis and Chloe, Suite No. 2, Pavane for a Dead Princess;—Debussy:Three Nocturnes
  DG 415 370-2. BSO, Abbado

Respighi: Orchestral Works

Ottorino Respighi (1879-1936) achieved world-wide fame by virtue of his three symphonic poems on Rome each celebrating some aspect of the Eternal City. The first was *The Fountains of Rome*, next *The Pines of Rome*, and the third *Roman Festivals*. Harmonic and orchestral color-effects derived from Impressionism are evidenced throughout; Debussy's contribution intermingles freely in these works. Effects of mist and haze, intimations of familiar natural sounds, leaves rustling, birds twittering, children's laughter, bells tolling, sunsets pellucid and evocative, a subtle synthesis of early morning stillness, exotic languor and inarticulate nostalgia created by the intricate filigree work for harps and celesta, and diaphanous writing for multi-divided strings impart a freely sensuous conception that blends Straussian pictorialism with Debussian Impressionism.

I think it was the legendary conductor, Otto Klemperer who said, "Anybody who used a canned cuckoo in his music ought to have been taken out and shot." Well, this may be *Kitsch*, all told, but it is the best, most aurally gratifying *Kitsch* in the recorded literature. Respighi certainly could orchestrate, and the atmosphere and environment he creates to depict the pines and fountains of the city of Rome, as well as the festivals occurring within the city, probably could not have been pulled off more effectively by any other composer at any time.

I was justly accused of enjoying loud, boisterous music with lots of cymbal crashes as a child, and I would say that this trilogy of works has the highest "crash coefficient" in musical literature per unit time with the exception of the Tchaikovsky *1812 Overture* using real carillons or the Dvorak *Husitska Overture*.

Historically, it was considered that the great performances of the work were those by Toscanini and the NBC Symphony Orchestra, and Reiner and the Chicago Symphony Orchestra. I have to exclude Toscanini, not by virtue of the age of the recording as it really is one of Toscanini's efforts in the studio and is reasonably well engineered despite the dead acoustics of NBC Studio 8-H, but because the performance is relentlessly loud and unremitting. Toscanini was considered by many to be a great conductor; I found him routinely inelegant and I agree with many who feel that his musical performances showed very little variety or tonal color to distinguish between composers—that is, everything he performed almost always sounded the same.

Fritz Reiner's legendary and pioneering performance of the *Pines* and *Fountains* of Rome (no *Feste Romane*) is one of the great contributions to the gramophone, and it should be heard despite its forty years of age. It is not, however, any longer a sonic spectacular that it has been touted by RCA as being.

With that said, there are probably two dozen outstanding performances of these works in the catalog, and I will simply mention the names and orchestras of those who have yielded outstanding modern digital interpretations, any of which will please the listener. Between these I have very few particular favorites, but will leave my current top choice as the recommended version of the entire *Roman Trilogy*.

Due credit should be awarded to Jansons and the Oslo Philharmonic Orchestra, Muti and the Philadelphia Orchestra, Maazel and the Pittsburgh Symphony Orchestra, Karajan and the Berlin Philharmonic Orchestra (no *Feste Romane*), Dutoit and the Montreal Symphony Orchestra, Sinopoli and the New York Philharmonic Orchestra, and one earlier recording, just after the Reiner recording historically, with Ansermet and the Orchestre de la Suisse Romande (again, no *Feste Romane*).

Despite the excellence of these recordings and probably let alone two dozen others which I have failed to mention, all inadvertently, the one recording I would obtain at this time is shown below. It possesses the excellent qualities of all those mentioned previously, plus has a certain degree of innocence and discovery as if each work is being heard for the first time.

- Roman Trilogy (The Pines of Rome, The Fountains of Rome, Feste Romane)
  BMG/Conifer 75605 51292 2 Orchestra of the Academy of Santa Cecilia, Daniele Gatti

Stravinsky: The Rite of Spring

When Igor Stravinsky (1882 - 1971) was once asked to name the composer who had influenced him the most, he replied: "The musicians of my generation and I myself owe the most to Debussy." No other Russian composer has responded so positively to Debussy. And *The Rite of Spring* remains the acme of Russian musical Impressionism. However greatly the essential fabric of *The Rite* may differ from

Debussy, Stravinsky uses sound in exactly the same way to appeal to the musical sensitivities rather than to musical reason, and his use of orchestral color is no less Impressionistic for being barbaric rather than sophisticated in temper.

Like Debussy, Stravinsky seeks the musical expression of a fundamental truth, of a primeval facet of the human consciousness, of the abyss that was primordial chaos. The beginning of all things is the ritual of spring, and Stravinsky musters, in varying degrees, all the language of Impressionism to articulate in music this most fundamental of all impulses. And the direct effect of Impressionism is most immediately apparent in the preludes to the two parts of *The Rite*.

The introduction to Part I is intended to represent the awakening of nature, the scratching, gnawing and wiggling of birds and beasts. Primitive man, too, was not greatly elevated above the animals he hunted or which hunted him; he was direct, harsh and brutal, and so is *The Rite*, often. And a complex tissue is built up from the accumulation and intensification of a number of subtly-differentiated melodic and rhythmic shapes rather than actual motifs: color is all important, the scoring for the wood winds strikes an appropriately acrid, almost physically painful, note, with the plucked strings giving unobtrusive support to the wood winds.

In the opening of Part 2, the music depicts a melancholy that is almost pain, that partakes of the character of grief. But it is the searing and wrenching that accompanies birth and fertility—the birth pains of a world, rather than the spiritual and subjective sorrow of death. The musical textures are more lush, the lines less sharply etched, and gentle oscillating chords dissolve effortlessly into each other in a typically Impressionistic nocturnal evocation. All is a vague, tenuous fluidity. But the intricacy of the cross-rhythms, the constantly changing tempos, and the complexity of structure built upon all manners of different permutations and combinations of the notes demonstrates the affinity between empirical primitivism and a sophisticated nervousness that is the essence of Stravinskian Impressionism.

The Rite of Spring has been brilliantly served since the beginning of long playing microgroove, from memorable recordings by the composer himself in early stereo to recent contributions by major domestic and European orchestras. There are probably no fewer than sixty good performances of the work, any of which would bring pleasure to the novitiate and probably, equally easily, to the experienced listener.

I first learned *The Rite of Spring* on the four-hand performing piano versions in an EMI performance by Michael Tilson Thomas and Ralph Grierson, which was issued in 1968-9. I still own this LP, but unfortunately it has never seen reissue in CD. It is my understanding that as a young man, Michael Tilson Thomas met the composer Stravinsky, and had the opportunity to discuss music with him in some degree of depth. Perhaps that, and his own intellectual pursuits, resulted in what I consider to be the most idiomatic performance of the work since the composer's own interpretations for CBS. During his tenure as assistant conductor of the Boston Symphony Orchestra, Tilson Thomas recorded the premier of *King of the Stars*, a seven minute cantata for chorus and orchestra. This was followed by an essentially definitive *The Rite of Spring* performed in Symphony Hall, and both the acoustic and performance could not have been better realized at any other time. Everything is in proper perspective and in proper place, and the recorded sound is much like DG's product in Symphony Hall: sumptuous and realistic. Some feel that the LP release of the recording is better than the CD. The CD is accompanied by a rather decent but underwhelming performance of *Petrushka* by Charles Dutoit, with the exceptional contribution of solo pianist Tamas Vasary. Dutoit's second performance of *Petrushka*, with the Orchestre Symphonique de Montreal, is a far more engaging adventure, and should be owned.

There are countless other excellent performances of *The Rite of Spring* by such conductors as Solti and the Chicago Symphony, Salonen and the Philharmonia Orchestra, Abbado and the London Symphony Orchestra, Levine and the Metropolitan Orchestra, Sir Colin Davis and the Amsterdam Concertgebouw Orchestra, and Kent

Nagano with the London Philharmonic Orchestra. Unfortunately, there are so many good performances that I have enjoyed over the years that I simply can't even begin to list them all, which is unfair to those musicians who have brought me great pleasure in the rehearing of this favorite work.

Stravinsky, in my mind, knew his works best of all interpreters concerned. I possess his recordings, and despite their age, they are delightful. I do not think, however, in the end, that his versions give as much listening pleasure as the interpreters named above. Indeed, Stravinsky himself had suggested that composers might not be their own greatest exponents.

- The Rite of Spring
  DG 435 073-2 GGA. BSO, Michael Tilson Thomas
- The Rite of Spring; Petrushka; The Firebird (Suite); Pulcinella
  DG 453 085-2 GTA2. LSO, Abbado

Modern Music

In the arts, modernism is a particularly gossamer term, for what may have been truly modern at one time may at a later date seem commonplace. There are elements in music that have had a peculiar appeal in their time but have proven to be incompatible with true and permanent greatness. Often, the more sudden and sensational the initial success, the less it has been likely to endure. Also, the degree of modernism in music has depended upon the experience and taste of the audiences. Some have regarded as modern only that music which, when it was created, departed from previous convention and was not readily accepted. Humans are by nature too complacent to change, and audiences have typically reacted with a dim view to the "modern" music of their time.

What is the value of any contemporary art? No rule applies. At times, once again, it is a function of the subjective views of the audience. Everyone can perceive only in proportion to his or her capacity; no one beyond it. A profound work may easily fail of response, as many works in music have done in the past, because the average caliber of an audience is too shallow, though it may deeply stir an exceptional few. And though it is a fact that few decisions have been made during the lifetime of a composer, is it possible that an obscure Mozart may never find his acclaim? It is frightening to think of such a chance: it seems a little akin to the danger of being buried alive!

In 1896 Bruckner passed away, a year later Brahms left this world, and Richard Strauss gave the first performance of *Also Spracht Zarathustra*. By 1918, the creative work of Strauss was essentially done. A new era had begun in music. Like two highways leading in different directions, the old and the new stood at a crossroads, and a new generation of young musicians now began to attract the attention of the musical audience. As the First World War destroyed the Europe of old, the new music could no longer sing of dreaming and painting, and mood and emotions. The new musicians, disillusioned and hostile, wanted no part of romanticism—people had become skeptical towards big words and ringing phrases, or idealistic dreams and romantic fantasia. The bold egotism of Berlioz, the *grande geste* of Liszt, and the erotic sensuality of Wagner now seemed to be nothing but exaggerated playacting. The opera with its symphonic music and *leitmotif* became a thing of the past. The ground over which blood had been spilled in streams was shaking; the air was filled with the moans of the dying and the cries of revolutionary masses. Realism, not Romanticism, embodied the spirit of the new age. And the most forceful representative of this change was Arnold Schoenberg.

The New Music became akin to architecture, not to poetry or painting. The orchestral instruments no longer applied color nor were they carriers of feeling, but became parts of a structure. Uncloaked and unadorned, this music utilized the tone material as aptly as the stonemasons of the Middle Ages who had created the Gothic windows and gargoyles of the big cathedrals from granite blocks. The musician no longer played the philosopher or poet or painter; he lived in tones and thought in tones. And like every big revolution, Schoenberg's music was considered to be life destroying and menacing.

Whereas musical thoughts hitherto had delved in length and breadth, modern music stepped into depth. And all its forming and shaping took place not in that old intimate tone sphere that had been divided by the seven-tone scale, but in a space of twelve tones where a composer's imagination had to search anew for tones and tone combinations, and themes and thematic treatment. Here was a substitute for the familiar concept of tonality. Here was music especially suited for an era suffering under heavy social and economic problems and expecting a cure from rational science. It was a music without color decoration, without literary facade, without illustrating tricks, without theatrical attitude; music that did not dissolve into subjective moods but was all form and figure. The singing voice neither sang nor spoke, yet every one of the new and unaccustomed tones, and every tone blend, was nevertheless logically intelligible. Here was a new music that was practical and concrete with the brightness of the conscious, yet extended into the dark of the unconscious and the dawn of an unknown, unreal world whose figures were not physical shapes but spiritual ones, albeit often merely in the embryonic form of thoughts. Here was music with an identity. And yet, some composers like Rachmaninoff remained faithful to a noble romanticism. To this great modern master, the piano was still the old romantic instrument that had tones for ecstasy and radiance, for a sighing heart and a yearning spirit.

From out of the Second World War, in which humanity had staggered into death and destruction again, America emerged as victor. After years spent in a blood bath, the world needed stimulation, and a new music with strong rhythms was required for a revitalization of its worn-out nerves. The post war generation was unromantic; there were no tone areas or expanded harmonies in its orchestra—just spasmodic, gesticulating, forcefully drawn lines. The landscape of the new continent, with its gigantic spaces, its forests and canyons, the prairies and cotton plantations determined the character of its music—new colors, new tempo, a new vitality and a new humanity. And in his music, Aaron Copland drew inspiration from small and big towns, from saloons and dance halls.

American music is necessarily a record of a score of different tendencies and efforts in different directions, efforts of uneven value, but all attesting, in sum, to the rapid artistic growth of a nation born of a multitude of races which make up the warp and woof of American national life. And it is just such an amalgamation of divers peoples and spiritual forces that offers the broad and exceptional promise for a new song of the millennium when composers will give the sound of music the dignity of a great symbol that can spread the calm light of a higher law upon a struggling world.

Richard Strauss: Tone Poems

Franz Liszt invented the symphonic poem; Richard Strauss (1864 - 1949) developed and perfected it, and rechristened it the tone poem. He provided it with the realistic colors of a virtuoso, and spread it out to paint giant symphonic tableaux. The basic feeling of his music is still romantic, but his means of performance are realistic. Each of his poems are different from the others in mood and feeling; each is intrinsically linked to the poetic idea the composer wishes to convey. Each is music as expression. And the variety and complexity of the tone poems demonstrate that Strauss, once he was seized with an idea, could develop and execute music with extraordinary talent.

Death and Transfiguration, his first tone poem to become popular, describes the sufferings of a sick man and his ultimate release through death and dissolution. The music is wrapped in a dreamlike aura that can be sensed at once in its soft introduction where the mood is established by the uneasy and irregular pulse of soft strings while a flute heaves a pathetic little sigh. The music is extraordinarily graphic in its mortal aspects, when human suffering is described with an almost clinical accuracy that depicts the writhing pain, the hammer blows against the brain, the tortures of fever, the horrible nightmares, and the contortions of the nerves. The orchestra moans and groans and thrashes in pain, and breathes feverishly and heavily. All is reality and pathology, not just imagination. But as much as his musical genius soars in the earthbound portions, it falls during its ascent to the sky. The "Transfiguration" music is less successful and less noble. Some have suggested that it fails to inspire because the composer was not deeply concerned with religion or the religious. He lacked involvement with God, and felt none of the passion of faith. His passion lay in psychological probing; it was in his expression of character that his talent showed itself.

If a humorist is an artist who can not only create funny works but can voice grave thoughts lightly, then Strauss excelled as a humorist. *Eulenspiegel* in German means an owl's mirror. Whether the owl here serves as a symbol of wisdom, and the mirror as a reflection of man's foibles, remains uncertain. *Till Eulenspiegel*, Strauss's altogether brilliant composition, tells the story of a figure that has been invented in the literature of nations in one guise or another because there is need for him: he shows that the simple are superior to the educated, the poor cleverer than the rich, that the strolling beggar is able to best the seated dignitary, that the liar often speaks the truth, and that he is strongest armed who can summon impudence! The music is melodiously easy and charming without a stretch of philosophic meandering. The musical episodes are varied and consistently entertaining yet strongly realistic—the clattering pots of the women vendors as Till rides into the village square, the mumbling of the monks, Till disguised as a priest preaching a greasy musical sermon, Till glowing with love, Till humming a folk ditty, the trumpet tones pronouncing his death sentence, and so on until his last expiring squeak on the gallows; we seem to see the events pass before our very eyes! In a word, *Till* is a heartwarming and happy masterpiece.

Beethoven once said that music is a higher revelation than philosophy. But can music really reveal philosophy? Can anyone possibly express in music a complete philosophic thought process, or portray in sound a specific philosophic system or a detailed philosophic teaching? To the extent that Strauss attempts the impossible he fails. In the most beautiful prose that he composed in his prose poem *Also sprach Zarathustra*, Nietzsche conveyed an idea of the evolution of the human being and race from its origin that, through breeding, education, hard thinking and harder egotism, rises above mediocrity and conformity to the idea of a Superman. The road lies beyond good and evil; all means that will propel humankind along it are recommended. To reach the higher state, says Nietzsche, all weak institutions that advocate the sanctity of humanity in general must be destroyed. Christianity must be destroyed, democracy abolished. And Nietzsche clothes his ideas in robes of multicolored language. He sings as he teaches, he rhapsodizes as he expounds.

The music of *Also spracht Zarasthustra* is a work of curious anomalies, divided against itself. Within its thirty three minutes are moments of superb beauty and passages of gripping intensity, side by side with amorphous sections and technical cleverness. From the stunning opening of the sunrise—man undeveloped, man ignorant, man unfired by a will to power—to the beautiful *Epilogue* that ends the composition in an aura of peace, the music overwhelms with its opulence and bores with its stuffiness. It is inspiring and professorial, fulsome and fabulous, bursting with both romantic exuberance and doughy pedantry.

The two celebrated Spanish dons, Don Juan and Don Quixote, are citizens of the world. They transcend countries, nationalities and time. *Don Juan*, Strauss's second tone poem, (*Macbeth* was the inferior first), was hailed as the extraordinary success of a youthful composer who had touched a beating vein in the young generation that he represented. For, in a new language, he had captured the spirit of the times! Here was expressed openly erotic desire, voluptuousness and rebellion, both virility and femininity and, at the close, weariness and satiety, and death in a useless duel. The spirit of the music is purely subjective in which the symbolic figure of fickle desire moves through scenes of enchantment to a climax of barren despair. The music begins in an impetuous main theme mingled in a spirited song that plunges into the fullness of life, much like the sudden flame of a desire that is kindled anew. The sounds become sexual and ravenous, flaring up like a torch that is dissipating energy. The realism is not confined to individual episodes, or to the musical description of the women that the hero sets out to conquer. It is felt in the general mood of the entire music. Strauss does not defy tradition by ending this poem in triumph—a final elemental burst of passion stops abruptly before a long pause. The end comes in dismal, dying harmonies—a dull sigh of emptiness, void of joy, and even of the solace of poignant grief.

Don Quixote can forever be interpreted afresh. And Strauss gives a wondrously quickening and realistic interpretation, as in the battle with the windmills, the bleating sheep herds, the water dripping off the clothes of the knight as he emerges from the water, and the litany of the monks. The music has what is needed to make the Don come alive: irony and derision, affection and sympathy, sadness and comedy. Complex, ingenious and technically marvelous as it is, it strikes one as natural and indeed as simple. "Whether he was a fool or a wise man is not clear, but surely he entered heaven," concludes Cervantes of his hero. Strauss does him justice.

It was the conductor Hans Knappertbusch who referred to Richard Strauss as follows: "I knew him well. I played cards with him one afternoon a week for forty years. He was a pig." It's often been said that Strauss wrote his tone poems simply for the money, and performed them likewise. Whether this is true or not, Strauss was a brilliant orchestrator, and his conductorial and compositional skills are exemplary. Even in Strauss' own time, recordings of the works, demonstrating their brilliant orchestration, were very successful.

Also Sprach Zarathustra is famous for its *Dawn of Civilization* introduction in the film *2001: A Space Odyssey*, but obviously this is only the first three minutes of a 35 minute work. This is a glorious exercise for large orchestra, but unfortunately, in hyperbolic performances, it can have a windbag-like character which bloats the intellectual content of Strauss' writing. Therefore, I believe a thoroughly emasculating performance of the work often is the most illuminating and, as such, pride of place goes to Bernard Haitink and his mid 70s performance of the work on Philips at mid price. The Contcertgebouw Orchestra performs brilliantly, and the recorded sound is limpidly clear and precise. A no-bonus addition to this work, a truly anemic performance of *Don Juan* is included, but this performance of *Also Sprach Zarathustra* is one of my *Desert Island* favorites.

There are a number of other outstanding performances of the work, notably the first DG recording by Herbert von Karajan and the Berlin Philharmonic dating from approximately 1974, and that of William Steinberg and the Boston Symphony Orchestra from 1972, a truly brilliant tour de force which benefits from some of the greatest recorded sound I have encountered from this time period. There are probably forty other excellent performances of the work, but with anyone of these three, one could not go far wrong.

Don Juan is a seventeen minute tone poem illuminating the character from the written literature. I was first introduced to this work when seeing Zubin Mehta conduct it on a televised broadcast in which he used only his right hand for the conductorial exercise of presenting this work. I was rather surprised by this, but he appeared to impart all the expression he needed with his right hand, and the performance was illuminating. This broadcast occurred somewhat after his initial recording of the work as the first recording of the Dorothy Chandler Pavilion of the Music Center in downtown Los Angeles. This recording is still available on RCA and is quite good, but others have surpassed it.

I would say that Sir Georg Solti and the Chicago Symphony have one of the most dramatic presentations of the work available, and it was featured on one of the original LPs produced in 1972 in Chicago: *Solti Chicago Showcase*. The Chicago brass are absolutely unbelievable, and the hair trigger accuracy of the playing has never been bettered by anybody.

Karajan, Bohm, Kempe and Szell have all committed outstanding renditions of the work to disc, and any of these would also be an excellent choice, especially Szell who, with his outstanding Cleveland orchestra, delivers almost as exciting a rendition as Solti. Please note that I am not equating the recent Solti/Berlin Philharmonic account of *Don Juan* or *Also Sprach Zarathustra* with either of the specific recordings mentioned above.

Don Quixote has been well served on record since the early stereo era, and my favorite recordings remain that of Rostropovitch and Karajan with the Berlin Philharmonic from a very early stereo performance, or Janigro and Reiner with the Chicago Symphony, or Hlinka and Mehta with the Los Angeles Philharmonic, all of which are eminently satisfying performances. There are newer, more modern renditions available, but none are better than these.

Till Eulenspiegel is a tale of a prankster which brings great pleasure. It demonstrates Strauss' incredible tone color painting better perhaps than any other single orchestral work he composed. Again, Solti and the Chicago Symphony have demonstrated their apt ability in this work, and the performance they generate for their all-Strauss recording from the '70s is quite unbelievable. This remains my preeminent choice, although Reiner and the Chicago Symphony many years earlier had evoked similar excitement, albeit in less good recorded sound. Kempe, Karajan and Previn have all produced excellent versions of *Till*, and any of these would also make satisfying company.

Outstanding performances of *Death and Transfiguration* are provided by Karajan and the Berlin Philharmonic Orchestra and by Levine at the MET.

- (i) Also Sprach Zarathustra; Death and Transfiguration; Don Juan; Ein Heldenleben; Till Eulenspiegel; (ii) Der Rosenkavalier: Waltz Sequence
    Ph Duo. 442 281-2 (2) Concg. O, (i) Haitink, (ii) Jochum
- Death and Transfiguration
    DG 447 422-2GOR. BPO, Karajan
- Also Sprach Zarathustra
    Ph. 420 521-2 PSL. Concg O, Haitink
- (i) Don Juan;Till Eulenspiegel; Also Sprach Zarathushtra;
  (ii) An Alpine Symphony; (iii) Ein Heldenleben
    Double Decca 440 618-2 (2) (i) Chicago SO, (ii) Bav RSO
    (III) VPO, Solti
- Don Quixote; Don Juan
    RCA 09026-68170-2, Janigro, Chicago SO, Reiner
- Burlesque; Also Sprach Zarathushtra; Rosenkavalier waltzes
    RCA 09026-68638-2, Chicago SO, Reiner

Elgar: Orchestral Works

The phenomenon of greatness in English music vanished from England with Purcell, and it was more than two hundred years later that there came upon the English scene a young man from the west country without a musical degree, who proceeded calmly and sweetly on the unconscious assumption that he was by nature and destiny one of the great composers. A certain unmistakable royal pride and temper was hinted on occasion, but normally a less pretentious person could not be found. One could meet him and talk to him for a week without suspecting that he was anything more than a very typical English country gentleman who did not know a fugue from a *fandango*. But his music took away your breath!

It was Sir Edward Elgar's (1857 - 1934) *Variations on an Original Theme*, called the *Enigma Variations*, that first brought him out of obscurity to fame. And what a gallant idea for a theme and variations: fourteen character sketches in sound of the composer, his wife and twelve personal friends—the fourteen variations—all derived from a gentle, hesitant violin theme. The score is prefaced by a series of initials, each set of initials depicting the close friend whom one of the variations portrays. The profiles in music are crystalline, stamped with good breeding, and reveal a tenderness and emotional beauty, and a flowing lyricism, that are refreshingly different in modern English music. The first variation, eloquent and poetic, is a musical portrait of Elgar's wife who was the greatest single influence in his life, and the final variation is a self portrait. The composer called the variations *Enigma* because he suggested that there was a hidden alternative theme in the music which, though never actually played in the work, was supposed to accompany each and every variation, thus persisting through the entire work as a silent accompaniment. It has been proposed that the silent theme is the motto melody of Wagner's *Parsifal*, but the mystery has remained unsolved.

Pomp and Circumstance are a set of six patriotic military marches that were composed for the coronation of Edward VII. It is the first of these that is the most commonly played, and is akin to being England's second national anthem. The first march is in two parts: a brisk and nervous passage that forms a prelude to a flowing, majestic melody.

The title of the popular and happy overture, *Cockaigne (In London Town)*, denotes the ancient square mile of old Londinium where the Cockneys ply their trade. But it paints a larger portrait of a big city, and the music depicts the varied experiences crowded into a few hours of London life. To some, it will be purely classical music, telling no stories external to itself and the listener. Others may hear in it all sorts of footsteps and to them it may tell all sorts of stories, complete with Westminster chimes, snatches of Yip-i-addy, and a march of the costermongers to Covent Gardens. The musical canvas evokes a series of pictures—serious, humorous and romantic—that spans the grace of Knightsbridge and the expanse of Hampstead

Heath. Here is average, middle-class London, London optimistic and by no means uninteresting, London of the garrulous creatures and assoiled shows, merry London, and London tragic and terrible. And though the music abstains from revealing its sordid and steamy side, the tone pictures are a splendid time capsule of a magnificent city and its people.

The three works discussed here by no means epitomize the significant output of Britain's perhaps most famous composer, but they are so representative of this composer's highest quality output that they can be considered as a group for his orchestral music. I did not warm to Elgar until I was in my thirties. I really had never heard his music, but had erroneously presumed that he was simply a second class composer and that I probably would not really find his music stimulating. Well, I have eaten my words more than once in my life, and I would say that I listen to Elgar as frequently as any other composer whose music rests on my shelves. There is a certain kind of wistful melancholy to the works presented here which descends upon the listener only after repeated hearings.

The *Enigma Variations* depict in musical caricature, friends, associates and significant others in the life of the composer. The composer himself apparently has depicted his own persona in the final variation. This is as great a work to me as the Dvorak *Symphonic Variations* or the Brahms *St. Antoni Variations*, and fortunately, it has been brilliantly recorded.

The conductor Sir Georg Solti recorded the work twice, once with the Chicago Symphony Orchestra and once with the Vienna Philharmonic, the latter being one of his last recordings. How a Jewish émigré from Hungary could become so steeped in understanding of the music of Sir Edward Elgar may defy logic, but Solti, who lived in the United Kingdom for perhaps thirty years and ultimately became a British subject, plumbs the depths of these works effortlessly. The Chicago Symphony recording is somewhat craggier and more characterized than the Vienna Philharmonic recording, but either will bring great pleasure to the listener. I must have them both, because to me they are so different. The recorded sound of each is excellent, and the playing of each is highly refined.

Leonard Bernstein and the BBC Symphony Orchestra recorded the *Enigma Variations* in 1982 for DG. I think the British at first revolted upon hearing this recording because of its extreme willfulness and distortion of the score. This may not be a first choice for listeners to learn, but it is a performance that all should hear. This is my single favorite performance of the work, if there was one, notwithstanding a *Nimrod* variation which is literally twice as long as it should be. The orchestral playing is brilliant, and the dynamic range of the recording is concussive. This is only available by import presently and hopefully it will be reissued some day at mid price.

Other recordings of the *Enigma Variations* which are noteworthy are those of Sir Charles Mackerras on Argo, Giuseppe Sinopoli and the Philharmonia Orchestra, and that by Eugen Jochum and the London Symphony Orchestra recorded in 1975. In North America, the conductor David Zinman has recorded the work with the Baltimore Symphony Orchestra for Telarc in what may be sonically the best presentation of the work I've encountered. Any of these performances will please the listener, amongst the dozens in the catalog.

The *Pomp and Circumstance Marches* curiously are not widely available as a complete set. Many recordings just present two or three of the five marches, and they should all be heard. They will remind you of high school graduation, but they are orchestral miniatures that are giant musical thoughts. Sir Georg Solti and the London Philharmonic recorded the five *Pomp and Circumstance Marches* for London in the seventies. His performances are highly idiomatic and sensitive, besides which they are brilliantly recorded. Daniel Barenboim and the London Philharmonic Orchestra recorded the works for Sony Classical in 1976, and the performances, while less idiomatic, are nevertheless exciting.

A rather willful interpretation of two of the *Pomp and Circumstance* marches are by Leonard Bernstein and the BBC Symphony Orchestra. These are absolutely worth hearing because of their willfulness, let alone because they can bring tears to your eyes. I am not quite sure how the BBC Symphony Orchestra musicians reacted to the making of the Bernstein CD, but it remains a staple for my sanity.

The *Cockaigne (In London Town)* has been well depicted on CD by Sir Georg Solti, Sir Alexander Gibson, Giuseppe Sinapoli, and Sir Adrian Boult, among others. One of my favorite records is a series of Elgar Overtures with the Scottish National Orchestra with Sir Alexander Gibson on Chandos which is worthy of seeking. I love all of the Elgar Overtures, and they should find a place on your shelves.

- Enigma Variations; Pomp and Circumstance Marches; Cockaigne overture
    London 417 719-2-LM. Chicago SO, Solti
- Enigma Variations
    London 452 853-2-LH. VPO, Solti
- Enigma Variations
    DG 413 490-2GH. BBC SO, Bernstein
- Pomp and Circumstance Marches
    Sony SBK48265. LPO, Barenboim
- Overtures (incl. Cockaigne)
    Chandos 8309. Scottish National O, Gibson

Stravinsky: Petruschka

When Igor Stravinsky (1882 - 1971) was twenty years old, he met the greatest living Russian composer Rimsky-Korsakov. And then and there he abandoned a promising law career to take on music. A decade later, when in Rome, he composed the ballet *Petrushka* based upon the carnival story of a doll, a superfluous puppet-like man, who is the helpless victim of a brutality that he cannot combat.

The exquisite and tender music of *Petrushka* is Stravinsky's age of innocence. Everything in this music is new and personal; everywhere the roots of this music arise from primitivity and folk lore. There is a startling mechanical rhythm, appropriate to its subject, that is breathtaking in its virtuosity and brilliantly colorful orchestration, but it was its harmonic innovations that made it so controversial. A shriek of two trumpets in different keys is Petruschka's theme, and for musicologists, this created mayhem. For, if one combined two keys, then what happened to tonality? The new technique was labeled polytonality, and a whole French school sprang up after it.

The tragedy of Petrushka, gripping for its laconism, has been variously interpreted. Let us not admit anything lest we weep! The music reflects everything with reckless mastery: the bustle and tumult of the carnival crowd permeated with Russian folk melodies and street songs, the gait and aspect of each leading figure, and the grotesque agonies of the helpless one. The Stravinsky orchestra is not a colorful or exuberant one that is singing of landscapes, steppes and forests; it is hard and bound to the depths of the earth itself, where the rock forms hard masses. And the rhythm is not a spiritualized rhythm but a primitive one stamping with rough high boots, strong as peasant soil, wild as untamed nature, whirling in circles.

The peoples' hustle and bustle at the fair and the puppet play are the substance of *Petrushka*. Crowds and mass movement are set in contrast to the performance of the wooden puppets where love, jealousy, despair and death become theatrical play. There is always a very strong motion in the music, the harmonies play the turmoil, chords pile up against each other, and chromatic tones swim in circular motions intensified to orgiastic proportions. Everything in this music is strongest life, tumultous reality. From this raw underground of moving harmonies, short themes arise like primitive music, and are whirled around with ever new rhythmic accents. Not for one instant does the rhythmic energy lose its strength; with every passing moment the orchestral timbre increases its vitality with shrill colors. Its seems as if a monstrous mechanical apparatus has been set in motion to transform the demonic music into a rhythmic orgasm.

From out of this mass commotion emerges the play of the marionettes—sharp, clinking and porcelain-like. Ghostly, too, is the mood of Stravinsky's music. When Petrushka is repelled cruelly by a kick, the music sounds like breaking glass. Petruschka's collapse is veered to the grotesque by scurrilous passages on the piano, and the end of the scene gives the impression of a china doll falling to the floor and breaking into a million pieces. In the death scene the spookishly bizarre yet fantastic themes are folded together like figures placed in a box when the game is finished. The music ends in a grand manner to prove that there *was* life in the marionettes, a soul even in the wooden puppets, vindicating the old Oriental faith that in the play of marionettes lies an image of exalted life.

Stravinsky's *Petrushka* was first composed in 1911, and revised in 1947. This is perhaps Stravinsky's second greatest ballet after *The Rite of Spring*, and it is a delight from start to finish. The work has been extraordinarily well served, especially in modern recorded sound, and there are probably fifty at least good performances of the work dating back as far as 1955. Due to the dynamic range of the work, and the demands placed on the orchestra by the score, I would suggest that the listener obtain as modern a recording as possible, of which there are several which I prefer.

My single favorite performance is probably not yet available on CD, and is the 1974 version by James Levine and the Chicago Symphony Orchestra on RCA. If the reader can find this recording in a used record store on vinyl or cassette, the rewards are innumerable. The playing is beyond reproach, and the recorded sound, engineered by Jay David Saks, remains outstanding despite its 1978 publication date.

Outstanding versions of the score have been provided by Abbado with the London Symphony Orchestra, by Chailly and the Royal Amsterdam Concertgebouw Orchestra in a truly stunning performance, Bernard Haitink and the Berlin Philharmonic Orchestra, and by Sir Simon Rattle and the City of Birmingham Symphony Orchestra. There is very little to choose from any of these modern recordings in terms of performance, depth of understanding of the score, and recorded sound.

The reader should also study the performance by the composer, recorded in the early sixties for Columbia Masterworks and reissued by Sony Classical a number of years ago. I don't believe that Stravinsky was the greatest conductor of his own works, but it is clear from the outset of the performance precisely what the composer had intended. It is also remarkable to see how elegantly the aforementioned conductors, in more modern sound, have adhered to the composer's intentions as depicted in the score.

- Petrushka; Pulcinella
  London 443774-2 LH. Royal Amsterdam Concertgebouw O, Chailly

Rachmaninoff: Symphony No 2

"I compose music because I must give expression to my feelings... it is the product of the sum total of my experiences." This remained Sergei Rachmaninoff's (1873 - 1943) creed—embedded in the warm temperament of melody and the natural harmonic fabric most suited to it lay the composer's whole personality. Recovering from a severe depression and an emotional crisis that had been precipitated by the luckless hearing of his first symphony, Rachmaninoff left Moscow with his wife and baby daughter for a long sabbatical to Dresden. Here, in the virtual seclusion of his comfortable little house and garden, he composed one of his best symphonic works: Symphony No. 2.

Much has been read in this music of which the composer himself remained non committal. Some have called its theme *Momento mori*, with the threatening, heavily oppressive chords seeming pregnant with the premonition of death, and the trumpets and violins swelling to a desperate groan that collapses and dies away. The dull inflexible chorus at the conclusion of the Scherzo also seems to cut in with its gloomy warning of death, even in the carefree exuberant moods and the most ecstatic moments of the music. Others have found in its attitude a Tolstoyan resistance to evil, the brooding and somber reflective state of a soul that endures the sight of the dark aspects of Russian life, indeed of all life, more as a seer than a rebel. The music seems to look out at a somber world of dim distances, of golden lights and shadows, of fateful and steady motion—impersonally, dispassionately, and with moderation.

It is true that the nature of Rachmaninoff's premises demands a sense of tragedy. Yet the larger part of this work is serene or even frankly exuberant. The main argument is virile, not resigned, and the finale is joyous.

The symphony was composed in 1908, and performed the following year in St. Petersburg under the baton of the composer.

Rachmaninoff's Symphony No. 2 is one of the most beloved romantic works of its era, and it has been well served since it was written in the recorded format. Curiously, two of the most unique recordings of this work are on one label, both relatively recently introduced to the catalog.

Mikhail Pletnev, in his own right one of the master pianists of the current generation, has turned conductor and has developed a hand-picked body of musicians to form the Russian National Orchestra that was assembled after the fall of the Iron Curtain. Using what I believe to be the intended score for the performance, Pletnev models a dramatic, incisive and potent version of the symphony, without histrionics and overly emotive flair. This is again one of the great recordings of all time in my mind, though many will disagree and find certain aspects of it contrary to their recollection of how the work should sound.

For those who wish a version of the score with which we are most accustomed, I would suggest an excellent recording of poetic beauty and overall competence from the early 80s performed by Vladimir Ashkenazy and the Concertgebouw Orchestra on London. There are very few performances of this symphony, let alone all three Rachmaninoff Symphonies, which are so eminently successful as Ashkenazy's foray into this repertoire.

The great East German conductor, Kurt Sanderling, recorded the Rachmaninoff Second Symphony in 1956 for DG in mono. This recording has resurfaced on DG Originals recently, and it has to be one of the stellar classics of the gramophone. I don't want to say too much about this recording other than it really ought to be heard by lovers of this work, as it is again a basic staple of the Rachmaninoff diet. It is by no means a first choice amongst performances by virtue of its recording date, and I would say that although the sound remains quite good, the work has more to offer in stereo than it does in multi-microphone technique monophonic recordings of the era in which it appeared. Nevertheless, it can be strongly recommended.

- Symphony Nos 1-3
    London 448116-2 LF2. Concertgebouw O,
    Vladimir Ashkenazy
- Symphony No 2
    DG Originals 449 767-2 GOR.Leningrad Philh. O,
    Kurt Sanderling

Rachmaninoff: Piano concertos

Right until his death in World War II America, the Russian composer Sergei Rachmaninoff remained faithful to a noble romanticism. His heroes were Chopin, Liszt and Tchaikovsky. He was the greatest master of the piano in the modern era, and to him it was still the old romantic instrument with a nature sensitively attuned to beauty and gaudy melancholy that had the tones of ecstasy and radiance to express the singing of a heart. The Liszt arpeggios that rippled like harps, and Chopin's melismata that gleamed like a string of pearls, were very much still a part of Rachmaninoff's piano music. He opened no new worlds: he was satisfied to recreate old ones, nostalgically and eloquently, to expound the doctrine of beauty. He was the Russian soul in modern music—emotional, hypersensitive, moody, elegiac, at alternate moments brooding and savage.

The First Piano Concerto, like his First Symphony, was a failure. But the Piano Concerto No. 2, perhaps his best known, reflects the vitality and freshness that he felt as he took on a new lease on life after months of psychotherapy for a despairing, all-possessing apathy. Few of his works are so richly filled with intoxicating melodies; few seem to have arisen from such soaring flights of inspiration. From the majestic opening of the first movement to the stirring and eloquently lyrical melody for oboe and violas in the final movement, the music teems with exciting, moving, passionate and tender ideas that pour forth inexhaustibly. The second movement is a particularly poetic piece, at times sentimental, often nostalgic, snappily dour then rhapsodic, but always deeply felt and sensitively expressed.

Written almost a decade later, the Third Concerto is radically different in style and spirit. Here is not Rachmaninoff the dark Romantic, but a serious composer concerned with symmetry, development, form and conclusion. It is less emotional and nostalgic, bolder and freer in its musical conscience, with intensely expressive themes and a more symphonic breadth.

The Second Concerto was first performed in Russia in 1901; the Third was introduced in New York. In both places, the virtuoso-composer played the solo piano parts; Gustav Mahler conducted the New York performance.

I must confess not to be enamored of any of these works, but I do know they are great, let alone very popular. The movie *Shine* brought to fame the Third Concerto as far as the public's eye was concerned, and I have recently studied this work and have found one indispensable performance to own.

If you're in the market for a comprehensive analysis of the concerti expertly performed and played, I would suggest that you find the recordings on London as played by Vladimir Ashkenazy and conducted by Andre Previn. These performances are stunning from start to finish, and will compliment any collection as a highly prized commodity.

As for individual performances, I have a special place in my heart for Sviatoslav Richter's performance of the Second Concerto with Stanislaw Wislocki and the Polish National Radio Symphony Orchestra on DG Originals. This is an indispensable reading and, despite its greater than thirty year age, has stood the test of time both in terms of performance integrity and the preservation of very decent sound.

As for the Third Concerto, I have a special place in my heart for a live recording from the Berlin Radio Symphony as broadcast on *Sender Freies Berlin* and released recently on CD by Philips. The performance is played by Martha Argerich—and it is stunning because of her technique and/or command of the instrument and the work, conducted by the Italian Riccardo Chailly. One audition of this performance will tell you why it's my personal favorite, and why the work is such a great work! This particular performance, which is complimented by an equally fine Tchaikovsky's *Piano Concerto No. 1* conducted by Kiril Kondrashin, makes an outstanding coupling. Another seminal and monumental recording is the 1951 Horowitz/Reiner performance which is as good a choice as any to introduce the inimitable magic of this piece. Indeed, Rachmaninoff himself had said that Horowitz was the only pianist who played the piece better than he himself did!

- Piano concertos 1-4
  Decca Double 444 839-2. Vladimir Ashkenazy; LSO, Previn
- Piano concerto No. 3;—TCHAIKOVSKY: Piano Concerto No 1
  Ph. 446 673-2. Martha Argerich; Berlin Radio SO, Chailly

Prokofiev: Symphony No 1 (Classical)

In opposition to the Romanticism of Rachmaninoff, Serge Prokofiev (1891 - 1953) placed a modern classicism in his art—his music contains clear rhythms, simple melodies and lively tempi, often with humor and laughter. He is witty and alive without solemnity or attitude, and his music lets the light stream in through many windows without dreamy corners or dark recesses. "There is a return to classic forms which I feel very much myself." he declared, "I want nothing better, nothing more flexible or more complete than the sonata form, which contains everything necessary to my structural purpose."

It was in such classic forms that he composed his "Classical" Symphony No. 1 during the Russian Revolution. And with it began the neoclassical movement that swept the world of modern music soon after the First World War. It is witty, lively, melodic music in which a modern composer imitates at least Mozart's serenity, if not his blithe spirit and great soul. Prokofiev's music has no transcendental background. It consists almost entirely of melodic lines with little role for tonal quality, or the magic of color, or the poetic mood. No mistaking those clipped phrases, those mocking themes, those

308

capricious rhythms, those piquant insolent gestures that appear and reappear throughout the work! There is a technical spirit here, for the simplicity of his music is the product of education: his hand was skilled in the elaboration of things. But his classicism was not the creation of a classic imagination; rather, it was the idea of an artist. It was the reaction of a modern musician toward the style of the Impressionist era. The classic forms are used for the facade of a modern house but the walls are smooth and without ornaments, and in it resides a brilliant man.

This is one of the earliest works that I learned, and such is probably the case with many a young listener's exposure to symphonic literature. It is a brief work, hardly sixteen minutes, and it well demonstrates the broad spectrum of instrumentation and orchestration in an elegant, simple, but by no means unsophisticated way. To me, virtually everything this composer wrote after his First Symphony, not unlike Shostakovich, was a downhill course, but perhaps that is both provincial and narrow minded of me!

In his earliest years while at London Records, Claudio Abbado recorded the Prokofiev Symphony Nos 1 and 3 with the London Symphony Orchestra. The recorded sound was good, and the performance of Symphony No. 1 was well nigh perfect—just about as perfect as I thought it could be. I was wrong! That original record, London CS6671, may or may not have seen reissue on CD, but Abbado has outdone himself. For, several years ago, Abbado recorded the *Classical Symphony* for DG with the Chamber Orchestra of Europe, and this performance is one of the great recordings currently available of this work. It is joyous, alive, and blissful, and it should be heard.

There is really only one other competitive recording with the outstanding version by Abbado, and that is with the Los Angeles Chamber Orchestra and its conductor, Gerard Schwarz. This recording was made at Bridges Auditorium, I believe, on the campus of Claremont College by Delos Records, a local concern, and it is one of the most outstandingly engineered performances of any work that

I have encountered. The dynamic range of the recording is almost assuredly near 10 decibels, and this is not heard to full effect except in the finale. The LACO certainly has one heck of a timpanist! It is a shame that the orchestra has not blossomed with respect to its programming schedules and steady leadership, as it is truly an ensemble of outstanding proportions, far outclassing other national orchestras.

- Symphony No. 1 (Classical)
    Delos DCD 3021 Los Angeles Chamber O, G Schwarz
- Symphony No. 1 (Classical)
    DG 429 396-2 GH. Chamber O of Europe, Abbado

Bartok: Concerto for Orchestra

The music of most of the talented composers of the modern era that spanned the two World Wars was mobile, something more like wax that absorbed the impression of the spiritual, literary and artistic movements in Europe, carrying ever new forms. For the Hungarian genius Bela Bartok (1881 - 1945), however, music was something permanent and strong like a signet ring that puts its own mark on every note. Bartok lived in solitude and he went his own way. And his path led him over Hungarian plains and across the Rumanian mountains, through hamlets of poor but gaily painted peasant houses, where he collected the music of his native folk songs and folk dances. He was the only one of the modernists whose music, despite its bold innovations, remained tied to folk music. In a changing world it was the source of his strength—the great nature whence all forms were descended, the elementary force of the world.

But Bartok was no romanticist. He was not interested in their national content and coloring or their primitivity but in their melodic and rhythmic qualities that filled the folk music with such energy. Here was concise and condensed music that could compress the contents of a song into a few expressive bars much like a wizened face that is marked by years of experience, of grief, lament and longing that brings eternity to its expression. And out of this substrate he created new patterns, new harmonies and new rhythms. There is a rich humaneness in Bartok's music, but the quality is the common human quality, not humanity in its universal confines. Regardless of how much he condenses and reduces his music to the very essentials of tone and rhythm, his music remains an art of the soul, of its joys and grief and sorrow even when he seeks heights where the atmosphere becomes thin and cold. And the songs of the people from which Bartok's music is descended continue to resound in the lonely spheres in which his spirit descends to seek new truths, and capture the light of a new beauty that glows at the edge of his own fantasy.

When Bartok undertook a commission to compose the *Concerto for Orchestra*, he knew that he was dying—he had been repeatedly hospitalized, his strength was ebbing, and his weight had sunk to eighty seven pounds. The title of the work explains his intention to treat the single orchestral instruments of a virtuoso orchestra in a *concertant* or soloist manner. The general mood of the *Concerto* passes from the sternness of the first movement to a jesting second one, then a lugubrious death-song ends in an assertion of life in the finale.

This sublime work has fared extremely well since the beginning of long playing microgroove, and one of the earliest successes in that era was the performance by the RIAS Symphony Orchestra conducted by Ferenc Fricsay. This recording has been reissued on DG Originals recently, and is paired with an equally excellent performance of Bartok's *Music for Strings, Percussion, and Celesta*. The sound holds up admirably well despite the greater than forty year age of the recording.

A somewhat later recording, in early stereo with Fritz Reiner and the Chicago Symphony Orchestra is considered by many to be the epitome performance of the work, and it might be difficult for me to disagree with this. It is a wry spirited performance, in reasonably good sound, that captures the brilliance of the orchestra and Reiner's understanding of the score. A more recent performance with the Chicago Symphony by Conductor James Levine is less scintillating, but improves upon the Reiner recording in terms of recorded sound. An even more recent recording by Pierre Boulez with the Chicago Symphony is truly stellar, but it may lack the final degree of Hungarian refinement afforded by Reiner. Those looking for the most modern of recorded sound would be wise to consider Boulez, regardless.

In addition, in approximately 1981, Lorin Maazel recorded the work in one of DG's first digital productions. I still find this performance a technical knockout, both sonically and performance-wise, and it has been reissued on DG Classikon which is presently available only in Europe and the UK. Readers who come upon this recording in a used CD bin, or who travel abroad and find it, would be wise to consider it.

Finally, a poignant performance of the work by Rafael Kubelik and the Boston Symphony Orchestra is available on DG Galleria. This is an extraordinarily heartfelt performance played by the orchestra for which the work was actually commissioned. The orchestra has this music in its blood, and the interpretation, while a personal one, is quite idiomatic and extremely well played.

- Concerto for Orchestra; 4 Orchestral Pieces
  DG Dig. 437 826-2. Chicago SO, Boulez

Barber: Adagio for Strings

A suave style combined with elegant workmanship has made Samuel Barber (1910 - 1981) one of the major new voices in modern America. His deeply poetic temperament, and his simple yet powerfully moving writing, is reflected in the subtle moods and atmosphere that characterize his music. The poignant *Adagio for Strings*, composed in Rome in 1937, sustains a poetic mood throughout. The work, which is a slow movement of a string quartet, is based upon a single lyric theme that is announced forthright by the first violins. It is taken up by the violas in imitation, and then appears in the other voices until a rising climax is reached in the high strings. There is a pause, and the music comes to a tranquil close.

The *Adagio* was first performed in New York by the NBC orchestra conducted by Toscanini.

Barber is one of the great composers of our century and his work is known by people in music, but outside of musical circles he is almost a nonentity. The movie *Full Metal Jacket* spotlighted the Barber *Adagio for Strings* a number of years ago, but this hardly represents the composer's overall importance to the musical litera- ture. Barber's orchestral music, including his *Essays for orchestra Nos 1-3*, *Overture to the School for Scandal*, and *Medea's Meditation and Dance* are all works which should be heard by the novitiate listener and committed to memory. He is a distinctly American composer, unlike Copland who had quasi-Hebraic overtones in all of his writing.

Great collections of Barber's orchestral works are few and far between. One of the earliest, and most satisfying of all, is that by Thomas Schippers, a man who died in his late 40s of lung cancer from smoking. Schippers was a genius at the podium as well as in the opera house, and an amalgam of Barber's greatest orchestral pieces has recently been reissued by Sony Musical Heritage at mid price. This is too good to miss.

Leonard Slatkin and the St. Louis Symphony have recorded on EMI an amalgam of Barber's orchestral works which is also durable and eloquent. The St. Louis Symphony plays brilliantly and with feeling, and the recorded sound is also outstanding in these recent releases. Leonard Bernstein has recorded the Barber *Adagio for Strings* with the Los Angeles Philharmonic Orchestra with DG as late as 1984. It is a somewhat willful performance, but well recorded and well played.

Finally, perhaps the best of all demonstration-class discs is that by David Zinman and the Baltimore Symphony Orchestra for Argo which is, much like the Schippers' recording, an amalgam of several different works representing a broad period of the composer's life. It is this disc which I would recommend as a starting point for new listeners, and then obtain Schippers' to supplement it.

For those looking for only a recording of the *Adagio for Strings*, there is a very interesting compilation on BMG (RCA) of the *Adagio* that is played a number of different ways: with full orchestra, vocal ensemble, and chamber groups. This is a mid price disc that is worth hearing from the standpoint of creativity, uniqueness and reorchestration. I was initially somewhat negative about this recording when I first saw it, but upon repeated hearing, clearly, it has a secure place on my shelves.

Finally, for those who wish to hear the *Adagio* written as it was first thought out by the composer in its original quartet format, I recommend obtaining the Barber *String Quartet* performed by the Emerson Quartet for DG. This is a worthy acquisition not only for the full quartet, of which this is a single movement, but also for the accompanying music on this splendid CD.

- Adagio for Strings; Essays Nos 1, 2; Music for a scene from Shelley; Overture: The School for Scandal; Symphony No. 1
  Argo Dig. 436 288. Baltimore SO, Zinman

Copland: Appalachian Spring, Orchestral Suite

The music of this ballet takes as its point of departure the personality of Martha Graham who in 1944 produced, choreographed and herself danced in this work. The following year Aaron Copland (1900 - 1990) arranged an *Orchestral Suite* from his ballet. The title *Appalachian Spring* was chosen by Miss Graham from a heading of one of Hart Crane's poems. The ballet describes a celebration in spring around a newly-built farmhouse in the Pennsylvania hills in the early part of the last century. The music expresses the emotions, both joyful and apprehensive, of their new domestic partnership, suggests here and there the strange and terrible aspects of human fate, and ends with the couple left quiet and strong in their new home. The simple story notwithstanding, the music is evocative enough to create pictures in one's imagination, and conjure images of a not too distant American past.

There are two performing versions of this work, one for chamber orchestra and one for full orchestra. Both, in their own right, are excellent, but my preference is for the scaled down chamber orchestra version because of its elegance and certain endearing qualities which cannot be depicted in words. To that end, I know of two outstanding chamber orchestra versions, either of which I would recommend handily.

The first is by Keith Clark and the Pacific Symphony Orchestra in a pioneering digital recording on the Reference Recordings label. This performance was taped at the Orange County Performing Arts Center and was issued on audiophile vinyl LP and on CD, and there is nothing in the catalog which surpasses it.

As the Clark recording may be difficult to find due to its limited distribution, I would recommend the performance by the Orpheus Chamber Orchestra as an excellent option for a chamber orchestral version of this work. The Orpheus Chamber Orchestra is a conductor-less body, and has produced a wonderful CD of several Copland favorites, all of which are worth learning.

Of full orchestra versions from modern times, I believe there are a good half dozen performances, all heartfelt and all worthy. Two distinctly American conductors probably have reached the heart of this work better than any others, and I would suggest that the listener find either Leonard Bernstein's New York Philharmonic recording on Sony Classical although it is not digital, or the more recent performance by the St. Louis Symphony Orchestra and its conductor Leonard Slatkin. Both are warm, effusive statements which will bring great pleasure to the listener.

- Appalachian Spring (Chamber Orchestra Version)
  DG 427 335-2GH. Orpheus Chamber Orchestra

Bernstein: West Side Story, Symphonic Dances

New York City! Throughout his life, Leonard Bernstein (1918 - 1990) depicted the tragedy and squalor, the glitter and glamour, and even the poetry and pathos of this great city. And in the Broadway musical *West Side Story*, reminiscent of the German *Singespiele* (song-plays), he captured the spirit of inner city youth, the tragedy of urban violence and young delinquency, and the tale of the star-crossed lovers, Tony and Maria, caught in the tangled web of teenage gang rivalry. The dances that form this music are called *Symphonic* not because they are arranged for a symphony orchestra, but because they grow out of a few basic themes that are transformed and combined to express the variety of moods and actions that unfold in this tragic tale of senseless violence and young love.

There are really only two studio recordings of *West Side Story* which are not "sound track" performances to the original movie. Both are conducted by Bernstein, and both differ in temperament and presentation.

The original CBS (now Sony Classical) performance depicts the work as Bernstein saw it in the early sixties, with a cast of American soloists which differed in character from a sound track recording which was made at another time. I remember the work this way, and I know that many listeners of my generation will.

Bernstein re-recorded the work with a pickup orchestra of "friends" and soloists including Jose Carreras, Kiri Te Kanawa and Tatiana Troyanos as the leads, and I fear that while this is technically a far more polished performance, one that perhaps even demonstrates the drama and ethos of the music, there is something odd about the recording in that neither of the lead singers speak English without accents. Therefore, there is some comedy to the presentation, and although it is highly unintentional, it does not destroy the integrity of the performance. It just doesn't seem all quite "there" to me, however, and my preference would be for the original recording on Sony Classical whenever it becomes available. For now, the modern recording will have to suffice.

Zinman's Baltimore Symphony Orchestra record of the *Symphonic Dances* are my current favorites.

- West Side Story
  DG 415 253-2 GH2 (2) Orchestra conducted by
  Leonard Bernstein
- Symphonic Dances
  London 452 916 LH. Baltimore SO, Zinman

Part II
The Lifetime Listening
Program

The essence of this section lies in its title: it is a *lifetime* listening program. The orchestral and instrumental works listed herein may take several decades to cover, or may be heard in a much shorter time. The point is that what they offer cumulatively is of large dimensions, and they are intended to be an important part of a whole life. They can be a major experience, a source of continuous growth. Hence the word Lifetime. These composers are life companions; once part of you, they work in and on you and with you. They should not be heard in a hurry, any more than friends should be made in a hurry.

The Program is simple. It is designed to fill the mind slowly, gradually, under no compulsion, with what the greatest composers have thought, felt and imagined in their music. And even after we have shared these thoughts, feelings and images, we will still have much to learn. The authors claim no particular competence in compiling this list other than tradition and their own experiences. Its purpose is not to exhibit the erudition of the compilers (limited enough in any case) but to be of service to the reader. The music is listed alphabetically, by composer, and it may be explored and re-explored in any preferred order. *Works that are already discussed in Part I are not duplicated.* The music lover may choose a topic, a century or a specific composer. Women have contributed to the rich heritage of classical music in their own way, and their rightful place in our musical legacy is amply recognized. Indeed, this book begins with music composed by a woman. The classical music tradition is still alive and thriving in our own lifetime, and the works of leading living composers are also included. Recordings are identified by price: budget ($), mid-price ($$) or full-price ($$$). Selections in this list that are part of our *Desert Island Collection* are highlighted by **bold facing**—they are outstanding recorded performances whose magical quality make them a special treasure that is uniquely valuable, no matter the price.

The Lifetime Listening Program

Johann Sebastian Bach

- **Violin concertos Nos. (i) 1-2; (ii) Double violin concerto; (iii) Double concerto for violin and oboe in C min**
  Ph. 420 700-2 Grumiaux (ii) Krebbers (iii) Holliger (i-ii) Les Solistes Romandes (iii) New Philh. O, Edo de Waart $$
- **The Well Tempered Clavier (complete)**
  Sony Classical M3K 42266. Glenn Gould (Piano) $$
- Cello suites Nos 1-6
  EMI Dig. CDS5 55363-2 (2). Mstislav Rostropovitch $$$
- Cello suites Nos 1-6
  Sony S2K 63203. Yo Yo Ma. $$$
- St. Mathew Passion
  DG Dig. 427 648-2 (3) Monteverdi Ch. E. Bar. Soloists, Gardiner $$$

Bela Bartok

- String Quartets Nos. 1-6
  DG 423 657-2GH2 (2). Emerson Qt $$$

Amy Beach

- Symphony in E minor (Gaelic) - BARBER: Symphony No 1
  Chandos Dig. CHAN 8958. Detroit SO, Jarvi $$$

Ludwig van Beethoven

- (i) Piano concertos Nos 1-5
  Ph. 456 045-2PH3 (3). Brendel, Chicago SO, Levine $$
- Piano sonatas Nos 27; 28; 29 (Hammerklavier); 30; 31; 32
  Ph. Duo 438 374-2, Alfred Brendel $$
- Piano Trios Nos 5 (Ghost); 7 (Archduke)
  Sony SBK 53514, Eugene Istomin, Isaac Stern, Leonard Rose $
- Piano trios Nos 7 (Archduke); 9 in B flat
  EMI Dig. CDC7 47010-2, Ashkenazy, Perlman, Harrell $$$
- (i) Violin sonatas 1, 2, 3, 4 & 5; (ii) Romances for violin 7 orch. Nos 1-2
  Ph. Duo 446 521-2 (2) Henryk Szeryng (i) Ingrid Haebler; (ii) Concg. O. Haitink $$
- Violin sonatas 6, 7, 8, 9 & 10
  Ph. Duo 446 524-2 (2) Henryk Szeryng, Ingrid Haebler $$

- Missa Solemnis in D
    DG 447 922-2 (2). Concg. O, Bernstein $$
- String Quartets Nos 1-16
    DG 423 657-2GH2. (7). Emerson Qt. $$$

Alban Berg
- Violin concerto; - RAVEL: Tzigane; - STRAVINSKY: Concerto
    DG 447 445-2. Itzhak Perlman, Boston SO, Ozawa $$
- Violin concerto;- RIHM: Gesungene Zeit; Time Chant
    DG Dig. 437 093-2. A-S Mutter, Chicago SO, Levine $$$
- Lyric suite; String quartet, Op 3
    EMI Dig CDC5 55190-2. Alban Berg Quartet $$$

Hector Berlioz
- **Harold en Italie; Overture: Le Carnaval romaine**
    DG 415 109-2. Wolfram Christ. Berlin PO, Maazel $$$
- Requiem Mass (Grande messe de morts); Overtures: Benvenuto
    Cellini; Le Carnaval romain; Le Corsaire.
    DG Dig 429 724-2 (2). BPO, Levine $$$

Leonard Bernstein
- (i) Candide: overture; (ii) On the Town: 3 dance episodes; (i) West
    Side Story: Symphonic dances; (iii) America - BARBER: Adagio; -
    GERSHWIN: Rhapsody in Blue
        DG Dig 427 806-2 (i) LAPO; (ii) Israel PO; (iii) Troyanos with O,
        Leonard Bernstein $$
- Symphonies Nos (i) 1; (ii) 2 for piano and orchestra
        DG 447 953-2 (2) (i) Christa Ludwig (ii) Lukas Foss, Israel PO
        Leonard Bernstein $$
- (i) Symphony No 3; (ii) Chichester Psalms
        DG 447 954-2 (i)V Boys Choir(ii) Soloists from V Boys Choir,
        Israel PO, Leonard Bernstein $$

Georges Bizet
- **Symphony in C; - BRITTEN: Simple symphony;—**
    PROKOKIEV: Symphony No 1
        DG Dig 423 624-2 Orpheus CO $$$

Alexander Borodin
- Prince Igor: overture; Polovtsian Dances
        Virgin/EMI Dig CUV5 61135-2. Royal Liverpool PO Ch. & O,
        Mackerras $$

Johannes Brahms

- **Hungarian Dances Nos 1-21 (complete); Variations on a Theme of Haydn**
  DG Dig 431 594-2, VPO, Abbado $$
- (i) Clarinet Quintet in B min; (ii) Piano quintet in F min; String Quintets Nos 1-2
  Ph. Duo 446 172-2. (i) Herbert Stahr (ii) Werner Haas, Berlin P Octet $$
- (i;ii) Clarinet trio in A min (iii) Horn trio in E flat (ii) Piano trios Nos 1 in B; 2 in C; 3 in C min; 4 in A
  Ph. Duo 438 365-2 (2) (i) George Pieterson (ii) Beaux Arts Trio (iii) Francis Orval, Arthur Grumiaux, Gyorgy Sebok $
- **Eine deutsches Requiem**
  Ph Dig. 432 140-2 Monteverdi Ch, ORR, Gardiner $$$

Benjamin Britten

- (i)Young Person's Guide to the Orchestra; (ii) Simple Symphony; Variations on a Theme of Frank Bridge
  Decca 440 321-2. (i) LSO (ii) ECO, Britten $$

Max Bruch

- Violin concertos Nos 1, 2; Adagio appasionata; In Memorium; Konzerstuck; Romance , Op 42; Serenade, Op 75
  Ph 432 282-2 (3). Salvatore Accardo, Leipzig GO, Masur $$

Anton Bruckner

- Symphonies Nos 1-9
  DG 429 079-2 (9) BPO and Bavarian RSO, Jochum $$
- **Symphonies Nos 1-9**
  DG 429 648-2 (9) BPO, Karajan $$
- **Symphony No 6**
  EMI CDM7 63351-2. New Philh. O, Klemperer $$

Emmanuel Chabrier

- Espana (rhapsody);
  DG 447 751-2GH. VPO, Gardiner $$$

Frederic Chopin

- Piano works
  RCA GD60822-2-RG. (11) Artur Rubinstein $$
- Piano sonatas Nos 1, 2 & 3
  Naxos Dig 8.550363. Idil Biret $

- Piano concertos Nos 1 & 2
  Naxos Dig 8.550123. Istvan Szekely; Budapest SO.
  Gyula Nemeth $
- Polonaises 1-16
  Decca Double 452 167-2 (2) Ashkenazy $$
- **Waltzes 1-14**
  EMI CDH7 69802-2. Dinu Lipatti $$
- Les Sylphides (ballet); RAVEL: Bolero; DELIBES: Coppelia: Suite;
  GOUNOD: Faust, Excerpts., OFFENBACH Gaite Parisienne: Ex-
  cerpts; TCHAIKOVSKY: Sleeping Beauty (suite)
  DG Double 437 404-2 (2). BPO, Karajan $$

Claude Debussy

- Preludes, Books 1-2 (complete)
  EMI mono CDH7 61004-2. Walter Gieseking $$
- Etudes, Books 1-2
  Ph Dig 422 412-2. Mitsuko Uchida $$$

Frederic Delius

- **Brigg Fair; Dance rhapsody No 2; Fennimore and Gerda;Inter-**
  mezzo, Florida suite; Irmelin: Prelude. Marche caprice; On
  the hearing of the first cuckoo in spring; Over the hills and
  far away; Sleigh ride; Song before sunrise; Summer evening:
  Summer night on the river; (i) Songs of sunset
  EMI CDS7 47509-2 (2) RPO, Beecham (i) with Forrester,
  Cameron, Beecham Ch. Soc. $$$

Antonin Dvorak

- **Symphonies 1-9; Overtures: Carnival; In nature's realm; My**
  home. Scherzo cappricioso
  Decca 430 046-2 (6). LSO, Istvan Kertesz $$
- Serenade for Strings; Czech Suite
  Erato/Warner Dig 2292 45928-2. Lausanne CO, Jordan $
- **Cello concerto; - TCHAIKOVSKY: Variations on a rocco theme**
  DG 447 413-2. Rostropovich, BPO, Karajan $$

Edward Elgar

- **Symphonies Nos 1-2; Overtures: Cockaigne; In the South**
  Decca Double 443 856-2. LPO, Solti $$
- Violin concerto in B min. Op 61
  EMI Dig EMX 2058. Nigel Kennedy. LPO, Handley $$
- **Cello concerto in E min; Sea Pictures**
  EMI CDC7 47329-2. Du Pre, LSO, Barbirolli $$

Manuel de Falla
- (i) Nights in the Gardens of Spain; (ii) El amor brujo (ballet, complete); RODRIGO: Concerto
  - Decca Dig 430 703-2;(i) De Larrocha, LPO, Fruhbeck de Burgos (ii) Tourangeau, Montreal SO, Dutoit $$
- **The Three Cornered Hat (ballet): complete; El amor brujo**
  - **Decca Dig. 410 008-2. Boky, Tourangeau, Montreal SO, Dutoit $$$**

Cesar Franck
- (i) Symphony in D minor (ii) Symphonic variations for piano and orchestra (iii) Prelude, choral and fugue
  - Errato/Warner Dig. 4509 92871-2 ORTF Nat. O, Martinon $

George Gershwin
- An American in Paris (i) Rhapsody in Blue
  - Sony SMK 47529-2. NYPO, Bernstein (i) Bernstein (piano) $$
- Porgy and Bess; Symphonic picture
  - Decca 430 712-2. Detroit SO, Dorati $$

Philip Glass
- Dance Pieces: Glasspieces: In the Upper Room: Dances Nos. 1,2,5,8,9
  - CBS Dig. MK 39539. Ens., Michael Riesman $$$

Alexander Glazunov
- Violin concerto; -SIBELIUS: Violin concerto; - TCHAIKOVSKY: Violin concerto
  - EMI mono CDH7 64030-2. Heifetz, LPO, Barbirolli $$

Mikhail Glinka
- Ruslan and Ludmilla:overture - PROKOFIEV: Alexander Nevsky
  - RCA GD 60176, Chicago SO, Reiner $$

Henryk Gorecki
- Symphony No 3 (Symphony of sorrowful songs)
  - Elektra Nonesuch Dig. 979282-2. Dawn Upshaw, London Sinf David Zinman $$$

Percy Grainger

- Molly on the Shore; Blithe Bells; Country Gardens;Green Bushes; Handel in the Strand; Mock morris; My robin is to the greenwood gone; Spoon River; Shepherd's Hey; Walking Tune; Youthful Rapture
  Chandos CHAN 6542. Bournemouth Sinf, Montgomery $$

Edvard Grieg

- (i) **Piano concerto in A min**. (ii) Holberg suite, Op. 40; Lyric suite Op. 54; (iii) 4 symphonic dances Op. 64 (ii,iii) Peer Gynt (incidental music): suites Nos 1, Op. 46. 2, Op. 55; (v) (Piano) Lyric pieces, Op. 12; Album leaf; Arietta; Fairy dance; National song; Norwegian melody; Popular melody; waltz; Watchman's song, Op. 43; Butterfly; Erotik; In my native country; Little bird; Solitary traveller; To spring.
  Ph. Duo 438 380-2. (i) **Kovacevich, BBC SO, C.Davis,** (ii) ECO; (iii) Raymond Leppard; (iv) Philh O; (v) Zoltan Kocis $
- Lyric Pieces
  DG 449 721-2, Gilels $$$

George Frederic Handel

- **Concerti grossi (12)**
  Decca 444 532-2 (3). ASMF, Marriner $$
- **Messiah**
  Decca Double 444 824-2 (2). ASMF Ch & O, Marriner $

Josef Haydn

- Symphonies Nos. 6 (Le Matin), 7 (Le Midi); 8 (Le Soir)
  Naxos Dig. 8. 550772. N. CO. Ward $
- Symphonies Nos. 45 in F sharp minor (Farewell); 48 in C (Maria Theresa), 102 in B flat
  Naxos Dig. 8.550382; 4550382, Capella Istropolitana, Barry Wordsworth $
- **Symphonies Nos 82 (The Bear), 83, (The Hen) 84, 85 (La Reine); 86, 87 (Paris Symphonies)**
  Ph. Duo 438 727. ASMF. Marriner $$
- Trumpet concerto; - HUMMEL: Concerto
  Sony CD 37846. Marsalis, Nat PO, Leppard $$$
- The Creation (complete, in English)
  Decca Dig 430 397-2. New College Oxford Ch, AAM Ch & O, Hogwood $$$
- The Creation (complete)
  DG/Archiv 449 217-2AH2. Monteverdi Ch., ORR. Gardiner $$$

Paul Hindemith
- Mathis de Maler (symphony); Concert music; Symphonic metamorphoses on themes by Weber
    DG 429 404-2. Israel SO, Bernstein $$$

Gustav Holst
- Military band suites 1-2
    Telarc Dig CD 80038. Cleveland Symphonic Winds, Fennell $$$

Imogen Holst
- String Quartet No 1 - BRIDGE: 3 Idylls; - BRITTEN: String Quartet
  No. 2
    Conifer Dig. 74321 15006-2. Brindise Qt. $$$

Alan Hovhaness
- Symphony No 2 (Mysterious mountain); And God created great
  whales; Alleluia and fugue; Prayer of St Gregory; Prelude and
  quadruple fugue
    Delos Dig DE 3157, Seattle SO, Schwarz $$$

Charles Ives
- Symphony No. 2; Central Park in the dark; The gong on the hook
  and ladder; Hallowe'en; Hymn for strings; Tone roads No 1; The
  unanswered question
    DG Dig 429 220-2. NYPO, Bernstein $$$
- (i) Symphony No. 4; Robert Browning overture; (ii) Songs: An
  Election; Lincoln the great commoner; Majority, They are There!
    Sony MPK 46726 (i) NY Schola cantorum (ii) Gregg Smith
    singers, American SO. Stokowski $$

Josquin des Pres
- Antiphons, Motets and Sequences
    Meridian ECD 84093. New College Oxford Ch., Higginbottom $$$

Zoltan Kodaly
- Concerto for orchestra; Dances of Galanta; Dances of Marosszek;
  Harry Janos: suite; Symphony in C; Summer evening: Theater
  overture; Variations on a Hungarian Folksong (The Peacock)
    Decca Double 443 006-2. Philh Hungarica, Dorati $$

Franz Liszt

- Dante Symphony; (ii) Dante Sonata
    Teldec/ Warner Dig. 105807, BPO, Barenboim, (ii) Barenboim
    (piano) $$
- A Faust Symphony
    DG 431 470-2; 431 470-4. Kenneth Riegel, Tanglewood Festival
    Ch, Boston SO, Bernstein $$
- Annees de pelerinage, 1st year (Switzerland); 2nd year (Italy); 3rd
  year (Italy)
    DG 437 206-2 (3). Lazar Berman $
- Piano concertos 1, 2; Totentanz
    DG Dig 423 571-2. Zimmerman, Boston SO, Ozawa $$$

Gustav Mahler

- **Symphony No 3**
    RCA RCD2 1757. Horne, Chicago SO, Levine $$$
- Symphony No 3
    Sony SK48380. LAPO, Salonen $$$
- (i) Symphony No 4; (ii) Symphony No. 2 (Resurrection)
    DG 453 037-2GTA2. (i) VPO; (ii) Chicago SO. Abbado $$$
- (i) **Symphony No 4;** (ii) *Lieder ein fahrenden Gesellan*
    Sony SBK 46535. (i) **Judith Raskind, Cleveland O, Szell;** (ii)
    Frederica von Stade, LPO, A. Davis $
- **Symphony No 5**
    DG Dig 427 254-2. Chicago SO, Abbado $$
- **Symphony No 6; Songs from Ruckert**
    DG Dig 423 928-2. Chicago SO, Abbado $
- **Symphony No 7**
    RCA RCD2 4581. Chicago SO, Levine $$$
- Symphony No. 8 (Symphony of a Thousand)
    DG Dig. 445 843-2 (2). Tolz Boys' Ch., Berlin R. & Prague Philh
    Ch., BPO, Abbado. $$$
- Symphony No. 8 (Symphony of a Thousand)
    Decca 448 293-2. V Boys' Ch, V State Op. Ch. & Singverein,
    Chicago SO, Solti $$$
- **Symphony No 9**
    DG 410 726-2. (2). BPO, Karajan $$
- **Symphony No 9**
    DG 435 378-2. (2). BPO, Bernstein $$
- Symphony No 10 (Unfinished; Ed. Deryck Cooke)
    EMI Dig. CDC7 54406-2. Bournemouth SO, Rattle $$$

Fanny Mendelssohn
- Piano trio in D — CLARA SCHUMANN: Trio in G min
  Hyperion Dig CDA 66331, Dartington Piano Trio $$$

Olivier Messiaen
- Turangalila Symphony
  DG Dig 431 781-2. Bastille O, Chung $$$

Wolfgang Amadeus Mozart
- Symphonies Nos 28, 32 (Paris), 40
  Naxos Dig 8.550119, Capella Istropolitana, Barry Wordsworth $
- **Symphony No 36 ("The birth of a performance"); 38**
  Sony SMK 64474. Columbia So, Bruno Walter $$
- **Symphony No 39; 35 (Haffner)**
  CBS MYK 38472-2. Cleveland O, Szell $$
- **Piano Concertos Nos 9, 15, 22, 25, 27**
  Ph Duo 442 571-2 (2), Alfred Brendel, ASMF, Marriner $$
- **Piano Concertos Nos. 20, 21, 23, 27; Piano sonata No. 17;**
  Rondo in A minor
  Double Decca Analog/ Dig. 436 383-2 (2). Vladimir Ashkenazy,
  Philh O. $$
- Clarinet concerto; Flute concerto No. 1; Andante for flute & orchestra; Flute & harp concerto; Oboe concerto; Horn concertos Nos 1-4; Rondo for horn & orchestra.
  Ph. 426 148-2 (3). Brymer, Monteaux, Ellis, Black, Civil, ASMF, Marriner $
- Serenades Nos 1 (Haffner); 9 (Posthorn); 13 (Eine kleine Nachtmusik); Serenata notturna
  Decca Double 443 458-2. Vienna Mozart Ens. Boskovsky $
- Requiem Mass in D min
  Ph Dig 420 197-2. Monteverdi Ch., E. Bar. Soloists, Gardiner $$$

Jacques Offenbach
- Gaite Parisienne
  RCA 09026 61847-2. Boston Pops O, Arthur Fiedler $$

Carl Orff
- **Carmina Burana**
  DG 447 437. Schoneberger Boys Ch. Berlin German Op
  Ch & O., Jochum $$

Niccolo Paganini
- Caprices (24)
    DG 429 714-2. Salvatore Accardo $$

Serge Prokofiev
- Symphonies Nos 1 (Classical), 5; Romeo and Juliet: Excerpts; Chout: Final dance
    RCA mono 09026 61657-2. Boston SO, Koussevitsky $
- (i,ii) **Peter and the Wolf**; (iii) Lieutenant Kije suite; (iv) Love for 3 oranges suite(ii) Symphony No 1 (Classical);
    Decca 433 612-2. (i) **Sir Ralph Richardson** (iii) Paris Conservatoire, Boult (iv) LPO, Weller $
- **Violin concertos Nos 1 & 2; - STRAVINSKY: Violin concerto
    Sony SK 53969. Cho-Liang Lin, LAPO, Esa-Pekka Salonen
    $$$**
- Piano concerto No 3 ; - Ravel: Piano concerto in G
    DG 447 438-2. Argerich, BPO, Abbado $$

Camille Saint Saens
- Carnival of the Animals; Danse macabre; Suite algerienne: marche militaire francaise; Samson et Dalila:Bacchanale; Symphony No 3
    Sony SBY 47655. Phd O, Ormandy $$

Arnold Schoenberg
- Verklarte Nacht
    Hyperion Dig. CDA 66425. Raphael Ens. $$$

Franz Schubert
- String Quartet Nos 12; 13; 14 (Death and the Maiden); 15
    Ph Duo 446 163-2 (2), Italian Quartet $
- Piano sonatas Nos 19; 20; 21; 3 Impromptus (Klavierstucke)
    Ph Duo 438 703-2. Brendal $

Clara Schumann
- Piano Trio in G minor
    Hyperion Dig CDA 66331. Dartington Piano Trio $$$

Robert Schumann
- Humoreske, Op 20; Kinderzenen, Op. 15 (Scenes from childhood); Kreisleriana, Op. 16
    Decca Dig 440 496. Radu Lupu $$$

- Piano concerto in A min; Novelettes 1 & 2; - LISZT: Piano concerto No. 1
    RCA 6255-2RC. Rubinstein, Chicago SO, Giulini $$

Dmitri Shostakovich
- **Symphonies Nos 1; 6**
    Chandos Dig CHAN 8411. SNO, Jarvi $$$
- Symphony No 5
    EMI Dig CDC7 49181 -2. Oslo SO, Jansons $$$
- Symphony Nos 6, 12 (The Year 1917)
    Decca Dig. 425 067-2. Concg O, Haitink $$$
- Symphony Nos 1, 7 (Leningrad)
    DG 427632-2 (2). Chicago SO, Bernstein $$
- Symphony No 9
    Chandos Dig CHAN 8567. SNO, Jarvi $$$
- Symphony No 10
    DG Karajan Gold 439 036-2, BPO, Karajan $$$

Jean Sibelius
- Karelia Suite, Op 11; Scenes historique; Festivo, Op. 2513; The Chase; Love song; At the drawbridge, Op. 6611-3; The Tempest (incidental music) suites 1-2, Op 109
    EMI mono CDM7 63397. RPO, Beecham $$
- Symphonies Nos 3, 6, 7; (i) Violin concerto in D; Finlandia; Legends: The Swan of Tuonela; Tapiola
    Ph Duo 446 160 (2) (i) Salvatore Accardo; Boston SO, Sir Colin Davis $$
- Symphonies Nos (i) 4; (ii) 6; (i) The Bard, Op. 64; Lemminkainan's return, Op. 2214; The Tempest: prelude
    EMI mono CDM7 64027. (i) LPO, (ii) RPO, Sir Thomas Beecham $$

John Philip Sousa
- Marches
    Mercury 434 300-2. Eastman Wind Ensemble., Frederick Fennell $$

Igor Sravinsky
- **The Firebird (complete); Fireworks; Le chant du rossignol; Scherzo a la russe**
    Mercury 432 012-2. LSO, Dorati $$

Peter Tchaikovsky
- **Symphonies Nos. (i) 2 (Little Russian); (ii) 4 in F min**
  DG 429 527, (i) New Philh. O, (ii) VPO, Abbado $

Georg Philipp Telemann
- (i)Viola concerto in G; (ii) Suite in A min for recorder and strings; Tafelmusik Part 2; (iii) Triple violin concerto in F, Part 3; (iv) Double horn concerto in E flat
  Naxos Dig. 8.550156 . Capella Istropolitana, Richard Edlinger $

William Walton
- Balshazzar's Feast; Coronation March; Crown Imperial, Henry V (incidental music)
  Decca Dig 448 2134-2. Bryn Terfel, Bournemouth SO, Litton $$$

Ralph Vaughan Williams
- A Sea Symphony (No. 1)
  BMG/RCA 60580-2-RG. London Symphony Ch., LSO, Previn $$
- A Pastoral Symphony (No 3); Symphony No 4
  BMG/RCA 60583-2-RG. LSO, Previn $$

Heiter Villa-Lobos
- Bachiasnas brasilieras
  Hyperion Dig CDA 66257 Jill Gomez $$$

Carl Maria von Weber
- Overtures
  Capriccio Dig. 10052. Staatskapelle Dresden O, Gustav Kuhn $$$

Selected Bibliography

Abraham, Gerald, *The Music of Sibelius* (W W Norton & Co.,Inc., NY,1947)

Apel, Willi, & Daniel, Ralph, *The Harvard Brief Dictionary of Music* (Pocket Books, Simon & Schuster, NY., 1960)

Barzun, Jacques, *Classic, Romantic and Modern* (Doubleday Anchor Books, NY., 1961)

Barzun, Jacques, *Berlioz and his Century* (Meridian Books, NY., 1956)

Berger, Melvin, *Guide to Chamber Music* (Anchor Books, Doubleday, NY., 1990)

Bernstein, Leonard, *The Infinite Variety of Music* (Simon & Schuster, NY., 1966)

Calvocoressi, MD, *Mussorgsky* (Collier Books, NY.,1962)

Carter, Harman, *A Popular History of Music* (Dell Publishing Co., NY., 1956)

Clement, Catherine, *Opera, or the Undoing of Women* (University of Minnesota Press, MN, 1988)

Copeland, Aaron, *What to Listen For in Music* (The New American Library, NY.,1959)

Conrad, Peter, *A Song of Love and Death* (Poseidon Press, NY.,1987)

Crompton, Louis (Ed.),*The Great Composers: Reviews and Bombardments by Bernard Shaw* (University of California Press, Los Angeles, 1978)

Downes, Edward, *Guide to Symphonic Music* (Walker & Co., NY., 1981)

Drew, Elizabeth, *Poetry, A Modern Guide to its Understanding & Enjoyment* (Laurel Editions, Dell Publishing Co., NY., 1959)

Evans, Edwin, *Tchaikovsky* (Avon Books, NY., 1960)

Ewen, David, *Music for the Millions* (Arco Publishing Company, NY.,1944)

Ewen, David, *Romain Rolland's Essays on Music* (Dover Publications., NY., 1959)

Frankenstein,Alfred, *A Modern Guide to Symphonic Music* (Meredith Press, NY., 1966)

Forbes, Elliot, *Thayer's Life of Beethoven* (Princeton University Press, NJ., 1979)

333

Gartenberg, Egon, *Mahler, The Man and his Music* (Schirmer Books, NY., 1978)

Geiringer, Karl, *Haydn* (Anchor Books, Doubleday and Company, NY., 1963)

Geiringer, Karl, *Brahms* (Doubleday & Co., NY.,1961)

Goepp, Philip, *Great Works of Music* (Garden City Publishing Co., NY.,1913)

Graf, Max, *Modern Music* (Philosophical Library, NY., 1946)

Grove, George, *Beethoven and his Nine Symphonies* (Dover Publications, NY., reprinted 1962)

Gutman, Robert, *Richard Wagner, The Man, His Mind, and His Music* (Harcourt, Brace Jovanovich, NY., 1968)

Hildesheimer, Wolfgang, *Mozart* (Farrar, Straus & Giroux, NY., 1982)

Hill, Ralph, *The Symphony* (Penguin Books, NY.,1949)

Howard, John Tasker & Lyons, James, *Modern Music* (Mentor Books, NY., 1942)

Hurwitz, David, *Beethoven or Bust* (Anchor Books, Doubleday, NY., 1992)

International Library of Music, Vols. 1-4. (The University Society, NY.,1925)

Kamien, Roger, *Music: An Appreciation* (McGraw Hill Inc., NY., 1982)

Kerman, Joseph, *Listen* (Worth Publishers Inc., NY.,1972)

Kinscella, Hazel Gertrude, *Music and Romance* (RCA Manufacturing Co., Inc.,NJ., 1941)

Krenek, Ernst, *Gustav Mahler* (Greystone Press, NY., 1941)

Kupperberg, Herbert, *Felix Mendelssohn* (Charles Scribner's Sons, NY.,1972)

Landon, H.C. R, *The Symphonies of Josef Haydn* (London, 1955)

Layton, Robert (Ed.) *A Companion to the Concerto* (Schirmer Books, NY., 1988)

Layton, Robert, *Sibelius* (Schirmer Books, NY.,1992)

Layton, Robert (Ed.) *A Companion to the Symphony* (Simon & Schuster, NY., 1993)

Le Mee, Katherine, *Chant* (Bell Tower, NY., 1994)

Longyear, Ray, *Nineteenth Century Romanticism in Music* (Prentice Hall Inc., NJ.,1973)

Machlis, Joseph, *The Enjoyment of Music* (W W Norton & Co., NY., 1984)

Magee, Bryan, *Aspects of Wagner* (Oxford University Press, Oxford,1988)

Marek, George, *Richard Strauss, The Life of a Non-hero* (Simon & Schuster, NY., 1967)

McKinney, H & Anderson, WR, *Discovering Music* (American Book Co., NY.,1934)

MacDonald, Calum, in *The Symphony, Past, Present, Future* (BBC Music Magazine, Summer Special, 1995)

Marx, Milton, *The Enjoyment of Drama* (Appleton, Century, Crofts, Inc., NY., 1961)

Moore, Douglas, *From Madrigal to Modern Music* (W.W. Norton & Co. Inc., NY., 1942)

Mordden, Ethan, *A Guide to Orchestral Music.* (Oxford University Press, NY., 1980)

Newmann, Ernest, *Stories of the Great Operas* (Garden City Publishing Company, NY., 1930)

Newmann, Ernest, *Wagner as Man and Artist* (Garden City Publishiung Co., NY., 1941)

Newmarch, Rosa, *The Concert-Goer's Library of Descriptive Notes , Vols 1-5* (Oxford University Press, London, 1931)

O'Connell, Charles, *The Victor Book of the Symphony* (Simon & Schuster, NY., 1935)

Palmer, Christopher, *Impressionism in Music* (Charles Scribner's Sons, NY.,1973)

Parrish, Carl & Ohl, John, *Masterpieces of Music Before 1750* (WW Norton & Co., Inc., NY.,1951)

Reese, Gustave, *Music in the Middle Ages* (WW Norton & Co., NY.,1940)

Robertson, Alec (Ed.) *Chamber Music* (Penguin Books, NY., 1957)

Robertson, Alec, *Dvorak* (Collier Books, NY., 1962)

Robertson, Alec & Stevens, Denis (Eds), *The Pelican History of Music, Vols. 1-3* (Penguin Books, NY., 1968)

Robinson, Paul, *Opera & Ideas* (Harper & Row, NY., 1985)

Rolland, Romain, *Beethoven the Creator* (Harper & Brothers, NY.,1929)

Rosenfeld, Paul, *Musical Portraits: Impressions of twenty modern composers* (Harcourt Brace & Co., Inc., NY., 1920)

Rudel, Anthony, *Classical Music Top 40* (Simon & Schuster, Fireside Books, NY., 1995)

Sabor, Rudolph, *The Real Wagner* (Sphere Books, Penguin Group, NY.,1987)

Saltzman, Eric, *Twentieth Century Music: An Introduction* (Prentice Hall Inc., NJ., 1967)

Scherman, Thomas & Biancolli, Louis, *The Beethoven Companion* (Doubleday & Co., NY., 1971)

Schumann, Robert, *On Music and Musicians* (Pantheon Books Inc., NY., 1946)

Seigmeister, Elie, *The Music Lover's Handbook* (William Morrow and Company, NY., 1943)

Sethna, Dhun H, *Classical Music for Everybody* (Fitzwilliam Press, CA., 1997)

Simpson, Robert (Ed.) *The Symphony 1. Haydn to Dvorak* (Penguin Books, NY., 1966)

Spaeth, Sigmund, *A Guide to Great Orchestral Music* (The Modern Library, NY., 1943)

Stringham, Edwin, *Listening to Music Creatively* (Prentice Hall, NY.,1946)

Sullivan,JWN, *Beethoven. His Spiritual Development* (Mentor Books, NY., 1937)

Taylor, Ronald, *Franz Liszt, The Man and the Musician* (Universe Books, NY., 1986)

Time-Life Records. *The Story of Great Music: A Listener's Guide to the Recordings* (Time-Life Inc., NY)

Thomson, Oscar, *Debussy, Man and Artist* (1937, reprinted 1967, Dover Publications Inc., NY.)

Tovey, Donald Francis, *Symphonies and other Orchestral Works* (Oxford Universitty Press, NY., reprinted 1990)

Upton, GP & Borowski, Felix, *The Standard Concert Guide* (Blue Ribbon Books, NY., 1940)

Vallas, Leon, *Claude Debussy, His Life and Works* (Oxford University Press, 1933; reprinted 1973, Dover Publications, NY)

Van Doren, Mark, *The Noble Voice* (Henry Holt and Company, NY.,1946)

Vienus, Abraham, *The Concerto* (Doubleday, Doran and Company, NY.,1944)

Walker, Alan, *Franz Liszt: Vols 1-3* (Alfred A Knoft, NY.)

Watson Derek, *Liszt* (Schirmer Books, NY., 1989)

Wilson-Dickson, Andrew, *The Story of Christian Music* (A Lion Book, Oxford, 1992)

INDEX

Academic Festival Overture, 216

Adagio for Strings, 312

The Age of Elegance, 45-50

The Age of Opulence, 189-190

Aida, 185

Also spracht Zarathustra, 293

Andante Cantabile (Tchaikovsky), 168

Appalachian Spring suite, 314

Appassionata sonata, 105

L'apres-midi d'un faune, 270

L'Arlesienne Suite, 249

Artist's Life waltz, 192

ars antiqua, 10

ars nova, 10

Bach, Johann Sebastian, 25
- B minor Mass, 35-37
- Brandenburg Concertos, 28-31
- Goldberg Variations, 33-35
- Orchestral Suites, 31-33

Balakirev, 164

Ballades (Chopin), 149

Barber, Samuel
- Adagio for Strings, 312-314

The Barber of Seville, 156

The Baroque World, 21-26

baroque music, 45

Bartok, Bela
- Concerto for Orchestra, 310-312

basso continuo, 23

Beatrice and Benedict overture, 130

Beethoven, Ludwig van, 70-71
- Overtures, 99-102
- Piano concerto No. 5, 107-109
- Piano sonatas, 102-106
- Symphony No. 1, 73-75
- Symphony No. 2, 75-78
- Symphony No. 3, 78-83
- Symphony No. 4, 83-86
- Symphony No. 5, 86-88

Symphony No. 6, 89-91

Symphony No. 7, 91-93

Symphony No. 8, 94-96

Symphony No. 9, 96-98

Violin concerto, 109-111

Benvenuto Cellini overture, 130

Berlioz, Hector
- Overtures, 129-132
- Symphonie fantastique, 126-129

Bernstein, Leonard
- Werst Side Story, 315-316

Bizet, Georges
- Orchestral works, 249-252

The Beautiful Blue Danube, 191

La Boheme, 159

Bolero, 279

Borodin, 165

Brahms, Johannes
- Orchestral Works, 216-219
- Piano concertos, 209-213
- Symphony No. 1, 198-201
- Symphony No. 2, 202-204
- Symphony No. 3, 204-206
- Symphony No. 4, 206-208
- Violin Concerto, 213-215

Brandenburg Concertos, 28-31

Bruckner, Anton
- Symphony No. 4, 194-196
- Symphony No. 7, 196-198

Calm Sea and Prosperous Voyage
    overture, 138

cantus firmus, 11

Carmen suite, 250

Chopin, Frederic
- Piano works, 148-151

Choral Symphony, 96

Classical Symphony (Prokofiev), 308

Cockaigne overture, 298

concerto, 47

concerto grosso, 23, 47
Concerto for Orchestra, 310-312
Copland, Aaron
    Appalachian Spring suite, 314-315
Coriolanus, 99
The Creatures of Prometheus, 99

Daphnis and Chloe, 279
Death and Transfiguration, 292
Debussy, Claude, 268-269
    Orchestral works, 270-272
Dido's Lament, 41-43
Don Juan, 294
Don Quixote, 294
Dufay, Guillaume, 11
Dvorak, Antonin
    Slavonic Dances, 170-171
    Symphony Nos. 7-9, 240-246

early music, 7-11
Egmont Overture, 100
1812 overture, 167
Elgar, Edward
    Orchestral works, 297-301
Emperor Concerto, 107
Enigma Variations, 298
En Saga, 183
Eroica Symphony, 78
etudes (Chopin), 149

The Fair Melusine overture, 139
Fidelio overture, 100
Fingal's Cave (Hebrides overture), 139
Fireworks Music, 37
The Flying Dutchman overture, 258
folk song, 11,16
Fountains of Rome, 282
The Four Seasons, 27

Goldberg Variations, 33-35
Great Symphony (Schubert), 115
Gregorian Chant, 9,12
Grieg, Edvard
    Peer Gynt suite No. 1, 180-182

Handel, George Frederick, 25
    Music for the Royal Fireworks, 39-40
    Water Music, 37-39
Haydn, Franz Josef
    String Quartet No. 77, 53-55
    Symphony Nos. 93-104, 51-53
Hebrides overture (Fingal's Cave), 139
Hildegard von Bingen, 12-14
    Gregorian Chant, 12-14
Holst, Gustav
    The Planets, 273-276

Impressionism, 267-269
Italian Symphony, 134

Jeux d'Eau, 279
Josquin des Pres 4
Jupiter Symphony, 59

King Lear overture, 130

Lemminkainen in Tuonela, 183
Les Francs-Juges, 129
Leonore overtures, 100
lied, 71-72
Liszt, Franz
    Symphonic poems, 151-154
Lohengrin prelude, 259
London Symphony (Vaughan
    Williams), 276
London Symphonies (Haydn), 51

Ma Vlast, 177
The Magic Flute, 64
Mahler, Gustav
    Symphony No. 1, 220-222
    Symphony No. 2, 223-225
Machaut, 9
madrigal, 17
Marche Slav, 167
Mass 8-10,16, 35
Mass in B minor, 35
Mastersingers (see Meistersinger)
Mazeppa, 153

Index

mazurkas (Chopin), 149
Die Meistersinger von Nurnberg, 252
Mendelssohn, Felix
    Overtures, 138-140
    Symphony No. 3, 132-134
    Symphony No. 4, 134-136
    Violin concerto in E minor, 136-138
La Mer, 271
A Midsummer Night's Dream, 138
Missa Papae Marcelli, 18
modern music, 289-291
Moonlight sonata, 103
motet, 17
Mozart, Wolfgang Amadeus, 49
    Overtures, 55-56
    Piano concertos, 60-64
    Symphony No. 40, 57-58
    Symphony No. 41, 59-60
    Die Zauberflote, 64-67
Music for the Royal Fireworks, 39-40
Mussorgsky, Modest
    Pictures at an Exhibition, 172-175

nationalistic music, 163-166
New World Symphony, 240
nocturnes (Chopin), 149
Nocturnes (Debussy), 271
Nutcracker suite, 239

Orchestral Suites (Bach), 31-33
opera, 23-24, 48-49, 124-125
Organ Symphony, 246
organum 10
Orpheus, 153

Palestrina, Giovanni Pierlugi da,
    Mass for Pope Marcellus, 18-20
Pastoral Symphony (Beethoven), 89
Pathetique Symphony, 230
Pathetique sonata, 102
Peer Gynt, 180
Petrushka, 301
Pictures at an Exhibition, 172
Pines of Rome, 282

The Planets, 273
polonaises (Chopin), 149
Pomp and Circumstance Marches, 298
Prelude a l'apres-midi d'un faune, 270
preludes (Chopin), 150
Les Preludes, 152
Printemps, 270
Prokofiev, Sergei
    Symphony No. 1, 308-310
Puccini, Giacomo,
    La Boheme, 158-159
Purcell, Henry,
    Dido's Lament, 41-43
Pushkin, 164

Rachmaninoff, Sergei
    Piano concertos, 306-308
    Symphony No. 2, 304-306
Rapsodie Espanol, 279
Ravel. Maurice
    Orchestral works, 278-282
The Renaissance, 15-17
Renische Symphony, 145
Respighi, Ottorino
    Orchestral works, 282-284
Resurrection Symphony (Mahler), 223
Rimsky-Korsakov, Nicolai
    Scheherazade, 176-177
The Rite of Spring, 248
Rob Roy overture, 130
Roman Carnival overture, 130
Roman Festivals (Respighi), 282
Romanticism, 121-125
Romantic Symphony, 194
Romeo et Juliette (Berlioz), 130
Rossini, Gioachino
    Overtures, 155-158
Ruy Blas overture, 139

Saint-Saens, Camille
    Symphony No. 3, 246-249
Scheherazade, 176
scherzi (Chopin), 149
Schubert, Franz, 71

Piano Quintet in A (Trout), 117-119
Symphony No. 5, 111-113
Symphony No. 8, 113-115
Symphony No. 9, 115-117
Schumann, Robert
Symphony No. 1, 140-142
Symphony No. 2, 142-145
Symphony No. 3, 145-146
Symphony No. 4, 147-148
Scotch Symphony, 132
Semiramide, 156
Sibelius, Jean
Symphonic poems, 182-185
Symphony No. 2, 159-161
Slavonic Dances (Dvorak), 170
Sleeping Beauty, 239
Smetana,Bedrich
Ma Vlast, 177-180
Spring Symphony, 140
Strauss, Johann
Waltzes, 191-193
Strauss, Richard
Tone Poems, 292-297
Stravinsky, Igor
Petrushka, 301-304
The Rite of Spring, 284-287
suite, 23, 31
Swan Lake, 239
The Swan of Tuonela, 183
symphonic poem, 151, 292
Symphonie fantastique, 126

Tannhauser overture, 258
Tapiola, 184
Tasso: lamento e trionfo, 154
Tchaikovsky, Peter Ilyich
Ballet music, 238-240
Orchestral works, 167-170
Piano concerto No. 1, 233-236
Symphony No. 4, 225-228
Symphony No. 5, 228-230
Symphony No. 6, 230-233
Violin concerto, 236-238
Till Eulenspiegel, 292

A Time to be Free, 163-164
A Time for Revolution, 69-72
Titan Symphony (Mahler), 220
Toreador's Song, 250
Tragic Overture, 216
Tristan und Isolde, 259
Trout Quintet, 117

Unfinished Symphony, 113

Vaughan Williams, Ralph
Symphony No. 2. 276-278
Verdi, Giuseppe
Aida, 185-187
Vienna Blood, 192
Vivaldi, Antonio,
The Four Seasons, 27-28
Voices of Spring, 192

Wagner, Richard
Die Meistersinger von Nurnberg, 252-256
Overtures, 256-265
waltzes (Chopin), 149
Water Music, 37-39
Waverly overture, 130
Weber, Carl Maria von, 72
Wedding March (Mendelssohn)
West Side Story, 315
William Tell overture, 156
Williams Vaughan, Ralph
Symphony No. 2, 276-278

Die Zauberflote, 64